W9-AFN-782

.91
.5
G44
2011

What People Are Saying about Valerie Geller's
Beyond Powerful Radio

"Imagine having one of the best radio practitioners in the world help you see the world you work in, in a new light. That's what this book does ... It's a great primer for anyone who loves radio — either learning the profession or already working in radio — who wants to learn how to approach their daily craft in a way that will build audiences, help you connect with those who listen to you and produce material they want to hear. This book will make you think again about how you communicate. From the basics of the language you use to the bigger picture of connecting across your radio station, marketing your station, promoting it as well as producing talk and news, this is a fascinating and invaluable guide. Whatever stage you are at in your radio career — student, journalist, music jock, manager or broadcast award winner — read Geller's books ...

Excellent, thought provoking and with a proven track record, this book will change how you broadcast and show you a new way to communicate. Just read it and see."
— *Liz Green, Talk Show Host, BBC Radio Leeds, UK*

"If you want to understand what makes radio work, read this, then read it again."
— *Jon Faine, Air Personality, ABC Radio 774, Melbourne, Australia*

"I highly recommend this to anyone interested in radio broadcasting. [Geller's] books should be in all broadcast schools and radio stations. Valerie Geller explains important techniques for helping the beginner all the way up to the most seasoned pro. We all need reminding of how to create powerful radio."
— *Rusty Humphries, Syndicated Talk Show Personality*

"An invaluable resource for professionals and students alike."
— *Michael C. Keith Ph.D., Boston College, Author of The Radio Station*

"If you want to achieve compelling radio and increase audiences, read this book immediately! Using these methods, LBC 97.3 in London experienced massive growth."
— *Scott Solder, BBC Radio 5 Live, London, UK*

LIBRARY
NSCC WATERFRONT CAMPUS
80 MAWIO'MI PLACE
DARTMOUTH, NS B2Y 0A5 CANADA

DISCARDED

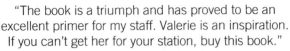

"It's my bible!"

— Åsa Paborn, Program Manager, Sveriges Radio, Sweden

"The book is a triumph and has proved to be an excellent primer for my staff. Valerie is an inspiration. If you can't get her for your station, buy this book."

— John Ryan, Managing Director, BBC Radio Manchester, UK

"Making it in broadcasting takes more than just luck. Think of *Beyond Powerful Radio* as your 'Road Guide' to success in radio."

— Andy Vierra, Program Director, KNUU, Las Vegas

"I recommend it to everyone and I use it in my classes. I love this book."

—Jo Maeder (The Rock 'N Roll Madame)
Air Personality, Author, Broadcast Instructor, New York University

"*Beyond Powerful Radio* is a fine guide for people inside the radio biz and an explanation of that biz to people outside, including the people who would like to get in. It's the kind of book where the reader thinks, 'Oh that's why they do that.'"

— David Hinckley, New York Daily News

"Packed with insights, well written, and fun to read. It's obvious why so many radio people consider this book 'a must'!"

— John Sawatsky, Professor of Journalism, Carleton University, Ontario, Canada

"*Beyond Powerful Radio* is a must-read/must-live-by if you want to succeed in talk radio. When I interview job candidates, if they have not read *Beyond Powerful Radio*, AND the companion *Powerful Radio Workbook*, I tell them to read them and come back. If you want to win in radio, you're taking an important step in that direction when you not only read *Beyond Powerful Radio*, but when you live, eat, drink, and personify the concepts Ms. Geller has so generously shared to help broadcasters and communicators move to the top of their game!"

— John McMullen, Director of News Talk & Sports Programming, Morris Desert Radio Group

"Anyone even considering a career in radio should read this!"

— Adele Scheele, Ph.D., Career Strategist, Author of Skills for Success

Beyond Powerful Radio

A Communicator's Guide to the Internet Age

Beyond Powerful Radio

A Communicator's Guide to the Internet Age

News, Talk, Information & Personality
for Broadcasting, Podcasting, Internet, Radio

VALERIE GELLER

Edited By Turi Ryder

AMSTERDAM • BOSTON • HEIDELBERG • LONDON • NEW YORK • OXFORD
PARIS • SAN DIEGO • SAN FRANCISCO • SINGAPORE • SYDNEY • TOKYO
Focal Press is an imprint of Elsevier

Cover Design: Kelli Grisez
Author Photo: Henry Leutwyler

Focal Press is an imprint of Elsevier
The Boulevard, Langford Lane, Kidlington, Oxford, OX5 1GB, UK
30 Corporate Drive, Suite 400, Burlington, MA 01803, USA

Second edition 2011

Copyright © 2011, 2007, 2006 Valerie Geller. Published by Elsevier Limited. All rights reserved.

No part of this publication may be reproduced or transmitted in any form or by any means, electronic
or mechanical, including photocopying, recording, or any information storage and retrieval system,
without permission in writing from the publisher. Details on how to seek permission, further information about the Publisher's permissions policies and our arrangement with organizations such as
the Copyright Clearance Center and the Copyright Licensing Agency, can be found at our website:
www.elsevier.com/permissions

This book and the individual contributions contained in it are protected under copyright by the
Publisher (other than as may be noted herein).

Notices
Knowledge and best practice in this field are constantly changing. As new research and experience
broaden our understanding, changes in research methods, professional practices, or medical treatment
may become necessary.

Practitioners and researchers must always rely on their own experience and knowledge in evaluating
and using any information, methods, compounds, or experiments described herein. In using such information or methods they should be mindful of their own safety and the safety of others, including parties
for whom they have a professional responsibility.

To the fullest extent of the law, neither the Publisher nor the authors, contributors, or editors, assume
any liability for any injury and/or damage to persons or property as a matter of products liability,
negligence or otherwise, or from any use or operation of any methods, products, instructions, or ideas
contained in the material herein.

British Library Cataloguing-in-Publication Data
Geller, Valerie.
  Beyond Powerful Radio: A Communicator's Guide to the
  Internet Age—News, Talk, Information & Personality.
  1. Radio Broadcasting. 2. Radio Broadcasters. 3. Broadcast
  Journalism. 4. Webcasting. 5. Internet Radio Broadcasting.
  6. Communication.
  I. Title
  384.5'4-dc22

Library of Congress Control Number: 2011920373

ISBN: 978-0-240-52224-1

For information on all Focal Press publications
visit our website at www.focalpress.com

Printed and bound in the United States

11 12 13 14   10 9 8 7 6 5 4 3 2 1

Working together to grow
libraries in developing countries

www.elsevier.com | www.bookaid.org | www.sabre.org

ELSEVIER   BOOK AID
              International   Sabre Foundation

Other books by Valerie Geller

Creating Powerful Radio:
Getting, Keeping & Growing Audiences-
News, Talk, Information & Personality

By Valerie Geller
Edited By Turi Ryder
Focal Press/Elsevier (2007)

The Powerful Radio Workbook:
The Prep, Performance & Post Production Planning

By Valerie Geller
Edited By Turi Ryder
M Street Publications (2000)

Creating Powerful Radio:
A Communicator's Handbook for
News, Talk, Information & Personality

By Valerie Geller
Edited By Turi Ryder
M Street Publications (1996)

Note: A full Instructor's Manual is available for
Creating Powerful Radio – including complete lesson plans
created by Melissa McConnell Wilson and Linwood Hagin Ph.D.

Contents

Foreword

By Tom Taylor

Watching Valerie Geller at work is exhilarating. Whether it's a roomful of people at one of the seminars she leads around the globe, or a small session, you feel possibilities opening up. You have those "Aha!" moments. You understand why one approach works and creates "powerful radio," and another is a blind alley. Valerie has that effect on people: They see more clearly, they become more focused, and they become more "themselves," because that's what Valerie is after. She shuns clichés and urges authenticity. And not wasting the listener's time. That's a big one: "Tell the truth, make it matter, never be boring."

So you leave a session with Valerie, and you want to keep that inspiration alive in your heart and mind. You've scribbled your notes and you've got your memories. But the rest of life takes over, and old habits are ingrained too deeply. That's why you've got this book. And if you've never had the privilege of being around Valerie and seeing through her eyes—well, that's also why you've got this book.

"Common sense" is one description of what Valerie teaches. She makes communication understandable, step by step. That common sense works not just in traditional radio, but in all the other platforms, whether they're called "new media" or "social media" or some kind of media that hasn't even been invented yet. Good storytelling always works.

Who is this book for? People already "in the business," such as journalists, reporters, news directors, talk hosts, managers, and anybody else who wants to sharpen their communications skills. Also people who want to break into the business, who've got a laptop and a microphone and the desire.

What's in this "Communicator's Guide to the Internet Age"?

You'll learn about:

1. *Creating content for any platform.* You learn how to put together a show, from prep work to performance to making yourself better

with the best techniques for airchecking. How do you create a talk show? A music show? What makes local different from national?

2. *Storytelling and voice.* How do you find and purify that unique voice that's inside you? How do you identify the living elements of a story and present them in a compelling fashion?

3. *Working across multiple platforms.* How do you translate content from one medium to another, being sensitive to the nuances of each?

4. *Marketing content.* How do you brand, and do, promotion, for whatever you're producing?

5. *News*—writing it, delivering it, and knowing: "What to do in the case of emergency." That could be a lifesaver for your audience.

6. *Understanding the audience.* That means the life stages of your audience, and understanding research, and ratings tools like the People Meter and diary.

7. *Making money.* How do you effectively communicate in sales? How can you create commercials that produce results for the client and keep the audience engaged? How do you generate effective fundraising, for the station or for charities, whether it's an immediate cause like disaster relief or an ongoing effort?

More than fifty media pros contributed their wisdom to this book—all top experts in their fields, from PDs and consultants to talk show hosts and professors.

There's a reason why Valerie's previous books, *Creating Powerful Radio* and *The Powerful Radio Workbook,* are being successfully used in sixty countries and have been translated into several languages; they work for people, consistently. So congratulations. You're making a smart investment. As Valerie says, "Do the work." If you do, the investment in time and thought will pay off. Because ultimately, what you're investing in is yourself. You'll discover you can be better than you ever dreamed. Isn't that what you really want?

—Tom Taylor
Executive News Editor
www.Radio-Info.com
Radio's online community since 1999

Introduction

> "Art happens—no hovel is safe from it, no prince may depend
> upon it, the vastest intelligence cannot bring it about."
> —*James McNeill Whistler*

The curse of our business is that it looks easy. Everyone can talk, so people believe they are experts, and that *anyone* can do it. That's because the great talented broadcast personalities and communicators make it *look* so effortless. But communicating powerfully in a way that will get, keep, and grow audiences is not easy. It is very hard work, requiring craft, skill, desire, experience, and training.

If you have the desire for the work, this book will give you the methods and professional standards that can help you succeed, wherever you are in your broadcast career, whatever your skill level, whether you broadcast on air, or online. It's intended for people at every level of broadcasting whose jobs are to face the blank page and create compelling programming using their personalities, listening skills and powers of observation and communication.

Beyond Powerful Radio is my fourth book. Though it's a new title, this is actually an update (with new material) of *Creating Powerful Radio: Getting, Keeping & Growing Audiences*.

Since the first edition of *Creating Powerful Radio* was published, satellite delivery, along with digital technologies, interactive mobile media, and the Internet, has emerged. With more available platforms and better technology and interactivity, we can reach an even broader audience. But, no matter the delivery system, there will always be a need to tell a story and for a storyteller who makes it matter.

The Creating Powerful Communicators techniques work in every culture, language, and country because they are based on the common denominator of universal principles—human connection and communication.

Radio holds up a mirror and reflects life as it is at the moment. Broadcasting stays interesting because, just as it does in life, it is in a state of constant change.

The three proven Creating Powerful Radio/Creating Powerful Communicators principles are: Tell the Truth, Make it Matter, and Never be Boring. (Notice how *you* tune out if you are bored?) All of the work I do is based on these three principles.

In *Beyond Powerful Radio* you'll find a wide array of proven techniques to make any subject come alive, with tools you can use to create compelling content no matter what the topic or how many times you've done it.

When *Creating Powerful Radio* was published in the mid 1990s, I had no idea that it would find its way around the world, and be translated into several languages. It was mostly intended for my clients as a written summary of ideas we'd worked with to get stations and on-air personalities and journalists to the next level. I wanted to leave them with something tangible and permanent that would last after either a Creating Powerful Radio or Powerful Communicators workshop or a consultation visit—something to avoid that "back to normal slump" that hits a few weeks after the consultant leaves. But *Creating Powerful Radio* became much more than that. It has served as a calling card in 33 countries. Over the years I have had the opportunity to work with more than 500 radio and TV stations. Each increased their listeners and viewers by working with the Creating Powerful Communicators methods which have helped thousands of broadcasters and students succeed.

If you have a copy of the first or second editions of this book, you will find, along with the new title, there is much new material here. There's much more on talent development, on-air performance, and airchecking, and expanded sections on news, interviewing, selling, and understanding more about your audience in expanded chapters on research and LifeStage Demographics.

The new chapters reflect an emphasis on the changes in the industry: Citizen Journalism; In Case of Emergency; Branding—Building the Brand Beyond Radio; Becoming a Powerful Storyteller; Your Voice—Improving Your Instrument; Audio Communication Across Multiple Delivery Platforms; Fundraising & Giving; Local vs. National Programming; plus an expanded chapter on Sales & Commercials.

For a fuller understanding of these techniques, delve into the book. If you follow these principles, and your goal is to engage an audience, you'll succeed.

On the next few pages you will find a *Quick Start* guide. These handy reminders are the proven principles of powerful radio, which are the core of my work. Because these pages ended up posted from Stockholm to Swaziland (people literally tore them out of the book), they are included here.

But again, these are just ideas. Creativity and radio is NOT "one size fits all." The way *you* create powerful radio, or communicate on any platform, is a highly personal effort. Your show is unique. No one can tell you how to do it. While the ideas in this book can serve as a guide or "road map," each broadcaster must find their own way.

If you would like further information about Geller Media International, one-on-one individual coaching, or the Creating Powerful Communicators seminars and Creating Powerful News workshops, contact:

Geller Media International
Consulting/Training/Seminars/Workshops
Phone: (+1) 212-580-3385
E-mail: Valerie@gellermedia.com
www.gellermedia.com

GELLER MEDIA INTERNATIONAL'S
TOPICS

FOCUS

ENGAGE

OPINION/
POSITION

STORYTELLING

Beyond Powerful Radio: A Communicators Guide To The Internet Age
By Valerie Geller, President, Geller Media International
copyright 2011. Reprinted with permission.
www.gellermedia.com

GELLER MEDIA INTERNATIONAL'S

CREATING POWERFUL COMMUNICATOR
PRINCIPLES

- ▶ Tell the truth.
- ▶ Make it matter.
- ▶ Never be boring.
- ▶ Speak visually, in terms your audience can "picture."
- ▶ Start with your best material.
- ▶ Address the individual, use "You" — talk to ONE person at a time!
- ▶ Do engaging transitions.
- ▶ Promote, brag about your stuff.
- ▶ Brag about other people's stuff.
- ▶ Be who you are on the radio.
- ▶ Take risks.
- ▶ Dare to be great.

Beyond Powerful Radio: A Communicators Guide To The Internet Age
By Valerie Geller, President, Geller Media International
copyright 2011. Reprinted with permission.
www.gellermedia.com

RULES OF ENGAGEMENT

ALWAYS ASK :

▶ What's in this for me—
   your listener?

▶ Is it relevant?

▶ Does it matter?

▶ Do you care?

▶ Can you make the
   audience care?

Beyond Powerful Radio: A Communicators Guide To The Internet Age
By Valerie Geller, President, Geller Media International
copyright 2011. Reprinted with permission.
www.gellermedia.com

AIRCHECK CRITERIA

Are you:

- Speaking conversationally, directly to each listener?
- READING?
- Sounding as though you are reading?
- Making smooth transitions? Are there "brick walls" between the elements or does the presentation feel seamless?
- Speaking visually?
- Telling powerful stories?
- Introducing the audience to characters they can care about?
- Funny? Is there humor?
- Taking the audience on a journey?
- Presenting moments of truth that connect?
- Including what's NEW?
- Including authentic self-revelation? — Do I know YOU, from this show?
- Going "personal" without going private?
- Boring? Did anything go too long?
- Taking risks? Any surprises in this show?
- Providing "talkable topics" for your listeners for later in the day to discuss with others? If so, what?
- Having fun?
- Giving your audience enough to make them want to come back?
- Serving your listeners? (Entertained, Informed, Inspired, Persuaded, Connected?)
- Compelling? Would your listener sit in a parked car and keep listening?

Beyond Powerful Radio: A Communicators Guide To The Internet Age
By Valerie Geller, President, Geller Media International
copyright 2011. Reprinted with permission.
www.gellermedia.com

PART I

Beyond Powerful Radio
Tools: Creating Content for Any Platform

CHAPTER 1

Beyond Powerful Radio
Creating Powerful Content—
No Longer "Just Radio"

"The experimental test of whether this art is great or good, or minor or abysmal is the effect it has on your own sense of the world and of yourself. Great art changes you."
—*Art historian Sister Wendy Beckett*

"Art is accusation, expression, passion."
—*Günter Grass*

Sitting on a shelf, in your bag or in a car dashboard, it's merely a box full of wires and silicon chips. The outward appearance gives little indication of the magic contained within. The radio is clearly one of the most ingenious devices ever created, yet to understand its power fully, it may help to view radio with primitive eyes.

You may have heard the story of natives in Papua, New Guinea, who, upon seeing and hearing their first radio, demanded to see the little man inside. A magic man, obviously, to fit inside so small a box. In the Pidgin of Papua, radio is in fact known as "Bokis, he cry," or "the box that cries." Primitive, perhaps, but accurate in a philosophical sense.

Radio is an almost magical extension of the human spirit. It can "cry out" and make a listener feel, laugh, and think. Powerful radio rings true and evokes a reaction. It also makes the listener want to keep listening in the hope that this will happen again.

Radio, no matter the delivery method, is very, very personal. People no longer sit around in groups listening to it. Today, much listening is done alone, almost in secret, through headphones, computers, on mobile devices, or in the steel-and-glass-enclosed privacy of a car.

One by one, the listeners are hunting for that connection, that powerful magic which is often missing from audio media today. Watching an average listener punch through the buttons on the car radio, or scan the Internet, is proof of that. One station after another is rejected. Many of these stations are simply unknown to the listener. But whether the "radio" comes in online, or through your phone or another mobile device, once that magic contact is made listeners won't go unless given a reason to leave. Your job as a radio professional is to entice the listener through the radio door, and then keep them coming back. This calls for powerful communication and connection. It goes way beyond "just radio."

In working with individuals and stations around the world, I've noticed that certain common threads run through each great radio moment, whether online, satellite, HD, or terrestrial radio. First, the audience must care about what is said. It must matter to them. It must touch their lives. The content or topic must reach them in a real and true way. And the topic can never be boring, or the audience will tune out.

Before anything goes on air, ask yourself:

- Is it relevant?
- Does it matter?
- Do you care?
- Do your listeners care?

While it may be the music or the news that first touches a listener, I believe the richest source of powerful radio comes from the personalities of the performers.

The key to personality radio is, logically, having a personality. This means having a rich, full life and drawing on all of your experiences. How you relate to life is how your audience will relate to you. The best broadcasters are great observers of life. They filter what they see going on around them through their unique creative process, and send it back out to the world. They talk about what they see, notice, think, and feel. They share their real selves. They mention what irritates them, what excites them, what saddens them. They react honestly to the news, current events, and the music they play. They are good storytellers.

If an air personality is doing the job right, audience members will feel that they are being addressed individually. The words "Hello, everybody" or "Good morning, St. Louis" will likely not be heard. The listener should feel that the person behind the microphone is like a friend. The air personality won't seem like a star but more like someone they would know in real life—a person with daily struggles, life experiences, and problems. Humor helps. You don't have to be a funny person to recognize a funny moment. This is a key element in creating powerful radio.

The points in this book are a basic recipe for communicating powerfully and creating powerful radio. You will read more about each of them in the rest of this book.

Every element of *Beyond Powerful Radio* relates back to these ideas. You can apply them to all facets of on-air work, including music presentation, talk shows, news, commercials, public service announcements, promotions, and more.

Let It Grow

Even the most powerful radio programming will take time to build an audience. Growing tomatoes takes a certain amount of time. So does building a news-talk or any radio station or program. Music stations or programs tend to grow a little faster. Obviously, standing over the tomatoes yelling "hurry up" is futile. Though it may seem ridiculous, it's amazing how many people expect that approach to be effective with creative talent and sales. Managers and owners hate to hear this, but in my experience, with few exceptions, it takes about three years to build a talk station.

The "overnight success" of Los Angeles Talk Station KFI is a good example. In 1988 every single bus board in traffic-infested Southern California was plastered with KFI ads. You could hear the station playing everywhere. People were talking about then-newcomer Rush Limbaugh. The *Los Angeles Times* printed six huge cover stories in its entertainment section about the various KFI hosts. Still the numbers hardly budged. Former owner Cox Broadcasting persevered. The company had spent money on programming,

Valerie Geller's Guidelines
for Creating Powerful Radio

- Speak in terms your listener can "picture." Use details. Describe the little things so your audience can "see" what you are talking about.

- Always start your show with something *very* interesting. This ought to be obvious but often isn't.

- Tell the truth. Listeners can tell when you don't.

- Never be boring. If you are bored, your audience will be too.

- If something big or important is happening today, go with it. It may be a pain to change your program or reschedule a guest, but it's worth the trouble.

- Listen to your station, even when you are not on (and check online content).

- Make your program matter. Use your own life as a show resource. Always answer: "Why is this on the air? Why should someone listen to this?" Would you talk about this OFF air?

- Bury the dead. If a topic is overdone, drop it.

- If you are live on air, anything goes! But anything pre-recorded should be perfect.

- It's okay to brag about your stuff—if it's good. Promote it.

- Brag about other people's stuff. If another host on your station had a "magic moment," talk about that too.

- If you don't know something, it's okay to say so. Actually, audiences love it when they sense that you are like them.

- Do smooth and interesting segues and transitions to other hosts and shows. Support them sincerely.

- Be who you are on the radio.

- Risk. Try things. Dare to be great!

talent, promotion, and an award-winning news department, so they hung on without making major changes. Three years, or about a thousand days after it signed on, KFI became an "overnight success." Years later it remains one of the most listened to news-talk stations in the USA.

Give It Time

People are busy and have short attention spans. But just as it takes time to grow tomatoes from seed to fruit, developing an audience is something that takes time to grow.

It is appalling to observe various local stations and networks hire and fire an on-air personality in haste if the show is not a "two-book wonder." Because of the new methods of "instant" electronic measurement, many managers give in to the temptation of throwing out a show that doesn't work *immediately.* But that is wrong. One of the problems with our industry is a lack of commitment on the part of management, to the talent and to taking the time it needs to develop and grow programming.

Brain researcher Dr. Evian Gordon writes, "It takes a thousand times of a repeated behavior to rewire the human brain to change a habit," including changing the listener's habits. Building an audience for both talent and a format is a process. It is tempting to pull the plug if results are not immediate, but a little patience and consistency can go a long way toward success.

This is human nature. Take some examples from years past. The original *Star Trek* TV series was canceled after just three seasons, because it had "failed." It took reruns for the audience to discover the Starship Enterprise and get hooked on the show. *Star Trek* in television spin-off shows, movies, and books broke records for decades.

American TV comedy star Jerry Seinfeld exhibits a framed memo from NBC-TV declaring that the initial research on his then new situation comedy showed a weak response, a poor supporting cast, and that most viewers who had seen the test pilot would not want to watch it again. The network ordered only four episodes. But somebody had faith in the series, and it paid off with many years of success for that network. Broadcasting is filled with stories like these.

If you can create quality programming, and consistently stick with a host, program, or format over the time it takes to find its audience, you will likely have your own success story.

CHAPTER 2

Beyond Powerful Radio
Are You a Generator or a Reactor?

"It's not what you say, it's what they hear."
—*Red Auerbach*

Putting Your Personalities in Power: Are You a Generator or a Reactor?

Have you ever noticed that some on-air personalities, while they may be completely professional, are somewhat boring by themselves? But the minute someone else walks into the studio, they seem to come alive and get much better. Some personalities seem more talented when they are performing live in front of an audience. Others are funnier, sharper, and more creative by themselves. It turns out that talent usually falls into one of two categories: generators or reactors.

In order to coach talent effectively, it helps to identify the talent's strengths and natural abilities. Sometimes that can be achieved by clearly defining the talent's roles. Consultant Dan Vallie advises, "There must be an anchor or director, a creative chief, a producer, etc." But before you define the role, knowing the type of performers you are working with lets you guide them toward their maximum performance. The programmer is then able to design powerful radio by making the shoe fit the foot, instead of trying to do it the other way around.

What Is a Generator?

The natural skill of a generator means that he or she can easily work alone or as part of a team. A generative talent can easily visualize original ideas. (These ideas are not always *good* or usable ideas, but generators do tend to come up with a lot of them.) A generator has a strong, independent imagination. The generator comes up with a myriad of topics, undaunted by the blank page. True generators are rare. Generators can be the "life of the party." Something interesting happens when a true generator enters the room.

What Is a Reactor?

Reactors are also creative individuals. A reactive talent takes existing ideas and comes up with numerous ways to make them better or more workable.

No less talented than a generator, the reactor nonetheless has a very different style. A reactor alone faces the blank page with terror. However, the moment a reactor comes in contact with a generator, he or she can instantly and very cleverly pick up on remarks, comments, or nuances and be very funny.

A reactor is usually the one who responds to just about any stimulus with an insightful or witty remark. Reactors can have a lot of fun talking back to their TV sets and radios.

If you've ever listened to a talk show that seemed to have a slow start, but then picked up after the interview or calls began, you were likely listening to a reactive talent. The minute the host can "react" off of the callers, or interview guest, generating for him or her, the show comes alive.

Many stand-up comedians are reactors. Although they might seem to be generative—after all, they're standing up doing a monologue in front of a live audience—in reality, if you put those people in a studio, alone in a room, without that live audience generating for them, they may be less colorful. Reactors work best with other people in the room to spark their creative energy.

Both types of talent are valuable and good, but the right casting here is the key. Forcing a reactor to carry the show as a generator doesn't work, and forcing a strong generator into an equal or subordinate partnership with another generative talent can lead to an almost painful on-air clash. The trick is to identify each person's specific strengths and then to encourage the person to develop those strengths.

Putting two generators together as co-hosts or as a team can sometimes be a disaster. They tend to battle for the microphone, seldom listen to each other, and compete for attention. The show sounds like two kids fighting at the dinner table. It is hard to listen for very long.

Putting two reactors together is not much better. The audience hears them casting a net for ideas over and over again. The process is dull, and, if nothing swims into the net, the show becomes weak and boring.

Electric connection with the audience happens when you have a balance of both elements.

How Do You Tell the Difference Between a Reactor and a Generator?

It is fairly simple. Generators have a lot of ideas and energy. They take huge risks and worry about it later. They have moments of brilliance. They sit alone in a room, and their minds overflow with ideas.

That is not to say that every idea a generator produces is a perfectly conceived show, but consistently they seem to be practically exploding with new material.

If you are looking at a reactive talent, you will notice that he or she is quick with a story, a memory, an imitation or a line for any topic you could give him or her. But you must lead the reactor by giving that first push, that suggestion, or a good opening. Leave the reactor alone in a room with no external catalyst for the show, and he or she is miserable. Reactors may do brilliant interviews, or pick things out of the newspaper that are unique, but they need some kind of initial stimulus to begin the process. But again, you probably have a reactor on the air if he or she is dull until the news person shows up or until the calls begin.

Generators are scarce. Most people are reactors. It is a little like being left- or right-handed. One is no better than the other. If absolutely necessary, right-handed people can adapt to use their left hands, and vice versa. You can certainly force people to improve in the area where they are weaker, but in most circumstances it is best for the station to take advantage of their natural inclinations.

A Cast of Dozens

You might think it takes a generator to host a morning show. That is not always the case. One reactor, "Casey," found a cast of generators in his listening audience. "Rita" owned and operated a local beauty salon. She was also Casey's loyal fan and listener. Rita started calling in on a semi-regular basis to chat about hot movies and goings on around town. She was funny and charming and had unique views. Rita became a regular on the show. The listeners started calling in wanting to meet Rita. She participated at station events and appearances.

Next, Casey added another regular listener, a talkative cab driver. Then he found a local construction guy with fix-it tips, who also happened to be 28 years old, dating regularly, and happy to talk about his adventures.

Using interactive media, Casey continues to add appropriate players as they appear. He now has a winning show with lots of generators to show off his reactive talents. He assembled his own generator–reactor team.

If you are an on air personality, it helps to know your own strengths, are you a generator or a reactor? And if you are a manager or programmer, it is your job to identify each person's specific strengths and then to encourage each one to develop those strengths. Once you know who your generators and reactors are, you can get onto the business of creating powerful radio.

CHAPTER 3

Beyond Powerful Radio
Personality Radio & Morning Shows

"An artist's working life is marked by intensive application and
intense discipline."
—*John F. Kennedy*

Why is the Morning Show Different from the Rest of the Day?

Morning drive is traditionally the most listened to daypart in radio. It starts the day, commands the highest ad rates, and requires the most up-to-date information so the listener can get out the door and face the day. A solid morning show can set the foundation for a solid radio station. On music stations, morning drive is the last bastion of personality radio.

If you play music on your show, a word about the music from the Australian Broadcasting Corporation's Jeremy Millar:

> Most listeners believe *you* choose all the music you play, and while sometimes that is the case, it is not always. The audience is at a loss to understand why you would play something you don't like. In focus groups around the world, listeners frequently say they think the host is an idiot for playing songs he or she doesn't like. They don't blame the station, they don't know about the playlist, so they blame the DJ or presenter

13

(and they say it's worse when it is a song they like!). It's important not to "diss" [or be negative about] the music you play. Someone, *somewhere* does like it. Obviously there will be many times when you have to play a track you don't like, but if you care, you can find a way to make a listener care. There are many examples of struggling stations that have improved their ratings by simply cutting their playlist. Sometimes less is *more*."

Most stations come up with the basics of traffic, weather, music, news, and sports scores, and other elements that drive a morning show. But what is unique to each show are the hosts and personalities. That is what the other stations cannot duplicate.

"Toothbrush Radio" or "I Hate to Get Up in the Morning"

A favorite research survey asked people in a Midwestern American city about their morning routines. The purpose was to look at listener needs, i.e., how each used his or her time in the morning, in order to improve programming during morning drive.

This survey showed listener habits. The list on the next page shows what that study found to be a "typical morning routine" for a "typical listener."

Of course, habits vary, and the list is a sample composite, but the research did show that people are creatures of habit and rarely vary from their personal morning routine. Based on my years of experience, below is an analysis of listeners' morning habits.

Attitude

- People do not like to get up in the morning. They are tired, groggy, and do not feel like hopping out of bed on a dark, cold winter morning if they do not absolutely have to.

- People feel that from the moment the alarm rings to the moment they get to their jobs, they are on their boss's time, not their own. Many people do not love their jobs and there is resentment of the morning rush. Because of this, humor on the radio in the mornings is especially important. If you can make a bunch of grouchy, groggy people smile or laugh when they don't feel like moving, you can keep them listening!

Reality

- If the radio gets boring, there's more to choose from. Listeners tune out and turn on TV in the background or go online. The Internet also offers immediate news, weather and sports and TV has gotten smarter, too. Those morning or "breakfast" shows now offer all the elements a radio show has—with the option of pictures.

- People want and need to know what time it is. Yes, they do have clocks in every room and some even wear watches. But it is easier if the radio tells you every couple of minutes what time it is so you know if you are on your morning schedule or running late.

THE ROUTINE

5:30 a.m.—the alarm clock rings

5:45 a.m.—the snooze alarm rings

5:50 a.m.—actually get up

5:51 a.m.—go to bathroom

5:55 a.m.—start coffee

6:00 a.m.—feed dog

6:02 a.m.—enter shower

6:08 a.m.—shave/brush teeth/blow-dry hair

6:20 a.m.—drink first cup of coffee, look at newspaper headlines

6:21 a.m.—listen for weather report

6:32 a.m.—wake the kids

6:35 a.m.—get the kids in and out of bathroom/get dressed for the day

6:58 a.m.—feed the kids and eat breakfast

7:15 a.m.—pack lunches

7:25 a.m —organize the kids' stuff for school and various other activities for the day

7:30 a.m.—organize your own stuff for the day; find kid's lost sock

7:35 a.m.—final house check, grab jacket, check for wallet, cell phone, keys/ lock door/out

7:40 a.m.—drive to work

What They Need

- When people wake up to face the day, they need to know basic information: What happened while I was asleep? Did anything explode? Are we fighting World War III? Can we drink the water? Is it safe to go out? What will everyone be talking about today at work? If I don't have time to read the paper this morning, or check my e-mail, I still don't want to look like an uninformed fool. What can I hear on the radio that will put me a bit ahead of my colleagues?

- Give the time and weather a lot. Listeners want to know: How cold is it out there? Do I need my boots? Do I need a raincoat? Do I need an umbrella? How do I dress my kids? Will it take extra time to get to work?

More Reality

People are creatures of habit. Personally conservative, they do not like changes at any time, least of all in the morning, when they are tired and cranky.

Powerful Morning Radio

Up the pace, not the volume, for morning drive. Move it along. The people listening now are in a hurry and don't have the time to get deeply involved in long, in-depth interviews or ongoing sagas.

Understand your listeners; less is more in the mornings. But make what you do *count*.

Mornings are when show prep and planning your time on air matter the most. Your awareness of the brevity of the listener's attention span in this daypart is key.

Air personality Jonathon Brandmeier explains his method for a successful morning show: "I break my show down into hours. Every hour should be a different show. If you continue something you did from 6 to 7 all the way until 9 to 10, the guy from 9 to 10 just waking up doesn't know what you're talking about."

Small Packages

Consultant E. Karl wrote in his report *State of the Art*:

> In the morning, if you get your listeners listening for an average of fifteen minutes an hour, you're doing pretty well. So, look at each hour as a package that has four fifteen-minute shows in it. . . . Each segment [should] contain all of the key elements you would have in any one whole hour of a morning show, e.g., entertainment, music, news, weather, and the other services.

Remember, it's important to:

- Prepare
- Read everything
- Make it matter
- Be real
- Have fun

It's Hard to Get Up in the Morning

Don't mention how tired *you* are. It's your job to get listeners out the door with your morning show, to motivate and get them going. If it is already a drag to get up early and get out, the least you can do for people is give them some help in facing the day. Maybe they'll feel better about it because they heard your show. And don't get too wired on coffee. Frenetic energy makes people nervous.

What Time is it?

Give the service elements a lot: time, weather, traffic updates, and quick news headlines. Give people what they can use both now and during the day.

Morning drive radio is the place where music radio and talk radio most intersect. Here are some thoughts and ideas from those who know what it takes to create a powerful morning show.

Boston morning man and air personality Matt Siegel offers the following points, important in creating powerful radio, no matter what your format or daypart:

What It Takes

- *Be honest.* Praise what you like . . . rip up what you hate . . . don't lie for the sake of a joke. This is how the audience gets to know you.

- *Use your own life as a source of material.* It's amazing how the audience always seems to know what's real. If they don't get to know something about you, they won't be loyal.

- *Be funny.* Don't forget you are entertaining them. This is radio, not therapy.

- *Be specific.* Name names—your wife's name, your boss's name, your friends' names, etc. That's what makes it real, thus scary, thus interesting. [In my opinion it is better to use a pseudonym or leave out identifiable details. Be aware of the rules about slander and libel and the possible legal ramifications when naming specific people, companies, products, etc., in your show.]

- *Be vulnerable.* Say something that you think might be inappropriate or a little personal. Be a grown-up. You can play the latest teen band's hit song and you can talk about the artists, but if you act like you are 18 when you are 35, you sound like a jerk.

- *Don't put women down.* It's cheap and you are better than that.

- *Be nice.* No matter how far you want to go, no matter how wild your act is, let the audience see something in you they like or, eventually, you will start to annoy them.

- *Don't be a wimp.* If you think it's funny or important, say it. Stop looking over your shoulder.

Ross on Radio

Edison Research programming consultant and Radio-Info.com's columnist Sean Ross has worked as a program director and record company executive. He writes a weekly column as well. Ross's thoughts on creating powerful radio are valuable for programmers and morning shows of any stripe.

Sean Ross's Top Ten Tips for Powerful Radio

- *Program for yourself.* Despite all the dogma about thinking like a listener and not a radio programmer, if you don't enjoy the product yourself, how can anybody else?

- *Use your special gift.* If you are going to do something anybody else can do on the radio, why did they need to hire you?

- *Some of those old wives were pretty smart.* Do not reject the "old wives tales" of programming out of hand. A station will not live or die if there is a power record out of the stop-set, tempo at the top of the hour, etc. But it WILL sound better.

- *When you become the 800th person to defy a cliché, you're not defying a cliché.* If your taxi driver is really a natural, put him on. But if 799 others have already cluttered the airwaves with local politicians, punk rockers, and orthodontists, a good DJ will be just fine.

- *Hire writers.* Only somebody who can write is going to be able to sell the same record, the same contest, the same crossplug 37 times and do it 37 different ways.

- *Yes, talented people ARE supposed to be difficult.* But don't waste your time on anybody who abuses the privilege.

- *If you are lucky enough to be working in live and local radio,* use the station you now have to do great local radio that entertains or touches the listeners with every break.

- *You gotta believe.* The world is full of successful stations with no money, bad signals, etc. Clearly, nobody told them they had a problem.

- *Don't use the signal to hurt people.* There ARE listeners who will let their dog eat dog food out of their mouth to win concert tickets if you insist on searching them out. It's no big deal to them, because many folks with REAL jobs endure degrading existences anyway. But wouldn't you rather make people feel better than feel stupid? The latter takes a lot more talent, especially now.

- *Every generation's music will become an Oldies format someday.*

American music industry icon Dave Sholin is a legendary disc jockey, program director, executive, and editor. He has helped a lot of budding young talents become more powerful broadcasters. Sholin figured out early on that the secret to success in radio is to be yourself.

Dave Sholin on Creating Powerful Radio

■ Always keep in mind the first eight letters of the word "personality": P-E-R-S-O-N-A-L. Whether one million listeners or one hundred, each one should feel that the conversation is being directed to them.

■ Trendiness has a short shelf life. Reflecting trends is quite different from embracing the flavor-of-the-month approach.

■ Origination always beats imitation. Allowing unique and likable qualities of your personality is the goal.

■ Don't feel the need to be funny on every break. Forced humor often sounds that way.

■ Try and avoid the echo technique, repeating what the caller just said.

Example:

"Hi, who's this?"

"John."

"Well John, where do you live?"

"Hillview."

"Oh, Hillview, etc. . . ."

■ Don't be afraid to push the envelope and try different or improper techniques. Though batting a thousand is unlikely, play the percentages.

■ Anyone in a music format needs to remember that the music is the star. Leave the negative personal opinions at the door. The songs must be great; otherwise, why play them?

■ Become an expert on the varied interests of the local community. Get connected to those in the know. Before mentioning any well-known local figure or local town, make sure your pronunciation is correct.

■ Less is more. The fewer the words, the greater the impact.

■ So-called rules should be considered as guidelines. In some cases, they need to be twisted or broken.

Air personality Ross Brittain has been on stations around the country combining humor, heart, and reality with an edge. This list comes from his days of doing mornings on Z-100 in New York.

Ross Brittain's Tips for Jocks

- Over-prep the day before.

- Do the things your listeners do.

- Make things bigger than they really are. Use theater of the mind—produce BIG or overproduce.

- Structure your breaks BEFORE the mic opens. Use Post-it notes to remind yourself.

- Remember your audience composition when building in features.

- Don't get caught up in "information overload." DELEGATE!

- Cluster your commercials correctly and clean up your talk breaks to avoid clutter.

- Speak concisely. Edit copy or write down important items so you won't get lost. Remember to use your sense of forward motion to move, or not move, your show.

"That's not my political opinion. That's just stuff I hear on the radio."

CHAPTER 4

Beyond Powerful Radio
From Rock to Talk
(and for Anyone Who Wants to
Do a Talk Show)

"Don't walk in front of me, I may not follow. Don't walk behind
me, I may not lead. Walk beside me and be my friend."
—*Albert Camus*

"The great 'end' in life is not knowledge but action."
—*T. H. Huxley*

It's been a long time since the truly "full service" radio station disappeared.
Most listeners in the United States have only heard of, but never actually
heard, a station where music, interviews, news, sports, and personality call-
in segments were equal parts of the programming day.

Not only that, but even the highly formatted stations have narrowed
their focus into subcategories of their genres. For example, in talk radio
there are "Hot Talk" stations, "Lifestyle Talk" stations, "Truck Talk"
stations, "Political Talk" stations (which include their own sub-genres—
some political station formats are geared toward either the left or the right
wing), "Sports" stations, "Religious" stations, and "Women's Talk" stations, just to name a few. With the advent of high-definition, online, and

satellite radio, formats now target audiences in ever greater detail, and the trend is likely to continue. If a "full-service" station appeared today, it would probably be researched and designed to fit that small subsector of the listening audience who have been determined to need nightclub music, political polling data, volleyball scores, and agriculture reports.

In music-based formats, personality elements tend to be restricted to morning drive, or have been done away with altogether. Morning shows tend to be filled with so many commitments—news, sports, commercials, business reports, traffic, weather, and promotions—that there is often little time for personalities to emerge.

The Great Ones Make It Look Easy

One of the last bastions of personality radio seems to be in the talk formats. That is where people perceive an opportunity to be free to creatively express themselves. Consequently, we're seeing an influx of people who want to do talk radio, many of them smart, hardworking, and funny, but often having no experience in the format. And they all have one thing in common: They think it's going to be easy. After all, anyone can talk. It must be simple—right? Wrong. As with any other demanding occupation, from pro football to ballet, the great ones make it look effortless, but if you've ever tried to toss that ball 50 yards or do a grand jeté, you know that's not the case. This book can train you in powerful radio methodology, and the craft of broadcasting. You can improve your skills. But the one thing no one can teach you is talent. That is a gift you were born with. And even the most talented broadcasters work very hard if they're successful.

Talk show hosts as individuals are a diverse group, with a common element. They all tend to have strong opinions, they are funny or at least have a sense of humor, and they have original things to say. They stay topical, are interested in listeners' opinions, and enjoy interacting with people. These hosts connect with people in a real way. It is a real relationship, even though it often happens with one person in a small room with a microphone and the other in a kitchen, at a desk, or in a car.

It hit me years ago hosting overnights on talk station KOA/Denver. Taking late-night calls from people in thirty-eight states all over America, I learned how people needed to be heard, how talk radio eased the collective loneliness of those glued to their radio dials all night long. How powerful radio could be. In his book *Radio Waves*, Jim Ladd writes about "sitting around the glow of the radio campfire, hungry for the sound of the tribal drum."

If you are working in a music format, you are ahead of the curve when it comes to launching a talk radio career. Many music radio air personalities turn out to be just the right people to handle talk radio. They have a range of interests and understand the time constraints of radio. They also have been schooled in the basics of formatics and why they are important.

Maintaining an audience requires great storytelling. In music radio, the songs are often the stories. When music hosts decide to become talk radio hosts, it is often a case of wanting to talk about the stories that are inspired by stories that songs are telling, or the stories behind the songs.

Music radio hosts are comfortable working with all the properties of sound. Most of the good ones know how to edit sound, use it to set an emotional tone, and understand how sound affects thought and mood. Those skills are a great asset when making the transition to personality radio.

Among the better known of the "rock-to-talk" personalities is syndicated host Rush Limbaugh. His show advocates an agenda in much the same way music radio in years past picked up on politics, pop culture, and issues of the day. Rush adds excitement to his show by employing music radio production values, sense of timing, produced bits, jingles, and parody songs, all mixed in with a heavy dose of his conservative politics. A talk radio pioneer, Limbaugh took the format of "serious" or political talk radio, something that had been traditionally stodgy, and added the element of fun to a format previously unblemished by humor.

People ask me all the time, "What's Rush like?" When I worked with Rush at WABC in New York, the thing I remember best about him is that he was a pro and he worked hard. He'd be in the office hours before his show, going through dozens of newspapers looking for material and doing show prep. He didn't make life difficult for management, and he was a fun guy to have a cheeseburger with.

Limbaugh explains his success this way in his book *The Way Things Ought to Be*: "[On station KFBK in Sacramento, California] I was allowed to be myself." He says it was the first time in seventeen years on the radio that he was allowed to be who he was on the air. Limbaugh warns, "You'll never be your best doing it someone else's way." He says his show has been so successful because he entertains audiences, not because of his right-wing politics.

One of the few other conservative political radio personalities with the same kind of following was the late venerable newsman and commentator Paul Harvey, and for almost the same reasons. Harvey was a master storyteller and was fun to listen to. When his broadcast was on, you could see people parked in their cars, captivated, during the lunch hour listening to Paul Harvey.

The moral for success here: No matter what your politics, be unique. Be yourself. Create your own style.

Play the Calls Like You Play the Hits

Another secret of Rush Limbaugh's success is that he "plays" callers like a DJ plays songs. Talk radio is not public service radio. Rush understood that you have to entertain listeners. Just because someone calls the show does not mean he has a God-given right to be heard on air. Rush says:

> The primary purpose of callers on my show is to make *me* look good, not allow a forum for the public to make speeches. I, after all, am the reason people listen.... Two minutes of a boring caller is the same as playing a record nobody likes. What do you do when a song you don't like is played? You go looking for a song you do like.

Despite radio's long-running emphasis on targeting a youthful demographic, it's a mistake to let age be a prominent factor when judging talent. It pays to remember: Whether a person is eighteen or eighty, if he or she captivates you with original thought and storytelling, can relate his or her own take on the truth, and communicate an interest in life, you'll have a winner!

What Else Does a DJ Bring to the Talk Table?

Talent can take you a long way, but it must be strengthened by experience. Good voices in talk radio are secondary. It's what you say that matters most.

Timing

A real advantage the rock-to-talkers have is timing. You can hear the polish and experience of a personality trained by years of short segment breaks on the air. They know how to hit the point, get to it fast, and get out of it.

Less is More

Former music jocks have learned when to end a bit. In listening to audition material, you can hear the difference between an experienced talent who has fought the clock and won, and a talented beginner who doesn't quite get the timing. That training, which only comes from experience, is invaluable and shines through in talk radio, even without the tight restrictions of short songs and a format clock. The lesson here: Just because you get a couple of hours to play with, don't waste it!

How to Rock the Talk

Another DJ who made the transition is broadcast personality Phil Hendrie. After a successful twenty-year career in music radio, Hendrie was feeling cramped by the lack of freedom and formatic restrictions while doing morning drive at a Los Angeles rock station. When his station decided to make a change, Hendrie begged for a chance to try his hand at talk. A new LA talk station gave him an opportunity to host a weekend show.

Back then, Hendrie was a creative guy with huge potential. He spent years as a radio vagabond, honing his talk skills. Hendrie has become famous for his amazing talent of hosting a show where he plays his own callers, using dozens of voices who take on their own personalities. Callers become the "hits" of the show when they take the bait and phone in to argue with one of Hendrie's characters. Hendrie observes life, filters what he sees, adds his unique talent, and lets it roll. His career path has moved toward television and movies.

Phil Hendrie on Creating Powerful Radio

- *Get in there and flop.* Try everything. Powerful radio is experimentation. If the station you're now at doesn't appreciate it, sooner or later you'll find one that does.

- *Be a popular culture junkie, but not just TV and movies.* It means noticing dress, road signs, vending machines, faces, accents, window tinting, houseplants, snippets of conversations, drool, etc. Record all of it.

- *Forget callers.* Prep your show so that the material is interesting to you first, your listeners second, and your callers third.

- *Be absolutely clear and focused as to what your show is about.* Management tends to push around and overconsult talent that isn't. You'll be getting and taking a lot of bad advice.

- *Keep your show lean.* It's about you. If you don't need them, lose the sidekicks, the happy talk with the newsperson, the chronic callers.

- *Don't pre-record bits.* Do them live. So what if you screw up a sound effect or a line. Your chances of succeeding with a bit go up a hundred percent when you do it live. And don't overwrite. Keep your ad-libbing skills sharp.

- *Throw away the listener mail.* If they have something to say, they'll call. Listeners who write to talk show hosts are oddballs.

- *Listen to one aircheck a month maximum.* Listening to too many airchecks will only depress you as you nitpick every little thing. If you hit a home run on the air, you'll feel it.

Music Hosts:
Are You Ready to Make the Move
From Rock to Talk?

Do You...

- Listen to talk radio and like it better than music radio?

- Get really mad when things are clipped out of the newspapers, or when you can't find anything heavier than *USA Today or People* around the station?

- Have a home subscription to ten or more magazines or newspapers?

- Spend hours and hours online reading news and editorials?

- Find yourself calling talk shows?

- Resent your program director telling you to "shut up and read your liners"?

- Hate the "hits"?

- Check your watch a lot and feel mostly bored during your airshift?

- Enjoy taking calls on the air or do more phone bits than you're supposed to?

- Like doing interviews and wish you could do more?

- Long for more airtime to talk about things that matter—what's happening in the news, in town, etc.?

Trial by Fire is Not for Everyone

Even if you get a chance for that on-air audition, it may not be the best way to strut your stuff. An audition is not the best of circumstances. Being on the hot seat is a nervous thing. It's been my experience that people who audition well are a bit like people who do well on tests at school. Those who "ace the tests" are good test takers, but they are not necessarily the smartest or best and brightest talents. Programmers can be fooled. They can hear a great demo or audition night, hire the person, and then be very sorry later when they are not as good as expected.

Ex-music jock Turi Ryder expresses it another way:

Every person in the world is capable of three good talk shows. Each individual has a few things that he or she cares passionately about, at least for a few hours. After that, it gets much harder. Creative people constantly find new interests, new subjects they need to entertain themselves. That is how they come up with different shows every day.

Ryder was working as a disc jockey for a well-known music station when I met her. Her Top 40 DJ days included some of the best stations in America. She was bright, fun, loud, and lovable, but with a definite dark side. I thought she'd be perfect for talk radio. She has gone on to enjoy a career as a major market talk show host, writer and now is the host of *"Turi Ryder's Exception to the Rule"* a short-form nationally syndicated feature for CBS radio.

Tips from Rock-to-Talker Turi Ryder

- Audition as the entertainer you are, not as the host you think "they" want.

- Don't be afraid to say "I don't know" on the air. Audiences prefer honesty and ignorance to artifice and arrogance.

- A little silence can be a valuable thing.

- "Nice" is a luxury you can't always afford.

- Establish rules for your show, then play by them.

- You have 50,000 watts and a microphone; the callers have only a phone and a radio. Give them a break.

- Never make fun of a caller after he or she is gone. Exception: if he or she hung up on you.

- Changing the names of businesses and people lets you tell either more of the truth or bigger, better lies.

- Not everyone who has done something interesting IS interesting.

- EVERYTHING IS MATERIAL.

How Do I Break Into Talk?

As a radio consultant who is constantly on the lookout for talent, I find that while listening to airchecks is important, the best way to find tomorrow's stars is not necessarily airchecks. Airchecks can be heavily edited to sound great, especially since many people now have home editing software. But from a talent's perspective, all that home audio capability can be a great thing. You can use it to put together an "audition" show and post it on your website. Talk programmers are also giving audition opportunities to podcasters and bloggers in their quest to find new talent. Some talk personalities have independently set up their own website "stations" and are hosting their shows—bypassing broadcasting or working at a radio station altogether, and a number of Internet-only talk networks have emerged.

But if you are seeking a job at a radio station or network, whether you have a studio available or some simple computer recording equipment, it's what's on your audition effort that counts.

The Audition

I often ask the host to interview himself or herself and record it—by this I mean starting with a question, then moving to a descriptive monologue from the potential host's unique point of view. That's how most actual talk shows open every day, and you don't need callers to come up with an interesting fifteen-minute conversation.

I'm also listening for the likeability factor. An air talent may be brilliant, but if you would not want to take a five-hour car trip with them, why would you put that person on the radio and ask your listeners to do exactly that?

Think of your audition as a spoken autobiography or narrative, where you are free to tell your favorite stories about yourself and your life. This not only showcases your storytelling ability—a very important part of talk radio—it lets people get to know you in a very personal and powerful way. Some of the best auditions tell of meaningful experiences that have changed or moved people, experiences that have made them the way they are. The more personal a story, the more universal it often is.

Another method for programmers who are considering an untested talent is to ask the host to do a hypothetical talk show. Ask, "What would you talk about if given a few hours on air?" Ask the host why he or she cares about those subjects—why would they be interesting? Ask the host to do an opening monologue for his or her "show" with opinions and personal stories or about some event of the day. You can offer a studio for recording this if you have one available.

I once had a client—a news anchor, author, and expert in finance—who had never before hosted a talk radio show and wanted to try it. She recorded a charming story of two little old ladies who came to her for financial help and discovered they were nearly millionaires as a result of their hobby of collecting antique dishes. A ten-minute recording got her the opportunity to audition and substitute-host on some of the top stations and networks in the country, without any actual talk radio experience.

Still, without an aircheck, it's definitely harder to find a program director who will risk putting you on the air. So how do you come up with some kind of presentation that will showcase your personality and potential as a talk host? How can you convince a programmer to put you on as a substitute host to "audition" on the air? Your best weapon in getting a shot at an audition shift on air will be a powerful demo.

Creating a Powerful Demo

No one likes making a demo. Talent will take any excuse to hem and haw and procrastinate when a program director says, "Send me your stuff." The general feeling is "I don't know what to put on my demo. I am the worst judge of my own work. How will I know what is good and what is garbage? What really represents me?" I once waited five years for a talent to send me his aircheck. This is where having your own website can really help you. When you have your own site, you don't have to choose one particular type of show or talk format to submit; you can post several, with descriptions, and a program director can simply click on the topics and styles that seem to work best with his or her needs. You will have to sort through or create work that you feel represents you at your best. Even the most experienced talk hosts tend to avoid this task.

Here are some ideas and techniques to help hurry along those facing the excruciating dilemma of creating an audio demo.

1. **The aircheck should always leave the listener wanting more.** The worst thing you can do is offer too much. It's like overfeeding a fish until it dies. If you are sending a disc or posting audio files, be sure to segment them into tracks or subfiles. That way the program director can skip around more easily, or dip in and out of your show. If you leave your audience just a little bit hungry, it will pique their interest in you. Your goal is to get the PD, manager or anyone who can hire you, to ask for more.

2. **Don't get paralyzed deciding what to post or burn.** If you have an hour showcasing your versatility, use that. If you have a great hour showcasing only one aspect of your personality, use that. Then let me ask you for more. Most PDs look for talent who are equally good with humor, substantive issues, interviews, and breaking news.

3. **Show your heart.** Show what you care about on your demo.

4. **Show your stuff.** Showcase your technique. News executive Bernard Gershon suggests, "If you are the person preparing that demo, put your best stuff up top—even a montage of some highlights—then more details. If you are weeding through audition audio tracks, listen for that spark—the edge that, with your guidance, will make that person a pro."

5. **This is your self-portrait.** This demo should be exactly as you want to be perceived by a potential employer. As air personality Turi Ryder advises, "Make your demo or audition not for the job you currently have but for the job you want to have or the show you want to do. Keep in mind, the people listening want to hear not only what you have done, but also what you can do for them."

6. **Be Yourself.** There is nothing worse than being told that "you were never as good as your demo." As Ryder puts it:

   > "It should be like a good, but not a rare, hour—one where you really do not want to edit anything out, but not as if a perfect human being with your voice was sitting in for you. I want whoever hires me from that demo to know what they are getting before I move my furniture."

   On your website you can create a perfect self-portrait, but, for your own good, make it an accurate one. Ryder warns music and talk hosts:

   > "If in your typical day, a caller changes your mind or you must admit ignorance of which drug the murderer was on, or screw up the name of the Afghani foreign minister, then that is the show you do."

   She points out that the exception is in the case of news. There, an error-free audition is preferable.

7. **Showcase your most individual work.** I like to hear shows that originate in people's lives. One example I use for coaching came from veteran Swedish radio personality Jesse Wallin.

Jesse decided that he wasn't going to mix the formula for his new baby's bottle. He said it was easier to just spoon in the powder. That way, when the kid spits it up, all you'd need for cleaning would be a dust-buster or a vacuum. It takes a father who has cleaned up a lot of baby spit to think of that. I laughed, I was moved, and I cared about him.

8. **Think like a program director.** Imagine your disc arriving in the mail, or opening your link online. Now it is in the player, with an attentive, hopeful, and open-minded program director beginning to hear your work. Then the phone rings. Ask yourself, would the PD stop listening and get the phone, or ignore it because he or she was too absorbed in hearing your work?

Looking for Talent

Make an audition that commands attention. Music radio consultant Guy Zapoleon puts it this way: "There is an 'X' factor. It is the feeling I get from listening to the talent." What do I listen to? Everything that comes in. As Bernard Gershon says, "You have to review demos, place ads, network, and listen to your competition in both smaller and larger markets. Try to find someone who you think 'gets it,' who has an original sound. If the person truly has potential, the rest can be learned." With most stations and satellite radio available via the computer, it's easier than ever to hear any host in any market in real time. Hosts should always remember, when designing their websites, to make it as easy as possible for a potential employer to connect to their stations during their airshifts.

What am I listening for? Anything that keeps me in a parked car in a dark garage with the groceries melting in the back seat, because I have to hear the rest of the show, is a keeper. If I cannot leave until I know what is going to happen next, you're in.

When listening to a personality music show, Guy Zapoleon asks:

- Do they connect with the audience?

- Are there great phone calls where you get the feeling from the listener that they and the jock are truly friends?

- Are they creative at selling the radio station, using promotions, using liners?

- Do they still get excited by something that radio pros take for granted, but the listeners don't . . . the music?

Programming executive Denise McIntee sifted through New York City's radio applicants for years. Here is what she looks for in demo airchecks:

> Do I laugh? First and foremost, I want to know if the host has a sense of humor. Do I want to keep on listening? Would I want this person as a friend? What did I learn from the host? Did I walk away from the show with a new perspective on a topic? Was the host able to persuade me to change my opinion? Is the host respectful to those who disagree? Can he or she "fight fairly" with a strong, intelligent caller?
>
> The host should have talent walking in the door. That is a given. But, developing energy, communication, and humor is tough. If a host does not possess these important vital traits, you should re-examine your hire. Very few people have it all. That is why there is a shortage of "genius-level" talk-show hosts and entertainers. Most times, a leopard does not change his spots. If you start without the basics, you could end up stuck with a host you are constantly trying to change, rather than coach.

News executive Bernard Gershon has hired many news writers, anchors, and reporters. Most of what he wants in a candidate would be necessary qualities for anyone working on the air as well as for managers.

When searching for talent at any level, look for three primary qualities:

- Intelligence

- Desire

- Sense of humor.

Intelligence does not just mean being book-smart or having a high IQ. Intelligence means the ability to solve problems, to complete complex tasks with resourcefulness, initiative, and resolve. A good job candidate also needs to be intuitive, to understand what is on listeners' minds, what will get them to tune in.

So, if you are interviewing potential talk-show hosts or newscasters, you need to find out what they are interested in, what stories push their buttons. Even if those story ideas sound boring to you, let them explain. They may win you over. That is what makes a talk host or newscaster great—the ability to communicate and excite.

An Intelligent Job Candidate Will Also Be Looking for New Challenges

If you are interviewing someone who has seen it all, done it all, knows it all—move on. Curiosity is key to intelligence. Do not be fooled by a long résumé with important-sounding titles and degrees. I look for job candidates who have traveled, and have taken an eclectic mix of courses in college. I hold nothing against history or economics majors, as long as they have the ability to communicate. Look for a sense of humor, but you are not looking for a wiseguy or a stand-up comic. But you are looking for a good communicator and storyteller, someone who can roll with the punches, take criticism, and still take his or her job seriously, someone who can relate well to fellow employees and diffuse difficult situations with humor and aplomb.

Getting a Job: The Demo is Done, Now What?

You have made the perfect aircheck. It represents your best work. Your personality shines through. It is visual, informative, inspiring, funny, has tons of truth in it, and you know if you can just get the right person to hear it, it will get you a job.

You will now learn one of the most disheartening lessons in radio: Getting someone to listen to your work is harder than you thought. Programmers, consultants, station group heads, and everyone else who can actually hire you are very busy men and women.

Consultant Jaye Albright explains, "It takes time to do justice to material people send. That is why I do not have time to do this sort of in-depth listening and thinking about more than one or two auditions per day."

Talent is very sensitive. If a talent calls a programmer, sends a demo, calls again to follow up but doesn't hear back, he or she is likely to get discouraged. My advice? Don't be.

Jock auditions tend to be three to five minutes long, and they arrive by the pound. Many of the people who send them have at least some experience, though not always. Talk airchecks are longer—they can be around thirty minutes. It takes longer to listen to them. Whatever the format, there are always a lot of airchecks waiting to be heard, and the number of auditions I receive from complete amateurs is staggering.

Talk radio is an art, not a science. Finding those artists requires spending time sifting through the plethora of auditions that are e-mailed, mailed, handed out, or even dropped off at your door.

Here is how it happens for me: Typically, whenever I attend a talk radio conference, or present a seminar, I collect around fifty CDs or weblinks in less than six hours—all personally handed to me by hopeful talent. When I return to my office, there are dozens more waiting in my e-mail and regular mailbox, and my voicemail is filled with broadcasters asking, "Have you heard my show yet? I sent it a month ago!"

When I walk in the door after three weeks on the road, jet-lagged, hungry, and exhausted, that is not the time you want me to hear your work. Please cut consultants and program directors some slack. You want me to listen when I am "in the mood." And that mood is not on a reliable, methodical timetable. When I was an air talent, I never understood that things happened on *their* time, not mine.

Don't Rush Me

Programmers generally listen to new material when they are in the market for talent. It would be nice if stations' needs always coincided with hosts' availabilities. Unfortunately, it seldom works that way. Sometimes PDs miss their chance at a great hire.

I once did a talent search where I listened to dozens of shows I had stowed away, and found a young guy I really liked. I heard a lot of potential there. I called him in St. Louis, and he picked up the phone just as the moving van was arriving to pack up his stuff. He had accepted a job in Milwaukee two weeks before and was on his way. Although his work had come in to my office four months earlier, I hadn't gotten around to hearing it—my loss.

Don't Develop "Attitude"

Unfortunately, when a programmer fails to respond promptly to an aircheck and résumé, the talent can get really mad. Many lean toward the touchy side anyway. They take it personally. Some simply give up. If they are extremely annoyed at you, they could ruin great opportunities for themselves.

Talent may think: "I have called, written, e-mailed, and faxed. I put in a lot of work on that demo. My work is good, and I want somebody to hear it and find me a job. Hire me, or at least tell me 'no.' It has been two months." Or, "What a jerk this guy turned out to be. He [or she] never even acknowledged receiving my materials. They couldn't pay me enough to work there now!"

In truth, it is entirely possible that the programmer has been busy, has not gotten around to hearing your work, and does not want to call and say "no"—at least not yet. However, if you call fifty times, you may get a "no" from a programmer just to get you off the phone. You can be sure that if you become a pest, your audition has very little chance of being heard at all. Most PDs would interpret an overeager host as someone who would be a pain to have around the station if he or she were actually hired. The goal is to be politely persistent, not obnoxious.

Sometimes It Pays to Be Aggressive

Decades ago I went after a job I wanted very much. I knew the PD had offered it to someone else, but I wanted him to hear me before he committed to the hire. I called him up and played my aircheck for him over the phone. It was too late to get that job, but my tenacity impressed the programmer enough that he recommended me for other positions.

When to Send Out Your Work

A logical time to start looking around is when you know people are hiring, unless you just want to make a connection for later. In the United States, it generally happens twice a year, like clockwork, just before the fall and the springtime Arbitron ratings periods. Although some stations do post openings, not all of them will. Be sure you have every e-mail subscription to every trade you can (many are free of charge). If you can't afford some of the pricier newsletters, ask a trustworthy friend in the business to forward any leads to you.

Pay special attention to the websites that show the ratings for markets where you want to work. If you see a station on a downward path, chances are they may be open to making some changes. Do a little sleuthing when you're trying to contact station management. With a little ingenuity you should be able to figure out the e-mail addresses of anybody you want to find. Make sure you read online the newspapers from the cities where you hope to work, particularly their media columns. You can contact those writers directly through their websites, and they may have some good leads for you.

"Sorry, Your Show Is Garbage": A Programmer's Horror Story

When I programmed WABC in New York, I was fairly organized about the hundreds of applications that came in, especially because we had a well-publicized opening. It is my policy to listen to everything.

In the days before you could electronically and easily send sound files, I had a system that included three big brown cardboard boxes. In the first box, which I kept on the floor by my desk, I had the "keeper shows." Next to it was the second box, where I kept the "possibles" or people from whom I wanted to hear more. I kept the third, the box of "unlikely" candidates, on top of my desk so that my assistant could write polite "no thank you" letters to them.

Late one night, a new cleanup crew, thinking that the two boxes of audition demos on the floor were trash, threw them away. I came in on Monday morning and looked around for the "good" batch, but it was gone. Of course, the demos in which we were not interested were still there, right on top of my desk.

It was humiliating to have to put an item in the trades saying, "If you sent material and an application for our morning show, please resubmit it. The janitor threw it out." On the other hand, if you really want to hear all about certain individuals, by all means put their discs or business cards on top of your desk. It won't be long before you hear, "Oh I see you're talking to Brian . . . he's looking for work again?" Or "Is that Sue Smith's demo? Her auditions sound great. Too bad she can never do a show to match them!" And here is the best comment I heard from a staffer who noticed a package on her boss's desk: "Oh him . . . he's great on the air, but let me tell you about the time we had to bail him out of jail for drunk driving after he hit an old lady. Another time he showed up for work handcuffed to his date, and we had to hire a locksmith to get him out so he could do his shift."

Heed this warning: Unless you truly want feedback from the staff on potential candidates, and do not mind if they go ballistic reacting to what is on your desk, do not leave anything out for them to see.

If you are a talent who cannot risk having the world know you are looking to move on, use e-mail and a website, or, when you send your work, try saying, "I know some of your staffers. Whether or not you decide to hire me, I'd appreciate it if you kept my application under wraps." Most program directors will respect your confidentiality.

Finally, be sure to fully label everything you send with your contact information.

REMEMBER, materials get separated. WRITE YOUR DATA ON EVERYTHING!

Library, Nova Scotia Community College

CHAPTER 5

Beyond Powerful Radio
Local vs. National Programming

"People will forget what you said, people will forget what you did,
but people will never forget how you made them feel."
—*Maya Angelou*

When you tune your radio to hear a favorite program or music, do you know where the show originates? Is this show coming from your town, or from New York, London, Chicago or Los Angeles? If you're listening because you like a certain personality or the content of a show, do you care where it comes from?

In America, and throughout the world, radio stations are licensed to cover local communities, and to serve them. Yet, mainly for economic reasons, many stations have opted to broadcast a full slate of programming generated elsewhere. Others provide a mix of both local and national or international shows. Very few stations broadcast one hundred percent locally produced programming.

There is no question that local news and current events should be covered by a local radio station. Our first and most important responsibility as broadcasters and communicators is to keep the public safe from harm. If there's something happening locally that affects the health, well-being or safety of our audience—that *needs* to be covered. But aside from local news and coverage of community events, does it really matter where it's produced, if it's *good* content?

The following story is from Native American storyteller Ron Evans, with thanks to Joel ben Izzy:

The Storyteller

Villagers in a remote African tribe had been living just as in years past. Their homes were constructed of grass; their water collected from a nearby river. They planted and gathered their crops by hand. Nothing they used or did required electricity. In fact, they didn't have electricity at all. Each night, as was their custom, the tribe gathered and listened to their village storyteller. Through the stories, the people maintained their history and learned of their ancestors.

A foreign anthropologist came to Africa to live with the tribe, to study them. It was rare to find a group of people who were living in the same manner as their ancestors had lived for generations. Soon after he arrived, electricity came to the village. The country's government believed that electrical power would improve the villagers' day-to-day lives, and make everything easier for them. Not long after that, a television was plugged in.

Now, instead of gathering around a storyteller, each night, the people of the village could watch the television. And they did—for one week. Then, they turned the TV off, and went back to gathering in the evening around a fire and listening to their own storyteller.

The anthropologist was puzzled. He asked, "Why go back to the storyteller when there are so many more stories on TV?" One of the villagers replied, "Yes, you are right. There are many more stories on the television. But here in *my* village with my tribe, the storyteller knows *me*."

Storytelling is powerful. It's true that it might be better to be in the very same room with someone who knows you personally. But if you can't have your own storyteller, one of the definitions of powerful radio is when a listener forgets they are listening to radio and just feels that he or she is *in the room with you.* When you tell a story, on radio, or in a podcast, in a movie or a novel, so that the listener feels "my storyteller knows *me*," that's when communication is at its most powerful. Your audience forgets *where* the voice they hear is coming from.

If a personality connects with an audience, if the information is relevant, and the stories powerful, if audiences feel that the storyteller "knows them," then it does not matter whether the storyteller is sitting in front of a microphone a few city blocks, or thousands of miles, away. The storyteller knows *you* if, when you feel lonely, you can tune in to that storyteller and no longer feel alone.

In America, most audiences say they really don't care that certain personalities are national rather than local broadcasters. One example is Oprah Winfrey, a national broadcaster. Oprah's audiences feel a connection to her and feel that they *know* her. The issues Oprah talks about are important subjects in her audiences' lives.

If you create programming that is relevant, and if it's presented engagingly, is useful or fun, if it informs or entertains, showcases human experiences and if your stories inspire, persuade and connect with the audience— it's going to succeed, no matter where it comes from.

"How about a little music to push the plot along."

CHAPTER 6

Beyond Powerful Radio
Performance & Formatics

"To escape criticism—do nothing, say nothing, be nothing."
—William Teacher

"If you bring forth what is within you, what you bring forth will save you. If you do not bring forth what is within you, what you do not bring forth will destroy you."
—Jesus

Performance

Now that you are on the air on a regular basis, you know what hard work it really is. When you listen to the radio, you notice people who sound spontaneous. They make their work look natural and easy. It seems these people never make a mistake on the air, or, if they do, you hardly notice, or the show takes an unexpected twist and gets even better.

Then there are broadcasters who seem pained and uncomfortable when things go astray. It can make you very nervous to listen to people reacting to a situation that way. How can you make sure you sound like one of the naturals?

The difference between accomplished professionals and talented neophytes is that the seasoned air talent always give you the feeling that they are in control, no matter what happens.

This skill can be learned. The people you admire on the air have mastered some basic techniques that carry them through the most difficult situations. Their experiences—successes as well as failures—are what make them so adept now. You cannot avoid some of the unpredictable aspects of this business, but you can learn reliable techniques to improve your show. You can escape certain traps by practicing a few elementary performance points, and there are things you can do to "self-correct" should the show begin to take a turn for the worse.

Performance Points

1. **Pick Topics about Which You Really Care**

   A great talent or personality can make selecting a sofa interesting. Boring people, on the other hand, could ruin a conversation about the discovery of human life on Pluto. If you are *interested,* you will make it *interesting.*

2. **Use a Strong Show Opening or Monologue**

   Be sure to do the following:

   - FOCUS the topic.
   - ENGAGE the audience by forming a question.
   - State your OPINION or POSITION on a talkable topic.
   - Explain your view through example, experience, or STORYTELLING.

   Do not read entire prepared speeches. If you must read on air, do not *sound* like you are reading.

3. **Never Be Boring!**

   Get rid of dull guests immediately. Remember, if you are bored, it is boring. If a guest starts out great, or was selected as an expert, but in fact turns out to be stiff, too nervous to think clearly, or is in any other way non-communicative or inept as a storyteller, get rid of that guest.

   How often have you checked your watch when a guest is talking, or have taken a mini-vacation in your head? If this is happening, try a few direct questions calculated to raise the energy level in the room. If that does not help, dismiss the guest.

If this is a problem for you, have a prearranged signal with your producer just as couples do at parties. News people can be sent in waving copy. Anything that allows you to shove a dullard out the door is fair. Make a transition, and immediately try doing something else.

Remember, you are probably more interesting than a boring guest. Be flexible and protect your air product. If the guest is great, keep him or her with you longer.

Why is getting rid of a boring guest so difficult?

It is surprisingly hard to speed the departure of a guest because we are trained from childhood to consider the feelings of others. As professionals in polite society, we do not wish to be rude. But it is ultimately better to be abrupt with one guest or caller than to be impolite to an entire listening audience, boring them because we feel uncomfortable cutting off the discussion. The audience is under no obligation to be polite to you, the host. They feel free to leave if things get dull.

What if the expert is in the room staring at you, expecting to go on the air for the full show?

With live radio, it is especially difficult to ask the tough, meaty questions or to cut off a boring guest if that person is in the room. Do it anyway. You should not have promised a guest more than a few minutes of airtime. Your producer can explain the show's "policy" on the matter.

It is easier for some hosts to exercise the "cutoff" switch if the guest is on the telephone rather than live in the studio. Try sacrificing a little sound quality by using a phone connection if this makes it easier for you to end an interview. One famous American host has created an environment designed to simulate the listener's experience. She places the guest in another studio, without eye contact, so that the conversation relies solely on listening and verbal communication. You may find there are some advantages to conducting an interview this way.

4. Don't Take Calls Just Because They're There

Program director Alan Eisenson has rules for guests and callers. He says, "Guests and calls are simply tools for the host to use to make a better show. I would rather hear a strong air personality than boring callers or guests. It is up to the host to determine when a guest or call gets boring. Some guests could be great for three hours and others are only good for five minutes. Some callers could go on for five minutes, but are only worthy of five seconds. A good host and producer should be able to tell the difference and pace the show accordingly. Only use callers to enhance the show."

Talk personality Turi Ryder's theory is that many "callers will make their point, then begin to make it a second time if left unchecked. The trick as a talk host is to get them off the air when they finish their best material, before they say: '...*oh, just one more thing*' and before they start to loop around again."

5. What If the Interview or Topic Goes Wrong?

Sometimes you ask a wrong question, or don't frame your talkable topic/engaging question well. If you are not getting the desired response, perhaps it is time to change the story or example a little, or recompose the question to engage the audience differently. Do not be afraid to reset your topic going into or coming back from a break. But do not repeat your topic exactly. Add something new.

6. You Can Change Your Mind

Your opinion may change. As Alan Eisenson points out: "Views may change as an issue evolves over days or weeks. Do not be afraid to change your opinion as more facts become available or if a caller or guest persuades you with a strong argument to change your mind. Do not stick to your guns if you find you are wrong. Remember, always tell the truth. And don't be afraid to admit you don't know something. You're not expected to have all the facts about every issue all the time."

7. Take a Risk on the Air

Sometimes you head into a danger zone with a comment, view, question, or decision you make about what goes on the air. Understand that not everything you say will be popular, even if you feel it is true.

A lot of what you can get away with depends on your relationship with management. Even more depends on your level of success. Proven personalities can get away with much more than an unproven talent or new arrival.

If you know you are heading into a controversial or "gray" area, sometimes it is better to ask permission from your boss. A powerful show is not one where a host lives in fear of getting the axe. Note to managers: If a talent calls you and lets you know he or she is about to move into a potentially dangerous topic, make a decision. If you need to take a moment to consult a lawyer, or another manager, do it quickly.

Is it better to beg for forgiveness than ask for permission? That depends. Trust your instinct or gut feelings, but try not to hold yourself back from potentially powerful moments. Do not be so afraid of failure or getting into trouble that you lose your spontaneity and sense of discovery, risk, or adventure on the air. Live radio is a live experience.

Broadcast executive Mel Karmazin always backed multi-media performer Howard Stern. When they worked together at CBS radio, no matter what Stern said, if he "crossed the line" and got the network into trouble, Mel Karmazin paid the penalty fines. As a manager, Karmazin believed in Howard and liked the profits generated from the show. He understood that talent cannot be restricted. If you want the great moments, you must assume some risk.

Some talents, like Stern, have chosen to move their entire shows to alternative distribution systems. There's less risk of fines or public outrage if your programming comes via satellite or the Internet. Alternative platforms are fairly unlimited when it comes to what language can be used, although many cable networks choose to maintain over-the-air broadcast standards. Over-the-air terrestrial radio and TV continue to have limitations as to what words cannot be broadcast. Because of the number of incidents where restricted language has been accidently aired, and large fines have been levied, many over-the-air stations have increased their time delay during live events. There's usually someone standing by with a finger over the "dump button." If you hire a talent who is used to broadcasting in an unrestricted setting, make sure he or she understands the standards you expect, and the risks you are, and are not, willing to assume to support creative content.

In America, there is often greater concern over offending special interest groups than over the occasional expletive that may slip out. Either way, great talent who have strong management backing them up will have a better chance of surviving and achieving success.

The best managers behave honorably. As a manager, if you tell your talent it is OK to do a certain type of show, you are honor bound to live by that commitment until you mutually agree to change it. Do not fire talent for your mistake. If you say, "Go ahead and speak your mind, create discussion, we do not mind controversy," then be prepared for the consequences. Your phone will ring constantly with angry listeners. Your mailbox will be filled with hate letters. Fifteen people may march in front of the station, threatening to boycott your biggest advertiser, and your spouse may be embarrassed to tell friends where you work. If you are not ready to live with that on a day-to-day basis, then do not hire people who do those types of shows.

Talent will occasionally do things you would rather they had not done. However, not all talent live on the cutting edge—most operate somewhere between the safe and the daring. But the more artistic and creative the talent, the greater the risks that artist is likely to take. The payoff can be enormous, but it may cost you your serenity and security.

In Chapter 8, *Airchecking,* you'll find various examples and methods of guiding talent to say what they want to say while generating less hostility or controversy. It is best to establish a line of communication where managers know what is happening and can choose what fights to support. Managers do not like unpleasant surprises.

8. Use Your "Off" Switch

From the wisdom of consultant Jaye Albright, "Master the use of the most difficult piece of equipment in the control room: the 'off' switch on your microphone. Practice moderation. Learn to recognize when a bit is over, and stop talking at that point."

9. The Day You Wished You'd Stayed in Bed

Not every show will be your best show. Even your favorite air personality has the occasional bad day. Sometimes you just can't hit the ball, no matter what you do. Your rhythm may be off, or you may not be feeling well.

When you had a show that did not work, it is important to do a quick analysis. Look for an easily identifiable reason why your show didn't work. Not enough sleep? Hungry? Inadequate show prep? A fight with your former spouse just before you went on the air? If it is fixable, fix it. Do it differently next time.

Perhaps you simply did a poor job of it. There are two things you can do: You can choose to pick it apart over and over and beat yourself with the aircheck, making yourself feel terrible, thereby ensuring you will do a worse job tomorrow, or you can let it go. Regular listeners who like you will forgive one bad show. Tomorrow someone will be listening who has never heard you before. That person will not know about today's bad show. Forgive yourself and move forward.

10. Treat the Staff You Work with Respectfully

Whether you know it or not, they have a lot of impact on your performance. The station's staff can help you or sabotage you in a million ways. A miserable team will cost you more than you think.

"It's not enough that we succeed. Cats must also fail."

> "Art lives from constraints and dies from freedom."
> —*Leonardo da Vinci*

Formatics

Listeners like formatics. They provide structure, like the walls of a house. People want to know to whom and what they are listening, and they like to know what time it is. Jaye Albright says:

> For most of us in most situations, formatics are absolutely essential. They are like "the blocking and tackling" exercises of our sport. And, as in the NFL, where spring drills begin with the statement, "This is a football," before you dispense with formatics, you must execute them naturally, flawlessly. Formatics are all about memorability, habit, and familiarity. It is these things that can make ratings, unless your content is constantly superior and compelling.

For a programmer, making sure the formatics are properly done is the easiest part of an aircheck session. The aircheck tells all. If anything is missing after a performance, follow it up in the session. Call attention to it and make it a goal for the next session. Sometimes new talent do not understand the importance of formatics to ratings results. Explain the necessity of getting this part right. As long as ratings are counted by recall, although it will matter less with PPM (Personal People Meters), this is one element of success that is up to each host.

It makes sense to do everything we know to win. Repetition stimulates recall. It is that simple. Your station will be marketing itself to advertisers with hard data about website visits, store traffic, etc. Make sure you are doing your part by giving the information you are asked to communicate.

With the advent of PPM, where listening is measured in real time, without the listener or viewer having to recall his or her habits, or keep a diary, some types of formatics have become far more important, while others are not quite as vital as they once were. One of the facts of life that has not changed is, in the words of the Australian Broadcasting Corporation's Jeremy Millar: "It's easier to get existing listeners to spend more time with you than to recruit entirely new listeners. Because ratings share is a function of both Cume (numbers of listeners) and TSL (time spent listening), it's intuitively appealing to encourage existing listeners to listen longer. You're pushing on an open door, because you've already got their attention, and are just seeking a little more."

How much more? Millar suggests you set as your target:

"Five More Minutes"

"We're too busy," Millar continues, "dropping kids off, juggling phone calls, checking messages, thinking about how to say 'no' to that holiday visit, and listening to radio. Mental multi-tasking is at an all time high. We've all seen the statistics on how much information we're bombarded with each day. You want me to listen longer? Can I give you another quarter hour of my time? As they say in New Jersey, 'Fuggedaboudit.' Five minutes more? Keep going. I'm listening.

If all your listeners gave you five minutes more every day this week, your share would move in a very positive direction."

So, how can you use formatics to get those extra five minutes? Here are Millar's suggestions to make your station "sticky."

1. *Invite.* Don't tease. And invite like you mean it.

2. Invite a mere five minutes ahead.

3. Like a magician, don't do the full "reveal." Keep something up your sleeve by inviting with a "hook" that tells your audience what's in it for them.

4. Invite frequently. Invite five minutes more listening any time there's something telegraphing, "you might want to leave us now." *For example*:

   ■ At the top of the hour, invite across the news and make people feel included in what follows the news, or promote what we're about to learn in the news.

   ■ As you change topics, or switch to something new, invite the audience to stay, and tell them why this is going to be good.

   ■ As you go into a song (someone might not care for this song, so invite people to listen to what's coming *after* the song).

   ■ Prior to the next guest, invite the audience to listen in, or join in.

Make an Appointment

What if you decide you want to invite your audience *more* than five minutes ahead? That's "Appointment Listening." Jeremy Millar describes how to create "appointment listening" to increase your station's ratings: "Pick a single show highlight, not a menu of options. Give the listener the exact time they can hear it. If they're interested, but you're vague on the time (i.e., 'coming up,' or 'later on this morning,' 'soon,' instead of 'in ten minutes,' or 'at the end of this song' or, 'at 7:15') they won't bother. Tell people *exactly* when they can hear something, and they might make the effort. Research supports this technique, and it's easy to do."

You Are Invited

If you download a podcast, or watch a YouTube video or even broadcast TV, you no longer have to come in during the middle of a show. You can digitally record it, and begin at the beginning. But live radio is still one place where you join the action "in progress." So, it's important that listeners feel that they can join in at anytime and are always "invited" into your program.

Dennis Clark is Executive Producer for the Ryan Seacrest morning show on KIIS-FM in Los Angeles. Clark explains how the Seacrest show invites the audience to join in *anytime*:

> Have you ever been to a social function where the first thing you observe when you arrive is people standing around in small groups, chatting and drinking? You pick a group and approach them—in a nanosecond you know whether you're welcome to break into the circle, or whether it's best to detour to a new group. This is "The law of party throwing." It means that we want to make the show sound as accessible and welcoming as possible. We want listeners to feel it's OK to break into our circle. We invite listeners with the underlying sentiment, "Jump on in, the water is fine."

Overcoming Resistance

Programmers around the world share a common frustration and ask the same question of talent: "Why don't you simply do the formatics as you are told? How hard can this be? We have talked about this over and over again!"

Talent says: "You care more about call letters and time checks than you do about content! A monkey or a robot could do formatics. I am an individual. I got involved in what was happening at the moment."

Some managers take it too far and become obsessive about the number of call letter and dial position mentions. Although it is my belief that you can never say the name of a station enough times, New York City program director and personality Scott Shannon makes this important point: "Great stations are not built on hot clocks and contests, they are built on heart."

Why rebel with formatics or forget to do them? The reason is that many on-air personalities do not believe it is important. Because they already know who they are and where they work, it becomes boring to them to repeat their name and the station's dial position and call letters.

If the talent does not understand the absolute importance of formatics, they will not be a priority. Ask talent to imagine how they would feel if someone heard their show in a cab and wanted to listen again at home, but couldn't, because they couldn't remember the station's dial position and call letters. Not giving your call letters is like asking someone to find your house when you have no street sign or address out front. It is to everyone's benefit if talent understands how listeners listen. Make it clear that the audience has a short attention span and often uses radio as background. As a last resort, if a talent continually forgets to do formatics, try helping out with produced elements. If you have ever listened to a radio show and wondered, "Who is this person and who is he talking to?" you will understand the need for resetting and formatics.

Credit Where Credit Is

I once consulted a station with famous, historic call letters. Everyone associated with it was proud to work for this radio legend. They assumed that people were familiar with their station. Many were, but most of their actual listeners seldom heard the call letters or station name and had trouble remembering where they were tuned.

We increased that station's ratings seventy percent in one ratings period by saying the call letters and the name of the station every time we took a call, gave the time, started the news, and opened the microphone. I would love to say we added seventy percent to our listening audience, but the truth of the matter is we simply made it easier for people writing in their Arbitron ratings diaries to remember where they were tuned. With accurate electronic measurement this may not be as crucial, but if you are getting "credit" for listening based on recall, you can never say the call letters or the name of the station too many times.

Be responsible for eliminating what Arbitron terms "Phantom Cume," i.e., those people who listen but can't exactly remember the dial position,

DENNIS THE MENACE

"I LIKE THE WAY YOU DON'T EVER TAKE A BREAK FOR COMMERCIALS."

Internet address, or name of the personality or of the station. If your station is using a recall method for ratings, then every fifteen minutes you are judged by what the diary keepers write down. That means every fifteen minutes hammer home:

- YOUR NAME

- NAME OF THE SHOW

- NAME OF THE STATION ("The Talk Station")

- CALL LETTERS AND DIAL POSITION

Repetition is the way we learn and memorize. Think of television's *Sesame Street*. Repeat and repeat and repeat until the audience learns it.

Talk Radio Formatics

Each format in radio has a slightly different structure. They all have one thing in common: Your listener should never feel the pressure you feel to execute formatics correctly.

Never let a listener feel the format

Don't use "radio-speak." Try not to use those words and phrases you say only when you are in front of a microphone, e.g., "segment," "this program," or "forecast." Try to keep your formatics as natural-sounding as possible. Always answer the question, "Why should someone listen to this?" Only mention the "clock" if there is a benefit to the listener.

If you say "Here's your traffic on the eights," it is helpful because the audience needs to know that you are keeping your promise to bring them traffic every ten minutes. You may also have a break at twenty minutes past the hour, but listeners should never feel your formatic restrictions. That's our problem, not their problem. They don't need to know when it's time for us to take a commercial break.

The structure of your show is there for a reason, mostly to market your station. But listeners care only whether it is interesting or relevant to them. Your audience should never feel your format—they should simply feel they are spending time with you.

For talk radio, the structure is more or less like the one Alan Eisenson uses:

Talk Formatics

- Open the hour with your name, the time, and the call letters.

- Do some short opening comments, if you have any that day which may or may not be your main topic.

- Launch into your monologue, i.e., engage the audience with your opinion/position and storytelling.

- Ask the question. This is your tightly focused topic.

- Give out the phone numbers.

- Take a break, using proper formatics: Use the term "up next" instead of "take a break."

- Open the floodgates (the phones) after your first break.

- Reset the topic by asking the question going in and out of each subsequent break (again, using proper formatics).

Resetting and Teasing

Broadcast instructor and former RCS executive Tom Zarecki spent years as a programming consultant. He says:

> Since new people keep tuning in, the host needs to frequently recap guests' names, what group they represent, and showing how the topic is interesting to a listener. Keep teasing upcoming show segments or features. Waiting five minutes in a drive-time interview to recap what's going on, or only teasing once or twice an hour, is simply not often enough.

Formatics do not have to be dry and boring. If you do them well, they can become a creative and exciting part of your show.

Formatics Tips from Consultant Tommy Kramer

Be sensitive to repetition. A good talent varies the way everything is done. The listener wants consistency but not predictability. Even if positioning phrases or branding should require that things be said in the same words all the time, the talent can still vary the inflection of the words. Repetition becomes boring quickly and is also an indicator of the deadly "automatic pilot" mentality that can bring down a talent or a station fast. Do your part. Keep the talent energized by pointing out good examples when they occur, or freshening things up that may have become tired sounding.

Here are more specific ways to use formatics to engage your audience from Tommy Kramer's *Coaching Handbook*:

■ **Pull the listener into the radio with you**

If you say "It's 72 degrees out there" you tell me, the listener, that I'm out there and you are not out there with me. You are somewhere else. In reality, I am in my car or at my desk and you are with me when I am listening. Why push me away? I've heard talent in Fort Worth [a suburb of Dallas, Texas] say "over in Fort Worth." Why? Just saying "in Fort Worth" will say it without distancing yourself from the Fort Worth listener. Avoid saying anything that pushes the listener away.

■ **Sell the benefit**

Always sell a benefit of the show or station. "Soft easy favorites" is not a reason for me to listen to you on my way home from work.

What is the benefit to me? But "soft easy favorites to make your drive home easier" gives me a reason to listen.

■ **Use real language**

What is more effective? "For further information and details, call 456-1111" or "You want to know more? Give me a call." How about, "It's just about forty-five minutes after the hour of twelve o'clock." Would you ever say that if I asked you what time it was? Wouldn't you just glance at your watch and say 12:45? Talk on the air the way you talk in life.

■ **Connect with the listener**

Tell me—don't read to me. Let your language and manner pull the listener into the radio. The legendary late newsman Paul Harvey used to write about a dozen key words on a card, then tell the story.

■ **The rule of one**

Do one main thing per break. Obviously, you need to identify the station and/or music, give the time and whatever your station's "formatics" are, but do that stuff briefly and then do the one thought you set out to do this break.

■ **Hit the target**

Many stations find it helpful to draw up a specific profile of your listener, complete with a picture if possible. Post it in the on-air studio. Speak to that one target listener every time the mike opens. Say things that will appeal to and interest him or her. For instance, if it is a soft adult contemporary station, you might not want to dwell on the hockey scores. And keep it singular. Do not say, "If some of you listening would like to go…" Instead say, "If you want to go…" Always talk to one listener at a time and aim at the target.

■ **Promote ahead**

Promote anything of benefit coming up on your show. Be truthful. Instead of "I'll have tickets to give away in a few minutes," try "This hour, you will have a chance to win Lady Gaga tickets!"

If you tell me something is coming up in a few minutes and I only have twenty minutes until I get to work, I'll be mad at you if you don't get to it by the time I shut off the car radio. But if you tell me it's coming up within the next thirty minutes, and I only have twenty,

I won't hold it against you. Never promote anything as, "coming up after the break." That is like saying, "I'm going away now."

■ Don't tell the listener what to think

It is irritating. "Here's one you'll really like" (How do you know? What if I don't?) or "You'll have a great time" (What if I have a lousy time?). Tell me that you like it and why (or why some people like it). Let me decide for myself. You may know the Chinese saying: "Tell me and I'll forget, show me and I may remember, but involve me and I'll understand." We do a lot of "telling" on air, which never seems to work as well as finding the way to "involve" your listener in your subject or topic.

■ Sell the dream first, before you give the information

In advertising, they say, "Sell the sizzle, not the steak." Seek an emotional link with the listener. Help me see why I want to win before I have to hear all the junk about how to do it. If you do not make me want what is being offered, there is no reason for me to care about all that technical information.

■ Have a road map

Know how you are starting. Have a destination in mind. Know how you are ending. Move on to the next element.

Often a talent takes way too long to get to the point. We have all heard breaks like: "WZXT 99 with Elton John and Rocket Man from 1973. You know, he's done a lot of great work over the years and this one is definitely one of the all-time favorites. Now let's go to the phones—Jennifer's on line three. Let's find out what her most embarrassing moment was. Jennifer, how are you this morning?" Tighten it up, cut to the chase! "WZXT 99 with Elton John. Jennifer is on the phone. Jennifer, what was your most embarrassing moment?"

■ How to edit phone calls

Keep the unnecessary parts of the calls off the air. "OK, Jane, thanks for calling in today" or "Thanks for having me on," or "thanks for taking my call," and other superfluous stuff does not need to be on the air. It is boring, slows momentum, and no one cares. Instead identify the station and keep to the point, "Jane, you are on Sunny 98.5. What weird gift did you get on your birthday?"

■ Formatics for callers

Dennis Clark uses a specific format for calls that go to air on the Ryan Seacrest Show. (More about how he handles callers in Chapter 14, *Call Screening.*) "Each caller is identified by name and place, and, after they make their point, they get a brief and sincere acknowledgement of their call." The standard format lets potential callers know that this is a safe place for them to call. Clark says, "They can join our circle with confidence. No listener should feel scared to call because they are worried they might be embarrassed or humiliated."

■ Reset the stage

Adopt an egg-timer attitude, and every couple of minutes briefly reset the stage for anyone who may just be joining the show. (One talent coach I know actually leaves a fifteen-minute hourglass on the studio console.) If the listener cannot quickly get what is going on, he or she might choose another station. If I tune in and hear "Florida's winning coach Steve Smith on Sports Radio 540, The Team,…this morning," I won't feel confused. Let the new listener know which voice belongs to which person and what that person's role is! "Celluloid Mike, our film critic is here. Mike, what should I take the kids to see this weekend?"

■ Break the habit of "taking a break"

Please do not use the word "break." It comes from TV, where they regularly do stop the action and break away from programming to do other things. But because everything on your radio station is a part of your total format, you are almost never "breaking away."

Do not "break now for the news." Each time you tell the audience there is a break, they think that they, too, can "break away." The whole show is yours. That includes sports, news, and anything else inside your show. Stations are rated not only on how many listeners show up, but also on how many listeners stick around. Try something along the lines of "Let's find out what else is going on. It's six o'clock and you are listening to WXXX. News is next." Do not throw away a single minute of your airtime, even if your station requests that you give a standard introduction to other elements. The mark of a professional is the ability to make every word his or her own.

■ Don't panic if you need a moment

Have you ever heard someone on the radio chattering aimlessly, verbally casting about for clarity of thought or direction? That talent has likely been taught to "keep the meter moving. Whatever else happens, keep talking."

However, that fear of "dead air" can provoke meaningless, manic episodes that will actually lose your audience. Do not be afraid of a moment of silence. The listeners will understand, and it beats the alternative. Do not panic. Take a pause if you need a few seconds to collect your thoughts.

Taking a moment of silence can also become a tool. Veteran New York radio host Bob Grant learned this trick and often paused for a few seconds after stating a powerful message to get the listener's attention. Grant, among others, learned that nothing can get the attention of the listeners more quickly than a second or two of "dead air."

Content Plus Formatics Equals Ratings

In addition to your content and style, here are some talk radio basic formatics that can make a difference and get you ratings.

Before each break

- Remember to tease what is coming up or reset your talkable topic or engaging question.
- Involve your audience. Use a cliffhanger to keep them coming back for more, staying through a break, or just listening longer.

After each break

Briefly reset your topic. A reset should include:

- Your name
- Dial position
- Topic: Ask your focused question or tease—preferably one that everyone listening to will have a burning desire to answer
- Phone number
- Time check (if relevant)

Example: "In case you've just joined us, it is 6:21, I am James Johnson and you are listening to WXYZ AM 690. Our guest is supermodel Christie Christensen, talking about her new book, *Sleep Your Way to the Top.* What do you think about using sex to get your job? Call us at 666-8255."

At first, working with formatics is a struggle. Aircheck yourself regularly. Keep practicing and you will notice improvement. When someone comes up to you in the hall and says, "You make it all sound so easy," you will know you have mastered formatics.

CHAPTER 7

Beyond Powerful Radio
Finding & Developing Talent

"Sometimes when you are leading [an expedition] you have to say whatever you can to keep people on your side. It doesn't matter if people believe what you say or not. They need to see you believe it. That's what leadership is about."
—*Philip Kerr (on leadership and mountain climbing)*

Where Do We Find Tomorrow's Talent?

In her novel *Star Country,* Jill Robinson suggests that "star potential," or raw talent, is easy to spot: "Long before the fame hits, the star's the different one. The leader—or the weird one. The motor's there. You want to feed off it; use its heat."

The stars of broadcasting share certain traits. Genuine talent are true individuals, gifted storytellers, and good listeners, as well as articulate communicators. They have original thought, intelligence, and passion. These people have a strong life force and a sense of humor. They have passion, and they get a kick out of things. They burn with curiosity. Some have a formal academic education; all have a lot of life experience. These are people who naturally connect with others—individuals with ideas and things to say. They tend to be a little ahead of popular trends. They have a strong need to be seen and heard.

It Takes Talent to Find Talent

Developing talent, product, and content requires another element: faith. There must be someone on the staff—a manager, producer, or programmer—who has the ability to find the right people and bring them into the fold. The ability to recognize talent is a talent in itself.

General managers and program directors would love to have a crystal ball they could consult to find out which personalities will work and which will flop. But there's just no way to do it with a new person the public has not experienced.

Take a chance. Give a talented prospect a shot on the air. Make it a weekend or fill-in slot. See how he or she sounds and trust your instincts. Don't pull the plug too soon. If you believe in a talent, hold on, even if not everyone in the building shares your belief.

A tip that can save you two ways: Never judge the talent on just one show. A talented host should be versatile and able to switch from light to heavy topics. I once heard a guy do a pretty decent show on the right way to hang the toilet paper. The next day he was interviewing the Secretary of State. It's just as important to know that the quality is consistent even if the topics vary wildly.

How To Find Talent

Station managers constantly complain that fresh, up-and-coming talent is hard to find. Where are the syndication superstars of the future? Because talent is born, not created, how do we spot it? Then how do we develop and keep talent once we have them?

Despite the spectacular growth of syndicated and satellite radio, only a handful of people have developed at the network level. Most successful national talent started on a much smaller scale, with daily or weekend shows in small to medium markets. When network talk or music shows are given to individuals who don't have much training or talent, they usually have some degree of fame, particularly in politics or acting. A lot of programmers get seduced by using a "big name" to draw an audience. Usually, this doesn't work out. Most successful hosts are people with strong backgrounds in radio. They've worked hard to learn their craft and often make the job look easier than it is. That illusion of ease is one of the reasons many managers think they can put any famous person on the air and have him or her succeed.

As more and more stations turn to syndicated programming, there is concern that the smaller-market, "farm team" method of growing tomorrow's talent is disappearing. Using a syndicated show may be cheaper in the short run, but developing your own talent can pay off down the line in ratings, revenue, and goodwill.

Programming executive Denise McIntee has years of experience finding and developing new radio talent. She advises:

> Be on the lookout for colorful characters in your everyday life. Ask friends, business associates, relatives, and neighbors. Often, they can tell you about an obscure cable-TV host on at 4:30 in the morning who was totally entertaining, or a local stand-up comic who had the patrons in stitches. Teenagers are a valuable resource as well. They hear about the latest trends or hottest acts about a year ahead of everybody else.
>
> Radio stations are loaded with born entertainers, and not just the people on the air.
>
> Look closely for the [off-air] employees who are surrounded by staff when they walk in the office. These are the people everyone looks to for entertainment. Their electricity may translate onto the airwaves.

Sadly, most programmers will not give an audition to anyone without an established track record or who has not honed his or her craft in a smaller market. These programmers lack confidence in their ability to discover a "diamond-in-the-rough."

Sometimes looking at the people working or just "hanging around" your radio station can bring big benefits. I have found and developed radio personalities who literally landed on my doorstep. At WABC/New York, we did a huge, nationwide talent search, looking for somebody fun, interesting, topical, and loaded with personality. I listened to hundreds of programs from all over the country and auditioned several people. None of them proved right for the specific profile of the station we were building.

When our afternoon call screener/board operator expressed interest in hosting a show, no one took him seriously. Then we talked to him. He had studied acting at Yale and had a real feel for radio and a wonderful ability to do impressions. He could sing and write parody songs, was original and creative, and was up on current events. He was also funny. His idol was the afternoon host, for whom he was running the board. We tried him out. He was hilarious. The show was a success.

Syndicated host Lionel was a listener. He was a lawyer who liked to call in to talk shows. He was so talented, verbal, and funny that the PD of a Florida station gave him a shot on the air. He wound up drawing such huge audiences that he was offered a job in New York.

Another example is TV and radio personality Danny Bonaduce, a former child actor from the popular 1970s TV show *The Partridge Family*. Chicago air personality Jonathon Brandmeier had a regular "Where Are They Now?" feature on his show. Brandmeier located Danny Partridge, alias Danny Bonaduce, in Danny's own words, "broke and starving" as a maitre d' at an LA restaurant. Brandmeier thought Bonaduce such an engaging personality that he helped him land a radio shift. Watch for talent wherever it presents itself.

Real-life characters are another way to jazz up your show. Include interesting folks from your community in your on-air cast. Many of the big morning show hosts in America have made "stars" out of peculiar people they encountered in real life. Brandmeier got enormous mileage out of "Piranha Man," a Pakistani immigrant who operated a donut shop. "Piranha Man," with his thick accent and his foreign ways, was endlessly amusing, but he also helped to familiarize other Chicagoans with a rather misunderstood ethnic group. "Piranha Man" eventually had his own theme song and even came out with his own line of cologne.

One BBC station in England has used a New York City taxi driver, "The Gabby Cabby," to keep listeners up to date on what's going on in America. His reports deal with pop culture, weird people, and odd occurrences. How did the station find this guy? He's the cab driver who happened to pick up a visiting British program director.

Another station uses a former flight attendant as their regular consumer/travel expert. Twice each week, she gives her humorous inside tips on the travel industry, and, like the cabby, she's developed into a genuine station personality. "Rita from the Beauty Parlor" is another "found" personality. She's funny and spirited. Rita reviews movies, gossips, and gives advice about love and relationships, all based on what she's learned while doing women's hair.

Don't exclude people who might be considered mentally ill. As it's known in politically correct circles, their "alternative reality" can offer a refreshing change from the everyday reality the rest of us have to deal with. If a listener insists that he is Napoleon, and seems sincere, give him a chance.

You can find unique characters everywhere. The only requirements are that they have lots of personality, are fun, and are good talkers. I've found talent in all kinds of unlikely places. I've worked with bartenders, teachers, musicians, writers, scientists, lawyers, doctors, university professors, pet groomers, athletes, pro-team coaches, priests and ministers, cops, and housewives, all of whom had personality and original things to say. Even those who did not work out were worth a try. The moral is: Always be on the lookout for talent everywhere, from the experts who make guest appearances on your station to the life of the next party you attend.

What to Look for in a Talent

So how do you get on the talent development track while continuing to provide a decent level of programming today? There is no easy answer. Asking experts in the field for help and advice is one way. Many PDs use the weekend, fill-in, or late-night shifts to find and develop people. Another tactic is to steal promising talent from the competition. Don't worry if your prospective host isn't perfect. Allow faults to show. That's what makes people interesting. Author Anne Lamott could easily be writing about air personalities as she describes the traits of narrators in her book, *Bird by Bird: Some Instructions on Writing and Life*:

> A person's faults are what make him or her likable. I like [for narrators] to be like the people I would choose for friends, which is to say they have a lot of the same flaws as I do. Preoccupation with self is good. As is a tendency toward procrastination, self-delusion, darkness, jealousy, grovelling, greediness, addictiveness. They shouldn't be too perfect. Perfect means shallow and unreal and fatally uninteresting. I like for them to have a nice sick sense of humour and to be concerned with important things... politics and psychological and spiritual matters.

Look for people who are unique, bright, and articulate. Find good listeners, with strong personalities and opinions and a variety of interests about which they are passionate. Most have a sense of joy and humor and are big readers. Often they are rebels. They should be fascinating. Sometimes they are angry. These are the "odd ducks." They can talk to anyone about anything. Most of all, great personalities possess a quality that is at once indefinable and compelling. Some call this quality the "X-Factor." Can you remember the last time you stood shivering in your towel in the morning, but couldn't turn on your shower because you had to hear what was coming next on your radio? Find people who can make you do that.

Humor has a place on your station. You might be surprised to find that humor has a place on every radio station. You do not have to hire funny people, just people who have a sense of humor. It is important that your staff and your station have an appreciation for the odd, the strange, or the quirkier aspects of life. Moments of levity can be found in topical stories, news, or issues. Even the most serious news programs save a "kicker" or feature for the end of the newscast.

Hire Storytellers

See if you can find someone who can tell a story three times, three different ways. Because many broadcasters work with subject matter that may not change very much over the course of days, weeks, or even months, they must be able to vary their storytelling. This keeps it interesting to an audience familiar with the material. It is as if you told your spouse a story. That night you have dinner guests and you tell the story again. The following day, you retell it to a friend over the phone. Your spouse has now heard the story three separate times. However, if you managed to vary your anecdote with different details or a new approach, it was not boring. If you have people on the air who can do this, you have the makings of a great radio station.

Finally, hire smart people. And when you find yourself looking for work, try to find the smartest people you can and work for them. If you are just learning broadcast management or any other aspect of the broadcast business, apprentice yourself as you would in any other field, from medicine to plumbing. Learn from the best—it will set a standard for you.

Right Casting

It is important when you have assembled a stable of on-air talent to make sure that each one is positioned to achieve maximum success. In my work, I call this "right casting." Understanding right casting is vital. If you were a movie director, you would not cast Arnold Schwarzenegger in the part of an old, bald, chemistry professor. He could play the part, but he is better playing his "strengths."

Once you've decided that someone has what it takes to be on your station, you still have some assessing ahead. I have found that talent tends to fall into one of two categories: more about this in Chapter 2, *Are You a Generator or a Reactor?*

Knowing the type of performer you have (or if you're on air, you are) lets you guide toward his or her maximum performance. The programmer or manager is then able to design a powerful radio program by building a show around the strengths of the personality instead of trying to do it the other way around by stuffing your performer into a role that does not fit. Broadcasters also need to know what roles they play best when they are looking for work. As a manager, the first and maybe best thing you can do to help talent do their jobs well is to make sure they are correctly cast and given the tools they need to work effectively.

Managing Off-Air Staff

Most people get angry at anything they perceive as unfair. Radio is definitely a business in which, as George Orwell writes in *Animal Farm,* "some animals are more equal than others." A lot of radio performers are, at least on a local level, "stars." They get treated differently, with a lot of extra privileges. They are stars because of their talent, and talent is not distributed fairly.

It takes many people working behind the scenes to support a star. Some people would be better off going for an on-air position in a small market rather than working in an off-air capacity in a large one, because their need to be the star is huge. Others are far happier remaining out of the limelight.

Lots of people are drawn to this business and take supporting jobs until they can be on the air, but until that happens, they need to be at peace with the job they are doing. A producer, glaring across the booth and thinking, "I know I could do this show so much better" is not likely to be helping your program.

Management can compensate for some of the attention that gets directed to the star, but is really owed to the supporting cast, by acknowledging the cast members directly. Still, if you have a chorus line that is miserable not being in the main spotlight, they will be angry and dissatisfied and will do your station very little good.

There is nothing wrong with ambition, but the people you hire must have the talent and desire to do the job they are currently doing. When they have mastered that position and are eager to move up, managers owe it to them to look at whether or not they would now be well cast in another job. If such a position is not immediately available, give them the option, even the assistance, to move to another situation where they would be better able to fulfill their goals.

Radio is a highly demanding business. Often the hours are long and the pay is low. It would be nice if one could staff a station entirely with workaholics, heirs to large fortunes, or those who never need to go home. Many jobs in broadcasting really do require huge amounts of time and commitment. If you enjoy your job, but it never seems to be over, you might find that other stations set up their staffs differently, hire more people, and pay them better. It may not be the type of work you are doing that is causing you difficulty, but rather where you are doing it. In other words, you could be correctly cast doing the same job somewhere else.

Right Person, Wrong Show

Sometimes a talent has what it takes to succeed but has been put into a situation that is holding him or her back. Perhaps it's the venue that's to blame. Not everyone is right for every job. The talent may be GREAT, but the setting or the city or the station is wrong.

One example is funnyman Jay Thomas, a talented DJ and actor who never achieved substantial ratings in New York. But when he moved to Los Angeles, he became a top music radio personality.

The first incarnation of the *David Letterman Show* was actually in the middle of the day. It didn't work very well, but the folks at the network felt they had something and the show metamorphosed into the hit *Late Night with David Letterman* show (now the *Late Show with David Letterman*). Less resolute managers might have thrown Letterman on the heap of former TV talk hosts. Believe in talent and take the risk.

Part of the right casting is learning the abilities of each performer. Do not expect a serious interviewer or journalist to go on the air in morning drive and be a comedian. That is not the nature of the individual's talent. Right casting is also about risk. Allow talent to fully realize their roles even if, occasionally, they go to the extreme. Do not be upset if your funny, childlike jokesters make the occasional inappropriate remark. They are exploring the limits of the roles in which you have cast them.

"Never, ever, think outside the box."

Right Casting and the Passion Quotient

You and your staff should be listening to the station on your own time because you like to and because you are proud of it. Many managers who have moved up through the ranks of sales sometimes do not understand that although all on-air talent enjoy earning a good salary, their sole motivation is not always strictly a financial reward. On-air personalities are strongly motivated by the chance to do creative work and perform for an audience. So when you are thinking about whether you or your staff are rightly cast at your stations and jobs, look for passion about the station, its place in the community, and the audience it serves. A talent who does not like, respect, or value the listeners is not likely interested in working hard to get more of them.

Though most people have to work to earn a living, many broadcasters, if offered their same career track again today, say they would pursue it, even knowing in advance about the hardships and obstacles ahead. In fact, if asked how their jobs could be improved, other than with additional financial rewards, most on-air talent I've met list ways their show could be improved and the station could be promoted.

Meet with your staff. Ask each member: "If I could offer you something to make your job easier, what would it be?" Those with a passion for their work often come up with ways they could do the job more efficiently, or better serve the listeners. They may surprise you. The following is from a news director's actual wish list: "Poor newsroom lighting and a dearth of natural light are creating lethargy. Proposed Solution: Reworking the lighting and hanging some drapes could improve the work environment and pay off in a more energized staff."

Notice this news director's commitment to the quality of the product and the well-being of her staff. She is successful in part because she feels strongly about doing a good job with the tools she is given—just the sort of person who is right for her job.

By the way, it is possible to kill an employee's enthusiasm by consistently saying "no" to small but practical solutions to real station problems. Wherever possible, say "yes" and build passion for the station and your product.

Find out why each member of your staff wanted the job he or she now has. The answers may prove enlightening. While some may have thought broadcasting would be an easy paycheck, others fought hard for a chance to be part of the station or on the air.

A lot of prestige and power comes with our titles. It sounds good to be able to say, "I am a journalist" or "I run a radio station." The actual work is another matter. Did you become a program director because you thought that was the next job to take after hosting your own radio show and now find that you miss being on the air every day? You may have lost some of your passion for this work, due to wrong casting.

If you became a manager because you were offered a promotion and now find yourself in sales meetings when you would much rather be working with talent and marketing, your station is losing the benefit of a great PD who cared about the creative side of the organization.

Even if you have the most successful morning show in town on your station, if a DJ is burned out, or exhausted from getting up at 3:00 a.m., the numbers will soon reflect that. Keep checking in with your staff to make sure they are still happy. Just because all was well three months ago doesn't mean that everything is fine today, especially if there have been changes. For example, a member of a team show may have gotten a lot of inspiration from his or her co-host but may not enjoy working with the new partner.

There are a lot of reasons people choose a broadcast career. Perhaps in the beginning a DJ liked appealing to the opposite sex, seeing the country, and the music he played. But today, that same man is married, owns a house, and cannot bear listening to the music on his playlist. Clearly, as people grow and change, the challenge for a manager is to make sure they are cast in a role that is suitable for who they are today. That Top 40 DJ might be better cast playing hits on an Oldies station or Gold Format, or hosting a talk show.

Consolidation of broadcasting properties has made it easier to hang on to good people. Frequently, it's just a matter of moving someone to the sister station in the studio across the hall to rekindle their passion for the work.

Someone who likes to write comedy and create clever parody songs may end up producing commercials for mattress stores. The payoff for this person could have been when clients and sales people request his or her spots because they work so well. If that is the case, as a manager, you should also make sure that you are spotlighting your staff's achievements by submitting work for awards and industry commendations. But if that same production director envisioned being part of a morning team and is utterly miserable putting his or her creativity to use in a more anonymous and isolated setting, all the awards in the world can't substitute.

It is possible that a few modifications would make somebody's job right again. This may be as simple as hiring an assistant for a production director who feels overwhelmed or finding the right co-host for an uninspired morning host. Maybe a change of daypart would enable a presenter to relax and rejuvenate with a favorite hobby in off-hours, bringing new life to his or her show.

One newsman I know takes several weeks off, with the blessing of the radio station management, during hunting season. When he returns, his work always improves. Another example: An album rock music host who was also a serious mountain biker was allowed to change shifts in order to have more daytime hours to pursue his passion. He enjoyed the change so much that he went on to organize station cycling promotions, which have benefited the station and several charities.

It is also possible that someone is incorrectly cast not because he or she cannot do a job, but because he or she does not wish to do it. If you notice an employee speaking longingly of a position you never thought he or she would want, ask the employee why it appeals.

At stations around the world, and at the Creating Powerful Radio seminars, people ask how they can tell whether they are rightly cast. The shortest answer is: That which comes easily to you is probably what you do best. How much of that do you get to do? Do you have many perfect days at work? What is a perfect day at work for you? Is there an opportunity to do more of what appeals to you in your present position?

As a manager, you would do well to learn these things about your staff: What comes easily to them? When do you notice them having the most fun at work? Where do they struggle? These are areas that each host, manager, and programmer should look at from time to time.

Right Casting for Everybody

Just as many fine actors also produce and direct their own award-winning films, you can have natural ability in many areas. So the question becomes what do you like to do best? How do you determine which job at a radio station is right for you? How do you find which shoe "fits your foot"?

How Do You Know if You Are Rightly Cast in Your Current Role?

■ If you look at the clock all day long and find the minutes inching by, perhaps you are not rightly cast. If you are a manager, ask: Do you like to manage others? Do you get as much satisfaction from someone else's good work as you do from your own?

■ If you are on air or producing but you find that directing and developing others is fun, perhaps moving from on-air to management may be the right casting for you. There are no rules. Though you can be successful either as a performer or manager or both, it's often easier if you focus on and develop one area.

How Do You Know You Are on the Right Track?

I cannot say this often enough: The skills that come easily to you are probably your strengths. But there is also a danger. Just as an opera fan who sings in the shower and joins the community choir may not have been blessed with a beautiful voice or perfect pitch, it is a sad but true fact that some gifted broadcasters waste years of their lives trying to make themselves something they are not. Sometimes the thing you love to do, or admire most in others, is not where your actual strength lies.

In her book *The Vein of Gold*, Julia Cameron explores this journey of discovering what you do best. Cameron quotes director Martin Ritt:

All actors have a certain territory, a certain range, they were born to play, that is their "vein of gold." If you cast an actor within that vein, he or she will always give you a brilliant performance. Of course you can always cast an actor outside his vein of gold. If you do, the actor can use craft and technique to give you a very fine, a very credible performance, but never a performance as brilliant as when he or she is working in his or her vein of gold.

On the following pages are some questions for broadcasters (talent and/or managers) to consider, to help you decide if you are rightly cast in your current job.

Talent

When it comes to your show, are you more comfortable playing it safe than taking chances on the air? Do you worry about looking foolish?

Superstar performers take a few chances. If they spent a lot of time being anxious about their images, they would miss opportunities to be great. It takes bravery to risk looking silly in front of an audience, but your listeners appreciate courage even if you fail. If the thought of looking undignified petrifies you, perhaps you should try something safer.

Talent/Managers

When there is a mistake on the air, is it always someone else's fault? Who is to blame for sloppy on-air presentation?

Successful talent take a lot of responsibility for their shows. If something goes wrong on the air, they do not throw up their hands, blame the equipment or the producer, and give up for the rest of the hour. They dump the boring guest, look up an expert's phone number, or carry the microphone down to the street. In short, they have courage to do whatever it takes to achieve a quality air product.

If the station has no budget for newspaper and magazine advertising, successful talent buy their own. If the station cannot afford a piece of equipment, motivated employees go out and find a sponsor who is willing to provide the product on trade. An executive producer I know once organized a collection among the staff to buy a much-needed piece of recording equipment. A manager went to the pharmacy and bought medicine for an ailing newscaster. A program director once told me, "I'd get down on my knees and shine (the host's) shoes if that would help him do a better show."

In a well-cast broadcasting scenario, if something goes wrong, each person involved, from the program director to the call screener, comes up with an idea of how he or she could help make it better the next time. If you are not willing to take responsibility for your product, ask yourself why you are doing this job.

How afraid are you of getting fired? Does that motivate you?

Everyone has a boss. If you live in fear to the extent that you are not willing to risk management's displeasure, you may be miscast. It is important that you feel strongly enough about your freedom to try new ideas on behalf of your station, your show, or your staff. You must be willing to incur a little fallout once in a while. Sometimes, the powers-that-be must be obliged, but there should be a little give and take here.

If you are immobilized by fear of losing your job, you should ask yourself the next question.

If you did lose your job, how easily do you think you could find another one?

If the answer is that you could not easily replace this job, then you may need to express your creativity in other ways. Technology has made it easier to do some of the work of our business outside of a radio station or broadcast facility. Many hosts, producers, and sales people have studios and offices in their own homes. That has cut down on some of the need to become a migrant worker for the sake of a broadcasting career. Still, if having to make sacrifices in the form of a move, pay cut, lifestyle change, etc., is something you are not willing to do, then seek out a job where you are more properly cast.

Managers

Are you willing to risk? Do you feel uneasy when you hear the format being broken?

If you know that nine times out of ten your format is going "out the window" for a good reason, then you are demonstrating the kind of flexibility that can come only when you have confidence in your air staff and are comfortable with your job.

Talent

Do you feel ruled and restricted by the station's format clock, or do you feel you have enough control and discretion to structure your show according to the needs of the moment?

If you are able to work within the confines of your format, yet have enough leeway to pursue the occasional "magic moment" or news emergency, you are probably working with supportive management in a role that fits you.

Talent/Producers/Management

Do you ever get ideas for somebody else's show or feature? If so, do you usually share them with the talent or keep them to yourself?

If you can pass material along or be of assistance, you are demonstrating courage, leadership, and a generous personality. You have a vision of the total health of the station. You are a team player. This attribute would serve you well either as a manager or as a member of a team show. You might do better working with a few other performers rather than flying solo.

Talent

Do you have total control of your show?

Almost nobody has that, unless you own the station. But, your goal should be to leave the studio each day feeling: "That was me. That was what I wanted to do on the air today." If you finish your show feeling as though you executed somebody else's agenda, with no personal stake in the outcome, you are probably miscast.

Managers

Do you feel you or your producers are constantly forcing ideas on the talent? Do you feel you must hold the reins tightly to ensure that he or she will do a particular type of show every day? Do you feel you are in a wrestling match with the talent for control of the show?

If so, you are controlling the show out of fear the talent is inept, or you are trying to put a square peg in a round hole and the talent is miscast, or you would prefer to do the show yourself.

Talent

Do you believe the work you do matters?

Having a microphone is not something one should take for granted. Because aspects of the job can become routine or mundane, it is easy to forget that listeners are giving you their most valuable resource—their time. There is a commitment on the part of the broadcaster to offer information, entertainment, inspiration, or whatever your station has promised to provide.

Talent/Managers

What is the best thing about your manager? What is the worst thing about your manager?

If you make an honest inventory of your manager's good and bad qualities, you may find that your job is better than you thought it was. What seems like an unsatisfied boss may actually be someone who is working very hard to bring you to the next level of performance. He or she may see potential where you see none. Although you might feel miscast in a certain job, you may be there to learn skills for the next position your supervisor has in mind for you.

However, you are probably miscast if you feel that your manager is the radio police, if he or she consistently makes you do things you don't want to do, or you work in fear of being caught making a mistake.

Managers
Are you proud to sell this product?
Would you be just as happy selling something more tangible or less controversial? While running a broadcasting operation gives you prestige, it also makes you a target. If you would be more comfortable managing a different type of company, give yourself permission to move on.

Managers/Talent
Finally, everyone should ask: Do any jobs at the station, other than the one you now have, seem interesting to you?
If they do, why not learn them? There are always vacations, emergencies, and fill-in opportunities. You may find another area of the business that is a better fit for you—one where you would be better cast. (Note: For more on this, see Chapter 20, *In Case of Emergency.*)

If radio does not fulfill your need to be heard and to express yourself creatively, if it drains rather than energizes you to create something new on the air each day, if you find you are upset or tired of taking irate calls from a community leader or offended politician, there may be some other work that might be more suitable.

Most creative people have a lot of artistic abilities, and radio may not be the right creative venue for you.

Similar Goals

Part of right casting is making sure that your goals and the station's objectives work together. Broadcast consultant Andy Beaubien puts it this way:

> As much as personalities would like to think that their show is their own exclusive artistic responsibility, it is nevertheless part of the station's overall effort. It ultimately must satisfy the station's goals. If the personality's

goals and the station's goals are out of sync, the result will be frustration and bitterness on both sides. In almost every case where there is a serious problem between management and an air personality, the underlying cause is usually a conflict between goals or, to put it in the language of the trade publications, "philosophical differences."

Talent may also have philosophical differences with the audience. That is fine in many cases, and some talent build careers by flying in the face of convention, but it can be a tough road. Does this mean you should alter your true self to keep your job? Programming consultant Jaye Albright speaks from experience when she says: "Radio does reward the craftspeople who most accurately reflect the current cultural realities. If you can find it within yourself to respect the prevailing value system, while still being true to your own unique creative voice, you may be more successful."

Tips for Finding and Developing Talent

Radio can be taught, but talent is rare.
If you find the real thing...MAKE THE HIRE!

1. Look for talent in nontraditional areas.

2. Make your choice and then stick by it.

3. Don't pull the plug if you don't see immediate results.

4. Have faith.

5. Motivate the talent with honest feedback and encouragement.

CHAPTER 8

Beyond Powerful Radio
Airchecking

> "No one can make you feel inferior without your consent."
> —*Eleanor Roosevelt*

The Aircheck Session

Talent Is Hungry for Feedback

"Management rarely fails to let me know when I screw up, do something wrong, or make a mistake, but then they can't seem to tell me what to do to get it right." This is a typical complaint I hear all the time from on-air talent throughout the world. Surprisingly, hosts often hire me at their own expense to conduct aircheck sessions with them, craving direction that their program directors cannot or do not have time to give.

Airchecking is more than just a show critique. One-on-one coaching, or airchecking, is a specific, focused way of working. It is not the only tool that can be used to develop, improve, and advance talent, but it is the best one. Airchecking is the process of listening to a show and, using specific criteria, determining what worked and what did not work. With a guide, airchecker, coach, or PD as your witness, you then decide what can be improved.

Even if you listen to archived audio of your shows religiously, you are likely to miss many nuances of the total performance. One air talent I work with says, "When I listen alone, I focus on how *I* did. I get critical of just me, not how the whole show went. When I listen with other people in the room, I focus on everything that is happening on the air: the guest being interviewed, sound effects, callers, and audio quality. I hear it all."

It can't be helped. Think of your school or family group photos. When you see one, the first thing you do is look at yourself. It is the same in radio. The natural thing is to pay attention to how you made a certain point or handled a particular caller. You are less likely to be aware of the subtleties of that caller's comments or the newsperson's clever contribution. There is something about listening to your show with a witness in the room that forces you to hear your work differently. Airchecking should be done in such a way that each talent sets achievable goals to fulfill his or her creative potential.

The Mirror

Talent, if you do not know what you sound like on the air, you are already in the danger zone. You are working with a handicap. Watch a child play by making faces in a mirror: "What do I look like if I'm mad? What do I look like with my tongue out? Can I see myself from the back?"

Airchecking is like a mirror. It allows you to determine the answers to the following: "How do I sound when I am sad or angry? How do I behave with a difficult guest? What happens when I try to sound smarter than my partner? Am I smarter than my partner? What happens when I pretend to know something about a topic I know nothing about? What happens when I'm bored on the air? How do I sound if I didn't get enough sleep? What kind of a show will I have if I have not been out of my house in a month except to go to work?"

Your audience knows, but without your aircheck as a mirror, you do not. Sitting alone with and listening to your show is like a single mirror. Working with a talented aircheck coach can give you multiple reflections of your work. There are other angles you cannot see with only one frame of reference. Viewing those other angles is the power of a good aircheck session.

What Exactly is an Aircheck?

That depends. One New York DJ defines an aircheck session as "a way for the program director to yell at us periodically." Says another: "Isn't it like a report card?" From a manager: "Oh yes, we do that once a year with talent. We analyze audio of a past show. The meeting takes an entire day. You can read the report in their file." And one industry professional simply asked: "Isn't it some kind of postmortem after a dead show?"

These comments all have a grain or two of truth, but try thinking of your show as a garden and airchecking the show as a weeding process. In order to maintain its health, growth, and beauty, you should regularly walk through your garden and take note of which plants are thriving and which need attention. Some parts of the garden flourish, some struggle to survive. But always you check to make sure your plants have the right sun, soil, etc. Your aircheck is like that walk to see how well your garden is coming along.

When done correctly, airchecking can be a solution to the dilemma facing managers and programmers around the world who complain: "I can't find any good talent. I've listened to dozens of on-air auditions and shows and they are all bad or mediocre." Or, "This is a good station in a reasonably sized market, and the job pays a decent salary. Why can't we find the right people?"

Exactly where are all those talented and creative people hiding? Where is the next generation of talent? You may get lucky and find a genius on the doorstep of your radio station, but one important task of radio programmers and managers is to find and develop new personalities.

Anyone who has done it knows that it is hard work to develop on-air personalities. Often it is less expensive and easier for stations to broadcast a syndicated national or network show than to have live, local talent on the air. But it is important to note that most syndicated programs were once local success stories. That is another reason it is important to work to develop new local talent now.

Even the strongest syndicated shows can be beaten by hot local talent. But looking to the future, what will stations do once today's syndicated shows run dry or move to television? Airchecking and developing talented people is one way to ensure that creative and powerful radio will continue.

> "One must be permitted to be clumsy and fail."
> —*May Sarton*

Basic Aircheck Rules

1. **Always work from the audio of the show you are discussing.** You may wish to transcribe it word for word to emphasize specifics. Keep in mind that a transcript can destroy context. Sarcasm, irony, and humor can all get left behind with the loss of vocal inflection. This often happens when a manager receives a nasty call or complaint letter with specific quotes included. Inevitably the context is missing. A discussion can degenerate quickly if the actual facts of the case are in dispute. Having a copy of the show on hand allows you to look not only at the content, but also the context of an event.

2. **Focus on one thing at a time.** Sometimes an aircheck session turns into a "dump" session, in which talent unburdens him or herself of a lot of thoughts having nothing to do with the show. A double standard applies here. It's acceptable, to a point, for the host to digress. After all, a PD is uniquely able to understand pressures talent may be under, and even, in some cases, to do something to alleviate them.

   As a manager, however, you are there to aircheck, not to vent. Listen to the talent. Should you hear the makings of a great show taking place in your office, encourage the talent to put that on the air.

   Don't let these diversions distract you from the aircheck session; just move the subject back to the archived show at the most appropriate moment.

3. **Tell the truth.** Trained communicators sense when you are fibbing.

4. **Reinforce the positive by starting with the good stuff.** Remember to acknowledge goals achieved.

5. **Be fair. Criticism goes in very deep.** No matter how angry you are, avoid verbalizing your negative reactions to a piece until you can express yourself calmly and rationally.

6. **Let the talent discover along with you what needs to be improved.** On-air personalities are often their own harshest critics and can mercilessly rip apart their own programs during an aircheck session, recognizing and identifying specific areas where they can improve.

7. **Outline strengths.** Ask a lot of questions. What worked? Why did you want to do this on the radio? What were you trying to say here? Did this connect? Was the language visual? Did you talk to the individual and involve your listener? Did this make you laugh?

8. **Have faith.** Believe in your talent's ability to improve.

9. **Close with achievable goals.** Always end an aircheck session with one or two mutually agreed upon "achievable goals." Pick at least one thing that can easily be accomplished by the next scheduled session. Try to let the talent initiate goal-setting.

10. **Is there promo potential?** Is there anything in the aircheck of your show that you could use as a promo?

> "Managing creative people is an oxymoron. You don't manage
> them at all. Instead you provide an environment in which they
> can be simultaneously stimulated and protected, challenged
> and encouraged, exposed and private."
> —*Nicholas Negroponte*

The Method: How to Aircheck

Unfortunately, there is no airchecking school for programmers. You learn by working with people, seeing what is effective and what is not. Some aspects of airchecking will vary greatly, depending upon the individuals involved. It is in the best interest of programmers and managers to learn to aircheck effectively. One size does not fit all, but if the talent wins, the station wins. There are a few things one must never do, but the only right way to aircheck is the way that works.

Without an understanding of what is required for an individual air talent to succeed, even the most gifted new hire may not reach his or her potential. In a case like that, it takes a year or two for the talent to leave or be asked to move on. What went wrong?

Let's go back to the garden analogy. You came home from the garden center with some big, fancy bulbs. The picture on the box showed a huge, exotic flower, but, unfortunately, the box was without instructions. How much water was needed? How much sun?

There may have been nothing wrong with the talent you chose, but when you have to play a guessing game, there is a good chance of damaging the talent, or at least failing to create an environment where talent, like that fancy flower, can blossom.

If you found something you did not recognize in your garden, you would not cut it back without knowing what it was. It could be something wonderful. The same goes for air talent. Consultant Dan Vallie puts it well when he advises programmers to "let talent go out on a limb as far as they can. Do not restrict them until you find their range of potential and limitations. It's better to reel them in after a while than to have to keep pushing them out there."

Fix It Today

A great aircheck session with a trained program director or consultant can move talent along faster than any other tool. Progress may be painstakingly slow. Talent improves step-by-step, day-by-day. Frustratingly, the process may sometimes seem to be working in reverse. There is a period of intense growth, followed by what sound like patches of mediocrity, where all coaching seems to have been in vain. What you may really be hearing is the talent searching for ways to implement suggestions and ideas you have discussed. Have faith and continue the process. If you are on the right path, positive change will come.

Several other experts have contributed their aircheck rules and philosophies to this book, including consultant Dan Vallie, a big believer in spending time to coach talent.

Dan Vallie's Talent Development Steps

1. Talent is the product. You can't develop talent if you do not spend time together. The talent will improve more quickly if time is taken for coaching and direction.

2. Do not criticize talent or tell them something was poorly done unless you direct them on how to do it better. If you cannot give them a better way, at least approach the issue with a team attitude, working together to come up with a solution.

3. Make yourself part of the show, as the director. Directing involves making sure the talent play to their strengths. Help to assist and make up for their weaknesses. Give guidance in those periods where the talent is at a loss as to how to grow next or how to handle an immediate topical event on the air. If your feedback is useful, talent will not feel the session is a waste of time.

4. If the expectation is not clear, the delivery will not be on target.

5. You can learn from the talent, just as the talent can learn from you. Do not direct by doing all the talking. It is frequently more important to listen. Be sincerely interested in the talent's views and understand their perspectives.

6. Be a good facilitator. Draw talent out and get them to verbalize their feelings and thoughts. Watch their body language. Show them that you care about them and the show's success.

7. If yours is a music-intensive station with most of the personalities on the morning show, meet with them every day. It does not have to be an aircheck session. The format and length of the meeting can vary. If everyone sees it as helpful, you will all make time to meet. If any of you thinks it is a waste, the meeting will frequently be canceled or dreaded.

8. Do not try to impress the talent with how much you know, where you have worked, or the fact that you are the boss. Just be honest, encouraging, supportive, and consistent with your direction and approach.

9. Great coaches give talent credit when they perform, and share the blame when something fails. These are the people who can get you to the Super Bowl or World Cup, but only when you work as a team.

10. Praise often in public and private—but criticize only in private.

It Cuts Both Ways

Mistakes occur when an aircheck session is mishandled. Just as a talent can get a reputation for being difficult to work with, your reputation as a programmer can be severely damaged by a bad relationship with a host in your employ. These people do talk to one another and to managers. It is possible that the person whose aircheck session you botched years ago can keep you from getting your next job or warn a show you are actively courting.

There are a lot of ways to mess up an aircheck session. If you have worked in the business for a while, you are probably familiar with some of them. Consultant Lorna Ozmon provides an all-too-accurate picture of what can go wrong:

> Let's examine the state-of-the-art model for critiquing air personalities. Typically air personalities are critiqued, on average, monthly. The aircheck sessions are often canceled or rescheduled due to an "emergency" usually having to do with sales. The talent and the PD meet in the PD's office with all its inherent disruptions and distractions. The talent hands the PD a copy of a show the PD has never heard, which the PD plays.
>
> As the show begins, the PD is thinking, "I hope I can come up with something to say and not look like I have nothing of value to offer." The talent is thinking, "I hope this is over soon and it doesn't hurt my feelings." After a few breaks, the PD stops the audio and, with a quizzical look, says, "There's something about that break that bothers me." At this the talent silently wonders, "What does that mean?" and says, "Could you give me something a little more specific?"

Feeling slightly inadequate, the PD gives the talent a healthy dose of "don'ts" and sends the talent out feeling confused, unmotivated, clear on what not to do but clueless about what to do. This traditional approach to airchecks has done much to close the minds and hearts of talent at radio stations everywhere.

How Airchecking Can Damage Talent

Lorna Ozmon takes a psychological approach to airchecking and has developed her own techniques. She has found that before she can begin to make progress with a personality, it is essential to explore what has been said to him or her over the years that created both the good and bad habits he or she carries. Ozmon's cardinal rule for airchecking comes from Hippocrates: "Make a habit of two things—to help or at least to do no harm."

Ozmon explains:

Before talent can move forward, you've got to get rid of the unnecessary baggage, stuff they've been told by bad PDs or people who influenced them when they were just starting out. That stuff really sticks.

I usually ask them to make a list of all the "orders" they have been given through the years. Then we look at the list and ask, "What no longer works?" The idea is to get rid of the "old tapes" from previous programmers. Old-time journeymen broadcasters have been hammered by dozens of PDs. It is time to get rid of what no longer works for the talent. It is not enough to haul out the clichés and tell someone to "be an individual," "just be yourself," or "be more conversational."

In order to be effective, you have to be very specific when you guide talent. You have to ask questions and point out what you hear and what you think it means.

Ozmon particularly warns against the "Frankenstein Syndrome," a persona copied from "pieces of others." She advises: "It is OK to use tactics learned from others, but do not cobble together pieces of what works for other people and imitate it. That doesn't work." Ozmon continues:

There is much harm being done to the performances, psyches, and potential of broadcast personalities today. Management tends to forget that people who are asked to risk parts of who they are every day must be managed differently than those who work on the assembly line at an automotive plant.

Many air personalities are now being managed by cops, not coaches. Cops punish people for mistakes and misjudgments. Coaches train, instruct, and inspire new behavior. Cops tells us what not to do. Coaches explain what to do and demonstrate how to do it. The result of the "cop mentality" in radio air personality development is a lot of time wasted in attempting talent development with disappointing on-air results.

What follows are ten complaints from talent who have expressed to Lorna Ozmon what they feel is wrong with the traditional aircheck or "critique" process:

- No, or too few, aircheck sessions

- Contradictory or inconsistent input

- Lack of praise for progress

- All negative feedback

- Lack of "how-to's" and creative input

- Vague input without specific examples

- Autocratic edicts without rationale to support or explain them

- Perceived personal attacks

- Criticism from a higher authority delivered as though it came from the program director

- Program directors who critique dishonestly, either because they do not believe a personality fits the station, or do not believe in his or her ability to succeed.

Lorna Ozmon's list spells out the damage that can be done to talent. Clearly, air personalities who have experienced some of these difficulties will be less trusting of the process than those with positive airchecking experiences.

A Cautionary Tale

Here is what can happen when you ignore the preceding list: John considers aircheck sessions just this side of a torture chamber. He has good reason:

> I know my PD uses these aircheck meetings to jerk me around. He makes me feel small, and he gets off on belittling me. He keeps these stupid lists of minutiae. I dread these meetings. They wreck my whole day. I hate being airchecked. Even if I make a change, he never says anything positive

about my work. I'm not convinced my PD knows why my show works when it does. I wish he would leave me alone. I get ratings, and I have been doing this for years.

If John works for you, you are either a sadist or something is terribly wrong with your airchecking technique. Because they are already in a very vulnerable situation, talent should be made to feel as much in control of their sessions as possible. Here is how:

- Let the talent choose the audio.

- If there are notes from the session, let the talent keep them.

- Give the talent access to positive feedback from anyone whose input is going to matter during the session.

- Always acknowledge progress and positive changes.

There are differing opinions as to the benefit of revealing research results to talent. Be careful. You do not want to withhold information, but you do not want to beat talent down with audience ratings so that they become discouraged. Consultant Randy Lane advises: "Keep the emphasis on the performance, regardless of the numbers." If there is a reason you are calling a meeting, let your talent know, if possible, what it is.

Why Don't More Programmers Aircheck?

Here are a few of the million reasons:

- **No time.** It takes as much as a two-hour session for each hour of programming.

- **Emotionally draining.** You are dealing with people's personal qualities and deepest feelings.

- **No confidence.** Most programmers have little training in this area and fear doing harm. One size doesn't "fit all" and each on-air talent may require a different approach. Also, talent can get pretty defensive about their work. Lorna Ozmon counsels PDs to prepare for this using a tactic called "Objection Busting." She says:

    You must mentally prepare for every possible objection to what it is you are trying to sell. In the case of an aircheck session, it is usually a change in behavior. If you have a logical response to every reason why the talent does not agree with your position, you will be more relaxed, focused, and effective while conducting your aircheck sessions.

- **No crisis.** Some only aircheck when things go drastically (think lawsuit) wrong.

- **Burnout.** Most PDs are overworked and overwhelmed with demands for their attention. (See 1st and 2nd reasons listed above.)

- **Don't like them.** Sometimes managers have a show or host that they find personally distasteful.

Using these reasons, many PDs recite an internal monologue such as this one:

Who am I to pick apart this show? These guys are professionals and have been doing it pretty well for a long time. I don't want to say anything to them that will break their stride. I know the show isn't as good as it could be, but I'm not sure why.

What if I'm just nitpicking on the little stuff?

What if I'm wrong?

What if I antagonize them? Then they will rebel and won't do anything I want them to do. Maybe I'm better off leaving them alone.

The end result of this internal discussion is that the aircheck session never happens, and the talent is deprived of an opportunity to improve his or her craft.

For program directors, the first step in making an effort at airchecking is acknowledging your areas of discomfort. Trust and truth must be established from both sides. This book cannot help you if you do not have good faith, a kind heart, and a desire to help your talent improve. If you are willing to overcome your resistance to airchecking, the rewards can be great. If you simply want a quick and easy way to strong-arm a performer into giving you the show you want to hear, this information won't do you any good.

Do not attempt to manipulate talent with false praise or threats. It is not right, it is not fair, and most of these folks are smart enough to know what you are doing. If you can only do one thing in your first aircheck session, pick out something you really did like and be specific about why. That would be an excellent start.

Knowing When the Time Is Right

Managers can aid talent by being sensitive to the right time for an aircheck. Educators call it the "teachable moment." Aircheck regularly at a mutually agreed-on date and place. As a guideline for newer talent, plan on a weekly session. Those getting started tend to require more attention from programmers, while more seasoned professionals may need only periodic airchecking to stay on track.

For talent who are not used to airchecking, the very idea of having to go through past shows with a PD can be unsettling. That is why consultant Tommy Kramer suggests: "Have your talent record every show. That way, you will always have access to a current show and your talent will get relaxed with the idea of being recorded. Plus, if something great happens on the air, you can have it on hand for a promo or sales presentation."

Lorna Ozmon feels strongly that full-time personalities should be airchecked once a month. She says:

People need time to process input and put it into practice for a reasonable period of time before they are ready to tackle a new concept or take the next step. Try to, as much as is operationally possible, make monthly sessions firm commitments. Although air personalities may say they dislike the aircheck process, nothing makes them feel less valued than canceling meetings with them.

For music program directors, Randy Lane uses this rule of thumb: "Have as much contact with your morning show as you do with the music and promotion directors." I agree with consultant Andy Beaubien when he says:

It is more desirable to briefly connect with an air talent on a very frequent basis than to rely on extended but infrequent meetings. The important thing is to maintain a continuing relationship. Some meetings should be in-depth discussions, while others may be brief and social in nature. Artistic growth can only come from the development of one's talent. Too often, once all the negatives in a person's style have been eliminated, there is nothing left but a bland and lifeless corpse.

Create a Safe Setting

For some, a "safe setting" may be a private office across a desk. Others prefer using more relaxed and casual settings away from the station with a glass of wine or cup of coffee. It does not have to be formal, but it does have to be regular and consistent.

Lorna Ozmon suggests:

> Get away from your phone, the sales department, and other distractions. Focus only on the air personality and the review. Go somewhere quiet and private enough to conduct the sessions effectively. Also, look for opportunities to be among people and observe life in your market at the same time. Meet over a meal if possible. People tend to be much more open to ideas when they are being fed.

Set the Scene

Tom Zarecki, consultant, programmer, professor, and former Radio Computing Services (RCS) executive points out: "The goal is to get the talent to enjoy aircheck sessions." He agrees that the setting for an aircheck is crucial:

> If you don't have a private area, use your car. Sit in the parking lot or go for a drive and critique the show along the way. No interruptions, no calls, very private. In case the talent needs to raise his or her voice, other staffers will not hear yelling from behind a closed door, which fosters gossip.
>
> Never go through a host's work with other hosts present. The only time aircheck sessions should be in a group is with a team show, like a morning show, where two or more people interact. Otherwise, do not review airchecks at an air-talent meeting. It is fatal. Don't try it.

What Can Kill a Session?

The absolute worst thing you can do is turn a session into a personal attack. No matter what you have to say to an air talent, if he or she feels berated or treated disrespectfully, you will make no progress at all. Lorna Ozmon advises, "If you are not clear of the difference between an assertive and aggressive statement, remember it is easy to add the words 'you idiot' to an aggressive statement. Continually remind your air personalities that it is what they do on the air and not who they are that is being airchecked."

1. **Avoid airchecking just prior to the show.** It always takes some time to digest new information, and, if the session was disturbing in any way, it could hurt today's show.

2. **Never ever, ever "hotline" a talent during his or her show.** Resist the temptation unless your station's license is in jeopardy or lives are at stake. Receiving a "hotline call" from the boss during the show is a sure way to frighten the host and throw the remainder of the program off rhythm. He or she stops thinking creatively and begins worrying. This is to be avoided at all costs. The hotline is not a rolled-up newspaper with which you may strike the talent on his or her nose. Even if the manager is calling with praise (and he or she should), it destroys the host's concentration to hear it during the show.

   The right time to aircheck or make any comments is once the show has concluded. It is best if the manager makes a note, considers the problem overnight, and then requests a meeting with the talent the following day. Try not to let a host worry for hours with an "I want to see you in my office" call that does not make the purpose of the meeting clear. If the show takes place outside of normal business hours, make an extra effort to aircheck at the host's convenience. Be flexible. Many top programmers are willing to come in on the weekends. An aircheck of the program in question should be available for the meeting. No matter how strong your feelings may be, come prepared to listen to a talent's reasons for handling something in a particular way.

3. **Don't build unnecessary resentment.** Be sensitive to your talent's schedules. For example, do not ask your overnight host to appear at a noon meeting when he or she would normally be asleep. If you aircheck the morning show, do not pounce on your team as they leave the studio. You are just getting to the station, but after several hours on air it is their lunchtime. They are probably hungry. They might be more receptive to your comments if their stomachs are full. Try taking them out or ordering breakfast. Hosts appreciate your willingness to take their odd hours into consideration.

4. **Airchecking is hard work.** All too often programmers hire and fire talent without ever having invested the time and energy that might have made a good host great, or enabled a talent to see the power of his or her work as well as its shortcomings.

   If you are a radio program manager and your air talent asks you, "What did you think of the show?" and you didn't hear it, or did hear it but didn't like it (but can't pinpoint exactly why...), or don't have time to deal with it now, *this* is the time to schedule an aircheck meeting.

Isn't There an Easier Way to Develop Talent?

Airchecking gets easier the more experience the talent and the coach have with it. Consultant Dan Vallie reminds us, "Coaching takes talent, too."

Airchecking is the power of one on one. It's being heard. It is someone rooting for you, being on your side. In sports it is the coach who pushes the athlete to maximum potential. Exercise makes sore muscles, but in the end it is worth it when you win.

Not only will you be pushing the talent on your staff to excel, but they will also be pushing yourself. A healthy aircheck session frequently features some strong differences of opinion. Most experts believe this should be encouraged.

Consultant Jaye Albright works with personalities who have differing styles and goals.

At best, I hope to get the personalities talking about what they were trying to do. That way, I can base my feedback on how well they accomplished what they wanted to do in terms of my responses. I try to communicate one or two key reactions I had in as nonthreatening a manner as possible. It is not important to me that they always do what I suggest, but it is important that they know why I feel as I do.

I ask that they hold me to the same standard. Was I prepared or on auto-pilot? Did I offer clichés, or did I spend time thinking about the work? I hope they will be as direct about these things with me as I try to be with them.

The longer I have worked with someone and the better I know that person, the more I tailor what I do to his or her communication style. Some people are so controlling that critiques only happen on their turf, and they change very little over the years on the things I fervently believe would benefit the individual.

In these cases, I keep singing my song to them in hopes that eventually the air talent will realize that there is a recurring theme in my advice and perhaps some grain of my truth will imprint.

In other, more common situations, even the slightest word can injure. In those situations, I attempt to be subtle and always carefully watch for body language indications of hurt, defensiveness, or misunderstanding.

It Does Get Easier

Sometimes a seasoned pro can be airchecked in a single word. A good example is an aircheck session that Los Angeles news presenter Susanne Whatley had with her then-news director Mark Austin Thomas.

> He was trying to get me to "brighten up" my performance. He gave me one word—"energy." Inside my own head I thought I was using enough energy, but when I tried it out his way, and then heard it back, my work sounded better! There is a lot of trust involved in doing what is suggested. When I first made the change, and pumped it up a little on the air, using higher energy, power, and pacing, it sounded silly to me inside my head, but when I heard it back, he was absolutely right.

Susanne is right. Things sound different in your headphones than they do coming out of a speaker. Encourage talent to grow independently by trying new ideas, experimenting on the radio, and "self-checking"; that is, listening to recorded shows on their own. You can also learn a lot from hearing others whose work you admire. You can even aircheck people you have never met by listening to their shows. It is a good way to see what qualities in their work are effective and might be adaptable to your individual performance.

Music radio consultant Guy Zapoleon "inspires hosts by playing a great talent example—past and present." A talent might wish to listen to a personality she looks up to in another market or, better still, someone who is on the staff who is philosophically aligned with her, and who can also be a mentor.

Every coach has a different method. Jaye Albright warns:

> Listening to your own work can be devastating. Seek objective feedback from as many directors as possible. Use what resonates truthfully with your own inner voice. Carefully consider the reactions of others, but do not ever take them personally. Their guidance is about their life experience and response to what you did. Try the things that seem sensible. Reject that which does not.

If there were an easier way, we would embrace it. Learning from others is something everyone does, but do not try to become someone else. Make it your goal to find your unique voice.

Getting It

The sections that follow contain some real stories of ways in which talent recognized and overcame obstacles using aircheck sessions.

"You Big Meanie!": Aircheck Success Story No. 1

Before her death, Mother Teresa, the nun who dedicated her life to caring for the sick and dying in India, was the subject of an hour's discussion. The host began the show by saying:

> I think Mother Teresa is a fraud. I have an article in front of me documenting her luxurious lifestyle, the money she has been given, private jet travel, and other perks of celebrity. It says here she accepted a huge contribution that turned out to be from stolen funds, and then, when asked, refused to give the money back. After all that, is she really a saint?

The host then took an hour of calls on what a fake he considered Mother Teresa to be. The following day, the program director was deluged with negative mail and angry calls. Much of the correspondence began by saying, "I usually love Dan's show but. . ." and ended with "I'll never listen to this radio station again!"

Why, the PD wondered, would this well-liked host generate such a heated reaction? The PD requested a copy of the show and found the problem immediately: Dan had introduced his supporting data only at the beginning of the hour. Listeners joining the program following the break, without having heard the show's opening, would have no idea what motivated him to say such angry things. It sounded like he was picking on Mother Teresa for no reason at all.

It would have been possible to listen to an entire half hour of Dan's show and hear him and the callers going back and forth about the saintliness or depravity of a prominent religious icon without ever knowing the revelations and allegations of her worldly shortcomings.

Using the audio from the program, the PD was able to explain to Dan that he had no problem with his opinion, however unpopular it might be. But he pointed out that Dan had not been heard or understood by a majority of his listeners, because he had not reset the topic on the air for the new audience tuning in. The host was so busy being angry and outraged, he forgot to mention periodically what had sparked his initial reaction. Dan had failed to explain again the reasons for his anger.

The result: To a majority of his audience, he just sounded mean. With the aircheck and letters from people who usually liked his show, the host could clearly see the result of not resetting a topic: He had been misunderstood.

Formatics Count

Resetting your topic at a minimum of every fifteen minutes is like giving your audience an on-ramp. Without resetting, it is like watching traffic on the freeway. You can see it go by, but you have no idea how to join in. Your show becomes accessible only to those who already got on the highway at the top of the hour. Resetting invites those listeners who are just joining in.

Have you ever walked into a room where people were in the middle of a big fight screaming at one another? You wouldn't want to be involved and would either avoid entering the room or leave as quickly as possible. But if they stopped the fighting and someone said to you, in a reasonable tone of voice, "Wait a minute. She says: 'Don't eat the butter, the bacon, the chocolate mousse; it will give you a heart attack.' But I say, enjoying my life is more important than living an extra ten years. What do you think?" You have now been invited in and may be willing to contribute your opinion.

As for Dan's show, the reset could have been done this quickly:

> I have an article that says Mother Teresa kept stolen money, demanded first-class air travel, feather pillows in hotel rooms, and gourmet food on the road. I have lost all respect for her. Some of you are telling me: "She is entitled to royal treatment for all the good work she does." What do you think?

Now the audience knows what is generating all that heat. They might not agree with the host or the callers, but they have a handle on what is going on. It no longer seems like an unfounded nasty attack against a saintly old lady.

"What Happened to You?": Aircheck Success Story No. 2

Rick had a weekend interview show covering serious issues. Around the station, he was charming and funny. Rick told such wonderful jokes and stories that management decided to give him a daily talk show of his own. It didn't work. Although his weekend show hadn't been a lighthearted affair, this new job was meant to be a smart, yet entertaining program. Unfortunately, every time Rick opened the microphone, he sounded stiff and authoritarian. Gone were the offhand anecdotes, the wry commentaries, and the relaxed original humor that everyone had enjoyed in the halls.

We scheduled an aircheck session with Rick. Something peculiar happened. Rick visibly bored himself. He skipped over dull calls. He yawned, doodled on a scratch pad, and looked at his watch several times. At one point in the meeting, Rick actually dug around in his pocket for change and got up to buy a soda. Obviously if the host is bored with his own show, the listener is not likely to find it riveting entertainment.

There was another problem. Rick did not notice that his attention was wandering. This was the conversation:

PD: "Rick, what did you think of this program?"

Rick: "It's OK, it's fine, this is how I do my show."

PD: "Rick, anyone who spends ten minutes in a room with you knows how funny you are. How come that's not on air?"

Eventually, we got our answer. It turned out that the reason Rick was holding back was because he was concerned about his reputation as a journalist in the community. He was afraid to have fun or loosen up on the radio for fear of not being taken seriously as an intellect. What would people think of him? He was worried he would lose his credibility, look foolish, or fail altogether.

At the end of one segment, there was a traffic report. The reporter got the hiccups in the middle of her story. All of a sudden, Rick forgot he was on the radio. A simple body function brought out his natural humor, if only for a moment, as he suggested possible cures. We used those few seconds of audio to demonstrate to Rick how his spontaneity and storytelling humanized him and made him a more likable air personality. We explained that that could be a powerful connection to an audience. Once Rick understood he could be the same person on the air as he was in the halls, he was able to make the change.

"Look Out the Window": Aircheck Success Story No. 3

The sun was shining and flowers were blooming in Florida, and a weird weather phenomenon was taking place. During the night, strong winds from Africa had blown sand from the Sahara desert to area swamplands, absorbing the usual stifling humidity in the air. On that day, the weather was dry, warm, and clear, instead of Tampa's usual unrelenting, sticky, tropical heat.

Blissfully unaware of the delightful spring afternoon in progress, the host on the air, a trained psychologist, broadcast two hours of carefully prepared and researched material on suicide and depression. The only people likely to have sat still for a show like that were probably incapable of physical movement. Great show, wrong day.

During the aircheck session that followed, the host was very defensive. "I did everything I was supposed to," she said. "We had powerful stories from individuals involved in the experience, presented problems with solutions, painted word pictures. The show was personal without being too private, why are you on my case?"

"What did you do for the rest of the day after you got off the air?" I asked.

"Oh, it was such a wonderful day that I went sailing with my boyfriend, drank wine, had a picnic on our boat—it was bliss."

"Would you have listened to your own show out on the boat?" I asked her.

Silence.

When programming, producing, or hosting a live show, it is always a good idea to literally take a look out the window and see what the day is like. It is part of what people are really thinking, doing, and talking about.

"Focus the Topic": Aircheck Success Story No. 4

PD Alan Eisenson relates the following story:

> We once had a talk host who found a great article in the Las Vegas paper. It was about a group of strippers bringing a class-action lawsuit against a chain of strip joints for not paying them the minimum wage, while also taking a portion of their tips. The host read the short newspaper article, but he never really focused it into a talkable topic. The show turned into a meandering discussion of stripping in general and ended up digressing into handicapped accessibility on public buses. (I still don't know how that happened!)
>
> When we were airchecking, I asked the host if he thought this would have been a great show had he only focused the issue into a tightly framed talk-show topic—for example: Are strippers second-class citizens? Don't strippers deserve the same workplace rights as everybody else?

It is the job of the program director to coach and direct talk talent and producers into thinking this way. Most good hosts and producers can smell a hot issue; the challenge is framing it into a talkable topic. When a host mentions a topic or issue, I always ask, "What is the point, or what is the question?"

Sometimes it is not so easy to see the point or a question in a subject. Then you have to go deeper to find the talkable topic. Peel away the layers. It may take careful thought to get to the real heart of an issue.

"Did I Do That?": Aircheck Success Story No. 5

Syndication executive Denise McIntee has the briefest but probably most common aircheck success story: "I once played an aircheck of a show where the host was talking down and being curt to a lovely, articulate woman. The host was truly stunned when she heard herself and realized how bad it sounded. She never did it again."

"Who Cares If You Don't?": Aircheck Success Story No. 6

Here is another story from Alan Eisenson's files: "I worked with a talk host who brought up the issue of drug testing. In listening to him, it became clear that he really did not care about the topic. Because he had no opinion about it, he had no story to tell. In that case, he never should have brought it up. He failed to engage the audience in the issue."

When this happens, the programmer should use the aircheck method and ask why the host chose his or her topic. If a show failed to engage the audience, the answer to this question tends to be something along the lines of "Well, it was on the front page, and I thought it would be good."

The PD should then ask some key questions to determine if there was a reason the host cared about their chosen topic which he or she failed to mention. If not, then this aircheck session can become an excellent opportunity to learn that you must care about your subject. As Alan Eisenson says:

> Always have a strong opinion about what you are discussing. Do not ever do a topic when you do not have an opinion, unless you have a guest on the show who has a strong opinion.

You engage the audience with your opinion/position or by telling a riveting relatable story about how the topic pertains to your life, or the lives of your audience. This is the churn, when your passion comes through and you can make your audience care about what you are saying. The show open or monologue is where you set the stage for your entire segment. If you do not care about your subject, you will not find a way to engage your audience.

It works better if the topic is something a host might easily discuss with a friend off air...and doesn't sound "manufactured" to fill a slot on the radio.

Make Time to Give Feedback

Programmer-turned-researcher Andy Beaubien warns that to neglect the talent may be just as dangerous and ineffective as bad airchecking. He recalls, "One person told me she made repeated attempts to arrange an interview with her newly appointed PD. After two months, she still had not succeeded. Various meetings had been planned, but the PD always canceled them. Feeling totally ignored and undervalued, she quit the station and took an on-air job with a competitor."

Randy Lane knows a DJ who says, "If you aren't getting feedback or being managed properly to perform at your best, tell your PD or GM what motivates you and what demoralizes you."

Talent Respects Talent

Sometimes an air talent will walk away from an aircheck session feeling as though he or she has been stomped on by a big boot.

Seattle air personality Dave Ross has worked for several PDs. He admits he does not care to be critiqued in the traditional aircheck session. Understandably, he finds it difficult to be airchecked by someone whose judgment he does not respect. "I resent that it is just one person's opinion of my work. I much prefer to get up in front of a group of people at a live remote or performance and get instant, immediate feedback that way."

New Territory

The first time I airchecked a morning show, I was one of those nervous programmers. I thought, "Gee, who am I to tell these guys what is wrong with their show?" The night before, I had listened to hours of their work, made lists, taken copious notes, and been too anxious to get much sleep.

After the next day's program, our three morning team members walked in, sat down, looked me in the eye, and waited for me to say something. This was back in the old days of cassette players. With sweaty hands, I put the tape in the machine. Before I could open my mouth, one host said:

> No, no, no, let's skip over that part, wait until you hear the next part, now that was funny. . . and wait, back it up . . . here's where we had that boring caller! Wait, oh here I stepped on you guys and we screwed up the call letters, forget that. . . and here's the part where the caller started complaining about the prize because the dinner for two was at a restaurant that did not have free parking.

This went on for about an hour and a half. I had not uttered a single word. At the end of the session, the guys stood up and smiled. "Valerie," one of them said, "you are great at this. It's the best aircheck session we've ever had."

These three broadcast professionals had known exactly what was right and what was wrong with their show. They just needed someone to be a visible audience for them and to witness their self-critique.

I learned something valuable that day from those hosts. This was my lesson: People already know their own strengths and weaknesses. All we as programmers and managers need to do is to help them emphasize their strengths and conquer or play down their weaknesses.

Sometimes, as Massachusetts Institute of Technology Media Lab professor Nicholas Negroponte says, "Management can be measured in its quality by its perceived absence."

Our areas of weakness are probably the things that are difficult for us or that we most dislike or avoid. That which comes easily is most likely our area of strength. This applies both to talent and to management.

Key Principles of Airchecking

1. **Define objectives and expectations.** Outline to the talent what you look for in a show. Make very clear what you expect of them, and who the target audience is.

2. **Do not lie.** If an on-air talent does not trust you or respect you, he or she will not listen to you. If something is not your favorite bit or moment, it can still have merit. Be clear about this.

3. **Know why the show is there.** Remind yourself and the talent of the program's value to the station.

4. **Provide necessary tools.** Do not expect talent to make up for broken equipment, inept performances of others, or things beyond their control.

5. **Ask more than you tell.** Find out why something was done before you react. There may be a good reason why somebody did what they did.

6. **Respect the individual.** Performers are not interchangeable talking meat. Do not force your talent to fit into a format or structure that is very wrong for them. Jaye Albright feels it is impossible to get anyone to do anything he or she really does not want to do with any degree of commitment and conviction.

7. **Preserve privacy.** Do not put copies of aircheck evaluations in the talent's personnel files. Nor should you discuss an aircheck session with others. Record a session only if the talent wants to listen to it again later. For trust to develop, these sessions must be private and confidential.

8. **Look for and highlight powerful moments.** What had you wanting more? As you listen to the aircheck, try to be aware of comments both on the air and from others on your show. Remember, it does not always have to be the star talent having the "power" or "magic" moments; they just have to occur during the show. Denise McIntee searches out these moments: "If a host is able to bring out a poignant story in a caller who was hesitant to tell his or her story, I point that out and praise, praise, praise."

Continued

9. **NEVER work without audio. Focus only on the show.** This is not the time to take up other concerns. Tom Zarecki cautions: "Sometimes the aircheck session spins into a discussion of station issues the talent may be concerned about. Music, production, news, remotes, advertisers, other talent may all end up woven into your aircheck chat. But keep them short. Just like the classroom full of kids who keep the substitute teacher distracted so he or she won't get to the lesson, make sure your talent isn't just trying to get you off the track."

10. **Keep egos out.** It is tempting for talent to remind the PD that they are superstars in the market. Try to remember that the PD is really there to help. Programmers, lower your ego shields. Be willing to listen to talent's ideas. Perhaps they resist direction because they think it could work better another way. They might be right. Ask them what their ideas are. If they have feasible suggestions, throw out your ego and use them. Does it matter where a great idea comes from if it works?

11. **Set achievable goals.** As Lorna Ozmon puts it: "Avoid managing by minutia. When you focus on smaller sub-issues, you are perceived by talent as 'picking on little stuff,' which they see as meaningless to their overall success. To recognize a big-picture issue, ask yourself, 'Will this behavior significantly affect the station's ratings or revenue?' If the answer is yes, it is a big-picture issue. Pick your battles. Fight for the big-picture issues, and let the talent win the minor skirmishes."

12. **Acknowledge accomplishment.** Give authentic feedback for good work. This is Denise McIntee's strategy: "I do not use the session to point out 'faults,' but I might mention that when the host handled a similar situation in a different manner, it seemed to work much better." Ozmon says: "Most performers are 'pleasers.' When you tell them what pleases you, they will strive to do it again." Dan Vallie recommends following up meetings of substance with a memo to recap what was discussed. Internet news executive Bernard Gershon stresses that you must "try to make it clear that the memo is a reminder for them, and for you—not 'evidence' to be kept on file so that you can fire them if they screw up again."

Choosing a Show

You are about to read the wisdom of several veteran aircheckers. Notice how different they can be. Once again, the "right" way to select audio for your aircheck session is the way that works for you. There are several ways to do it:

- Neither the program director nor the talent has heard the recorded show. However, because it is advisable for the talent to select a program to work with, more than likely he or she has a pretty good idea of what is on it. Talent may have notes of problems or questions requiring a second opinion.

- The PD can review the selected program before a session and review it, making note of comments and questions he or she would like to go over with the talent.

- The PD selects a specific show. He or she may or may not choose to preview it. Often the reason for doing it this way is that the PD heard it live and noticed an area for discussion.

- The selection is completely random. For instance, you can send somebody back to the studio to pull any hour he or she can find. While at ABC Radio, then-news director Bernard Gershon used this as a part of his development technique: "We had our on-air talent choose a favorite segment, then one of our managers selected a different one, and then one was picked at random. Usually, the talent went first. Many times they were much harsher on themselves than you or I would ever be. They heard their inflections and imperfections."

How to Listen

Remember that the reference audio must always be available at the aircheck session.

Tom Zarecki suggests: "Listen with the person in front of you. The talent at some point will want to respond to you. Maybe not at first, but it won't take long." Jaye Albright draws a distinction between someone you have worked with before and someone who is on a first "aircheck date" with you: "With new people whose styles I do not know, I begin by listening to a full, scoped half-hour of the show without comment. Then I solicit reactions to what we just heard to learn how they communicate, what they try to do on the air, how prepared they are, and what skills I need to focus on first."

Transcription

Consultant Lorna Ozmon favors transcribing a show word for word. Why?

> If you just listen back to the show, sometimes the talent gets distracted by the sound of their own voice. If the words are written out, it works better. Listen to at least two hours of programming. Set time aside to focus on the show you intend to use for the aircheck. Do this away from other distractions, and make detailed notes. Look for patterns. If you have made good notes, you will begin to see one or two recurring areas for development.

I use transcriptions only when working in a language other than English, but Lorna has specific reasons for her method. She explains:

> Transcription provides talent with specific examples and depersonalizes the critique process. The "script" is less threatening than "what I said." Don't pick out one bad break. Look for and transcribe breaks which show typical problems. This will deflect the impression that you are trying to find the talent doing something wrong and show that your intent is to help him or her.

Randy Lane favors transcription for slightly different reasons. He says:

> Experience the show as a listener. Listen to at least an hour of the show casually (as listeners do) and get an overall feel for the show. Literally transcribe at least an hour of the show while you listen. This enables you to be amazingly specific. Jot down the elements that you remember from the hour. This will give you an idea of what elements might be cutting through to listeners.

Use the Pause

Using a pause is Tom Zarecki's method.

> Try this: Establish the tone of the entire meeting by listening for about thirty seconds, then stop. Talk about what you liked and didn't like about the way he or she introduced the hour. Pause mid-sentence to compliment the talent on something specific. Nobody minds this. You can't do it too much.

> Nothing is more deadly and dull than pressing "play," then the two of you sitting and listening to a few minutes, or even the whole show, without anybody saying anything.

Ask Questions

Whichever way you decide to work with audio, there are some basic questions you can ask about any show that will help you evaluate its potential. This is my checklist of things I want to hear when I'm listening for powerful radio:

Valerie Geller's
Key Principles of Powerful Airchecking

1. Are you talking to *one* person? Is it conversational? Can an individual listener feel connected with the presenter, or is the host speaking to "all those listeners *out there*"?

2. Are you using visual language? Can you "see" the story?

3. Is there passion, fun, or humor?

4. Do you sound like you would rather be someplace else?

5. Is this a story affecting the listener's health, emotion, or money? Will this story inspire a listener to transform some aspect of his or her life?

6. Is there a "talkable topic" the listener can discuss later with others? Is this manufactured for air or would you genuinely talk about this off air?

7. Are there characters we can care about? Can listeners imagine this person?

8. Are you taking your audience on a journey?

9. Is this information that can't be found elsewhere? Is this information new?

10. Is it personal without being private? Do I get to know *you* as I listen?

11. Do I like spending time with you? If we took a five-hour car journey together would the time pass by quickly? Would it be fun, interesting and enjoyable?

12. Does this show feel too *long?* Is the time dragging by? If a topic is powerful, five minutes seems to pass in seconds. If a topic or host is boring or dull—a one-minute piece can feel like it goes forever.

13. Were you, as the host, in control of this show?

Questions to Ask at the Session

1. How does the talent want to be perceived by the audience? Have him or her pick three adjectives. Does she want to be seen as caring? Credible? Edgy? Funny? Intellectual? Is that happening?

2. Did the talent feel that the show worked? What parts were especially great? What bombed? Was there a talkable topic or engaging question? Was the topic or question focused?

3. Did the talent feel pressured to work with a subject from a producer or the front page of the newspaper even though he or she secretly could not have cared less about it? Did it sound "manufactured for air"? Did the show fit the day? Were there any breaking news stories or other events that should have been covered?

4. Was the talent nervous, unprepared, or anxious? Was the show accessible to people just tuning in?

5. Was the topic handled on our station in a way that was different or unique? Research shows that one of the reasons people leave news-talk radio is that they find it presents problems that leave them feeling hopeless and depressed. Did your host or program offer solutions along with the problems?

6. Was the talent trying to persuade the listener to take a particular point of view? What are the tactics the talent used to attempt to convince the audience? Did they work? What drew the talent to this subject? Does the talent have some kind of personal experience with this topic? Did the talent reveal that?

7. If the host could redo today's show, what would be different? Would a listener speak about things heard on your station tonight with a spouse at the dinner table? Was there anything that could be used to promote upcoming shows?

Ensure that your station always has something real and compelling on air to offer your listeners—not something "manufactured for air" and boring—which will result in increased ratings for your station.

Don't Be a "Call Counter"

Some programmers tally up the number of calls a show took during an hour at the aircheck session as if that number alone tells them anything about the quality of the segment. Air talent also do this: "It was a great hour. I got tons of calls."

Programmers and talent new to talk radio are often surprised when a program gets a lot of calls but is not successful in the ratings. It seems that getting a lot of calls should be a logical indicator of listenership, right? Wrong. The amount of calls received by a show is not a valid indicator of how well a program is working. This can be difficult to understand for those who like to see immediate response. It just seems so logical: If a show is working, people will call. But radio isn't always logical.

Shows are successful when created and performed for the ninety-eight percent of your audience who are listening, not for the two percent who fill the board with blinking lights. Personality Rush Limbaugh regularly reminds broadcasters about the importance of focusing on the content, without obsessing on the calls coming in. You could put a psychic on the air and you'll get the phone lines to light up, but the only people who will find the show interesting are the people on hold. Imagine a music radio station that gave concert tickets away for four straight hours every morning. The calls would be constant, but the ratings would be a disaster.

That's why programmer Jeremy Coleman refers to the full board of calls as "fool's gold."

Quality Callers

It's natural for some hosts to want to be polite to their callers, especially if they are worried about being perceived as "rude." But when a host allows a boring or inarticulate caller to wander on and on, that host is actually being rude to the thousands of listeners who are giving him or her their time. If a trade-off has to be made, choose your audience.

When airchecking, look for the quality of the calls that got on the air. Did the callers provide information, inspiration, or entertainment? Did they seem to know when you were kidding, when you were serious? Were they emotional? Articulate? Are you pleased with the duration of the calls? If you think a call went on too long, where should it have ended? Air personality (and editor) Turi Ryder applies what she calls "the rule of 'one more thing.'" She announces her policy of hanging up on any caller who utters that phrase, but tells her listeners it's because she wants them to look their best, and the information they'll give first is usually their top material.

Do you feel you understood the callers' points? If the host didn't understand, did he or she ask for clarification? Did the callers add to the show's momentum or drag it down? Did the host feel or seem to be in control of the calls? Did the host change anybody's mind or the reverse? Were any of the calls upsetting? Humorous? Aggravating?

Are you getting a representative cross-section of your targeted listeners to call in? Were any of these callers a potential resource for a future show? If so, did your producer get their contact numbers? Were you pleased with the mix of opinions and the number of calls you took? Do you feel the same way about all of this right now as you did during the show itself?

It is one thing to avoid confrontation between managers and hosts, but quite another to have a host who avoids it on the air. That is a sure way to a boring talk show. Tom Zarecki says, "Make the listeners like you, not the callers. Your greatest moments on the air may come from encounters with people who vehemently disagree with you."

Room for Risk

Ultimately, because the PD usually wins in a fight to the finish, it is important to allow talent to make a genuine mistake without getting beaten up. Talent will make mistakes, but, reminds consultant Andy Beaubien:

> Creativity cannot exist in a zero-risk environment. One of the PD's responsibilities is to encourage personalities to take calculated risks. Mistakes are a natural part of the creative process. That process involves dealing with unknown factors, the outcome of which is unpredictable. Conversely, making the same mistakes over and over again is not a sign of creative risk-taking but of carelessness and inattention.

If you want to show a talent what a bit could sound like if executed differently, you might try what consultant Guy Zapoleon calls the "before-and-after trick" of playing the original audio and then playing an edited version.

Jaye Albright uses the work of others on air to make her points: "It can be helpful to hear someone else successfully do the thing you are being asked to do."

Tom Zarecki's technique for listening includes the following points:

1. *Take notes during the meeting.* Have your own list of two or three points you want to cover. When talent comments on something you need to handle (examples: unreasonable demands from a salesperson, uncooperative screener, equipment problem), write this down and take care of it. Let the talent see you taking notes on their comments. This prompts them to make more comments.

2. *Create a short, numbered "what-to-work-on" list.* Your short list might be only one item! A typical list might say:

   ■ Make opening remarks shorter. Get to guest quicker.

   ■ Let callers provide the material. Don't be so quick to top them with your own lines.

3. *Make sure to date it.* It's important to put today's date, then you can chronicle the progress with subsequent shows.

4. *Avoid the novel.* Focus on the important things.

5. *Agree on concessions.* You and the talent may each end up with your own short list of priority points to work on.

Tips for Teams

Here are some thoughts from consultants who work with team shows. Tommy Kramer advises, "Team shows have some special needs. The objective is to avoid 'train wrecks,' where the listener cannot tell what is going on." Here are his tips for teams:

1. **Define roles.** The funny guy has to be the funny guy. To use a sports comparison, the play-by-play person and the color announcer have separate, clearly distinct roles. Cast them as you would cast a movie, and then get the talent to stay in their roles. Nothing is worse than hearing two people try to top each other.

2. **Listen to each other.** It is horrible to hear two people who each pay no attention to what the other says. How can they hope to connect with the listener? Tiny things can spur great moments on the air. But if the talent are not listening to each other, they will miss the cue.

3. **Use hand signals.** Most teams think they do not need them. That is why so many teams talk all over each other. There is nothing compelling about hearing two people talking at once. Simply pointing at the other person right before your final word can correct this and make it sound seamless. It takes only a moment to point at the phone to signal that you are going to a caller or the computer for music. Point at yourself to signal that you have something to say. Use the slit-the-throat signal to show "cut this off." Most teams get away from hand signals after a while, but if the timing gets off, go back to them.

Tom Zarecki's Thoughts About Airchecking Teams

- The thing you should not do in these team sessions is severely criticize any one person, especially the primary host.

- Most of any meeting with teams should be positive, upbeat, and motivational. As in individual sessions, if something is great, react accordingly. Applaud. Play it again. Compliment specifics.

- Continue to meet with your primary host, and other team members, separately, to reap the benefits of confidential sessions.

- Before your meeting ends, make sure to set the date for the next aircheck session.

Finally, as Guy Zapoleon says, "Every great team needs to practice; you have to dribble before you can dunk."

Don't Rely on Unreliable Feedback

The news director and staff of one of the most dreadful and lazy newsrooms I have ever seen felt no need to improve or change because they received the occasional fan letter. Remember, even the worst show has one listener.

Consider the talk host who opens the microphone and asks for comments on his or her show. Sure, there may be some helpful ideas generated, but if your goal is to increase your audience, the people you really need to ask are not listening at all. The feedback you are generating is not germane. If you ask a retired community leader what he thinks of the big modern rock station in town, his comments may be heartfelt, but they are useless.

Untutored feedback sources can be deadly. I once worked with a station where the manager's wife was offended by a single remark on the station's morning show. As a result, the morning show was canned. That air talent walked across the street, got a job at the competition, and became No. 1 in the market!

There is also a phenomenon where people may have a strong reaction to a personality and say they hate him or her, but they listen every day. The same person who strongly claims not to like a show can often quote you chapter and verse what he hated on the air that morning, and the day before.

The moral here is this: Powerful talent causes powerful reactions, both negative and positive. If your goal is to get ratings, understand what you are really hearing. Don't react to unreliable feedback.

One general manager actually fired a top talent because the complaint he received "was a particularly well-written letter that made an excellent case." Again, the talent simply packed up his huge audience and went over to the competition.

When radio consultant David G. Hall was a program director, he loved angry listener mail. On any given day, you could find the most vituperative letters tacked to his office door. You could hear the best irate phone calls by checking the station's website. Complaints, boycotts, and protests can also be a source of great free publicity for your station, ultimately generating new listeners.

Where is the Line?

With creative performers, there is a real danger of stepping over the line. Consultant Andy Beaubien points out that unreliable feedback can encourage talent to cater to an ever-decreasing segment of their audience:

> Content must be judged not only in terms of entertainment and information value but by legal and public-taste standards as well. Many personalities constantly test these boundaries. The PD's job is to help personalities to stay within the necessary parameters without compromising the creative process.

For obvious reasons, content that is offensive to the target audience or portions of it is to be avoided. Content that is acceptable to your target audience but not necessarily to the overall market may be permissible and even necessary.

Personalities often find that certain kinds of "on-the-edge" material are very well received by a particular segment of their audience. In reality, that segment may represent only a small portion of the target audience. However, minority audience reinforcement can be very influential. If a personality is allowed to be swayed by this narrow audience segment, the overall cume, or cumulative audience, will be reduced to an ever-shrinking core.

This phenomenon is a silent killer. Because the active core can be quite vocal about its preferences, the departure of the greater cume can remain undetected until long after serious damage has taken place.

When you drive away your audience—that is the line.

It All Works Together

The aircheck process can actually help with show prep. Lorna Ozmon suggests closing the aircheck session with a discussion of new ideas, including prep. She says:

> Look at the next month's calendar, and brainstorm for ways to capitalize on holidays or special events within the context of the talent's work on your radio station. Bring new books, magazines, and newspaper articles that could serve as new sources of creative inspiration. Even if none of the ideas discussed are ever used on the air, this process helps keep the seeds of creativity alive.

Everybody's a Critic

Airchecking works best if there is only one person doing the feedback sessions. It can be very frustrating to hear comments from too many sources. The talent already gets feedback from his or her audience, producer, spouse, children, and people around the station. If you have clearly established your objectives and criteria for deciding what a good show is, adding the opinions and standards of others can only muddy the waters.

CHAPTER *9*

Beyond Powerful Radio
High-Ego Talent

"Creativity takes courage."
—*Henri Matisse*

Perhaps you have had the experience of knowing people in the business who were great on the air, always got big ratings, but never kept a job for any substantial length of time? Many of these people "station-hopped" because they had demanding personalities and were tough to deal with off the air.

Often, great radio personalities have large egos and are not the easiest or most tranquil people to be around. But allowing your station's professional atmosphere to be blighted by tantrums is ultimately damaging. While managers need the skills to deal with touchy talent, no one can save a truly self-destructive host. Remember this when considering hiring a personality who has a "reputation."

One day, I was taking a break in the lunchroom of a client station. In between bites of sandwiches, staffers were talking about one of the station's most talented and successful broadcasters. Actually, he was one of the station's most talented former broadcasters, because he had just been fired.

"But he was so good on the air. I just don't get it," lamented the newest member of the staff. "I listened to him all the time. What happened?"

The room went silent. Had this guy done something truly terrible or maybe even illegal? Then one of the producers said, "Well he was kind of hard to work with..."

Another staffer chimed in, "Yeah, he could really get on your nerves. He complained all the time about everything."

A quiet young woman who had been working as an assistant producer to the ousted personality added: "If you weren't a big shot, he'd ignore you. He treated me like I was dirt, instead of a professional there to help him with his show. He made me feel like his personal slave. He'd order me to move his car or run outside to put money in the parking meter. He'd never ask or say please, just 'do it!'"

Having worked herself into a righteous frenzy, the young producer continued: "Whenever something went wrong on the show, like missing a network join, or a spot, or losing a guest on the phone, it was never his fault. He made a huge stink about it and blamed other people. He went through six producers in a year and a half."

"But the audience loved him!" argued the new guy.

"We didn't," said the PD, who walked into the lunchroom at that point, ending the discussion.

It has always been my belief that if people are difficult but truly talented artists, then it is worth some extra effort to put up with their nonsense, to a point. Talent is special, and artists are different. Gifts in this life are not distributed evenly. A person with abundant talent may have an equal lack of social skills. In her song about singer-songwriter Bob Dylan, Joan Baez wrote, "A savior's a nuisance to live with at home." And she's mostly right. True artists can be challenging to be around day to day. Sometimes they can be their own worst enemies. While we love and respond to their originality, creativity, and art, we have little use for their anger, insecurity, constant need for attention and approval, and lack of respect for authority.

The PD at the aforementioned station admitted that his former staffer had made him so anxious that he shut his door quickly or picked up the phone when he saw the "problem" air talent walking down the hall. Even so, he felt the dismissal was a loss both to the talent and to the radio station. It was a bad situation. However, I'm just the consultant and only looking at what went on the air. The rest of the staff had to put up with this guy every day. The station succumbed to the temptation of hiring a lesser talent because he was easier to live with.

How can managers effectively handle this type of personality? The answer is, very carefully. The first thing is to recognize that while the performer in question is an adult, legally speaking, that 40-year-old body may hide the emotions of a six-year-old. Don't be fooled by the long legs and beard. You can learn a lot about managing difficult talent by hanging around kids. Like children, they may be very insecure.

I walked in a day too late to save that situation. Had I had the chance to sit down and work with this talent and his manager before the situation blew up, here are a few of the points I would have communicated:

- Don't be a talkaholic. People are busy. Don't distract them. Let them go about their work.

- Don't send impulsive or angry texts or e-mails. E-mail can be harsh or misinterpreted. Wait a few hours and cool down before you hit "send." Use words carefully.

- Do it yourself. If you need special equipment and the station doesn't have it, consider buying your own headphones, microphone, etc.

- Be selective. Don't fight every battle. Save your energies for the important issues.

- Don't question authority until you've given the matter proper consideration.

- Have a little patience. Don't overreact.

- Your boss is not a mind reader. Tell your manager when you need attention. Set a time. It can't always be now.

- Don't ignore or mistreat those "below" you.

- Be a human being. Have a heart. Be sensitive to others.

- Save your show for on-air, not in the hall!

One of the challenges for overworked GMs and PDs is coping with the air personalities. Top radio talent can be sensitive, volatile, ego-driven, self-absorbed, insecure, and infantile. In other words, they are difficult to manage. They need a lot of time, attention, and positive feedback. These same "pains in the neck" can also be likable, charming, and tremendously talented. They perform and connect with the audience, and can potentially bring in huge numbers of listeners. It may be up to you to decide to make the effort to manage them.

It's worth developing people. If you can afford it, financially and emotionally, try it. When it doesn't work, remember right-casting: Someone who is not right in this job may be very successful in another situation. Even the failures can teach you something. Don't dismiss it, or worse, give up, just because it is the more challenging, risky route.

Talent vs. Management: Two Worlds

For a group of professional communicators, we often don't do a very good job of it amongst ourselves. Here is a typical unspoken dialogue between a manager and an on-air talent.

TALENT	vs.	MANAGEMENT
Pay attention to me!	vs.	Your listeners love you, what more do you want?
I'm important. Make me feel that way, NOW!	vs.	I have ten other things to do.
I'm a creative person, I don't like anyone telling me what to do.	vs.	We talked about this: I'm not changing my mind.
I want you to listen to my show and respond every day.	vs.	You leave me emotionally exhausted. I have a radio station to run and you're only one part of it.
I need positive feedback. Nobody appreciates me!	vs.	Why can't you just do your job and be happy with your big pay check?
I want to make a difference. I want to be great!	vs.	I just spent a half an hour on the phone with an angry listener.
Look at me! Listen to me! I want input into what I do here. I want to count!	vs.	I get this from my three-year-old at home, I do not need it from you at work.

CHAPTER 10

Beyond Powerful Radio
Avoiding Burnout

> "What was any art but a mold in which to imprison
> for a moment, the shining elusive element which
> is life itself—life hurrying past us and running
> away, too strong to stop, too sweet to lose."
> —*Willa Cather*

In your quest to create powerful radio, it is important to look at what can move radio forward, as well as to understand what can hold powerful radio back. This is why creative burnout is worth talking about. Burnout is an occupational hazard that sometimes happens to a performer under the daily demand of public scrutiny and constant pressure for consistently original output. While burnout can be a type of exhaustion, or energy drain, it is different from genuine clinical depression. While burnout can lead to a performer becoming depressed, the good news is that it can also be fixed.

Talent

How can you tell when talented people are suffering from burnout? They complain, they call in sick, they are late for work. Ideas don't come to them as easily. They watch the clock, counting the minutes until the end of their shifts. They fear the blank page and begin to rely on other people's ideas more than their own. They want more guests, interviews, and "easy" stuff. Their shows aren't as good as they used to be, and they just don't seem too excited anymore.

Managers

Exhaustion can lead to burnout for managers as well as on-air and producing talent. For economic reasons, many broadcast companies' resources have been stretched thin, making it necessary for individual managers to take on more and more responsibility. Even with improved time-management skills, many frustrated managers still feel overloaded with too much to do in a day. Unless companies provide realistic goals for managers, they can burn out as well.

Battling Burnout

When I wanted to learn more about ways to deal with creative burnout, I hosted a dinner party. Invited guests included actors, artists, a psychologist, a singer-songwriter, a film director, a textile designer, an architect, and some radio and TV people. Everyone in attendance made his or her living by facing the blank page and finding things to fill it. What did they do when the ideas stopped flowing? I gave everyone a pencil and paper. They began to write, talk, and argue. The following is what emerged.

Lower Your Expectations

No one is at his or her most creative all the time. Now may be the time to tap into the creativity of those around you. If your fire is burning low, try to rekindle your spirit and your ideas at the fires of others.

Are You Doing the Right Work for You, Right Now?

Determine what you enjoy about what you do. If the list is short, it may be time to rethink your job and find something else. Most people have many skill sets and typically will have several careers over a lifetime. As scary as change can be, it's better to make the switch than burn out in a job that's not right for you, or not right for you *right now*.

Artists, on the radio or elsewhere, need the right environment to grow. Managers need to understand that creative people are sensitive, introspective, and insecure. Talent need to understand that since you don't come with a list of "care and feeding" instructions, open communication with management is critical. Supervisors who don't take this into account will contribute to burnout.

Live a Balanced Life

It is easy to become driven to accomplish in this career and lose perspective on the rest of your life. Remember, you can love radio, but radio will not love you back.

- Do not become your work. Do other things that make you feel good and give you a sense of accomplishment. Create a balance in your life.

- Burnout occurs when you can no longer grow as a person. Don't let that happen. Challenge yourself to do new things outside of work.

Avoid Energy Vampires

You know the type, people who seem to suck the life right out of you by overwhelming you with their problems. They will exhaust you. Surround yourself with people who nourish you, who give, not just take.

Nourish Your Brain

Look at art. Go to a movie or attend the theater. Read. Talk to your kids. If you don't have kids, talk to someone else's or browse children's books. Play. Get out that set of watercolor paints in the closet and make some art. Listen to music. Try gardening.

Do something, anything, that will stimulate your own creativity and sustain you, even if you are not "in the mood right now."

Be Inspired by Reading

READ. You can easily go online and learn just about anything that may stimulate your creativity. Or take advantage of the plethora of books that inspire creativity. Important books for me include Julia Cameron's *The Artist's Way* and *The Vein of Gold*, Rollo May's *The Courage to Create* and

Anne LaMott's *Bird by Bird*. You can also ask a friend to recommend a biography or favorite book that might inspire you.

Do What You Want

On-the-air, whenever possible, follow your heart. Give others assignments that you don't particularly care about. Stick to what interests and matters to you. Look at what really makes you feel energized and passionate about life. Do those things. You'll minimize the risk of burning out if you maintain the integrity of your show.

Remember Why You Came

Rediscover your professional and personal roots. Take a look at what motivated you at the beginning of your career. What got you interested in doing this work in the first place? Why did you like being on the radio in the beginning? Why was it fun? Remember what led you down this long and winding road.

Take a Break

The root of the word vacation is "vacate," to leave. Take some time away: a day, a week, a month, a year. You may just need a brief change of pace in order to get new input, have experiences, meet new people. Go into "media or news *rebellion*." Turn off your computer, get away from all "screens" (except sunscreen!). Try to do something that will break the monotony of your daily routine and put it back in perspective.

Focus on the Positive

One station manager found that the right attitude can make a big difference and set a good example for the staff:

> I could easily become consumed by budget constraints, destructive corporate directives, any number of distractions, and the ever-decreasing amount of decision-making latitude I have as a PD. But I try to stay focused on the positive elements of my job: I have the rare luxury of a large and talented staff to work with and we are still the number one station in this community. The way to survive is to stay focused on the positive.

Managing Against Burnout

Program directors and other managers of artists and broadcasters have a special responsibility to guard against talent burnout. *Radio Sales Analyst* offered some worthwhile suggestions in this area under the heading "**Principles of Motivation**":

- The employee's behavior is functionally related to the way you treat them.

- People don't resist their own ideas.

- People will live up (or down) to your expectations of them.

- You must know the individuals you are trying to motivate.

- People will change only when they think they have to.

- Productive activity that is ignored will tend to decrease over time.

- Achievement and recognition are the top motivators at all levels.

Get a Life

The life of a performer is not always easy. A lack of stability can cause anxiety that can lead to burnout. Singer-songwriter Christine Lavin has lived through the ups and downs of the performer's life and offers this advice on what it takes to make it in a creative profession when times are tough:

> There is no dignity in starving. If you are not presently making enough money to support yourself with your [work], get a day job that will pay the bills while you work on your craft at night and on weekends.

Lavin worked temporary jobs for years while performing on weekends.

Her final words of wisdom, "Don't borrow money if you can help it."

Lavin's experience is especially applicable for radio performers. Weekends are often the easiest route to getting on the air, trying out in a new format, or working with new partners on the air. Weekend shifts will not interfere with your "day job," whether you have one in radio or an entirely different field.

The Radio Life Can Be "Rootless"

If you have been in the business for any length of time, you may have heard some variation on the following:

"The only job security is your ability to 'secure' another job."

"Radio is like winning a video game. If you win, you get to play another round."

"You can always tell how well a broadcaster is doing by the size of the U-Haul trailer behind his car."

As you may be aware, even before the global recession, commercial radio (or TV) in the United States has not been the most stable of careers. Often, you must move to a new city to have a chance to move up. You might find yourself out of a job at any time for just about any reason.

This insecurity adds stress and havoc to the already fragile life of the radio artist. A sense of humor helps, but some broadcasters can't take it and find other work. It follows that making your job a bit more secure would cut down on some of the stress-related burnout.

Writer, editor, reporter, entrepreneur and broadcast journalist Sheri Inglis warns: "To pursue a career in radio and live to tell about it, it is important to live a full life to be a whole person, not just living your life as a radio or TV person." The following are Sheri's ideas for people who "want to work in broadcasting and survive."

- **Look for a career in broadcasting as you would a marriage partner.** Don't get in because you think you can live with it. Get in only if you feel you can't live without it.

- **Diversify!** This is the single most important key to surviving the long haul in radio or television. Someone told me when I first began my career, "There ain't no gold watch in this business." Aside from a few rare exceptions, that is true. Resist the temptation to launch headlong into an "exciting career" as a disc jockey, talk host, news reporter or anchor, etc., and leave it at that.

While you're pursuing your radio career, also learn and grow another professional skill. Whether it is public relations, marketing, script writing, real estate sales, flower arranging, court reporting, or giving scuba lessons, you need something else to fall back on. I don't know of a single radio veteran who hasn't nursed a bruised ego at least a few times following an ownership change, budget cut, format shift, or political fall from grace.

Pursuing a second or third career admittedly takes extraordinary determination, but you'll save yourself and your family added financial devastation if you have a backup plan up and running. By not putting all of your "eggs in one basket," you also empower yourself to move on and, often, up in your radio career rather than simply accepting a bad or unchallenging situation out of fear of unemployment.

- **Be prepared.** Always have your résumé and updated demo materials ready at all times, no matter how happy or popular you are in your present gig. New opportunities will often arise on short notice.

- **Don't get involved in station gossip or politics.** You increase your chances of being spared through ratings dips and managerial changes if you keep your mouth shut and your nose clean.

- **Keep a good attitude about the station.** No matter how messed up things are, avoid complaining to management or coworkers. Be very selective about the battles you want to fight, then fight them with the highest level of dignity, professionalism, and maturity possible. If you are unhappy at a given station, move on.

CHAPTER 11

Beyond Powerful Radio
Show Prep

"Creating is never given to us all by itself. It goes hand-in-hand with the gift of observation. A true creator may be recognized by his ability to find about him, to the commonest and humblest thing, items worthy of note."
—*Igor Stravinsky*

"All truly wise thoughts have been thought already thousands of times; but to make them truly ours, we must think them over again honestly, until they take root in our personal experience."
—*Goethe*

Why Is Prep Crucial?

A general would never go into battle without a plan. A surgeon would never go into the operating room without a preliminary work-up. Yet it is surprising how many air personalities show up for work and just wait to see what happens. Some days they might get lucky, but for winning over the long haul, show prep is essential. If a talent is prepared, it does not matter if he or she slides in a minute before airtime. The prepared host can still do a great show.

It is never an accident when a show is number one. It takes very hard work. The best personalities compile a stack of material from various sources: articles from magazines or newspapers, written ideas, and material collected from the Internet along with stories they have picked up from life or have observed or overheard.

Syndicated talk-show host Rush Limbaugh is a master of show prep. He's disciplined. When I worked with him at WABC radio in New York, Rush would come in hours before each show. He didn't go on the air until he'd gone through dozens of newspapers, discussed ideas with his producer, and spent time on the phone talking with anyone from disc jockeys to political leaders.

Rush had concepts and stories, but no guests. He found things that interested him, collected them, and shared them with his audience. No one made him do this. Rush did it on his own, because he wanted his show to succeed. He realized the value of show prep.

Everyone has his or her own way of organizing show prep materials, but if a host sounds consistently disorganized on the air, try coming up with another system. If a host is prepared but cannot access an item during the on-air performance, all that prep is wasted and the show will wander.

Some talent are fortunate enough to have trustworthy people, usually producers, who do their show prep and planning for them. It then becomes the talent's job to creatively execute someone else's plan. Nevertheless, a plan still exists.

Creative talent are constantly doing show prep. Everything in their lives—what they read, eat, feel, experience, and even dream—all goes into their shows. Radio Personality Melissa McConnell Wilson says, "Twenty-four hours a day, seven days a week—every conscious waking moment, I'm gathering information to recall later to use on my show."

How personal can it get? With some air personalities, the best you can hope for in terms of confidentiality is that your name stays out of it. Managers beware: Your meetings or conversations with talent could become material.

There is a difference between personal and private. No one should be allowed to endanger others or personally harm them in any way. Not only can there be legal consequences to giving specific information about people's private lives, but there can be security issues as well. When in doubt, try asking: "Will the story of the car with the Picasso in the back seat be as compelling if I don't give the car's make and model?"

Oftentimes a little camouflage, using the essence of a true story, enables more creative and dramatic storytelling without risking someone's physical well-being or emotional embarrassment. What is your point? If entertaining your audience is the goal, then does it really matter if something happened to your wife or to "a woman I know...?"

Try television's Dragnet approach: "The story you are about to hear is true, but the names have been changed to protect the innocent."

Using Humor

Humor always attracts listeners. Some people are funny; others may not be funny but have great senses of humor. There are those who are hilarious in private but are not able to access those parts of their personalities on the air.

You can do show prep that improves your ability to be funny on the air. For example, you can learn to become a better storyteller. Consultant Jaye Albright offers this advice to those who would like to grow and develop in this area:

> Read every book in the library about humor. If possible, attend improvisation workshops. These can be mind-expanding releases of creative expression. [When telling a story] memorize specific and colorful details. There is nothing funny about the abstract—comedy emerges from specifics. Make note of them and use them; allow the child who lives within you to emerge. Tell your truth.

"When you start to take this job seriously, you're in trouble."
—*Jimmy Buffet*

"Use everything in your life to create your art."
—*Stanislavsky*

Rules for Powerful Prep

Here are some ideas and questions to look at when doing show prep.

Go with the Moment

This is also known as the rule of "out the window." If something spontaneous happens on the air that is better than what you have prepared, go with it! You would happily take a "side trip" to see the Grand Canyon while traveling through Arizona. The magic moments on radio—a breaking news story or a fabulous caller—happen when you least expect them, and when they occur it is wonderful. Although there is no substitute for walking into the station thoroughly prepared, you must also be willing to throw that stack of stuff "out the window" when something irresistible turns up.

Always Ask Why—Avoid Slot Filling

Always have a specific reason for wanting a guest. Avoid "guest-o-mania." If a guest has been booked for you, know the reason. Ask the producer, "What has this person done? Why is he or she special?"

Ask: "Will we enjoy this guest even if we are not familiar with his or her latest book or area of expertise?" Is this someone you would want to talk to off the air? Think twice before you take the easy way out and book a guest to fill an hour of airtime. If you have always wanted to meet someone, and he or she lives in your town or is coming to your area, it is perfectly acceptable to invite that person to be a guest on your show, provided that the goal remains to entertain or inform your audience.

Never promise a guest an hour. Instead, just ask for a few minutes of his or her time. Make it clear that because this is live radio, it is always possible that a guest may be preempted by a breaking story. You have now protected yourself from the potentially embarrassing situation of having to dump a guest if he or she is boring or if a bigger opportunity arises.

I am frequently asked for a rule about how to use guests. Unless you are doing an interview-based show, I advise using guests as spice. Like great seasoning in a bland meal, guests can be wonderful. Good guests can make a show, but they must be gifted communicators with passion, offer new information or have something relevant to say. The best guests are people who have personal experience, with a story to tell, rather than being just experts in their fields.

A guest can also serve as an unwitting foil for savvy hosts with barbed tongues. "John and Ken" in Los Angeles are famous for finding "village idiots" and using them on the air for comedic purposes.

Warning to Managers

Many managers like to hear guests on the air. It demonstrates that the host and producer have done some work to book the show and justify their salaries. They like to see bodies at desks for eight hours a day. Sales reps are asked to turn in lists of people they have called on, called back, or visited. Managers feel comfortable seeing people working. It's that "all in their places with bright shiny faces" song we learned in elementary school. We are accustomed to believing what we see. Management has a hard time accepting that a talent reading a newspaper, getting a hair cut, or fighting with his or her auto mechanic is actually doing show prep, but it can be true.

Broadcasting is not school, or a factory job where we punch in our eight hours a day. Radio work is different, more like art than manufacturing. A gallery owner would not call an artist at 8:45 in the morning and ask, "Are you at your easel yet? How many brushes have you used?"

The only hard rule for powerful radio is: Be prepared and on time for your show. What listeners respond to is the finished product. Our product is what comes out of the speakers on the radio. Our preparation is real but often invisible.

Be Prepared

Carry a recording device, camera or notepad at all times. Don't forget spare batteries for that device. If we were working as photographers, we would always have a camera ready. But we work in radio and our platform is sound. When was the last time you thought to yourself, "I wish I had a sound recorder right now?" They are small and light. Get one. Carry it. If you are not comfortable carrying one, at least keep paper and pen handy so that you can jot down a great idea before it is gone. Great ideas come in the shower, the car, and wake you up at night. Write them down.

Make Friends Outside of the Business

Spend time with normal people. If you only associate with journalists and broadcasters, you limit your vision. Expand your horizons. Talk to everyone. Your inner circle should contain people who work outside of radio and have a variety of interests and experiences. Listen to them. Find out what they are thinking, worrying, and talking about. It will help your show tremendously. Read everything. Watch everything. Find mentors. As consultant Randy Lane says: "Hang out with creative people, and learn from them. Study creative performers outside of radio."

Know Your Target

Know your audience. Do the listeners have a different lifestyle than the program host? Probably so. Perhaps the host lives in a busy urban center, whereas the bulk of the station's listeners are suburbanites. You need to know what goes on where they live, too. Read the local press. Drive around to get a feeling for your area. Attend neighborhood functions. Meet people. Get to know your city.

This is not *Lifestyles of the Rich and Famous*. Even if you do not frequent your local Wal-Mart, Ikea, or Home Depot, you should at least know people who do. Eat where your listeners eat; shop where they shop. Stay curious, alive, and interested.

Take a Test Drive

Discuss show ideas with somebody else. Prep is much easier when you have the luxury of working with a talented producer. He or she can help you focus ideas to help form questions you will ask on air and points you will make to engage your audience. Try bouncing the ideas off people around you: the call screener, the PD, the newsperson, or the station's security guard. It may help you focus on what is really interesting about the topic, or take it in a different direction.

Prep Warning

Do not do your show before the show. Testing out an idea should not be confused with rehearsing a monologue. Save your actual performance for the live microphone. It will never sound as good or as natural the second time around.

Pre-produce

Prepare the soundtrack for your show. Any bits, music, etc., that you think you might want to use should be close at hand. Inform your engineer or board operator well in advance if you will require any special technical assistance or equipment. Make sure your equipment is working.

Double-check

Before you go on air with a topic, ask: "Is it relevant? Does it matter? Do you care? Do your listeners care? What will I do if this topic gets boring? Do I have a fall-back plan?"

Be Generous

If you have found a topic that would be perfect for somebody else at your station, pass it along. Leave the article, book, note, etc., in that person's mailbox. E-mail them or give them a call. The success of your station depends on the efforts of all its creative members.

Experiment

Break rules if you can come up with a more successful method. Take what works for you, and leave the rest.

Surfing the Web

Most bosses frown on employees surfing the web during their working hours, but if you produce or host a TV or radio show (or podcast), part of your job IS surfing the web!

The Internet is a wealth of information and a source for material for your show. Nearly every newspaper and news service from around the country and around the world is available online—and on your mobile devices. Electronic press releases may fill your inbox, but take the time to plow through them. One or two out of dozens may offer a story you can use or build on for your program. Blogs are a great source of "talkable topics" and show prep material.

Another valuable way to check on trends, topics, and what people are talking about is to spend some time online. McVay Media's President of New Media Daniel Anstandig suggests, "If you take advantage of digital media, you can find out, up-to-the-moment, what your audience is talking about. You'll never need to guess the 'water cooler talk' for the day!" He recommends the following three websites:

Daniel Anstandig: Using Digital Media to Find Out What Your Audience Is Talking About

1. *Google Trends and Google Insights*. A quick visit to Google Trends can tell you what the hottest topics are *right now* on Google. This list, updated in real time, shows you what people are searching across the country in the Google search engine. You can also use Google Insights to determine what people in your market are searching. Google Insights offers the option to view the hottest searches over the last day, seven days, thirty days, ninety days, or twelve months. You can also narrow the audience down to your state or specific metro. Bookmark these sites: *http://www.google.com/trends* and *http://www.google.com/insights/search/*

2. *Twitter Trends with Trendsmap.com*. Using TrendsMap.com, you can find the most talked about topics on Twitter in your local market. You can see what keywords and topics are being tweeted the most by people who are tweeting in your town in real time.

3. *Yahoo Local News*. If you're looking for all of your community's news in one place, you'll find Yahoo Local News especially helpful. Visit the site, enter your location, and Yahoo will show you the big news stories from all of your local news outlets in one page. It's a quick and easy way to get up to speed on what is happening around town. Bookmark these three sites, and in moments you can be up to date on the hottest and more important topics in your market.

Tale of Total Show Prep

However you research your content, it's important to put in the prep time. The following "tale of total show prep" comes from consultant Tommy Kramer's *Coaching Handbook*. It illustrates what can happen when you do not do your homework thoroughly.

A talent called with a problem: He had overslept on Tuesday, had no time for show prep, and just barely made it in time for his morning-drive show. Yet he and his partner had a great show that day. The next day, the talent did two hours of show prep and arrived on time, but the show was difficult and out of synch. His question for me was, "Do I really need show prep?"

This guy got lucky on Tuesday. His creative side bailed him out. But it won't and cannot every day. Wednesday he did tons of prep, but all the work was informational. He had lots of things on tap but had not thought about where to go with them.

The answer is, "Yes, you need to do your show prep. But look for balance and prep your creative as well as your informational side."

Prep and Topic Selection

Method acting teaches that the actor must convince himself before he convinces the audience. If the on-air personality is genuinely interested in the topic, it will work better. Broadcasters organize their show prep in different ways. There is no "right way," just the way that works for you.

Dig Deep for Talkable Topics or Engaging Questions

Remember to look beyond page one for stories. Take notes from conversations you've had or overheard. Try to come up with at least one story or observation from your own life for each show.

Andy Beaubien and Jeremy Millar's Prep Methods

Basic preparation techniques are similar for every format. The actual protocol works as well for music as it does for talk radio. International consultant and researcher Andy Beaubien programmed many of America's top-rated Album Rock music stations. Beaubien, and the Australian Broadcasting Corporation's Jeremy Millar, outlined the following method for prepping and running a well-organized show: "Show prep is usually a team effort and not a task assigned to just one person. In most cases, the program producer becomes the official collector of show-prep material, since he or she is often more objective than the show's anchor."

Review

Ideally, show prep begins with a review (aircheck session) of the previous program. This is often accomplished at the daily meeting with the PD. Decide which segments worked and which did not.

Update

The producer updates the team on new material that has arrived. This may include items from publications, syndicated radio services, press releases, the Internet, and so on. The update should include a briefing on the latest news items that may fit the show. The availability of in-studio (or phone) guests should also be reviewed and the producer should be prepared to provide background information on them. It is also good to look at upcoming major news, sports, and show business events.

Sources

On the Internet and elsewhere, the local newspaper need play only a modest role in your show. If you find that you are depending on the newspaper for most of your topics, try a "newspaper-free" week.

Some teams hire writers who will generate exclusive material for their shows. You can often find talented freelance writers who will regularly deliver fully written, customized material for a surprisingly nominal fee.

Topics

Decide on a list of topics for the day's program, and assign a priority to each item. Gather additional information about items that have caught your attention. Often you may find that a topic which originally sounded interesting turns out to be a dead-end street. On the other hand, research may uncover amazing facts about a subject that had seemed limited.

If scriptwriting or pre-recorded material is to be used, the producer can assign these tasks to others on the team. Most talents prefer an outline to a written script, so they can deliver material in their own style.

Production

Pre-recorded material may include interviews with guests not available at airtime, on-the-street interviews, musical excerpts, sound effects, novelty voices, feature intros and outros, and highlights from previous programs.

Schedule

Schedule the program elements on paper. Make sure everyone involved gets a copy. Each program should be planned in quarter-hour segments (or smaller if necessary). Interview guests are also placed on the schedule at this time. The program schedule should be maintained on a daily and weekly basis. A good producer should always have a contingency plan, as last-minute guest cancellations are common.

Archives

An essential part of show prep is the maintenance of complete and accurate files. Include the following:

- A file of previous daily program schedules
- Copies of scripts and program ideas
- Background material by subject
- Audio files, including full-length recordings of previous programs and edited program excerpts.

Accurate records allow the team to recycle successful program features. Great guests and new show topics are not always available. A good library will keep the show afloat through slow periods.

Tommy Kramer points out that another nearly effortless way a team show continues to prep outside the station is to "communicate with each other off the air. An advance phone call or e-mail can prepare your partner or producer for a bit you want to do tomorrow. It gives the other person time to turn it over to his or her subconscious and think of creative ways to contribute. Time spent going to lunch or a ball game together can teach you things about each other's speech patterns, outside interests, etc., that could otherwise take months to learn."

Be Selective

It is great when you have ten fabulous ideas for a show but only need four. But how do you know which topics should make it to the air? Is there a set criteria for topic selection? Consultant Jaye Albright puts it very well:

> Do something that has something to do with me and my life. It can't be a cliché. It must be original and specific. If it is from your life, I hope that it becomes a metaphor for something about mine. Something that moves me emotionally, touches me personally, yet is delivered with spontaneity and the knowledge that my time is important. The less it has to do with me, the briefer or the more moving it must be.

WABC TV's Howard Price's job was to choose the stories that aired on top-rated *Eyewitness News* in New York City. Price knows how to spot popular issues and trends and, like many top producers, incorporates Frank Magid and Associates, research findings from years ago, which still hold true: Three subject areas listeners and viewers always respond to are stories about "health, heart, and pocketbook." He uses these criteria for topic selection:

- *You work for "WIFM"*—"What's in it for *Me?*"—and the "me" means your listeners.

- *Every day ask*: What are people really doing? What are they talking about right now at their desks or on the checkout line? How can my program engage in and advance the discussion? Explore problems and solutions. Unite your listeners with stories of personal crises or extreme viewpoints.

- *Have the vision and vigilance to spot trends, take risks, and exploit opportunities.* Do one thing, or a small collection of things, better, faster, and more reliably than any of your competitors. That is what builds your image in the minds of your listeners.

- *When selecting topics, ask: Will people expect us to cover this?* If your listeners know that you can be counted on for great coverage of sports, health, or politics, then they tune to you for those things.

- *People care about things that are close to them physically, emotionally, spiritually or intellectually.* They care about the security of their jobs, the education of their kids, the health of their parents, the cost of their homes, their favorite celebrities, etc. They care about the consequences of the decisions their leaders make. They want the answer to the question "What does this mean to me?"

- *Use radio's immediacy.* Radio can still get more places faster than TV. Do as much live as you can. If there is a current event where you can get a direct call through to the people involved, radio has the advantage while TV is still trying to push their camera in someone's front door. Pick that topic. Everyone has a telephone in the house, but hardly anyone has a satellite hookup in the living room.

- *Use the news.* Scan the wires, newspapers, magazines, newsletters, online services, and the Internet for stories that sadden, outrage, inform, enlighten, amuse, or frustrate.

- *Have a friend who has a friend.* Always get a phone number. Keep your database updated. Hang on to phone numbers of all sources. Take advantage of all the sources that offer free directories: the government, universities, TV and radio stations, public relations firms, etc. Keep "hot lists" of relevant phone numbers. Today's guests may be tomorrow's sources. Ask them to call you when things are happening.

- *Get a life.* There really is more to life than news, weather, and sports. Explore a broad spectrum of interests. Become a dabbler who knows a little about a lot of things. Be as worldly as your guests and listeners!

- *People want more than just the facts.* They want to understand why something is happening.

"ITS COME TO OUR ATTENTION THAT YOU HAVE A LIFE OUTSIDE THE OFFICE."

Prep for the Dull Day

Radio is easy when there is a lot going on and plenty to talk about. The real challenge of creating powerful radio is making it work on those days when nothing is happening. Sometimes it's hard to find things to talk about that are meaningful, entertaining, relevant, and significant.

The last thing you should do on a dull Monday is to start scouring last Thursday's paper for material. The urge to do this is often overwhelming. Resist! Use your own life experience instead.

Look Inward

Try using stories you have heard from family members or friends. One host got on the air and told about his grandparents, both in their eighties and somewhat forgetful. They resolved to keep lists of things to do. One day, Grandma asked Grandpa to pick up some ice cream at the store:

> "Do you need to write it down?" she inquired.
> "No. Just the ice cream?" he asked.
> "Yes," she replied.
> "I'll remember," he said.
> Grandpa came back with a dozen eggs, orange juice, a loaf of bread, and waffle mix.
> "I told you to write it down," said his wife. "You forgot the bacon!"

This sort of thing goes on in every family, and the more personal the story, often the more universal it turns out to be.

When I was running a news department, one of our reporters went through a bad night, waiting for her boyfriend to come home. She was a mess at work the next morning. I suggested she make a story out of her jealousy and put it on the air. She came up with an award-winning series called *Can a Man Be Satisfied with Just One Woman?* The more personal you get, the deeper you go, and the more likely you are to strike a universal chord.

Big Ears and Eyes

Sometimes you may overhear usable material. A writer who was supposed to meet her husband at an appointed time showed up hours late. He was rather upset when she finally arrived, but she offered this explanation: "I'm so sorry, but I was riding the bus and when my stop came, the people sitting in front of me were right in the middle of a story, and I just had to hear how it ended. I couldn't get off the bus!"

Sparked by this story, she wrote a book that was then turned into a movie. She became fabulously famous and wealthy, all because she overheard a conversation on a bus that she could use as material.

If a story interests you, find a way to make it interesting on the air. Real-life stories are all around us. Train your ears and eyes to catch them.

Bring an Idea to Work

After you have used up everything in your own life, create powerful brainstorming sessions. Contrary to rumor, genius is sometimes a collective thing. Ideas can be built upon, and they can come from anywhere. A "bad" idea can quickly become a good one if a couple of heads get together on it. Some of the best ideas come from the least likely sources.

Imagine that the "price of admission" for every employee at your station each day is to bring in one idea. They wouldn't necessarily have to be good ideas, just something someone noticed, thought about, or even experienced in the past twenty-four hours. All the ideas would be written down and go into a fishbowl.

Get the creative group together, then look at the ideas. Not all of the ideas would be good ones. Some might be truly awful. But if one or two were usable, you would be ahead. This works for programming, sales, promotion, research—just about everything you do, on the air and off.

One example from San Francisco: Our news department had just completed a ten-part documentary program on the slump in the computer business in the Silicon Valley. My entire brilliant, creative staff sat around racking their brains over a name for it. Overhearing us, our front desk receptionist looked up and asked, "How about, 'When the chips are down?' "

There was silence, then applause. That informal brainstorm session led to a catchy title for our series. You never know...and that's part of the fun.

More ideas on brainstorming come from broadcast consultant Michael Haas, who programmed Munich, Germany's Antenne Bayern. He taught his staff that an effective "bit" on the radio includes:

- Statement (headline)

- Elaboration (details)

- Kicker (climax and punch-line).

The seeds of an idea can be for any of those three.

Michael Haas's Brainstorming Rules

- During the brainstorm, there must be no judgment of ideas. No evaluation or criticism is allowed.

- Freewheeling is allowed and encouraged. The wilder and more outrageous the idea, the better.

- Look for quantity rather than quality. Try to end up with a long list of ideas. In brainstorming, quantity produces quality.

- Combine ideas. Make each idea better. In this case, only positive building is allowed.

- Every idea must be written down. If you choose not to write something down, you will have judged it, which violates the first rule.

- Every person taking part in the brainstorm is equal in rank. There are no bosses, no leaders, no hierarchy.

In order to come prepared to the brainstorming table, Haas reminds broadcasters to get a life. Listen to people and other stations. Read newspapers, books, and magazines. Watch TV. Notice billboards, commercials, and labels to get ideas. Use your life's experience, both private and professional, for material. Make friends outside the media world. Maintain your health with physical fitness and watch for stress. Bring some fantasy and idealism to the session. Have a positive attitude. Use empathy and people skills. Watch for trends. Keep in contact with listeners—drink at their bars, shop where they shop, etc.

"Hey, we're sheep. <u>Everything</u> seems like a good idea."

Ideas

Do not underestimate the value of living in the world as a source of show prep. Consultant Jaye Albright embraces this idea as well:

> Communication is more about listening and observing your target listener than it is about talking. Live a life. Build off-air relationships. Learn to expose your true feelings. Be vulnerable. Explore your own beliefs. Listen to others talk about their values and beliefs. Open a window to the inner workings of varying points of view. Experiment with safely expressing these differing points of view and then listen to what happens.

Scott Shannon on show prep

One man who never seems to run out of show-prep ideas is New York City's WPLJ (95.5 FM) PD, True Oldies Channel host and morning personality

Scott Shannon. You feel you know him when you listen to his work. Shannon explains his philosophy:

> There is no cookie cutter formula. You have to hit the listeners over the head with what you are doing. . . make your station sound different. I've always been able to figure out what people like, what's going to catch on and be popular...stay ahead of the curve. You could call me a "super-active consumer."

Scott Shannon's List for Creating Powerful Radio

- Carry a recording device (and camera) at all times.

- Carry spare batteries (or charger) for the recording device at all times.

- Read everything.

- Watch everything.

- Learn your computer and *all* your equipment.

- Answer your own telephones and talk to listeners.

- Hang out with normal people.

- Seize the moment.

- Create talk.

- Always remember these three words: PREPARATION, CONCENTRATION, and MODERATION.

CHAPTER 12

Beyond Powerful Radio
Producers — Facing the Blank Page

"The artist makes life more interesting or beautiful,
more understandable or mysterious or in the
best sense, more wonderful."
—*George Bellows*

The Powerful Producer's Challenge

Producing is a tough gig. When the show goes well, the host gets the credit; when it fares poorly, often it is the producer who is blamed. Good producer jobs are difficult to get. Most demand long, stressful hours for little reward and low pay. Although many music DJs and presenters produce their own shows, in talk radio, particularly in major markets, a producer can add significantly to the success of the program.

Finding the Right Producer

I frequently get calls from station managers and talent looking for the "right" producer. I also get calls from producers who are looking to move on for a variety of reasons, but mostly because they hate their hosts. They want the equivalent of a "radio divorce" but don't necessarily want to leave their "child," meaning the show itself.

As with any good relationship, the producer and the host must listen to each other. Both should share the same goals for the show. Hosts and producers spend a lot of time together. One of my favorite hosts in talk radio once said, "It was easier to find my wife than the right producer." So how do you find the "right" producer?

When you are on the air, it's almost like being naked in public. You are exposed and vulnerable. It is just you, the phones, and that big microphone. You need a producer who is on your side, supportive when you feel alone on the air, a presence beyond the glass wall. A producer is someone who believes in your show and wants to make you and the product sound great.

That is not necessarily the same thing as agreeing with the host's point of view. Some great producers give their all for hosts who are not of their own political stripe. Professionals can work with just about anyone. Of course the producer does not have to like a host or presenter to produce a successful program, but there must be respect. If the host knows that he or she has the support of a sharp and talented producer, the show works better.

Grow Your Own

Great producers are not born, they are developed. Optimally a good producer is a "fit" with the show and host. If you're hiring a producer, look for potential and promise. Ask: "Is this person bright? Good at handling pressure? Fearless? Can this producer pick up the phone and get the White House as easily as the local dogcatcher? Can he or she get along with the news department? Have ideas? Can this person say no? Does he or she like listening to talk radio and like listening to you?"

Do not hire someone who wants to be on air. It usually does not work out. The job of producing is more "directing" than acting. Though many hosts and personalities produce their own shows, successful producers who excel at this work enjoy the behind-the-scenes aspect of making things happen. Hosts should not have to worry that their producers are coveting their jobs and secretly working toward that goal, instead of putting energy and skill into producing a great show.

Sometimes you get lucky and the right producer finds you. Often the best producers are listeners first, people who enjoy the show. (These are people who enjoy listening to the program *without* being paid to do so.) One such listener and fan was Nuala McGovern, who became the senior producer for WNYC's Brian Lehrer program. In the beginning, she was a listener, who volunteered as an intern, learned the job, then was hired to produce one of the most popular public radio shows in New York City. McGovern served successfully in her capacity as executive producer at WNYC for many years.

Keep the Good Ones

Many American radio stations are sloppy about hiring and hanging on to good producers. They tend to promote secretaries, and hire minimum wage students or relatives. Good producers are often forced to go to TV or leave the industry if they want to be paid what they are worth. There is very little producer training or job security available. It is a trial by fire.

If you find a good producer, do whatever it takes to keep him or her. A good producer can contribute tremendously toward making your show powerful radio. A bad or angry one can damage you. Try not to upset them for no reason, and try to find it in your budget to pay them for the valuable work they do. When the right combination of host and producer comes together, it's a wonderful event. On that lucky day and forever after, the most important thing to remember about the host/producer relationship is this: Be patient. Be willing to work it out, not walk out.

Make your producer feel valued. Today's producers are tomorrow's program directors. When I am searching for program directors, I always take a serious look at who is behind the scenes screening and producing the best shows.

Share the Wealth

If you are a host, treat producers nicely. You get the glory, they're underpaid. You get the credit, they get yelled at. Share the perks, the books, the free tickets, and free meals. Take them to lunch or dinner. Give them honest feedback. If you blow up at them, apologize, and don't wait too long to do it. And if you get a ratings bonus, share some of that as well.

Thank Them Publicly

Lots of hosts take a few minutes at the end of every show to thank the producer, screener, writers, and the board operators by name. You should do this at the same time you thank your guests and listeners. Your producing team will feel appreciated, and that is worth it.

Don't Hire a Blind Date

Get to know your producer. Try him or her out before you make the final hire. Interns sometimes work out very well as producers after they get to know the ropes. Insist on having input into the hiring process. Again, get one who actually likes to listen to your show. Be open to working with someone who is not like you. Life-stage differences can be valuable. Let's say for example that you are an older male and your producer is a young female student. Now you have a couple of perspectives that can only help the show.

Hire Someone With Good Judgement

You should respect your producer but still be able to have an argument with him or her. Expecting not to have huge disagreements with your producer is unrealistic—as if expecting never to fight with your spouse. The producer–host relationship is intense. The disputes are never really fair because most of the time the host wins. Conflict can be healthy. A host should be able to freely express him- or herself with the producer. The producer should be able to do the same if the relationship is a fairly honest one. A "kiss up" trying to please you or agreeing with you all the time does not really help your show.

This is Show Biz

Choose a producer who knows you are doing a radio show and knows that the show must be fun and entertaining, rather than a forum for long-winded guests. Again, your job is to keep the audience engaged. Your producer should never promise a guest more than a few minutes on the air. If guests are boring, have the producer dump them. Thank them and get rid of them. Great guests can always stay longer or finish out an hour. Make sure your host has enough material to talk about, whether or not you have guests or calls coming in.

Get a Flexible, Not a Rigid, Person

Make sure your producers understand that a great talk show does not always stick to one topic or move from point "A" to point "B." Sometimes, it meanders like a river. A spontaneous incident on the air or a wacky call can take the show in a whole new, and better, direction. But if you have hired someone who can only move on a set schedule, you could miss a great radio moment like this one:

> Three politicians were on air discussing economic reform. A listener called in with a question. In the background dogs were barking so loudly, they could not be ignored. The host asked what size dog made such a racket. It turned out to be a Rottweiler, and there were several, because the caller was in the Rottweiler-breeding business. After some discussion of pets, another listener, this one a psychologist, rang through. He wanted to know what type of pets the politicians had. This psychologist had a theory about power and pet ownership. He reasoned that "cat people" need less control, because cats "do what they want." On the other hand, he felt control freaks would have dogs because dogs respond to commands. So what kind of pets did these politicians have? They all had dogs.

It's a good thing the screener-producer put through that psychologist, even though he was slightly off the point. It generated a magic moment.

Is There a Formula?

Although there is no crystal ball to see whether a host and a producer will take to one another, there are some personality traits that make for better matches.

Take a look at Chapter 2, *Are You a Generator or a Reactor,* in this book. Again, try to find the right "fit" with each host and producer. A reactive host will work best with a generative producer. To do his or her best work, a generative host needs a reactive producer. A generative producer, even one that is not on the air, must still come up with original ideas and be responsible for feeding the host talkable topics that can be worked into a theme for the show. There isn't a formula for choosing show topics either, but experience has taught me a few things that definitely do and do not work.

Avoid the "Manufactured Hour"

The closer the show sounds to real life, with genuine people having real conversations, the better it works. Try to avoid "easy" stories from headlines or from press releases—anything that sounds like: *"And now another topic manufactured to fill another segment of radio…"* If you wouldn't be talking about this *off* air, ask: WHY are you putting it on the show? Audiences prefer programs that sound as though the conversation could just as easily be taking place off the air.

Throw Out Stale Bread

Creating powerful radio—whether over the air or online—means never being boring. If a subject or topic has been extensively covered and there is nothing new you can add to it, ask yourself whether this is really "powerful radio."

Resist the temptation to book celebrity guests or experts just because they are available to you. Never book a guest without a reason. Ask: "Why should the listener care?" Your job is to get and keep audiences. The guest's is to publicize or try to get the people in your listening audience to buy their latest movie, book, project, and so on.

Don't book a guest just because you think he or she will generate phone calls. Sometimes a great show has few or no calls, and a bad show can have a full board of calls. Psychics on the air will net a full board of calls. Mostly it's boring. The only person interested in hearing the program is the person talking to the psychic. Why would the rest of the audience care? Meanwhile, the scientist with information on how to avoid Armageddon may not get any calls, because the audience is simply listening. They are taking in the information. Book guests and pick topics as though you had no phone in your studio.

Know Your Source

It is fine to use the Internet, prep services, current events, and news stories for content, but producers should also bring their own original ideas for the program. Producers should read widely, listen to the competition, and generate ideas based on life.

A cautionary word about the Internet. It's easy to Google guests and come up with names and sources, but be warned: The Net is not necessarily a reliable source of accurate information. The beauty of the Internet is that everyone has equal access. A lunatic in his garage can put up a website or create a blog that looks as convincing as a major university's. Some sites, such as those belonging to major newspapers, are more trustworthy than others. Sites with rumor, gossip, innuendo, and urban myth can still be useful, providing you acknowledge the provenance of the information and flag it accurately.

Do not undermine your credibility by presenting uncorroborated information as fact. There is room on radio and television for an entire range of sources and subject matter, from front page news to obscure phenomena, but be clear about what kind of a show you are doing.

In the Creating Powerful Radio workshops, producers are asked to bring in three items to work into talkable topics for show prep. The following simple techniques should bring several topics to the host that no one else will be able to cover in the same way:

1. **Your Life:** Bring in an idea from your own life, something that has happened to you.

2. **Overheard/Observed:** Something you've witnessed or heard about or directly overheard.

3. **News you'd talk about off air:** One item from the news that you would actually talk about with another person in real life, that is, if you did not have a radio show to produce.

In each case, find the "universal angle." A universal angle is a common thread or dynamic that affects everyone. Often the details of a story are interesting only to the participants and are no one else's business. While the personal is universal, the private can be boring.

Eavesdrop—Be a Snoop

Here's an idea where being a snoop paid off. On her way to work, Sara stopped for a take-out cup of coffee. Standing in line, she overheard a woman ahead of her in line on her cell phone, apparently breaking up with a boyfriend:

> WOMAN: No. John, it's really over. No, please don't do this. . .A weekend at the lake house is not going to change my mind. We are through.

John, this is the right thing to do. I am releasing you so that you can get on with your life and find the person who will be right for you.

The other customers were staring at their shoes, appalled and embarrassed. But it gave Sara, the producer, an idea for a question to engage an audience. She relayed the idea to her host and the show opened this way:

What possesses you to think you are alone in your living room when you are talking on your mobile phone? Have you ever overheard one of those excruciating conversations? You know, the kind where you would like the earth to just open up and swallow you because it is so embarrassing to hear? What is the most awful conversation you've ever overheard in public when someone has been on their cell phone?

The first caller to the program was a man who had had an experience that morning. On his way to work he, along with everyone else on the bus, overheard a fellow passenger *being fired*. The guy answered his cell phone and said:

MAN: What do you mean report to human resources? But what about the promotion? Jim got the job? But what about my PowerPoint presentation and the report? I have it ready to go here in my briefcase. Jim gave the report? Jim is in my office? I need to see Elaine in human resources?

It was a silent bus. Nobody could look at anyone else.

And that is how one producer's morning coffee stop led to a "universal angle" that created powerful radio—real people sharing real stories.

Use Your Life

Another producer helped his host get to the "universal angle" of a topic that came from the host's private life. "Bob," the host, had promised his wife he would paint their garage. But because Bob preferred to watch football on Sundays, they got into a huge fight. Bob and his producer decided that the paint, the garage, and the argument were Bob's private life...but there was a "universal angle."

Bob's question:

"Why do women nag? Why is it a woman will ask you over and over again to do something when you've told her ten times you'd get to it... it's on your list, you intend to do it?"

A female caller responded:

WOMAN: Well, if you guys would just DO the things we asked you to do, we wouldn't have to turn into these nagging shrews!

Meanwhile, the producer found a psychologist who had just published a study on male–female relationships. It seemed most men didn't care whether a woman gained weight or was a lousy cook—what they hated was nagging. Why? Because their mothers nagged them. The topic went for two hours, with lots of humor. It took a talented producer to help find the "universal angle" and focus it for air.

Formatics Count

It is important to have a producer who understands the logic behind formatics. Lots of producers know the basics but are never told *why* they matter so much. Why is it crucial to mention the station's name or call letters before each caller goes to air, and to reset the topic every few minutes—before and after commercial breaks?

With new electronic instant measurement techniques, this may not be as important in the future, but as long as we are working with ratings that are based on recall, what your listener remembers and reports to the ratings or research service will matter. Memory is not reliable. If people don't remember what they ate for breakfast, how can they remember what they were listening to at 7:17 in the morning last Thursday? How can they be expected to report accurately what they have heard to a monitoring service or market research interviewer? Of course they cannot.

Because of that, some radio listening, referred to as "phantom cume," is never counted in the ratings. Your staff needs to understand the importance of helping the listeners retain and write down your call letters by repeating them on air as often as possible.

Geller Media International's
Producer's Ten Commandments

1. Know your host/presenter, and his or her audience as well.

2. Do not covet your host's air shift, but be a faithful listener to it.

3. NEVER put a boring caller or guest on the air.

4. Have only ONE director or programming manager giving input.

5. Pay close attention to details so your host/presenter will not have to, and remember your address list or database and keep it up to date.

6. Be organized, able to easily and quickly locate a contact, and find the things your host/presenter puts down and loses. Never throw away a phone number, e-mail address, or a good take-out menu.

7. Know the Internet world *and* the real world. Read about and live in both of them.

8. Have a life outside the radio station. It will serve you as show prep, twenty-four hours a day, every day, providing you with creative topics and angles nobody else is doing.

9. Study the station, and learn to do everything. The payoff will go to the producer who can run the board, edit and assemble audio, set up a remote, screen calls, make coffee, and plan events or travel.

10. Foster good relations between your host/show and the rest of the radio station, especially the news and sales departments.

CHAPTER 13

Beyond Powerful Radio
Radio Talk Shows

"A picture is nothing but a bridge between the soul
of the artist and that of the spectator."
—*Eugene Delacroix*

"Talk radio—Because all great minds don't think alike."
—*T-shirt slogan*

Talk radio in America evolved from full-service personality music radio. Here is how it happened: At first, a few music hosts began taking calls on air between records, particularly on AM stations with strong personalities. Soon, there were fewer records and more listener phone calls. When it drew the listeners and advertisers, a few stations allowed the talk to stay, either in selected dayparts or, in rare cases, around the clock.

Talk Radio, When Talk Radio Wasn't Cool

When I entered the talk radio arena years ago, it was a format perceived by many as expensive, boring, and of no interest to younger demographics. Conventional wisdom held that talk radio was something your grandmother would listen to, and only dealt with events in her hometown.

159

Those of us doing talk knew this wasn't true. Our listeners were savvy, upscale, and worldly. Many were exceptionally well-read and well-informed. Generally, talk stations offering interesting programming produced healthy ratings, high revenues, and strong response for advertisers.

Even so, traditional talk radio stereotypes persisted until the early 1990s. That's when satellite program distribution and station economics helped to propel a talk radio revolution.

The "Rush" to AM Radio: The 1990s News-Talk Explosion

One important catalyst was personality Rush Limbaugh, whose unique combination of politics and wit brought unprecedented success to the format. Rush proved that a lot of the stereotypes about talk radio were wrong. The seismic impact of Limbaugh's nationally syndicated talk show, which drew large daytime shares on hundreds of stations, many of which had been steadily losing listeners up to that point, collapsed the notion that talk had to be local. Content matters, addresses don't.

Previous talk offerings such as the radio incarnation of the *Larry King Live* show had applied this principle and succeeded by syndicating on large numbers of stations in nighttime hours. Limbaugh amplified it and shattered the network talk taboo in the lucrative daytime hours.

The critics of talk radio were wrong and the numbers proved it. Limbaugh's talk listeners were young, hip, and savvy. And, as station managers quickly noticed, there were lots of them.

When Limbaugh's syndicated show debuted in the late eighties, it was carried on fewer than 100 stations; by the mid-nineties, it was on more than 650 stations. Program suppliers rushed to meet the demand, offering station operators easy access to satellite-delivered talk programming at all hours.

The news-talk format exploded. Once-dominant AM music stations, whose audiences had deserted them for FM, suddenly began doing talk. In the United States, markets that had one talk outlet suddenly found themselves with as many as five. News-talk is now the second most popular format in the United States. Hundreds of stations have switched to the News-talk format.

Talk saved many moribund stations from oblivion; but prospering in an ocean of talk competition means providing a better product than those of one's competitors. Fortunately, like all good radio, talk radio doesn't have to be more expensive to be more powerful.

Curious People

Talk radio listeners are curious people. They want to know nearly everything: what is going on in their town, their country, their world. They tend to listen when they are by themselves, so the more personable the host is, the better it works.

Talk radio is intimate while being anonymous. It allows listeners and callers to interact without exposing themselves to the dangers that might arise in a real-life confrontation. It's a strange sort of freedom and can result in a deeply honest conversation. Maintain control, and remember: You own the show. When a personal truth is well articulated, it touches the caller, host, and listener. It has universal and mass appeal.

Who Will "Make It"?

It's difficult to predict who "has it" as a host and who does not. Talent does shine through, but talent must be combined with a skill for communicating, watching, and listening.

Some of the best, most talented, and original "talkers" are lousy communicators because they don't listen. For example, stand-up comedians are often hired on the assumption that because they are smart, funny, and observers of life, they will be naturals on the job, but unless they are also good listeners they will fail miserably.

On the other hand, some of the most brilliant minds and greatest listeners are boring in a talk radio setting because they can't have a comfortable conversation in front of a microphone. The only way to know whether someone will make a good talk show host is to see how host and the audience respond to one another on the air.

Jack Swanson manages KGO-AM in San Francisco, one of the most successful talk stations in America, gives this sage and important warning, "Never be fooled into thinking that what you like is what your audience likes." An example is KGO's overnight personality. He gets huge ratings, but many sane and reasonable people find him hard to take for an extended period. However, he pulls in 25 shares, and you can't argue with that.

As a program director, you need to determine what you want from your talk show and what your listeners expect.

Listeners expect a talk show to present a point of view. Audiences also expect a talk show to expose them to new ideas so that they can learn new things. Famed CBS journalist Edward R. Murrow said of TV, but it is true for radio as well, "This instrument can teach, it can illuminate and it can inspire." A listener once commented in an Arbitron diary, "I didn't go to a college or university—talk radio is my college education."

NPR's Susan Stamberg writes in her book *Talk*:

Talk radio is a "rear view mirror" [of our time]. The talk comes from rage, frustration, pain, pride, exhilaration. It's public talk absorbed in private. That private experience called radio. It's also talk between strangers, although it can sometimes sound like friends. The "unearned intimacy" [photographer Richard Avedon's phrase] of a call or interview on a radio show can make deep connections, two people who have never met—trying together in a brief period of time for clarity, understanding.

Listeners expect talk radio to both validate and challenge their beliefs. Most of all, they want it to be interesting and fun. They want this entire process to be entertaining and a little bigger than life. When these expectations have been met, you have created powerful talk radio!

The Formula

Broadcast consultant and program director John Mainelli says: "Entertain informatively and inform entertainingly."

The following sections describe how to select and handle topics on the air. This will make your approach both personal and powerful.

Set Powerful Bait

The talk show monologue, or "churn," sets the scene for the show. The monologue, like the first page of a great book, should capture the audience with an original approach to your subject. There is no such thing as a boring topic, just boring hosts, and dull, unimaginative approaches to the stories.

Much like a fisherman baiting his hook and then casting the line, the host must first tempt the listener to engage and then think about the information, so that he or she wants to hear more. The churn must entice listeners.

It's up to you as the host to make *everything* you use work. Peel back each subject like an onion and find the most interesting ways to present your ideas. If the topic is truly interesting, it will also be genuinely interesting to you. And if it is interesting to you, you will find a way to make it interesting to the audience. Only use material you care about. If you can't make yourself care about it, don't use it.

Don't waste a minute of the listener's time on a list of boring stuff you feel you must discuss. The talk radio police will not be waiting outside to take you away should you forfeit discussing some big story of the day.

For instance, if your show starts at 10:00 p.m. and the TV news and the morning and afternoon papers have covered a story, it's all over the Internet and CNN's been hammering it for twenty-four hours, and it's been on your station all day, do you really want to keep talking about it? Do you have a unique view of what has been happening? Anything else to add or to say?

Think of how your audience must feel. Think twice about using something of which you are already sick and tired. Don't be an "actor." Real always works. Keep it fresh for you. Tell the truth. Focus. Use effective storytelling techniques and your show will never be boring.

As in Life, On the Air: Picking Topics That Work

Ever hear that old expression, "God gave you two ears but just the one mouth"? The most effective and powerful talk show hosts talk less and listen more to the world around them. Start each and every day with this question: "What are people doing—really doing—and what are they talking about—really talking about?" What people are talking about off air will work as topics on the air.

You can also USE YOUR OWN LIFE as show prep. If you spent an hour waiting in a wrong line for a new driver's license, chances are other people have too. If you have something to say about it, use it. If your child is having trouble learning a new school curriculum, chances are you're not the only bleary-eyed parent.

In all radio, but especially in talk, the audience feels they know you personally. You and your views are the product here. You have your life to work from. You are the quarter-hour maintenance. Being personal works.

It doesn't take much to see how it works. A popular talk host had a baby. After a brief announcement on the air that she would be taking extra time off because her new baby girl had to undergo a complicated surgical procedure, she was flabbergasted at the response. She heard from thousands of people, received e-mails, cards, letters, and even gifts from her listeners.

Most of the correspondence began, "You don't know me, but I listen to your show every night and consider you a friend." This host could not believe the level of support and, yes, even *love*, that came from total strangers who felt they knew her from listening to her talk show.

In addition to your personal life and experiences, you can, and should, scan the wires, newspapers, magazines, and the Internet for stories that outrage, sadden, amuse, or frustrate you. If it makes you laugh, cry, or bang your fist on the steering wheel, chances are it will have the same effect on your listeners and send them flying to the phones.

"It's always 'Get me a Godzilla type,' never 'Get me Godzilla!'"

Creating the Powerful Opening Monologue or "Churn"

Here is the method I use and teach at Geller Media International's Creating Powerful Radio seminars or when working with individuals:

DO:

- Find your focus. What is the issue or topic? What are you trying to say? Know your subject and know why you are talking about it.

- Engage the listeners. What do you want them to do with it? How do you want them to respond?

- Give an opinion. What is your position on this subject? What do you think about it? Why do you care?

- Tell the truth. Find your truth and what is meaningful to you about this topic or subject.

- Personalize the opinion through your storytelling.

DO NOT:

- Ramble.

- Appear aimless, scattered, or out of control.

- Talk about topics you don't care about (even if you feel you should care).

- Go too long before the punch.

- Be boring!

Scott Borden, a former manager of WNYC in New York, advises the following for talk show hosts and programmers.

Scott Borden's Creating Powerful Talk Radio Tips

- Radio is totally personal. When I listen, I should feel like it's just me and the person on the other end of the radio.

- People listen to radio in groups of one. Never talk to a bigger group.

- Radio, especially talk radio, is part of the "information age." We have to define our unique information niche and work it like crazy.

- Every listener letter or e-mail represents exactly one listener. Every listener phone call represents exactly one listener.

- Talk show callers do not represent the talk show audience. They are NOT as important as the host, who is the thing that all the listeners have in common. Callers are only good if they help the host.

- The late American radio legend Rick Sklar pointed out that the problem with modern research is it asks people to tell you what they think and do. When asked, people often lie about these things. Actions speak louder than words.

- Good radio is like obscenity—you can't define it, but you know it when you hear it. Sometimes you have to trust your gut instincts.

- People treasure memories. And the things we remember are the things that go really right or really wrong. Make the most of these moments.

- It's radio, not brain surgery. Failure does not equal a dead body on the table. It has to be fun for us too!

- You have to have a great plan for every moment on the air. And you have to be prepared to scrap this plan entirely the first chance you get.

CHAPTER 14

Beyond Powerful Radio
Call Screening

> "Talent hits a target no one else can hit;
> genius hits a target no one else can see."
> —*Arthur Schopenhauer*

The Art of Call Screening for Producers

If you take calls on your show, you already know that a great caller can make a show; a boring or bad call can be a show killer. You can almost feel the listeners tuning out. Like many tasks in life, screening appears to be easy. Answer the phone and put the call on the air? Not exactly. Screening involves being able to manage people. This job takes both art and skill.

When you turn over your broadcast to a caller, that caller becomes partly responsible for maintaining your audience. Dennis Clark produces the nationally syndicated *Ryan Seacrest* show. He says, "Think of the phone as a second or third microphone. It doesn't matter that it is located elsewhere, treat it as another guest mic."

Most producers have had the experience of putting what seemed to be a great call on the air and then watching it bomb. Sometimes a caller who seems like a long shot, slow-paced, slightly out of your demographic target, a little weird, will surprise you with his humor, passion, and a good story to tell.

How do you screen out bad or boring callers while attracting great ones? Are there methods to coach average or mediocre callers to become better and more powerful on air?

Contrary to popular belief, getting to speak on a talk show is not a given right in a free and democratic society. In order to qualify, you must have something to say. No matter what callers think or tell you, making it to air is not "their right." It is a privilege. Not everyone who demands to be on air is going to get on air, nor should they. Use your callers to the show's advantage, not the other way around. Do not put on a bad caller.

Hosts may panic when they see they have very few or no callers waiting to go on the air, but it is the producer's job to remind the host that less than one percent of the listening audience will ever call a talk show.

Sometimes a great show has very few or no calls. A bad show can have a full phone board for hours at a time. The number of blinking lights is a false indicator of how well a show is going. Unfortunately, hosts like to see a lot of calls or they get nervous. One solution is to cover the call lights so they cannot see who is waiting.

The job of the host is to focus the issue in such an engaging manner that interesting people with strong opinions and something to say actually want to call the show. But having no calls is not an indication that the station or show has no listeners. Sometimes a host can be so compelling, calls are not even needed.

Screening is a way to give power to a show by filtering out the elements that can hold it back and make it boring. It works best if the host does not make a big deal out of the screening process. Don't read off the computer screen.

Avoid ruining the fun for the listeners and for the host by telling them in advance what they will hear. Just give them a hint. There is no journey if the host gives the story away: "Mary on line three, my screen says you have a dog that found a million dollars in a garbage can?" That eliminates the surprise.

Keep a bit of the magic of radio. Work with and encourage hosts not to reveal what is happening behind the scenes. Try it this way: "Mary, tell us about your amazing dog." Or simply, "Mary, you are on WABC."

What Makes for a Good Caller?

You always know one when you hear the caller. A successful talk show may reject as many as fifty percent of the calls that come in. A good caller is relevant, interesting, funny, or poignant. This is a person who adds to the show and makes it better. Remember, normal people don't call talk shows. Sometimes so-called "normal people" aren't all that interesting. Often it's the weird ones, with the strange experiences and vision and stories to tell, who create those "magic moments" on air. A few tips:

- If you are bored *screening* the caller, how interesting will your audience find him or her?

- If you are discussing a human experience, it often works better to put on callers who have lived through that experience and have a story to tell rather than an academic or expert who is removed from the experience.

- Avoid multipart questions or a long, rambling preamble.

- Before you decide to put a caller on air, make sure the point he or she wishes to get across is concise, clear, and focused.

- If you are targeting a young audience, then it makes sense to avoid "older"-sounding callers. However, those who are under eighteen must be extremely articulate to be "good."

Dennis Clark advises, "No listener should ever feel scared to call because he or she might be humiliated or embarrassed. It's good customer service to thank each caller, but do this OFF the air."

[If you host live radio from a remote studio, and do not control your calls, choose a code word to let your engineer know you have finished with a caller. A quick "Thanks for calling WXXX" can do the job. Just make sure it's a signal to your engineer, not a long departure.]

For callers on air, Clark suggests the following system:

1. **Name and Place.** First, identify the caller and find out where they're calling from.

   Think locally whenever possible—suburb, city, state, etc.

2. **The Point.** Because most callers are not trained broadcasters, they may be repetitive (boring), or dilute their initial points. It's best to

go with the first point they'd like to make. Second and third points are usually weaker and may dilute the caller's initial point.

3. **The Close.** Closing the call is something of an audio "hug," not a "thank you for calling," but it should end in a positive or warm "close out." You can fade out the call, and then acknowledge the caller. The purpose is to let other callers know that this is a safe place to call, and that they can join our circle with confidence.

Jeremy Millar, of the Australian Broadcasting Corporation, advises to pre-record calls for music radio, rather than taking them live. "Pre-recording calls is a good way to make sure you're getting the best a caller has to offer. Let the interview go as long as you like, then listen back to it. Pick out a single point of gold. Then edit out everything that is not necessary to the call or the story."

Many stations want to air callers who sound most like the demographic group their station is targeting, but vital, passionate, interesting callers who have good questions, a sense of humor, are great storytellers, or have had personal experience of what you are talking about will always work, no matter their age.

The Short Hello

Train your callers. Avoid "greeting cards" such as "Thank you for taking my call" or "We love your show." Avoid "How are you today?" The host is fine. The caller is fine. Everyone is fine. Congratulations or greetings are of no interest to the listener. Get to topic. Don't be afraid to say, "Get to the point." We are very happy you love the show. The long hello is boring. This is a radio show, not a phone conversation, even though it may feel that way to you because you are holding a phone.

Give the callers your rules. "No reading of prepared statements or articles. You'll need to ask your question or make your comment without a long preamble. No multipart questions."

The Host Will Hang Up on You

To avoid callers calling back after they've been on the air and complaining that the host rudely hung up on them, alert callers prior to going on air that when the host is done, he or she will abruptly disconnect the line, and thank them before they go to air. While this may seem impolite, this is how it works.

The Pep Up

Before a caller is about to go on air, check back to be sure he or she is still waiting on the line and ready to go. You may need to remind the caller about the original point if they have been on hold for a while. Remind them again to turn their radios off.

Listen to the Show

Stay in communication with the host throughout the course of the program. Although you may be busy screening, do try to listen to the show and follow the thread of the program.

There Are Many Nice Ways to Say "No"

A screener needs a backbone. That does not mean being rude, but it does mean being firm. Get a screener who can tell people "No." Hire someone who can make a fast decision to get rid of a boring call. Ask: "Would this person keep a listener engaged?" If you think the caller or guest would be boring to a listener, do not put him or her on air.

Have a Sample Script for Screening Callers

- Answer the phone with the station's name or the name of the show: "KFIX Bill Johnson Show, what is your comment or question?"

- If the caller does not immediately come across with a concise point or opinion, help them focus. Ask: "What is your opinion?" "Why is this important to you?" "Can you give me a brief summary of your point?"

- If the caller still does not meet your criteria, he or she should be rejected.

- Remind the caller to speak clearly into the phone!

- You need to work quickly in order to have the next call up and ready to go. There should never be a time when the host cannot move on to the next call.

- If the caller meets your criteria, summarize his or her point and opinion on the computer screen for the host. That allows the host to take calls in the order he or she prefers.

- Clear audio is important. If someone is calling on a noisy mobile, not hearing the caller clearly will not help your show. No one likes to say no, particularly if the caller is a sweet lonely old lady who lives by herself with no friends and this call to your show right now is the only adult conversation she's had all week. But you must protect your product. Serve thousands, not one. It's hard to do, but it is your job to take care of the show, not the caller. Politely say, "No, I am sorry, but I am not going to be able to take your call, not today. Perhaps another time. Thank you."

Other Polite Rejections

"We are running out of time this hour," "Thank you, I'll pass your comment along" or "We cannot use your call today, but we appreciate you taking the time to call." Do not give them time to respond—politely disconnect.

Be tough but professional. Should a rejected caller become angry or try to engage you in an argument, do not get upset or rattled. If there is time, hear the caller out, and then hang up. The management has hired you for your ability to judge what will make a winning show. Most reasonable management will support you in your decision to protect your show from boring callers.

Avoid speaker phones or bad cell lines. If the reception is poor, do not put the call on air. Avoid callers with heavy accents who can't be easily understood.

You certainly don't want a producer to anger your audience. But your audience is really the ninety-nine percent of your listeners who will never phone.

A Rule About the "Regulars"

The only real rule about "regular callers" is this: Bad regular callers should not get on. Good regular callers should. In fact, we sometimes hire hosts who have been regular callers.

Your callers are your "active listeners." They are loyal, listen regularly, and are not too shy to call. One sharp producer made up a database of the "characters" or powerful callers to his show. He kept this list on the computer. Every now and then, when the board was slow and the night was long, he'd phone those people and ask them, by chance, if they were listening. If not, they'd tune in right away and usually come up with some good comments to move the show forward.

This producer also had a second use for his list of phone numbers and e-mail addresses. When the host was scheduled to make a public appearance or speech, he would e-mail an announcement to those listeners, who had asked to be included. Many enjoyed attending these events.

Sequencing Calls

- To best determine the order of the calls, keep track of the show topic and be aware of the points of view of the host and each guest.

- Conflict makes for interesting dialogue. If your host enjoys it, and it is appropriate for the program, move calls that do not agree with the host to the front of the line.

- If the show has guests representing several points of view, then alternate the caller's points of view whenever possible. In reality, you may not get an equal division or balance of callers reflecting pros and cons on any issue, but you can try, through the screening process, to eliminate clusters of similar callers and opinions. Push the interesting ones, the ones with passion, to the top.

- The first call on the show should be the best available caller. That first call often sets the tempo for the rest of the hour.

- Come out of each break with the strongest, most energetic and passionate caller you have waiting.

"She's Been Waiting for Forty-Eight Minutes . . ."

So what. The point is to make a powerful broadcast for the listeners. So if the host chooses to go with another topic or go long with a caller or guest, let them wait. Even if they get mad and yell at you, the first priority at all times is to protect the product on air and make sure it's powerful.

"He Sounded Fine When I Pre-interviewed Him . . . "

People get nervous when they actually go on air. Every call screener has had the experience of listening helplessly as a caller, who sounded so great before he or she hit the airwaves, flounders when the host takes the call.

Here's why: We are around live broadcasts all the time and forget that it can be a terrifying experience for someone who doesn't do this every day. Coach callers to take a breath, get right to the point, don't read from notes, be as you would in a normal conversation, forget the others listening, and don't worry about looking foolish.

Usually people lose the nervousness as soon as they get onto a familiar topic or subject about which they feel passionate. That is why we need to work with callers to help "get them there" as soon as possible in the call.

Put Yourself "On Hold"

If as a producer or screener you have not had the experience of calling a radio or television talk show, try calling somebody else's show. See how the process feels when you get screened. When the shoe is on the other foot, you will be amazed. When you understand what it feels like to be on hold, then it's your turn ... and when you are on air with a question for a host or guest, it will add another perspective and allow you to be more effective as a screener.

Messaging and E-mail

Hosts like to use interactive media, but the rule for including e-mails and instant messages is: "Is the content relevant?" During the business day, some people cannot use their phones to call a talk show, so you may be able to get more opinions on the air using e-mail or messaging.

Be aware that reading messages on the air is not as interesting as having the actual person delivering his or her thoughts in his or her own voice. Reading messages should be a second choice if you have a good call waiting.

Activating Text Messages

If you do use text messages from listeners on the air, try reading them with drama. Try introducing the sender actively, for example: "Carol, you're in Spring Hill. You say you've have been watching shoplifters at your neighborhood market ..." Using a "you" to address the sender makes the message sound more like a live conversation with a caller.

Go to Our Web Site for More

Stations that run edited interviews or performances on the air are allowing listeners to access the long form or complete versions from their websites. Your show or station website should also be used to move detailed content, such as a guest author's mailing address, a recipe, contest rules, out of your broadcast and make it available to the audience at their convenience.

As a producer, if your host promises listeners they will find a piece of information on your station's website, it is your job to make sure it gets there. If you don't, you make your host and your station look bad.

Geller Media International's Tips for Talk Show Producers and Screeners

Here are some methods and ideas that have emerged from the Geller Media International Producer's workshops over the years:

- Focus on your audience, not the one percent of the listeners who call in.

- Make sure your host has material to talk about if there are no calls coming in. Plan your show as if there will be no calls.

- Don't let all your lines jam. Screen out weak calls and keep some lines open so better calls can come in.

- If you don't understand a caller, nobody else will either. Get rid of the call!

- Get your callers relaxed and talking, but don't promise them that they will be on the air.

- Build a database of sources that you can use during shows for alternate/opposing opinions, or for emergency guests if the planned guest cancels. Cross-reference by areas of expertise, affiliations, etc.

- Build a database of great callers. On a quiet day, a savvy producer can use the list to find one to go on the air.

- Be sure to give guests specific instructions on how to get to the studio, and phone contact information. What if the station door is locked?

- Guests should fax or e-mail background materials ahead of time for the host to study. Guests should understand who their audience will be.

- Make sure guests know that the host will take care of any promotion for their book, their seminar, and so forth. There's nothing worse than a guest doing an awkward job of self-promotion.

- Develop a good relationship with your news department.

- If something major occurs, don't be afraid to cancel a guest! Radio's greatest asset is immediacy. Go with what's happening now and reschedule.

Caller Criteria

1. Can he or she offer an interesting personal experience pertaining to this topic?

2. Do you or the audience care about this person? Does this person sound like a distinctive "character?" (Hint: If you can "see" this person in your mind's eye, it's a good character!)

3. Is he or she a good storyteller?

4. Does he or she have a sense of humor?

5. Does this caller have strong passionate opinions on the subject?

6. Is this a person you would find fascinating or enjoy talking with off air?

7. Can this caller take the audience on a journey they cannot get to on their own?

8. Does he or she have something interesting, or of value, to say?

9. Can he or she offer new information about a story or subject or add specific knowledge or special expertise?

10. Is he or she entertaining?

"That's not what you told my screener you wanted to talk about."

CHAPTER 15

Beyond Powerful Radio
Interview Techniques — for Journalists, Talk Hosts & Music Personalities

> "Men are born with two ears, but with just a single tongue, in order that they should hear twice as much as they say."
> —*Charles Caleb Colton*

Interviews are a necessary part of the information-gathering process for both news and talk. A powerful interview can rivet the audience to their radios; a boring one can make them disappear.

Remember, your guests—whether rock stars, artists, politicians, experts, specialists in their fields, or "regular people" with stories to tell—may be nervous when they show up at your radio station. You go on the air every day and it seems routine to open the microphone and talk to thousands of people. However, this experience can be terrifying to "civilians," who may be nervous or forget what they want to say. They can become unsure of where they're heading with a point and become boring—talking endlessly, and saying nothing.

The purpose of an interview is to get the interviewee to open up and tell you things of interest. You may even get the person to reveal things he

179

or she does not ordinarily discuss in a public forum. You want your guest to share information, to tell stories.

A good interviewer knows that in order to get the most out of any interview, the person being interviewed must feel comfortable. Ideally, he or she should forget about the microphone. They should feel heard. If you catch your guest looking at their watch, there's a problem because during a good interview, time should fly.

One of the best things you can do to start your interview off well is to introduce your guest in a compelling way that will excite your audience, and make them want to hear what the guest will have to say. Of course, this will benefit you, by keeping your listeners waiting for the interview to begin. But your guest, who may be exhausted from a long book tour, or anxious about doing a good job on your show, may actually feel inspired to be more candid, and a better storyteller, because you've portrayed them or their work as exciting and interesting.

Here's a typical promo or introduction to an interview:

I hope you'll join us for a very interesting show tomorrow... Our guest is Dr. John Johnson talking about a new study from the Health Institute. This new report shows a higher percentage of children are now being diagnosed with autism. Dr. Johnson is an expert who works with autistic children. His latest book is *Understanding Autism*. To learn all about autism and children, join us here on KXXX at 10:00 a.m. tomorrow for our next show.

After a Creating Powerful Radio workshop, the host who had promoted this interview the day before, changed his approach and introduced his guest this way:

Imagine you're on a train in Japan. You don't speak Japanese and you don't know where the train is going. People are talking to you. Handing you things, some are yelling at you. They're asking you questions. They seem angry with you, but you have no idea what they want. You are completely frustrated. If you can relate to that, you now understand what every autistic child feels. Dr. John Johnson, author of *Understanding Autism* is our guest in studio...

It is up to you, as the interviewer, to present your guest so that the audience cares about what he or she will have to say. Grab their attention with powerful storytelling. You want your audience to stick with it, not tune out or start thinking about what they will be having for lunch or wondering if they'd turned on the washing machine.

You're the one who needs to keep things interesting.

Maintain Control

If the interview heads in a dull direction, grab it and steer the discussion elsewhere. For example: "I'm sure there are people listening now who fully understand the details of the photosynthesis process, but in layman's terms, could you explain why it's a bad idea to cut down the rainforests?" Your audience will appreciate it if you can keep your guests away from intricate and technical answers.

Often, you will be faced with an uncooperative interviewee, particularly in news situations. For example, politicians are notorious for not wanting to tell you anything substantive. They have their own agendas and want to use you and your airwaves to promote their ideas. Dealing with this tactic can be tricky.

Here is one method to get them to talk. It comes from Swedish newsman Stig-Arne Nordström. His technique is "getting it a little bit wrong."

Let's say you have a politician who is downplaying the significance of a proposed tax hike. You might say, "So your plan means no tax increases for anyone?" The politician will then feel frustrated and misunderstood. People in his profession can't stand that. He might come back with something like, "No, no, no, my plan would mean a uniform tax increase for almost everyone!" You've accomplished several things here. You got him to talk and explain it in a short form that is easily understood and you've landed the perfect radio interview sound statement. It is short, to the point, and cuts through the smoke and mirrors your interviewee was trying to use to hide his true agenda. Don't worry about the audience thinking that you are an idiot for "misunderstanding" your interviewee. If the interview is pre-recorded, you can cut out the "dumb" question and just air the tight, succinct answer.

CNN's former nightly talk host Larry King is notorious for asking the "dumb question." He claims he doesn't read the books of the authors he's interviewing. He also doesn't admit to much in the way of show preparation. Larry King's key is to ask the questions members of his audience would ask as if they had the chance to sit down and interview the guest, and his audience could comfortably relate to this more casual relaxed interview style.

This is how just one individual interviewer, Larry King works, and while it has been effective for him, it should not be construed as an argument against show prep, in which I strongly believe. Each interviewer and host works differently. But the secret of conducting a great interview is the ability to elicit powerful stories, and glean new knowledge and information in an interesting way, where you also get to know the person. In most cases, the more relaxed and "at home" the subject feels, the better it goes. The closer an interview can *be* to a "real" conversation, the better it works.

Here is another, somewhat controversial, trick for pre-recorded interviews. If a guest is nervous and the answers are too formal, stilted, long, and boring, try this: Wrap up your interview. Leave the recorder running (hopefully your guest won't notice). Then say, "Just to make sure I've got this right, could we go over it one more time?" The guest, now relaxed because the interview is "over," will often tell you, in a very conversational way, what the key points were. You can then "notice" that you left the recorder running and ask permission to use that interview, instead of the first, formal session. I don't believe this is an unethical technique. After all, your guest knew that he or she was talking to you for a broadcast interview, and this audio is often much better. Interview subjects are frequently grateful and will thank you for making them "sound so good."

The Art of the Interview: Powerful Listening

National Public Radio's Susan Stamberg got it right about interviews in her book *Talk*: "Talk always begins with a question. Listening. Listening for what's being said and for what is NOT said, listening for the silences, the cracks between the words, the hesitations, the contradictions, the glorious expositions."

Stamberg, like all good interviewers, understands that, in an interview, the "star" is the topic or the guest, not the host. It helps if you, as the host, can sublimate your ego somewhat and focus completely on what your guest is trying to say. Listening is the key.

The interview will go much better if the topic is something you care about, as opposed to something you think will be of interest to your audience. Remember, "interested is interesting." If you are bored by the topic, odds are your audience will be, too. Listeners can tell the difference between affected and genuine curiosity.

Like a fisherman going for the catch, it is sometimes necessary to use a variety of baits and lures for different types of interviews. Your opening questions will depend on the circumstances. Sometimes it pays to be tough. Other times, kindness, empathy, or humor serves you best. There is no one right approach to getting a great interview. Part of the skill and art of the job is to gauge the method needed to get the interviewee to open up and talk. That "sense of approach" is a skill you develop by listening.

Uh, Uh, Uh ... Nervous Guests?

Some stations actually hand out or e-mail a list of helpful hints for guests to read before going on the air. If you would like to try this, here are some points to include.

Tips for Interviewees

- Please be available and flexible. If the interview time has to be changed, be gracious. The station may call you in an emergency, if another guest has canceled, or if the station is in need of your expertise right now. Be willing to appear. The host and station will appreciate and remember you.

- If you want to make sure you get a copy of the show, have someone record it for you off the air.

- If you're an author, PLEASE don't repeat the name of your new book or your website over and over. Listeners will get annoyed. Your job is to be so fascinating that the listeners stay until the end of the interview because they want to hear the host repeat the title of your book. We will put your information on our station website if you give it to us in advance.

- Forget there is a larger audience. You will be much more effective if you speak to the host one-on-one, instead of addressing all those listeners "out there." The audience listens one at a time.

- Try to relax. Be yourself. Radio is personal and intimate. Listeners like to be spoken to that way.

- Watch your language. This is not a living room and certain expressions could slip out if you aren't careful!

- Keep to the point. If you don't have anything interesting to say, ask the host for another question.

- Turn off your mobile phone.

- Do not bring in a lot of notes to the studio and read from them. Hosts hate this and it can be boring.

- Ask for what you need. Do you have your reading glasses? A pen or pencil? Tissues? A glass of water?

- Do you understand the process? You should feel in control as much as possible. Ask how to use the cough button, just in case.

- Can you stop anytime? Is this being recorded, or is it live, direct, and "anything goes"? (If the interview is live but via remote, either phone, satellite studio or via SKYPE, what is the plan if anything goes wrong?)

- By the way, have you eaten? There's nothing more embarrassing than a microphone picking up the growling of your hungry stomach.

- Don't be rigid. As in normal conversation, the interview may take a turn that has nothing to do with your agenda. Be a good guest. The discussion may lead to even better things than you were originally prepared to talk about. A skilled interviewer does not stick to a script.

- Listen to the questions and answer them. If the host seems unprepared or unfamiliar with your topic, don't express anger or frustration. The audience is probably in the same boat. Just speak to the host as you would to a friendly, but uninformed, stranger you meet at a cocktail party or in the next seat on an airplane. If you can genuinely interest the host in your topic, you will also interest the audience, and will have a very good chance of being asked back.

Thoughts for Hosts and Interviewers

- Forget the long hello. Keep the introduction and greeting short and to the point.

- Listening is the key to successful interviews. Don't stick to a list. Often the best next question will come from the answer to the last one.

- Try not to ask "yes" or "no" questions. Ask the "how" or "why" questions. Ask how people feel, and have them explain things.

- If you didn't get enough of an answer, don't be afraid to ask again. This is especially important in recorded interviews when you are looking for that perfect sound bite.

- Curiosity counts. If you are genuinely curious about the topic, the interview will work.

- Ask "dumb" questions. Do not be embarrassed if you don't know all the answers; the audience probably doesn't either. That's why you are doing the interview.

- Get to the point. Don't clutter up the interview with lots of chit-chat. The audience cares about how what is being said affects their lives.

- Control the interview. Steer the subject in a better direction if the interview starts to get boring. Don't let slick-talking, verbally skilled guests get around you and not answer questions. Ask your questions again and again until you get answers, then move on.

- Focus on solutions, not just problems. Even if your guests have some pie-in-the-sky solutions or can offer nothing more than a phone number to call, that's better than ending an interview on some hopeless, downward note.

- Respect responses. Everyone is entitled to an opinion. If he or she is an idiot, that will come through loud and clear all by itself.

- End your interviews cleanly. Do a short goodbye. You don't need to recap points made during the interview. Trust that listeners got what was discussed and move on.

On Listening

Because listening is such a part of creating powerful radio, it's worth looking at separately. Years ago, at UCLA, a friend gave me a book called *On Listening* by psychologist Carl Faber. When I read the following passage, I was stunned. *On Listening* expressed what I felt in my heart about radio— about connecting and communicating.

On rough days, I still go back and read that book again. It always helps. Creating powerful communication means powerful listening.

Dr. Carl Faber taught courses on relationships, myths, men, and women. His early UCLA lectures were broadcast on Pacifica Radio in Los Angeles. The following is an excerpt from Faber's book.

From Carl Faber, *On Listening*

Most people have never really been listened to. They live in a lonely silence—no one knowing what they feel, how they live or what they have done. They are prisoners of the eyes of others, of the stereotyped, limited, superficial and often distorted ways that others see them.

There are no words to adequately describe what it is to be free with another person. It is most often a sensing that someone will let us be all of what we are at that moment. We can talk about whatever we wish, express in any way whatever feelings are in our hearts. We can take as much time as we need. We can sit, stand, pace, yell, cry, pound the floor, dance or weep for joy. Whatever and however we are at the moment is accepted and respected....

This experience of freedom and communion helps us to feel that someone is for us. And it is this deep sensing of someone, somewhere, being for us that breaks into the silent loneliness of our lives and encourages us in the struggle to be human. It helps us to break the tyranny of the strangers' eyes and to give to our lives all that we are capable of giving. Because listening can bring about such powerful healing, it is one of the most beautiful gifts that people can give and receive.

CHAPTER 16

Beyond Powerful Radio
Public Service Announcements

> "It is better to give than to receive."
> —*Acts 20:35*

It's generally understood that radio stations are licensed to serve the public. It can be radio at its best, or worst. In Europe, as well as in the United States, some radio stations exist entirely to perform public service, but what that means is open to interpretation. Most stations continue to solicit input from the community to determine its needs. These information-gathering efforts are called "ascertainments."

Smart commercial broadcasters know that assessing the true concerns of a community and addressing those issues can enhance a station's image and raise its public profile. Public service works best when the entire station is involved and the campaign is tied in to news, features, sponsorships, announcements, liners, and long-form programming to achieve a specific goal.

Fit Your Public Service to Your Target Audience

Let us say your target audience is adults twenty-five to fifty-four years old and you discover that their principal worry about their community is the school system. Your station might "adopt" a local school. Your promotions department, sales department, and even programming can put together a campaign to bring in volunteers, supplies, money, computers, and so on. Teenage listeners might have different concerns about their community. When you are deciding on content for your public service campaigns, try to find issues that not only are of importance to your listeners, but that also fit your target audience.

"Community service activities can be of tremendous benefit toward developing listener loyalty," says broadcasting executive Chris Berry. Here are some examples: WBBM-AM/Chicago sponsored the "Wreath of Hope" campaign every year to raise money for a variety of local non-profit agencies. The show's hosts broadcast live from shopping centers around the area while volunteers accept donations for the charities. Heavily promoted on air, the appearances help the charities, increase awareness of the station's personalities, and bring the call letters into the listeners' backyards.

At KGO/San Francisco, an entire programming day each year has been devoted to the "Leukemia Cure-a-thon." It raises money for research and victims of the disease. Producers and hosts design shows explaining the illness, the latest research findings, and the need for funding.

KGO's sister station, WLS/Chicago, has been holding its Cure-a-thon in a public place so listeners and organization volunteers can feel that they are a part of the event and meet their favorite personalities. Doctors, researchers, survivors, and families of victims are interviewed. The Cure-a-thon always has some very moving moments as family members describe the struggles of their loved ones. This special public service programming raises hundreds of thousands of dollars and the staff really feels good about participating.

WABC/New York has been among many stations helping listeners fight fraud and wrongdoing by directly connecting them with attorneys or volunteer agencies such as Call for Action. Aggrieved listeners could call a volunteer-staffed consumer line with their complaints. The station then used its firepower by contacting the business, employer, or other parties involved on the listener's behalf. They would usually get results.

Years ago KFWB/Los Angeles made earthquake preparedness its issue. Entire broadcast days were turned over to reports, and interview shows devoted to earthquake safety. The station published a free newsletter outlining everything from safety precautions to earthquake-proofing.

The pamphlets were available free from the station or at sponsors' stores. Several stations in earthquake-prone areas have launched similar campaigns.

Take advantage of your staff's creativity. One way to encourage hosts to support your public service commitment is to have them come up with their own ideas for a promotion. Sam Walton, who founded the Wal-Mart chain of stores, said, "People always support ideas they help create." Most hosts already have a "pet" charity or cause they feel connected to or would like to endorse. If your host feels the organization or issue is important, he or she can really get listeners excited about joining it.

The key to community service is to approach it like all other forms of powerful radio. Powerful public service programming is interesting and relatable, and it matters. Bad public service programming is wasted airtime. Nobody will hear about your good efforts if the presentation on the air is boring.

Include public service events on your daily or weekly calendar. Hold up the mirror that is your station and reflect back the true needs and concerns of your community. Be known as the station that always has something going on to help people. Hubbard Broadcasting Corporation executive and station owner Virgina Morris says she would not even consider hiring a manager who was not involved in the community—that is how strongly she feels about it.

Local or Not?

There is no wrong way to do good work. While local concerns or issues usually work better, stations that raise money for food drops in Africa or medical supplies to Haiti also create good feelings.

Since the Internet makes it possible to see extreme emergencies and disasters around the world, stations can easily get involved in helping people in their town or on another continent.

Whether your station is sending a truck full of supplies to hurricane victims ten states away or rebuilding a home for a burned-out family on the next block, you can use your station's website as well as its airtime to show need, organize help, and chart the difference your support has made. There are no rules here, but by finding a charity or cause about which your staff feels passionate, you'll do both your community and your station some good.

The Powerful Public Service Announcement

Most people hate "PSAs," and with good reason. They've traditionally been used as filler and treated that way. This need not, and should not, be the case. A public service announcement should *NEVER* be boring. Every moment on the radio counts, even those devoted to public service.

Here are two public service announcements on the same subject. They were heard within minutes of each other on different stations in the same market. Which do you think is more powerful?

Station 1

St. John's Hospital needs type O blood. If you are type O, here's the phone number to call ...

Station 2

There's a little girl, six years old, who's been badly hurt in a car crash. Both of her parents were killed. She's lying in a bed right now at St. John's Hospital fighting for her life. She might not make it, because she needs type O blood and the hospital has a shortage. If you're type O and want to help this little girl live, call us here at Z-97, and we'll tell you what to do. Z-97, the station that cares about our town.

If you can bring life to the story, your listeners will care about it, too.

You'll probably want to shy away from "produced" PSAs provided by outside agencies, unless they are great campaigns. For samples of some classics, you might want to listen to some of Dick Orkin's Radio Ranch spots or vintage Stan Freberg. If you can customize a campaign to make it sound like part of your station, you can make it work.

By being selective about the kind of public service announcements you use on your station, and by adding human and dramatic touches, you will turn what has long been perceived as a "tune-out" into an audience- and image-builder for your station. You'll find much more on public service and how to help organizations raise money, in Chapter 32, *Fundraising & Giving*.

PART II

Beyond Powerful Radio
Storytelling & Voice

CHAPTER 17

Beyond Powerful Radio
Becoming a Powerful Storyteller

If you communicate for a living, you work in the "story business." The purpose of storytelling is to entice the listener—to make the audience want to find out what happens next. It's not all that different from childhood fairytales: "*Once upon a time, in a far off land, there was a princess and a monster. Then one day…*"

Human beings love stories. We learn through them from the time we are children, and continue the tradition as adults. Most people find it very hard to resist a good story! If well told, they make us laugh, entertain, teach us about life, and, importantly, remind us of our humanity. Long before the printed word, every culture on Earth passed down its vital information, its ethics and morals, through storytelling, myths, and parables. Best-selling books, movies, television, and live entertainment are all based on great stories, and great storytelling.

Storytelling is one of the key points in the proven Creating Powerful Radio/Creating Powerful Communicator's process: focus, engage, opinion/position, and storytelling. There are those who are naturally powerful storytellers, and the art of powerful storytelling is a talent. Any topic in the hands of a truly talented master storyteller can come alive and captivate an audience. But the craft of storytelling is a skill that can be taught—no matter what your level or talent, *anyone* can become a *better* storyteller.

The pace is accelerating. Because nearly everyone has access to media and technology, it is your well-honed ability to tell stories within the limits of your medium that will allow you to get an audience, and to keep that audience's attention. In an over-communicated world where media is democratized and mobile and everyone can be a broadcaster, producer, publisher, director, actor, and storyteller: in a time when anyone from virtually anywhere can create and send pictures, words, moving images, and audio to anywhere else, and to anyone else—one person or billions, good storytellers will rule.

The audience for all that communication is overwhelmed. They have choices—what to read, view, listen to, comment on, interact with, and pass on to others. Whether it's a 140-character tweet, a thirty-second commercial, a sales presentation, or a full video production, if it is not a good story, it won't get attention.

The Creating Powerful Radio workshop mantra is: "There are *no boring stories*, only *boring storytellers*." Whether you work as a broadcaster (or communicator of any kind), your job likely involves powerful storytelling.

Storytelling trainer and consultant Jeffrey Hedquist says,

"Everyone—parents, teachers, managers, journalists, salespeople, advertising and marketing executives, and entertainers—all use stories. We either do it haphazardly, or with skill and effectiveness. You can use this inherent, powerful tribal communication skill to your advantage to influence, motivate, educate, sell or entertain your audience."

The basics of storytelling are covered in the chapters in the *News* section of this book, including: Who, What, Where, When, Why, and How. Beginning, middle, and ending. But it's the way you tell the story, using your own personality and tailoring it to your audience, that will make you a *powerful* storyteller.

Audiences connect to and respond to stories that reflect the basic themes of human nature: good and evil, right and wrong, humor, love stories, the ridiculous (life is absurd), or how an individual triumphed over the odds ("David and Goliath" or "revenge" stories). Rags-to-riches or riches-to-rags. Stories that show character and are hopeful, and teach, inspire, or move people, all work.

Tommy Kramer's Six Steps to Great Storytelling

Broadcast consultant and talent coach Tommy Kramer teaches storytelling. Kramer says,

> It looks easy, and everybody *talks* about telling stories on the air, but only a small percentage of people on the air know *how* to be compelling when they open the microphone.

> But the good news is that you don't have to be a born storyteller, this is a skill that can be learned. At its core, a story is simply a premise or situation that leads to some sort of resolution. What makes the average person a poor storyteller is that there is no resolution, no real "ending." It just slowly grinds down to a halt, or abruptly stops.

> Most "real people" (including guests and callers to your show) can't tell stories; they have to sort of be tricked into it. For a better result: Don't solicit stories on the air. Instead, just say something compelling enough to elicit an opinion or an emotional reaction in the course of the conversation. It's *your* job to wheedle the story out of them.

> Otherwise, you fall into the trap of having a lot of people who *think* their stories are interesting roll onto the air like a hand grenade rolling into the room with the pin pulled. It's not a question of whether or not it'll go off; it's a question of how many people it'll kill.

Here are the six steps Tommy Kramer uses to teach better storytelling:

1. **Start with the ending.** This may go against the grain of what you've been taught before, but as you prep something, start with the *ending*, then work *back* from there. A mystery writer *starts* with knowing who did the crime. Then he simply writes the story that leads to that being revealed. "Beginning–Middle–End" is the standard description of how a story unfolds, but in the Prep process, it should be "Ending–Beginning–Middle," because unless you know where you're going, you're going to be more likely to wander all over the place trying to find the "off" ramp.

   Remember that the ending needs to be something that we *haven't already heard.* Be careful about verbiage repeating. Many so-called stories on the radio start and end the same way, so there's no real "destination" to our journey. It's like we got in the car, drove around the block, and ended up right back at our own front door. Plus, when the end of a story is something that you've already said, it takes away the element of *surprise*—something that way too many radio stations have lost, ignored, or never learned in the first place.

The beginning comes next in the Prep process, because without a compelling opening thought, no one's ever going to stick around for the ending.

The middle part is about editing. You can take one step away from the "main road," but then come *back.* Again, it's like driving. One detour, then you get back on the highway—everything's fine. But take two detours in a row, and you feel lost. On the air, two "side roads" in a row means that the *listener* gets lost.

2. **Put yourself last.** Don't start by talking about yourself. Either [1] start with the subject, or [2] start by referencing the listener. "I watched American Idol last night" is just you talking about you. But "If you missed American Idol last night" draws me in. Since you pulled up a chair for me, now you're free to relate your story, give your opinion, etc. Or "Watching American Idol is like watching people run for Class President in High School" puts the subject "on the table." From there, with that "touchstone" established, you have license to give me your "take" on what happened.

3. **Never be typical.** Say what *only you* would say about the subject. If someone else would say it, *automatically reject it.*

4. **Use real language.** Use the language that actual human beings use in everyday conversations. When you get "presentational" instead of conversational, you've lost me. Don't "announce" anything. Just talk to me, like a real person—like you would by the grill if we were having a backyard barbecue.

5. **Don't read to me.** If you must quote something, say that you're quoting it, do it, then immediately return to just talking to me. (And make that quote a **short** one.) Radio is full of people reading a magazine or newspaper or website article to the listener. Just tell it to me, in your own words.

6. **Find another "camera angle."** This is the best thing you'll ever learn, which is why I saved it for last. When a great film director walks around, watching the actors rehearse, he's constantly thinking "Who do I show in this shot? Where am I going to put the camera?" A George Lucas or Steven Spielberg draws up "story boards" that are, simply, illustrations of what the camera angle for each scene will be.

Here's how the "camera angle" thing works:

Picture the Tournament of Roses Parade. Most people in radio (and especially in television) describe things from the judges' booth, watching the floats go by. "This float is the one the Tournament of Roses Queen rides. It's eighty feet long, made of over a million roses and chrysanthemum blossoms, and took ninety-four workers over two hundred hours to make." This is both typical and boring.

But what if you describe it from the Tournament of Roses Queen's perspective? She's ON the float, thinking "I've been waving to the crowd and smiling for two miles. My face muscles are screaming, and *man* is my arm tired—and we've still got eight more miles to go!"

Or you can describe it from the perspective of the marching band, walking in *front* of the float. From that "camera angle," it's probably something like, "What's *she* griping about? All she has to do is sit there and wave! But I have to WALK eight more miles—and lug this tuba!"

Each of those vantage points gives you a completely different view of the same event. The better and more adept you become at seeing different "camera angles," the more interesting and engaging you'll be. Just mentally put yourself in someone else's shoes, and describe how it looks and feels from there. "Camera angles" are the hidden secret to great storytelling.

There's at least one major way in which storytelling to a radio, TV, podcast or Internet audience differs from the kind of storytelling you might do around a dinner table: At the dinner table, it is considered very rude to leave if you are bored. But if you have not given your audience a reason to stay and hear it all, they won't feel obligated to listen for long.

So, it's important to put a few essential things up front. If you are telling a story outside of breaking news, it's necessary to immediately engage and captivate your listener. The trick is to get your audience to want to hear the rest of the story, and feel they need to know how it will end. In news there's a joke: "Don't bury your lead." As with anything you put on the air, ask: "Why should someone want to listen to this?" Give the reason someone should listen to your story before you do anything else.

If you've ever wondered whether you're really alone in the dressing room when you try on clothes, you'll want to know about the security guard who's going to jail today...

How do you find the reason? Before any story goes to air, take it apart, look at the facts and try to see it from all angles. Who are the players involved? How can you make your listeners care about them? Who will be affected by the outcome of what you have to say? Answer at least one of these questions, and put it right up front.

Looking Through the Prism

Similar to the "camera angle," one of the techniques to help people improve their storytelling is "The Prism Method."

Have you ever held a crystal prism up to the light and noticed that each time you move it, the pattern of rainbow colors dancing on the wall changes? While it's the same crystal, and the same light, and the same wall, when you move the prism, you change your perspective on the light, and you see a completely different pattern. Thinking of yourself as the prism through which the facts of your story will pass is a good way to imagine the many ways you can approach and tell the many sides to any story.

Here's an example of the "Prism Method."

Maggie, a reporter, waits in a shop to make a purchase. As she continues to stand there, Rachel, the owner of the store, is busy talking on the phone, making arrangements to close early tonight. Why? It turns out Rachel has to close at 3:00 p.m. because she's got to get to the airport on time to pick up her twin brother, his wife and their two-year-old daughter.

As the conversation continues, the story unfolds. Maggie learns through eavesdropping that the siblings have not seen each other for forty-seven years. They were twins, born in India, then were separated, after their parents divorced. The mother brought the baby girl to England, and the father took the boy to America. They hadn't seen each other since and neither knew what had happened to the other.

One day, the woman's teenage daughter asked about her uncle and was curious about her grandfather. She went online and conducted an Internet search. In less than four days, she'd located her mother's twin brother, living in the United States. Tonight was to be their big reunion at the airport.

Maggie was a reporter and this was a story. So she said, "Excuse me, but I couldn't help overhearing…" When Maggie asked if she could come along for the reunion, the woman agreed, and that's when Maggie learned the rest of their saga.

It turned out the brother had had a terrible life growing up in America. Their father, now deceased, had been an alcoholic, and had never kept a job for more than a few months at a time. He'd had four marriages. There were times when the boy was forced to live on the road with his dad, sleeping in their car. He'd gone hungry and had never finished a single school year in the same town.

Since the young man had had such an unstable upbringing, though he had steady employment, he chose not to marry until he was in his mid-forties. And he'd had his first child at forty-seven. So tonight, at the airport, the brother, his wife, and small daughter were meeting his twin sister and her family for the first time.

Now, there is no right or wrong way to tell a story, but you can use the Prism Method to find the *best* way for you to tell it. Maggie examined all angles of this story, to find the most powerful approach for her feature.

The Prism Method—Finding the Best/Most Powerful Approach

1. We are a global village. With the Internet, no matter how long someone's been missing, if you have the time and patience to look, with a bit of information, and a little luck (or maybe a small miracle), you can find nearly anyone.

2. Studies show that twins often feel incomplete if separated, even it if happened when they were infants. Do you ever wonder whether twins feel like two halves of one whole? If you're a twin, do you ever feel that you are "missing" your other half if you've been separated?

3. If you've never had a good parenting model, should you think twice about becoming a parent yourself? It's hard enough to be a good partner in a relationship, but if you've never seen love modeled—or watched a healthy relationship, how can you be equipped or prepared to be a good husband/wife or partner in a relationship?

All of these are acceptable angles with which to approach this story and they all would have worked. Maggie was trying to decide which she would use as she traveled to the airport with Rachel and her daughter. But when she saw the scene unfolding before her, Maggie knew her entry point would be the little girl. Here is the opening of her story, as it aired:

Two-year-old Liza with her dazzling smile, big blue eyes and blonde curls is sitting on her aunt Rachel's lap. Liza is exactly the same age her father and her aunt were when they were separated in India, forty-seven years ago...

This example shows how by examining the same story from all the potential angles and approaches, you can find the best, most compelling way to tell it. By using the Prism Method, you are well on your way to becoming a more powerful storyteller.

Where Do Stories Come From?

It's a popular belief that everyone has at least one good story to tell. In fact, this idea was the inspiration for a radio series, where people were urged to send in their stories, and then, if selected, narrate them on the air.

Unfortunately, having a good story solves only part of the challenge. Telling the story is, well, another story. That's how one of the most difficult-to-listen-to hours ever heard on radio came to be: People with good stories, who couldn't tell them, struggling to become storytellers in front of a studio microphone, broadcasting to potentially hundreds of thousands of listeners. I'm not sure they would have felt any better to know how it worked in practice. After a few minutes of "star-of-the-day" fishing through his vocabulary for words to describe his experience of delivering a baby in a parking lot, most of the audience had gone elsewhere for entertainment. It didn't help that the announcer of the broadcast had given the whole story away in one sentence at the beginning of the program. That's why storytelling is a discreet skill. All three basics of the Creating Powerful Radio principles apply:

- Tell the truth
- Make it matter
- Never be boring.

To accomplish this, there are also three more skills to practice. If you learn them, storytelling gets much easier. If you can learn to speak visually, emotionally engage your listener, and use the word "you" instead of "me", "we", or "I," you will instantly become a more powerful storyteller.

You don't need to hold a national contest to find good stories. They come from everywhere. Storytelling trainer and consultant Jeffrey Hedquist says, "You can get stories from your peers, clients and colleagues as well as from simple research [there is much more on this in Chapter 31, *Sales and Commercials*], but by far your biggest source of stories is you. Some of the best stories, or content for your material, come from the real lives of people you know or experiences you've had, heard about or observed.

Hedquist continues,

Your life is full of relationships and everyone you know has at least *one* story. Make a list of everyone you've ever known. It may take a while, and it's a list you'll continually add to, but do a little bit each day. Start with your parents, grandparents, spouse(s) and all your relatives, and work your way through to more distant connections, like bosses, customers, and club members. After every name, write as many words as it takes to remind you of at least one associated story. Some names will generate many stories. Every story has power because it's real.

When you need a story, scan your list and select stories that will work for your audience. Be able to tell a long and short version of the story. Flesh out each story, amplifying the conflict and drama. This chronological method seems to work for most people.

Don't spare yourself. Think back and make a list of those emotional markers in your life. What times in your life were the most emotional, defining, powerful, or life changing? You'll know because when you mentally relive them, you'll feel them in your heart and gut. Interestingly, if the stories are told well, that's exactly where the listener will feel them. And that's where most of our decisions are made—from the emotional center.

Can you remember when you were a "know it all?" Did you ever let someone down? Step out of your comfort zone and succeed? Lose a love? Lie, cheat, or misjudge? What experiences have changed your life?

If you ask yourself these questions or similar ones, you'll unearth memories, which you can use to craft stories for your show, your advertisers, colleagues, associates or employees. Write just enough description so you can recall the story later.

When you're under the gun to do your show, write a spot, give a speech, meet with a client or train an employee, it is not the time to make this list. Start it now, and add to it. Take five minutes a day.

Now that you have a method to pry lots of stories from your subconscious, how can you turn them into effective stories?"

Try focusing your stories using the following questions.

Jeffrey Hedquist's Ten Questions for Storytellers

1. Who is the story about?

Personalize the story. The most compelling stories aren't about a company, a station or an institution; they're about a person. This person is the protagonist, the hero. Your story follows the protagonist in pursuit of clearly defined goals. Ideally, make each member of your audience the protagonist, or someone your audience will identify with. Describe them well.

Give your protagonists detailed personalities. Name them [you may use fictitious names. Then you don't have to worry about hurting someone or legal repercussions, and you can make the names tell part of the story, too: "I had a crush on Miss Darling, my third grade teacher."] What do they look like? Be specific. Saying that someone has "curly golden hair with a mind of it's own," is a better description than "blonde." Next, think about quirks, blemishes, and oddities that make them unique. Include anything pertinent about their relationships.

To add visual spice, think of metaphors—what are they like? Is the person like a porcupine or a sleek Corvette convertible? Is your boss like Mr. Rogers or Tony Soprano? Think in terms of categories when you look for metaphors. If it will help them to understand the story, make sure your audience knows the relationships between characters.

2. Where are we?

Your audience wants to know. Once you tell them, they can follow the story more easily. Set the scene for your audience. Make sure they know:

Time: year, month, day, time, season, holiday...

Place: city, state, country, home, school, office, church, bedroom, attic, sidewalk...

Atmosphere: sunny, rainy, gloomy, tense, joyous, comfortable, uncomfortable...

Event: board meeting, wedding, vacation, dinner, baseball game, seminar, movie...

A longer version of the story will have more details, but even the short version should have some.

3. What's the goal?

What do your protagonists want or need to accomplish? What do they want to change? What are their dreams? Make the goal clear to your audience. Give them a reason to care about its attainment.

4. What's the obstacle?

It does not always start out that way, but the journey toward the goal can be one from safety to danger, from the known to the unknown. The obstacle is the challenge. It's what gets in the way of achieving the protagonist's goals. It is a *problem*, *dilemma* or *question*. It may be another person, something physical to be overcome, or something to be learned. Often it is an internal challenge. This conflict makes the story worth telling, gives it drama or makes the comedy work.

5. What's the process of overcoming the obstacle?

Your audience learns the most from how the protagonist overcomes the obstacle. It is the *method* that teaches the lesson. What memories did the encounter trigger? What inner demons did the protagonist face? Think minutia; think little steps. Tell the truth. The magic is in the details. Have your characters change, or evolve during the story. This keeps it interesting.

6. Are you showing instead of telling?

Use the active voice. Telling your audience someone was overcome with sadness is not as involving as saying, "As he heard the news, his lip quivered and a single tear rolled down his cheek."

Let your audience reach their own conclusions. Don't tell them how to feel. Give your audience the gift of discovery along the way.

7. Are you keeping it interesting?

Your story should intrigue and engage the audience from the beginning, and surprise them along the way to keep their attention.

8. What's the emotional connection?

You want your audience to care, to feel something from your story. We're all overloaded with too much information. Touch our emotions and you will get our attention. If we laugh, cry, get angry or sad, become frightened or shocked, get inspired or energized, we'll remember the story and the message you wanted to convey, longer.

9. What's the point?

Is there an "aha!" moment that allows your audience to discover a kernel of truth? At the conclusion, will your audience understand what the story was about? Will they have gained an insight?

10. Is there a clear call to action?

What should the listener do to get the benefits you've just told a story about? What could the listener do to apply the insight to his or her own life?

Jeffrey Hedquist's suggestions would work well for telling a short story, or writing a novel, but for most broadcasters, opportunities for telling long stories are rare. The norm is either short, or shorter. There are exceptions, of course. Public radio stations carry some popular shows where stories are told, or read, in long-form. But storytelling does not require great windows of time.

Commercials are some of the shortest forms of storytelling. You can probably recall at least one sixty-second spot that takes you two minutes to describe. Why is that? It's because writing "short" is almost always harder than writing "long." That's true for news, ads, and features. But if you can take someone on a complete journey in thirty- or sixty-seconds of air time, you are truly an adept storyteller.

Turi Ryder creates in both long and short forms. She's a talk radio host and a writer for the CBS radio news network short form humor feature, "Turi Ryder's Exception to the Rule." The comedy pieces are based sometimes on news, but more often on Ryder's personal life. You'll find it on top stations across the United States.

If you ask Ryder what it takes to tell a story in sixty seconds, she'll say:

A lot of time, first, I write the story without regard to length. Then, I look at it and think, "Well, most of this has to go." So I strip out every unnecessary word. I can come down to picking monosyllables over polysyllables, for timing's sake. Sometimes it makes me sad to have to hit "delete" and lose a great line. Actually, that's a lie. If I think the line or thought was really that great, I save it to use in some other, longer, form later.

You should probably keep all the original drafts of your writing, either because there may be material in there you can gather and use later for something else, or to make you appreciate how talented your editor is. The need to make every phrase count is a good way to ensure you use the most descriptive language possible.

It's also advisable to read the piece out loud a few times—for timing and for sound. Words can be funny, not only because of what they mean, but because of their actual sounds. Sometimes, I'll try on a few words for the same thing, to see which produces the desired effect. Since I'm writing something that I will voice, I try to take the opportunity to use my voice to paint part of the picture. It all has to work together. If you can believe this, there are actually numbers that sound sillier than other numbers.

Synonyms can produce wildly different effects. What's funnier: a baby shoe, or a baby bootie? An accident or a wreck? Three hundred, or two hundred and sixty-seven? And most people speak far less formally than they write. When you read your work out loud, you may be surprised at how unnatural it sounds, even if the words are yours. Sentences have to be simple. The action goes by pretty fast, and if you have lots of dependent phrases and clauses, no one will understand your point...unless your point is to sound long and convoluted.

The radio feature I'm working on may be based on a real news story, but if you're clearly creating a work of comedy, you can cover yourself with phrases like, "I imagine..." or "It seems that..." to let the audience know you're leaving the factual, and entering the fictional.

Pick the most dramatic language you can. Use your voice. You only have sixty seconds, so you have to make the listener's mind work along with yours to see what you see. By the time it's all done, you have spent two hours from start to finish on a one-minute piece. The ratio of raw milk needed to produce a pound of cheese is more efficient.

Jeffrey Hedquist suggests you examine every part of your station for places where storytelling could make a real difference. In how many areas are you using stories? Of course, these techniques apply in all the obvious places where you need content.

But Hedquist says, beyond your newscasts, morning shows, public service programming and commercials, there is need for good storytelling everywhere: sales proposals and your station's website, podcasts and promotional materials—even your Engineering department's training manuals. You'll be surprised how well your staff learns emergency procedures once they've heard the story of what happened when the last chief engineer forgot to fuel up the backup generator.

Because communication is really storytelling, you will find more information about how to tell powerful stories for a variety of platforms and purposes throughout the book.

CHAPTER 18

Beyond Powerful Radio
Your Voice—Improving Your Instrument

Taking care of your voice, learning its capabilities, and maximizing your ability to use the voice you've been given, is as important to creating powerful communication as storytelling itself. The voice is the instrument through which a story travels from the storyteller's mind to the listener. The voice gives the story shading, emotion, depth, humor, character. Your voice is the brush that paints the picture, and if it does not perform at its best, your story loses color, detail, warmth, and meaning.

"Now, What Are We Going to Do About Your Voice?"

One of the worst things I ever heard at an aircheck session was a PD asking the talent this exact question. Of course, the talent was devastated.

Fortunately, it is not your voice, but the content of what you say, that matters most. Audiences will listen to people who do not have great voices, but have something to say. They will spend very little time listening to a beautiful voice saying nothing.

Still, if you have ever gotten negative feedback about the sound of your voice, you know it can be hurtful, embarrassing, and frustrating. After all, what are you supposed to do about the voice you were born with? Range,

207

tone of voice, and how you sound are all variables. Not everyone was born with a beautiful voice, but with a little work, and some small changes, you can *improve* your voice, if you want to.

Some people are lucky, like "the screecher." The screecher was a bright, talented, articulate woman whose voice made her sound as if she were on the edge of hysteria. It was painful to listen to her, although the people who tried were rewarded by an interesting viewpoint and a good sense of humor. There was a general consensus that the show would be canceled unless the host got vocal coaching.

Finally, the desperate producer met with the PD to ask for help. "Turn up her headphones to maximum, and stick her microphone down her throat," was his advice.

The next day, four station employees literally ran into the office from their cars. "What happened to Liza? She sounds like a new person!" The improvement was instant.

Lesson: Sometimes a simple tip is all you need to sound better and fix your "voice problem."

Playing Your Instrument—Use Your Whole Body

One of the most brilliant and successful voice-over artists in the United States is Randy Thomas. In her book *Voice for Hire*, she writes:

> Your whole body from head-to-toe, is your instrument. In order to play good music, you must first learn to play the instrument. Never allow the confines of a voice-over booth, no matter how small it may be, to inhibit you. Your arms, shoulders, fingers, knees and hips can accentuate what you do as an actor, and let's not forget the face: There are more muscles in the human face than in the rest of the entire human body. That should give you some indication of the degree to which you can work your facial muscles to manipulate your voice, which is, after all, also a physical entity. No one cares what you look like in the booth. Frankly no one is watching, including you.

Yawn

Voice coach and author of the *Broadcast Voice Handbook*, Dr. Ann S. Utterback, stresses that a variety of problems with the voice can be fixed if you can work to correct your breathing. Often, the trouble is simply not getting enough air.

> Yawning has been used for centuries as a technique for relaxing the throat. Many times when I hear someone producing vocal sounds that seem to be caught in the throat, or when someone sounds tense or muffled and not projecting well, a good yawn relaxes the larynx and throat and promotes deep breathing. This is why it's important to breathe correctly. The voice does not begin with the vocal folds in the throat, it begins with the *breath*. It is the energy that provides the movement of the folds. Breathing also can eliminate tension or stress, which can create other vocal problems.
>
> Proper breathing begins low in the torso around your waist. You should feel your stomach expand as you inhale and contract as you exhale. One way to feel this is to lie down on your back, with a book on your stomach. If the book rises and falls as you inhale and exhale, while you're breathing comfortably, you're doing it correctly. Now try it standing. Place your right hand on your chest and your left hand at your waistline. Breathe so that you feel your left hand moving while your right hand remains still. This breathing will give you the best breath support for your broadcast voice and will reduce tension in your throat.

Utterback also advises that, because the voice is a muscle, it helps to warm it up with vocal exercises.

H_2O to Go

And then there's water. Utterback calls water:

> the magic elixir for your voice. (Actually, any decaffeinated, unsweetened, nonalcoholic fluid counts.) Moisture cushions the vocal folds as they open and close for speech. It works much like oil in a car to protect this delicate tissue. Gargling or just taking a quick swallow of water is not enough. We have to keep drinking fluid all day long for it to be effective.
>
> But the sad fact is most of us pay more attention to watering our lawns and houseplants than we do our bodies. This is despite the fact that even a small amount of dehydration (around 1% of body weight) can affect our physiological state and our performance. The 4 p.m. fatigue you may often feel could simply be dehydration. So, drink a lot of water!

Solving the Real Problem

One reporter I worked with said his voice was fine in the morning. But, he complained, after a full day in the field he sounded strained and tinny. After full days of running story-to-story, covering floods, fires, crime scenes and disasters, and filing for air, his voice was affected. It turned out that there was no problem with this reporter's voice. The hoarseness and cracking were a result of the tension of the job itself, caused by the exhaustion and the psychological demands of his work which involved seeing human distress and natural disaster, day-after-day. The young man's voice problem was miraculously cured when he learned to relax. His voice coach told him to make time to breathe deeply, drink plenty of water, and take breaks for things like yoga during the day, in order to alleviate his vocal tension.

Bad Writing!

Sometimes a problem with the voice isn't the voice at all. The problem is the copy. Good, natural conversational delivery starts with a good script. Utterback says,

> Often people who've been told they had voice problems really just had delivery problems caused by poor writing. One client thought she had breathing problems. She was shocked when I told her any broadcaster would have breathing problems reading her long, convoluted, complicated sentences! Another sounded choppy, but, again, it was the fault of the writing. No matter what good intentions you may have about sounding conversational in your broadcasts, if your writing isn't conversational, forget it.

There's a flow to copy when it's well written, but even the most gifted announcers have trouble voicing poorly worded copy. It's hard to read bad writing. If you have the ability to change the wording, do so. *Writing Broadcast News—Shorter, Sharper, Faster* author Mervin Block advises:

> Keep it simple. Avoid starting with the name of an unknown person or unfamiliar name. Also, if you can use a simpler easier word, do so. Avoid big words, wasted words, odd words, fancy words or clichés. Don't use long complicated sentence construction—stick to the "subject, verb, object" pattern. The more the writing sounds natural, the way you actually talk, the easier it is to read or perform on-air.

If you are already on the radio or on TV, you probably sound OK. You are likely a fairly good verbal communicator. Much of caring for your voice is just common sense. The best advice I have been given through the years includes the following:

- **Drink a lot of water.** (All of the voice experts recommend staying hydrated and all say "Carry a bottle of water with you at all times.")

- **Stand up in front of the microphone** (for more power and energy) instead of sitting.

- **Relax.**

- **Breathe deeply.**

- **Speak from the diaphragm.**

- **If you *really* have a cold, stay home.** You can ruin your voice by working when you're sick. You can also take down an entire radio station by passing your illness around.

- **Try hot tea.** People are individuals—each reacts in his or her own way to certain foods. What works for you may not work for someone else, but in my experience I'd suggest avoiding milk, cheese, popcorn, and certain carbonated drinks, before you go on air.

Berkley Productions CEO, author, and voice-over coach Susan Berkley works with public speakers and broadcasters. Here are some pointers from her book, *Speak to Influence: How to Unlock the Hidden Power of Your Voice,* to unlock the hidden power in your voice. First, Susan warns what *not* to do:

Susan Berkley's Tips
Avoid:

1. **Yelling.**

   Some people's voices are naturally loud and booming. Until you know how to do it properly, avoid yelling whenever possible.

2. **Not being physically fit.**

   When your overall physical vitality is down, your voice is one of the first places it shows.

3. **Calling in to the radio station by phone.**

   When reporting in by phone do not speak with the phone tucked between your ear and chin. To prevent yourself from sounding like a kidnapper calling to demand a ransom, use a headset. (Although wireless technology has made it possible to call in from nearly any place on earth, get to a landline if you can. It takes more vocal effort to use a cell or mobile phone.)

4. **Not warming up.**

Good speech takes muscle. There are many vocal warm ups. The simplest is to hum at a comfortable pitch out loud for a few minutes before you start your day.

5. **Speaking beneath your natural pitch.**

Some people habitually speak at the very bottom of their pitch range, mistakenly believing it makes them sound more authoritative and forceful. Unfortunately this puts great strain on the voice.

6. **Excessive throat clearing.**

It can damage the vocal chords. Some of the reasons for excessive throat clearing are nervous habit, and allergies. If it's a nervous habit, you can break it (listen for it on your aircheck). Instead of clearing your throat, take a sip of water. Replace a bad habit with a good one.

Here, Susan offers practical suggestions for ten common complaints:

1. *I hate my voice. I can't believe people pay me to speak. I'm just waiting for the day they come and tell me it has all been a horrible, terrible mistake.*

   Solution: Anyone who has had any success in the entertainment field has had this thought at one time or another. The voice we hear inside our heads is not the same voice others hear when we speak. Listening to a *recording* of your voice will show you the way you sound to others. This can be a shock, and can take some getting used to. If it's any comfort, most people hate the way they sound. Try to put these feelings aside and learn to critique your voice as if you were giving gentle feedback to your best friend. Work on your weaknesses, but also appreciate your strengths. In time you'll learn to take all of this much less personally.

2. *Get that "pukin' DJ" sound out of your voice.*

   Solution: You need to sound more conversational. Try working without headphones whenever possible. If you need them while on the air, keep the headphones on one ear only or turn the volume way down. As you listen to your aircheck, ask yourself, "Do I speak this way in normal conversation?"

The best radio creates the illusion of a one-on-one conversation between friends—not the "Voice of God" from Mount Olympus speaking to the little people.

Find a photograph of a loved one and keep it by the mic so that you can visualize speaking to that person when you're on the air. Better yet, if there's a human being in the room while the mic is on, look him or her in the eyes as you speak.

3. *Your voice sounds weak. You need more power.*

Solution: Psyche yourself up before you go on the air. Pro athletes do it all the time. Check your posture. Use lots of body language—gesture freely with your hands. Wear comfortable clothing that doesn't restrict your breathing. Start a fitness program. To get vocal energy, you need physical energy. Eat lean before you go on the air.

4. *You sound too breathy.*

Solution: There are two common problems with breathiness. The first is when the speaker, usually a woman, speaks in an exaggeratedly breathy manner. She often believes a breathy voice makes her sound more vulnerable and feminine.

The second problem is "misplaced breathing." The speaker exhales too much air in the middle of a thought and gives the impression that he or she is exhausted and gasping for breath.

Both problems can be cured by training yourself to breathe correctly and monitoring your progress with daily airchecks.

5. *You mumble. You need to improve your enunciation.*

Solution: Vowels add color to the speech. Consonants add clarity. If people are telling you that you mumble, you are probably dropping your consonants—most commonly final 'd's, 't's, and 'g's. You're also probably speaking too fast. Short daily practice sessions with a recording device are needed. Read from a newspaper or book. Go slowly, making sure you enunciate clearly.

6. *Your regional accent is too strong.*

Solution: Get a dictionary and study the diacritical markings. These will give you the correct pronunciations of the standard American vowel sounds. Practice them as best you can. Overall, this is a very difficult problem to cure without regular one-on-one sessions with an accent-reduction specialist. (There are "how to pronounce it" features on several websites. If you're not sure whether you're saying a word correctly, check. If you need to practice a more standardized American pronunciation, these can help.)

7. *You don't sound warm and friendly enough.*

   Solution: This one is easy—smile. A smile on your face will put a smile in your voice. Keep a mirror near the mic to make sure there's a smile on your face whenever the mic is on.

8. *Your voice is too high.*

   Solution: Not everyone was meant to sound like Darth Vader or Jessica Rabbit. Some of us are tenors and some of us are baritones. All voices are beautiful when properly played. One of the most common causes of a high, thin voice is nervous tension. Deep abdominal breathing will help you stay relaxed so that your voice can sound its best.

9. *By the end of your show, your voice sounds tired and hoarse.*

   Solution: When you are run down, your voice is the first thing to go. If you smoke, stop immediately. If you do not smoke, avoid smoky environments like bars and clubs. Make an appointment with a throat doctor to rule out any medical problems. A healthy voice should stay strong throughout an entire airshift.

   You could be suffering from allergies which could be irritating your throat. Avoid dairy products. Switch to unscented cosmetics.

   Drink at least eight glasses of water a day, especially while you are on the air. Avoid ice-cold beverages—they constrict the throat muscles. Drink warm water or herb tea while on the air.

10. *Your voice sounds boring and monotonous.*

    Solution: Put the fun back in your voice. Practice reading children's stories or trashy romance novels aloud in an exaggerated manner. Work with a mirror by the mic. Do not worry if you look silly or stupid. The sillier you look, the better you will sound. If there is emotion on your face and in your eyes, we will hear it in your voice. This is radio—no one can see you anyway.

Study the greats. Find and record voice models. Try and imitate them to pick up nuances of inflection and pacing. You'll find demos of top voice-over artists in the United States at *www.voicebank.net.* Listen to these men and women to model some of the best and most highly paid voices in the nation.

Remember, although not everyone can have a great voice, *all* voices can be worked with and improved upon.

PART III

Beyond Powerful Radio
Creating Powerful News

CHAPTER 19

Beyond Powerful Radio
Creating Powerful News

*"The essence of entertainment will not change. What has always
counted is the story and the skill with which it is told."
—Michael Eisner, former CEO, The Walt Disney Company*

News broadcasting is really two separate jobs. The first is covering the "big story," an event of such magnitude that it affects the lives, well-being, or safety of your audience. The other is covering everything else.

On "big news" days, it is not so important to worry about being creative. On those days, just gather the facts and get them on the air quickly. Give your listeners what they need to know. On slower news days (that is, most of the time), the news is like an insurance policy. Your newscast is in place, covering the day-to-day events of life, so that people know where they can find the information and where to go on the big news day.

Big news days are the days that journalists live for, when the adrenalin is pumping and the stories just seem to write themselves. But it's important every day to choose stories that are interesting. Every day, the stories you choose should affect your audience in some way. Pick items that connect listeners to what is happening in their community, what is new, interesting, or absurd. Give audiences talkable topics and entertain them with information.

Radio news can be much more exciting than many people realize. By doing what radio does best—getting information from the scene of an event to the air, quickly, and describing an event so listeners can visualize what is happening—we are using the most powerful tools we possess: immediacy and imagery.

But we are no longer just radio stations. Now every newsroom must function as a digital news organization. The mission is to inform, entertain and engage as many people as possible, as many times as possible across the day, on various platforms. FM radio, the web, instant messaging, "micro-blogging," HD Radio, Facebook, Smartphones and other applications are some of the growing list of media available to broadcasters. Stations have to use as many platforms as they can in order to get news to the audience in the form that's most useful to them. And your audience is using these platforms to send information back to *you*. Will you use it? How?

There's much more on this in Chapter 21, *Citizen Journalism*, but whether you're a professionally trained reporter or just happen to be on the scene when news is happening, if you've got a camera in your phone, you can contribute as a mobile media journalist to the on-air and online digital newsroom. Many TV reporters, also filing for the web throughout the day, are quickly becoming "backpack" journalists. The information age is not just radio anymore. What we look for now are smart people, with talent, who are very flexible. Then, we need to train those people to be good journalists.

Building a Great News Team

Network News Executive Bernard Gershon looks for these traits in a newsperson:

Desire or Hunger is Crucial

The best employees always want to improve their performances. They display this by asking for additional assignments, wanting to learn different parts of the business, asking to be sent to training seminars. They also understand that getting better requires hard work and long hours. Look for people who are aggressive when it comes to getting interviews, going after callers, going "prime time."

What We Look For

An effective newsperson is a storyteller who exudes "energy," someone who can generate enthusiasm and excitement from listeners and is interested in the topic, the caller, the job. My definition of dull? Demos of newscasters who sound like they are reading. Those can be identified in about thirty seconds—out they go. Yes, it is a cruel business, but everyone is busy.

Warning: I have seen far too many job candidates who expect to become radio or TV stars—or both—overnight. These people are usually too egotistical to understand that they have to work as a team, pay their dues, and gain a reputation. My suggestion…pass!

Most successful news operations hire reporters and staff with a sense of mission to both the station and the community, who understand that "super-serving" the listener is important.

Reward the Troops

Top-rated stations understand the importance of rewarding people for excellent work. It's not only important to hire right, but you also need to nurture your team. WTOP radio in Washington, DC rewards their all-news staff by regularly submitting their work for prestigious awards, which they often win. WTOP vice president of news and programming, Jim Farley knows, however, that you can't pay your rent with an engraved wall plaque, so he offers his staff bonus pay for increasing listenership and audience growth both online and over the air.

When he started at WTOP years ago, Farley says he couldn't imagine hiring anyone with less than five years of large market radio news experience. But a shortage of candidates forced him to reconsider. Today, his staff is a mix of both "graybeards" and young people, sharing their respective knowledge and insight. The junior recruits have taught Farley and his more experienced veteran reporters about digital editing, website design, and effective use of social networking. According to Farley, "the mix of both experienced and newer people has proven to be vital in the success of the station."

Farley says it's important that each reporter and news anchor understand the audience's needs:

Most listeners are interested in things that actually impact their lives: gas prices, traffic, new movies, tech toys, subway fare increases, personal relationships, romance, and health. They do NOT care about government process except when you tell them HOW it might affect them. Listeners want to know what does it mean for ME? Thomas Aquinas in his *Summa Theologica* defines passion as the sum of people's hopes, fears, needs, and desires. Got that? Hopes, fears, needs, and desires. Meet those needs and you create content that people become PASSIONATE about.

If a newscaster tells the truth in an interesting and, when appropriate, entertaining way, he or she can keep the attention of the listeners. A good reporter might cover a fire so descriptively that the listeners can almost taste the smoke in the backs of their throats. When you create "word pictures," your news story is almost like a movie. News should be great storytelling. Then it will never be boring.

There is concern within news organizations, especially in Europe, about keeping the news very serious and credible. While journalists have been trained to report accurately, there has been little emphasis on teaching them to attract or keep the attention of audiences. Their focus has been entirely on keeping journalistic integrity. This is admirable, but it does no good to be serious and credible if the results are so dull that listeners tune out.

Imagine being presented with a fourteen-course meal of totally bland cuisine. Nobody would want to eat it. What is the point of doing all the work of assembling a half-hour newscast that is so dry or arcane that most people cannot pay attention to it? Sure, there will always be somebody who can make it through to the bitter end, but most of your potential listeners will have given up and gone elsewhere. By making newscasts into compelling, powerful radio, you can have both credibility and interest.

Don't Be Interchangeable, Be an Individual

Information is available everywhere: on the radio, but also online, over the Internet, on mobile devices, in the paper, and on TV. So why should a listener come to you for information? Because that listener cannot hear *you*, the storyteller, anywhere else. Storytelling is the power you have to make the listener experience an event or take in information in a unique way. Be creative. Put your heart into it, keep your opinion out of it, and get your facts right. Find a way to make the story yours.

Here is an example from a Creating Powerful Radio news seminar that took place in Nairobi, Kenya. In this exercise, we gave the facts of one story to a dozen reporters. Here is the story we used:

A young woman had been arrested, tried, and jailed with a life sentence for murdering her father. She became pregnant while in prison, and gave birth to a baby girl. The question now was, "What will happen to that baby?" Should the authorities let the mother keep her baby in the jail? Or should they take away the child and give her to another family to raise? The woman's family wants nothing to do with this innocent baby. After all, the woman killed her own father. Her mother, who was his wife, had not forgiven the murderess. Perhaps the people who run the jail ought to allow the baby to stay for a little while until she reaches school age, then make a decision?

And who is the father? No one knows, and the woman won't say. This was a new situation for the jail. Everyone had an opinion as to what should happen.

Several journalists got to work, with this assignment: "Take these facts and report the story, but find your own unique and creative way to tell it. Use your voice, your personality, in the storytelling."

The result: One reporter, writing in Swahili, introduced the story this way: "The last immaculate conception happened two thousand years ago. The latest was yesterday, at the Nairobi jail... "

Another reporter, a woman in her early-twenties, wrote the story from the imagined perspective of the baby: "I do not know my father. I will never know my grandfather because my mother has killed him, and I may never see the light of day, for I am born in Nairobi jail... "

The Sound of the Story

The power of a story often lies in its sound. Whenever possible, record and use natural sound. If you are covering a parade, festival, or demonstration, this is obvious. Use the sound of the event underneath your report to give listeners the feel of "being on the scene." Less obvious, and less frequently heard, are the sounds of more routine events. Think creatively. Use sound to help you tell your story. If you are doing a story on day-care centers, it makes sense to record children at play and run that underneath your report.

Here's a story everybody does twice a year, done two ways:

"Daylight saving time is over. Don't forget to turn your clock back an hour at 2 a.m."

One reporter went to a clock store and recorded the clocks at noon. The story came alive with the sound of chimes, bells, and cuckoo clocks under the lead:

"This is the sound of time. Remember to turn your clock back one hour tonight."

That's more powerful. The sound makes it work better, even for an event that happens twice a year, like clockwork. Don't settle. It doesn't have to be boring.

Television has pictures, but now radio does too. Radio can become visual by posting photos and video on your website. But in radio the most powerful tool in our arsenal is still the imagination. By using sound and describing events and people in detail, we can stimulate imagination in a way television simply cannot.

One example comes from my former newsroom in San Francisco. A young reporter had spent all night covering a fire and was now at the station recording his reports for the morning newscasts. While the fire he'd covered was exciting, his reports were rather dull. I chalked it up to inexperience, and made a note to talk with him about it later. His story sounded like this:

> The fire burned throughout the night at the intersection of Powell and Main. The home was completely destroyed. No one was injured. It took two fire companies to extinguish the flames. The damage is estimated at four hundred thousand dollars. No one knows what started the fire.

When the reporter was done recording his story, he picked up the newsroom phone and called his girlfriend. Since he had been out all night, he needed to explain his whereabouts:

> You should have seen the fire! It was incredible! There was a full moon and you could see the black smoke billowing for miles around! All these people were out in their bathrobes and underwear watching it burn, with kids and dogs running around wild. They needed two fire companies to put out the flames because the first company couldn't get their hoses to work.
> So they lost the house and everyone had to wait for backup firefighters to show up. At one point, they thought there was a cat in the house, so all these firemen went in with oxygen masks to find the cat, but she was hiding under a car a block away! You could hardly breathe because the smoke was so thick and the wind kept changing, and they still don't know what started it. And that house! It's completely destroyed—nothing but ashes. They say it was worth four hundred thousand dollars! Can you imagine, even in that neighborhood, prices are up that high?

I impolitely grabbed the phone from the reporter's hand and asked why he couldn't put all that good stuff in his reports, instead of saving it for his girlfriend.

That reporter learned a lesson. Now he works for two national networks and has a wall covered with awards for making powerful radio.

Trying to convince a group of journalists that news does not have to be boring can be tough. They assume that some "important" details of a story have to be included, even if those details are not interesting. If such details do not interest you at the human level, it's likely that those details won't interest your listeners and they will probably tune out, leaving you and your "important" details behind.

If you feel you have not done your duty to your community unless you make every fact available, stash the minutiae on your website, where those who are interested can find and peruse them.

Again, if news is presented in a boring manner, listeners tune out or "zone out." Once, at a workshop in Finland with a group of radio journalists, I played them ten minutes of their newscast from the previous day. The group was sitting quietly and appeared to be listening intently. When it was over, I asked them, "What was the first story?"

Dead silence hung over the room. Not one journalist could remember. By the way, these were the same people who, the day before, had written, produced, and presented this newscast.

"What about the second story?" Silence. "How about the third?" No one said a word. Even though the group had just heard the newscast, the stories were so boring nobody remembered them. They had mentally tuned out.

Finally, I asked, "Does anyone remember anything from this newscast?" The only story anyone remembered concerned a church that was urging people to cremate their dead because it was cheaper than burial and the cemeteries were filled to capacity. The only story they could recall was a weird, interesting piece about cremation. Lesson: If you don't make the news interesting, listeners may "hear" the stories, but they won't sink in.

One broadcast reporter who is never boring is Mike Sugerman. At KCBS Radio and KPIX-TV in San Francisco, he has been known for taking the dullest stories and bringing them to life. Because he is creative, Sugerman's work is equally good on the hard news and lighter features. For example, take a "perennial" story like America's Academy Awards. Every year, reporters cover that story the same way: celebrity interviews, clips of the movies, and lists of nominees. Sugerman adds a dimension by doing his own "Oscar Poll." He asks guys named "Oscar" who ought to win. Nobody else does that.

When Sugerman does a story on the homeless, he gets into their world; he lives among them, gains their trust, and gets unique perspectives. Once he did a story about garbage by accompanying an apple core to the dump. He works with sound and humor. Sugerman retains his humanity and is never above the audience. Imagination and detail are part of what make him a master storyteller. Mike Sugerman advises reporters to take risks:

> First, learn the rules of traditional journalism. Then break them. After you learn what you are supposed to do, you can cover a story and figure out what all the other reporters will be doing. Then do something different. Often, the resulting story will generate comments such as, "What the hell was that?" But eventually the comments turn into, "Hey, that was good. How did you think of that?" Occasionally, you'll still hear, "What the hell was that?" But, if you don't make mistakes now and then, you aren't pushing the envelope far enough.

Mike Sugerman has only one warning: "Avoid making mistakes with actual facts. If you are factually challenged too often, you'll lose credibility, which is all a reporter owns."

Another amazingly creative reporter is Warren Levinson, head of the Associated Press Bureau in New York City. Levinson is a master of taking seemingly boring stories and making then fascinating. Because of his credibility and expertise as a newsman, Levinson has managed to do some of the Associated Press's best work.

Warren Levinson has some great tricks to make even an older story new without compromising any of the facts, like the time a burst water main in the city of New York had left some neighborhoods without water. Several streets and subways had been flooded for days. Because the problem was ongoing, people in New York were sick of hearing about it, even though their city was still a mess. Warren gave them what they needed to know in the following poetry-style report. Try reading it aloud.

The story has all the required news information—who, what, where, why, when—and it is fun to listen to, even if you've been listening to coverage of the problem all day, or all week!

Levinson says, "Newsmakers in their own words and their own voices are vital to good radio, but never forget that you are the storyteller. I have seen any number of reporters do verbal back flips just to work in a piece of audio better left on the cutting room floor. If you think that your voice cannot carry a story by itself, look to improve your writing or delivery."

Warren Levinson's AP Poetry-Style Report

(Opens with the sound of jackhammers, running water and construction noise.)

There are time bombs under New York,
aged a century or more.
The one that went off Thursday was put in in nineteen-four.
The water mains under Forty-Second Street gave way...

[Gaynor] ..."*Some of our older mains, that's safe to say*"

Dick Gaynor is a deputy of H-2-0 supply.
Half-gainer is the sort of thing that you or he or I
might have been tempted to attempt instead of catch the train,
since what subway tracks were under equaled forty weeks of rain.
And subway riders feeling more than usually harassed
sought detours. Were they mad?

[Martinez] ..."*No, New Yorkers are adaptable, they adjust fast*"

Manuel Martinez got them round the crippled four and five train
while road and track were closed to anything that has a drive train.
We don't whitewater raft here, but you could bob like a cork,
as you whoosh down Forty-Second, Warren Levinson, New York.

(Close with the sound of more running water, jack hammers, construction noises.)

Levinson also emphasizes the importance of ambient sound. "Don't overlook the sound that does not come in quotes: the street sounds of a fire rescue story, the special acoustics of an art gallery or museum." Levinson advises, "Don't use background sound for its own sake, but ask yourself, 'Are there sounds that can tell an aspect of this story more concisely than I can do in words?'"

Personalizing News—Put Your Self into it, But Keep Your Opinion Out of it!

Sometimes it works very well when a reporter expresses genuine feelings about a story. It would have been almost shocking to American viewers and listeners if reporters had managed to seem emotion-free during the events of September 11, 2001, or Hurricane Katrina. Stay objective with the facts, but retain your humanity. If you are genuinely moved by a story and you can personalize it in some way, the audience will be more likely to remember your work.

One CNN reporter covering the massive hurricane that overwhelmed the entire city of New Orleans changed many Americans' expectations of reporting from disaster zones. Anderson Cooper responded both professionally and personally to the story he'd been sent to observe. While people died waiting for help, their homes and neighborhoods destroyed, Anderson Cooper looked directly into a camera and voiced, to an elected official on dry ground, the outrage most Americans were feeling, "No one seems to be taking responsibility." The reporting Cooper did, with visual language and graphic storytelling, changed his career as well, making him one of the most recognizable faces of a major American news network.

Jim Farley says,

> WTOP routinely uses its muscle to make things better for the audience. During winter storm blizzards that shut down the Washington DC area, the station took the 'WTOP Pledge' to ride herd on the local power companies and governments until electricity was restored and streets were plowed across the region. WTOP's veteran traffic reporter Bob Marbourg is known for publicly berating anyone he thinks is hurting his listeners' commute: transportation officials, construction crews, the owners of double-parked 18-wheelers.... As a journalist, I make no apologies. Sometimes we have to advocate for the listeners.

While it's best to keep opinion out of the news, wherever there is a personal connection to a story on the part of the reporter, there is the potential for more powerful radio. One example comes from Sweden's Radio Jämtland. There had been a "mobbing" in a local school. A child had been forced down and beaten, then nearly drowned when his head was held in a toilet. The reporter remembered mobbing attacks from when she was a schoolgirl and how scary they had been. As it turned out, her daughter attended the school where the incident occurred. Like any decent mother, she was afraid for her child. She reported the story, but also told the audience she had special concerns about the safety of her own child. She brought her own life experience to the job. Any parent could relate to this story.

The Art of the Interview

The interview is the heart of the news story. When a reporter comes armed with a list of questions for an expert, spokesperson, or victim, it's easy to forget the most important thing—listening. The reporter is so eager to get to the next item on his or her list that the real story might be missed.

How many times have you heard an interview like this?

NEWSPERSON: So, Dr. Thompson, I understand you have discovered a new species of snake?
DR. THOMPSON: Yes. Its venom can be used to cure certain kinds of cancer, and the coating on its skin seems to protect it from radiation as well as heat.
NEWSPERSON: Interesting. Are you scared of snakes?

While this is a slightly exaggerated example, the failure to listen is not unusual. Your most important interviewing tools are your listening skills and natural curiosity.

Often, if you dispose of your "question list" and simply hear what your interviewee has to say, you'll ask smarter questions, get more interesting answers, and present a better story.

Ask simpler questions to generate simpler answers. When interviewing experts, there is a tendency to let them get away with giving long, drawn out, complex, and incomprehensible answers. The problem is that journalists don't like to admit that they don't know something or don't understand a complicated answer. But if you, a broadcast professional, don't "get it," what are the odds your audience will?

Nobody likes to feel or to look foolish, but it is your job to make sure that you get straightforward answers to your questions. Better to admit you don't understand something and try again for a simple answer than to leave your audience in the dark. After all, even your expert wants to be heard and understood. You'll find more on interview techniques in Chapter 15, *Interview Techniques—for Journalists, Talk Hosts & Music Personalities* in this book, but the basics are: be prepared, have genuine curiosity (it's obvious if you really *do* want to know something) and, of course, listen.

If you present the news in an interesting, topical and relevant way, the audience will consider it a reason to tune in, not tune out. Listeners will feel that they can't go a day without finding out what's going on, as explained through your newscast.

Top Tips from Reporters

Reporters from various newsrooms share their most important lessons:

- Talk to one listener at a time.

- Use silence; it's powerful.

- Avoid clichés.

- Get new ideas from calling on old story sources.

- "Off the record" means off the record. Don't "burn" your sources.

- Is collecting audio actuality or doing an interview worth the effort? Can you better use what little time you've got on another story?

- *Localize*. Know your city and use familiar terms for *things*.

- Keep a tease a *tease*. Make them want more later.

- Don't use the same lead that the reporter uses. It's lazy and boring and makes you look stupid.

- *REWRITE* all source material and use multiple versions. Don't use the eight o'clock copy at nine o'clock.

- Use one thought per sentence, one thought per actuality.

- Write to be *heard*. Maintain a sense of speech rhythm in your writing. Read it out loud before you read it on air.

- Avoid statistics if you can. Listeners don't usually remember them.

- No one knows what is in your sound recorder or computer but you. Only use the best and most powerful sounds.

- Save time by listening to recorded audio on the way back to your studio. Mentally have your multi-versions ready to go before you start editing.

- Make decisions. You will never get every detail into the story. Decide what goes in and what to leave out of each story version.

Valerie Geller—Geller Media International's Tips for Creating Powerful News

1. In the case of an urgent news story, get your facts first, and then worry about your presentation.

2. Describe things visually—paint word pictures.

3. Write shorter! Use fewer words but make them count. When in doubt, leave it out.

4. Use effective storytelling techniques; tell stories the way you would tell them to friends.

5. Use natural sound.

6. Stay objective! Keep your opinion out of the story, but put your humanity into it.

7. Really listen when you are interviewing. Ask simpler questions. Know when to ask a "what" and a "how" question versus a "yes" or a "no" question.

8. Understand your story well enough that if the copy blew away, you could continue the report.

9. Make the news part of your station's programming, not an interruption. Tease upcoming news between newscasts.

10. Present a solution for every problem, if possible.

More great ideas come from veteran newsman Ed Walsh. Walsh has worked with top stations and networks in Boston, Phoenix, and New York:

- Know when to file! The appetite of the news monster is insatiable. In the United States, radio news deadlines are rarely more than an hour away. Better to give the beast something accurate to chew on while you're collecting more information for a follow-up report.

- Wearing comfortable shoes cannot be overemphasized.

- The value of most press releases received rarely exceeds the cost of the bandwidth required to send them.

- In real estate, the top three attributes of a property are "location, location, location." In radio news, it's "local, local, local." That often means developing local angles to national or international stories.

- No verb in news writing is more overused than "say," as in, "Officials say…" Put some life into your copy! They don't "say": They "insist," "maintain," "claim," and so on.

- Avoid over-attribution. The name of the press flack for an agency is, in the vast majority of stories, not necessary to report. Officer Smith, in his capacity as spokesman, is "the police."

- Never lapse into non-conversational transitional phrases such as "closer to home" or "in other news." If you can't develop a clear, declarative lead, pose an interrogatory: "Have you ever…" It makes a much more plausible transition between stories.

- Establish presence by pre-filing when you won't be able to phone in, radio in, or send an audio file at the time of an event. If a reporter is to be at the airport for the Pope's 11:00 arrival, he can't file at 11:00; pre-file "The Pope is expected here shortly…"

- Remember, we're doing news, not history. Use the present tense wherever possible. Don't refer to "yesterday" unless chronology is crucial.

- Tell me a story—a true one, but a story.

- Never pass up a chance to go to the bathroom. Ever staked out a story in the early morning after having had too much coffee?

- Always say, "Yes!" when they offer you free food and drink.

Sharon Katchen is an award winning reporter. Her career has taken her from Denver to Los Angeles' all news KFWB. Katchen now reports for Fox News. Here is her advice to reporters:

Sharon Katchen's Creating Powerful Radio News Tips

- Quality never goes out of style.

- Don't run with rumors.

- Keep your views out of the news.

- Take notes; sound recording devices can fail.

- Accuracy; accuracy; accuracy.

- Report fully and fairly. Omitting major facts or viewpoints is bad reporting.

- It's not news to barge into a disaster or crime scene and ask a victim, "How do you feel?"

- Listen. The best questions come from answers.

- Good reporting and good sound make good radio.

- If it is not clear to you, it's not clear to the listeners.

Veteran newsman Mark Howell spent decades as the award-winning news director of KCWR/KUZZ in Bakersfield, CA. He now consults and teaches broadcasting. Howell passes along some of his wisdom:

Mark Howell's Creating Powerful Radio News Tips

- *Grab 'em with the lead.* Your first sentence must make listeners care, or they will mentally and/or physically tune you out.

- *Don't pull punches.* Reject euphemisms. Translate bureaucratic language to English. Speak the language of the common people, but clean up the grammar.

- *Concentrate on what politicians do, not so much on what they say.* Let those who are affected speak. Be skeptical of official pronouncements. Follow the money.

- *Natural sound* can be just as important as a talking head in helping to illustrate a story.

- *Every word must matter.* Leave out the adjectives and cut the clichés. Write the facts in your copy; let the sound supply the emotion.

- *When interviewing, LISTEN!* Use each answer to lead to the next question. The only stupid question is the one you didn't ask.

- *Look for story ideas in out-of-town media.* The Internet makes this easy.

- *Don't waste time* pursuing a story the local newspaper or TV stations have already done, unless you can genuinely advance it, not just repeat it with a sound bite. Look for the "what happens next" angle. Invest your time in stories the other local media haven't covered.

- *Get professional voice training* if you need it; it is worth the cost.

- *Understand the technical basics of sound reproduction* and develop an ear for high fidelity. Make sure you understand how to take care of your equipment and how to use it correctly. Then, don't accept bad audio in your own work. It's better to have no sound in your story than bad sound.

Denise Jimenez-Adams has worked in both TV and radio as a reporter and anchor from Chicago to New York City.

Denise Jimenez-Adams's Words of Advice

- Work as hard at communicating with your bosses and co-workers as you do with your audience. Communication is not an art well-practiced in the broadcast business.

- Know your boundaries—and those of the station.

- Practice, practice, practice ad-libbing factually so that your spontaneity with the news doesn't tarnish your station's reputation or your own.

- Words can be swords. Choose them carefully for an impact that enhances understanding of the story, not of you.

- News services are important resources, but not always an appropriate style to emulate.

- Read, read, read, for content and style, for emulation, and for information. Be a sponge forever.

- Don't assume:

  a) That you know more than your audience

  b) That your audience knows more than you

  c) That your opinion is welcome or important.

- Create your own style in writing and delivery.

- Experience what your audience experiences so you can ask the questions that matter.

- Communicate the facts that are needed and tailor the emotion to the situation.

- FEEL…and they will feel with you.

The résumé of award-winning writer, journalist, and author of *¡Se Habla Dinero!*, Lynn Jimenez, includes KCBS and KGO in San Francisco.

Lynn Jimenez's Creating Powerful Radio News Tips

- Take a breath.
- Pace yourself.
- Learn how to fix any equipment you use.
- Never throw away any phone number—EVER.
- The news crew is not your family, no matter what management says.
- Be comfortable with change. Versatility means survival.
- Have a conversation; don't lecture.
- You are a human being. You are worthwhile and so is everyone else.
- Remember that broadcasting is a small world.
- Have fun.

CHAPTER 20

Beyond Powerful Radio
In Case of Emergency

"The definition of insanity: doing the same thing over and over
again and expecting different results."
—*Albert Einstein*

Imagine the worst. If a radio station has limited news staff and most of the programming is syndicated or voice-tracked, how will you best serve your audience if an earthquake strikes, a record breaking blizzard or snowstorm hits, or there's a fast moving tornado, fire, flood, toxic spill, or a crazed gunman active at a local school? Are you prepared? What do you do? When disaster strikes, how can you be at your best, or at least not at your worst?

This has actually happened in several markets in the United States. Stations have failed the public in their time of need. And, next time, without advance preparation, it could be your city, your station, and your listeners. The answer is to prepare for *anything* that can happen and have a contingency plan in place so that all members of your staff know what to do when an emergency event occurs.

Because of economic demands and technological shifts, many stations have cut their news staffs. Some have done away with local news. Others have abandoned news altogether. If your station uses mostly network, satellite-delivered or even voice-tracked local programming, there may be times where there is no one at your radio station at all. So what can you do

237

when the big live news event happens? How do you respond when there is news so important that the lives, well-being, or safety of your audience is at stake?

One American "wakeup call" for broadcasting came on January 18, 2002 at 1:40 in the morning. It was a frigid night in Minot, North Dakota, when disaster struck.

Reporter Eric Magnuson wrote the story of the day the news went missing, for *The Nation* magazine:

> A freight train, barreling through the town, went off the tracks, causing freight cars to scatter along the rails like a loose pack of cards. Five tank cars carrying anhydrous ammonia ruptured, filling the area with a poisonous gas cloud. But a public warning over radio wasn't broadcast for nearly ninety minutes. One person died, and more than three hundred were injured in the incident. Jennifer Johnson lived two blocks away from the derailment. She heard the crash, then watched the ammonia cloud roll toward her house. She searched in vain for information on what had happened. The phone lines were out so she couldn't call 911. Johnson told the Bismarck Tribune. "The only thing on the radio was music—no one was telling us what happened or what to do." She tuned the dial through every station in town, but after an hour without hearing an announcement, she gave up and turned the radio off. She said: "We didn't know what the chemical would do to us."

What happened in Minot reflected what was to become a nationwide problem: media consolidation left many radio stations nearly empty at night. At the time of the accident, Clear Channel owned six of Minot's eight stations, including the designated emergency announcement station. The one person who was at the stations during the accident did not respond to local authorities' calls because phone lines were jammed by residents calling in. The authorities tried activating the radio's Emergency Alert System to notify the public about what to do, which can be done without station personnel, but the EAS failed. Authorities had to pull out a phonebook and call local Clear Channel employees at their homes to tell them to broadcast an emergency message.

Broadcasters took note, vowing not to let the same thing happen again. But it can, and it has. I began my career as a news journalist and reporter, later working as a news director, then a program director. Now, as a consultant, it's my job to make the news departments of stations I work with the crown jewels of the enterprise. I find it painful to see how we've cut news, putting at risk our ability to react quickly, confidently, comprehensively, and reliably to an emergency in the communities we serve.

The very best solution would be to bring back reporting and news coverage. Many of the program directors and managers I work for would be only too happy to restore full service news departments to their stations, but if they don't have that option, then what?

There are some practical ways to get information out to the public by using the staff you've got, a little creativity and pulling together during a crisis.

More and more stations now face the unpleasant reality that even when money is tight, they must find a way to serve their cities, and have plans in place for the day their communities need critical information.

Alan Eisenson, program director of the Clear Channel cluster of stations in Sacramento, including news-leader KFBK and talk stations in San Francisco, lives with the reality of a news staff that's a lot smaller than it used to be. Still, he's prepared. "Because," says Eisenson, "even if you have a skeletal news staff, when events happen, and calls start pouring into the station, the receptionist or board op or webmaster is overwhelmed, and the GM yells 'Do something!', you have to have a plan."

Partnering with TV

Jerry Bell, managing editor of KOA radio news in Denver, who has been a newsman for nearly thirty years, Lee Harris, morning anchor of 1010 WINS in New York, also a former radio station owner, and Eisenson all agree that it is important to "form a partnership with your local TV news station. A plan to partner with TV is not something you should leave until the moment you need each other. Nurturing a relationship that's mutually beneficial should start now, if it hasn't already. One of the goals should be to set up your station so that your local TV news team can send its audio feed directly over your airwaves, to your entire air chain, including your music stations."

Eisenson suggests that in times of dire crisis you consider partnering with other radio stations in your market. Two major U.S. broadcast organizations, usually competitors, Clear Channel and Entercom, came together and pooled their resources to serve their community during the Hurricane Katrina disaster in New Orleans.

Since you can't predict whose transmitter will still be functioning in certain types of emergencies, Eisenson suggests, "Arrange in advance for any stations in your cluster or area that have news staffs to record reports for stations that don't. Have them sent over by WAN, or any other method you can get onto your airwaves. You may need to use any or all of your frequencies to disseminate life-saving information." Offer the same courtesy to your local TV partner. And *it's vital* that you teach your staff, from the all night automation supervisor to the front desk receptionist, *how to flip that switch to halt your automation* or a show in progress so you can go live, or change over to a live feed from your TV partner.

That's not all you'll need to teach your day-to-day operations folks. *Everyone* in your building can learn to handle an emergency news situation should one arise. Just as you train for a fire drill, practice a news drill with everyone in your company, so you'll have "all hands on deck" when you need them. The basic things your staff should know, in case of emergency, are listed below.

Geller Media International's Emergency Preparedness Points

Does Your Staff Know:

- How to maintain credibility in order to collect, gather and verify that information is correct before it goes to air?

- How to get in touch with local authorities on the scene who can give you credible information?

- What is the right time and place for listener calls?

- What role should Twitter™ and other social media play in disaster or major event coverage?

Make sure your staff knows that broadcasters need to adhere to the first rule of the Hippocratic Oath, given to all new physicians: "Do no harm." Credibility and correct information are vital. If someone calls and tells you it is safe to go into a building where a shooting took place, but it turns out one of the gunmen is still inside, you may have made the situation worse. If you broadcast the wrong information, such as reporting on the death or injury of a person who is neither dead nor injured, you cause unnecessary pain and suffering to their families. And, there are legal issues. This is why extra caution should be used when giving names of people affected by a disaster before they have been officially confirmed.

Rita Rich, President of Rita Rich Media Services, has experience working in national newsrooms. She also produced *The Jim Bohannon Show* for several years. Rich now consults and trains media representatives, including staff at the American Red Cross. Rich maintains you can train just about anyone on your staff to give accurate information in a crisis.

Rich says:

With proper preparation, anyone can do it... I hate to give away a deep, dark secret: This is not exactly rocket science or nuclear physics. If you can turn on a mic, and speak clearly, you can be on the air and parcel out useful information. Most staff have some writing experience and, especially in a crisis, [are] able to use their natural curiosity about what is happening. Remember...protect the identities of innocent people, victims and the property of others. When questioning people, you don't want to broadcast to thieves and vandals where [they] are vulnerable. Individuals shouldn't be made inadvertent targets to those with devious motives... The problem with springing people into motion in a high-adrenaline situation is that in their hurry to get information on the air, they forget what it is to make sound decisions as they start chasing stories and make amateur mistakes.

What this means in practice is that you'll need to make sure that *every* member of your staff understands that he or she will be expected to get the names of people they talk to and, where possible, the locations of emergency situations.

But the audience, in most cases, does not need to be told, nor should they be, that, for example, "According to nextdoor neighbor Jessie Langmoor, the Hopkins family is still on their six month trip to Europe. They have no idea that a tanker truck exploded on their private property, just a mile away from their luxurious country house at 222 Farm Drive in rural Tucker County...All local residents are being told to remain indoors until authorities can confirm that the air is safe to breathe."

All they need to know is: "A tanker truck carrying agricultural chemicals has exploded on Farm Drive in rural Tucker County. Fire and safety officials have advised all residents of Tucker County to remain indoors until advised that it is safe to go outside. We will keep you informed." And, of course, again, all members of the station staff must learn how to interrupt regular programming and turn on a microphone. This may seem obvious, but a "Board Op 101" training seminar should be part of basic employment orientation if you have a very small operation, where there may not be a professionally trained engineer, news, or air personality available in an emergency.

Managers should be clear about what they can and cannot ask of non-broadcast staff. While it may be reasonable to expect a professional reporter to get up in the middle of the night and come in to the station when a big story breaks, it may not be reasonable or safe to request the same thing of your sales or traffic personnel. Someone needs to be the one who will make decisions about whether wall-to-wall coverage is needed or if periodic updates make more sense. Know in advance who that person will be. Have a chain of command.

Rita Rich offers the checklist below of what your staff will need. However, first, she suggests, assemble a book of contacts and e-mail addresses, complete with telephone numbers to call should your computers go down, and include the following:

- County Emergency Operations Center [if you have one].

- Local Sheriff's Department/Police Department.

- State police troopers' barracks numbers.

- Fire and Rescue media relations/public affairs office direct and cell numbers.

1. Home or cell phone numbers of public information officers for after hours calls. Staff Checklist. Make certain everyone on your staff is familiar with news or press releases. Don't assume the person in the building when something happens will know. (Also include emergency contact numbers for Public Information Officers, or PIOs, of high-profile locations such as airports, seaports, power plants, and utilities.)

2. Make sure you have the Department of Homeland Security numbers as well. Many jurisdictions now have, or are in the midst of, organizing a local office of homeland security.

3. Have a ready page of contacts for your local Red Cross Chapters, and their emergency operations centers. [Often there are other first

responder citizen support groups to list as well, such as the Salvation Army or local shelters for people and even animals. There may be people unwilling to evacuate in a crisis if they fear for their pets.] Keep in mind that emergency volunteers are a good source of leads for stories. However, most will not be authorized to speak "on the record."

4. Know and list which local weather service personnel, or weather information services, your station or group ownership has contracted with.

5. Contact information of local hospital emergency rooms and hospital media relations/public affairs personnel, to find out about injured or dead being transported from a scene.

While Twitter, instant messaging, and other forms of social media [such as YouTube] can be useful, Rich warns the information must be verifiable.

Jerry Bell also recommends that you keep a "how to" guide in your studio for emergencies. Here's his advice for how it should work:

Have a plan. Keep it in a red binder marked 'Emergency' in your studio. You can also put it on a computer, but what happens when the power goes out? Also, you can tear pages out of a binder if you need to. A lot of stations already have a printout and/or a computer file of emergency contact phone numbers including cell numbers of fire fighters and police, FBI and FEMA. But it's useless unless everyone in the building knows how to get hold of it. Copies of the emergency plan should also be in the general manager's office and the program director's Office.

Jerry Bell's Emergency "Red Binder"

1. **Emergency numbers and contacts (in a place where everyone can find it!).** Take the time to compile a list of contacts for people with police, fire, hospital, utility companies, and homeland security. Get more than office numbers. You need cell phone numbers, and e-mail and twitter contacts. *It will take a little time to get an initial list. But once you have one, test call every six months to make sure the numbers are current. Make sure you have numbers of people who are designated to go on the air.*

2. **A map of where staffers live and numbers where they can be reached 24/7.** Know where your staff lives. Whoever is closest to an event can head toward the scene. Since they work for you, you can trust their information. They can also explain local landmarks and help describe where something is taking place. They may even know people who live nearby.

3. **Guidelines for crisis coverage interviews.** Before I list them, let me say that I believe that managers should manage and stay off the air. In a disaster situation management is critical. Listeners should hear voices they are used to. Your regular DJ or talk host can handle the air work. A manager needs to listen to what's going out over the air and make decisions that guide the coverage.

   ■ Stay calm. Take notes and limit speculation.

   ■ When talking to the public, ask what can they see, hear or smell. Does the caller have any expertise to comment on a particular aspect of what is taking place? If someone tells you what they think or believe, remember to say you'll check it out with authorities. Do not accept it as fact.

   ■ Check with emergency professionals on a continuous basis. Ask them about observations from callers. Take notes. Repeat frequently what you have been told. Scene set every ten minutes. "Here's what we know right now…"

   ■ Put yourself in the place of someone who lives nearby. What would you want to know? That's what to ask.

   ■ If possible, have someone screen calls. If that's not possible, put your B.S. detector on. Hoax calls are a possibility. My experience is that young teens and adults in their 20s are the most likely hoaxers.

4. **Basic information about what to do for earthquakes, tornadoes, or terrorist events.** You can get great information from your State Office of Emergency services, weather service, and Homeland Security. They have simple instructions about what to do in a variety of situations. Sometimes this simple information is the best information you can impart in an emergency.

5. **Instructions about when to dump commercials.** (You don't want to broadcast a spot for an airline in the middle of coverage about a plane crash.)

6. **You need street maps of your area and state. Invest in a good quality street map.** It helps to pinpoint where something is taking place. If you have power, and can use a computer, Google maps is also great. Make sure you have a TV monitor in your studio. If there is TV coverage it helps if your on-air person can see what is happening.

7. **Create a mission statement for what you want your station to do during a disaster.** If there's a disaster, what do you expect? Spell out expectations. Then provide a framework for decision making. First order of business is to get a general manager or program director involved ASAP.

Rita Rich offers a few more suggestions about how your staff—even an on-air staff who are not in the building and are not necessarily trained news people—can swing into action to help the station cover an emergency:

Her first suggestion: "Get someone trained to turn on the microphone and who can read information." Then decide who can be on the air, and who will be the producer making phone calls, pre-screening and prepping those you want to have live and on the air. This is where a team effort comes in. It's nearly impossible for one person to do all of this. You will need help.

Rich continues, "If the emergency occurs in the middle of the night, your board operator, or even security guard, might have to be the one who opens the mic and gets the job done. I prefer a two person team: One on air, the other to sift out information and callers who claim to be experts, or authorities, about a situation." [As an example of phony experts, Rich uses the long running phenomenon of Howard Stern listeners who begin a sup-posedly serious call and suddenly lunge into "pranking".] Rich continues, "During a crisis, tabloid influences…are going to need to be tamed. Caller ID and a list of names of authorized public information officers or spokes-persons can help you screen the goof-balls from your airwaves." Jerry Bell agrees a screener is important, if possible.

Howard B. Price, Director of Business Continuity and Crisis Manage-ment at ABC News, shares a trick he's used to eliminate "prank calls" during live coverage. He suggests, "Try asking a 'check' question only a legitimate caller would be able to answer. For example, here in New York City, I'll ask anyone claiming to be a cop if they know anyone in the 35th precinct. There is no 35th precinct. So any answer they give other than that means they're bogus."

During the Crisis

Alan Eisenson warns that "even if you're faced with a frantic public and a panicked manager, it's almost never a good idea to simply start throwing callers on the air." Eisenson adds that if your station does not normally use live phone calls, it's still a good idea to make sure your phone system is wired so it can go live on air, and that it has a delay.

Get a Press Pass Now

Jerry Bell says music stations can plan in advance, especially stations *without news departments*. "Get a press pass. If you have a van you use for remote broadcasts, promotions or sales events, consider getting closer to the scene and anchoring coverage from there... many cities require a press pass for vehicles to get to a disaster scene. Make sure you have such a permit. Local press passes for some of your staff are also a great idea."

Develop a Clock

Rita Rich recommends, "Develop a broadcast clock, and stick to it during the time of emergency. In emergency situations, regular time checks are important. For emergencies lasting days -- time, day, date, and even a year can help a person who is trapped inside a building because of snow, or collapse, stay connected to the outside world and reality." If coverage of the disaster is causing your station financial hardship, or if money or goods are needed to help cope with the effects of a disaster, Rich advises turning to your sponsors. If you need it, during an emergency, the programming clock can, "provide opportunities for sponsorship or underwriting. Work with your station's traffic department to flesh out the possibilities (for sponsoring time checks, weather reports, etc)."

Prepare a Script

"Providing standard formats will help your station fulfill its obligation to get on the air with breaking news," Rich says, "even if an amateur needs to get the ball rolling, until professional air staff can take over. Provide the script so that an amateur can just fill in the blanks and get information out to the public. Script out what a person will say when a program is interrupted for an emergency. Script the questions a person should ask while screening a call for possible live broadcast."

Rich suggests any non-professional broadcaster who may be pressed into duty does the following:

- Identify the name and title of the person either calling in or who is being called.

- Where are they located? Get the location of the incident or the person.

- What is the situation they want to report?

- Find out (off air) the name and contact number of the person who is coming on duty next, who can continue to provide information for you.

- When might an update on the situation become available?

SUCCESSFUL COVERAGE — CASE STUDY
The Flood of the Century

On March 28, 2009, in Fargo, North Dakota, the Red River, driven by snow and rain, running over frozen ground, crested at nearly forty-one feet—twenty-two feet past flood stage. As the Red River began to rise, Scott Hennen, station co-owner and talk show host at AM 1100, "The Flag", and Eagle 106.9 FM understood the magnitude of the job ahead. He recalled the last time he'd been involved in a flood disaster. It was back in 1997, in Grand Forks. Hennen, then a program host on KCNN, would never forget broadcasting live in studio as flood waters were rising and a raging fire burned a few blocks away. At the time, a young student he'd met while guest-lecturing at the University of North Dakota had been a tremendous help. Mark Pfeifle volunteered by helping with late night airshifts and on the ground coverage. KCNN won an Edward R. Murrow award for the coverage that year. Now, without a news staff, Hennen knew he needed some help.

Hennen reached out again to that same young man. Mark Pfeifle, a former deputy national security advisor for communications and global outreach for the White House, was now working as Vice President, of S4 Inc, Systems Media Group. Pfeifle got on a plane immediately, bringing along others, including a web expert.

Hennen set the team up using the traditional tools supplied by his radio stations. Mark Pfeifle's crew of political campaign experts added their expertise of working across multiple media platforms that included: developing a website and using tools like YouTube, Facebook, Twitter and Flickr. In forty-eight hours, the team launched "The Flood Channel Network", a website carrying live updates, streaming video and announcements from FEMA officials and members of the city council. North Dakota State University journalism students, armed with mobile Flip-cams (personally purchased for them by Hennen), were able to provide first-hand reporting from the disaster area.

"It turned into C-SPAN for floods, essentially," Pfeifle says. "Student reporters were covering stories from places like Valley City, fifty miles away and posting on the website. We also got dramatic video from listeners. One showed a family rescued by helicopter as they were trying to save their house. They'd gotten trapped as their house became an island."

Corporate sponsors pitched in by supplying phones for emergency workers, supplies to keep volunteers warm, hamburgers and drinks to feed them. The effort worked far better than anyone had hoped. Hennen, Pfeifle and their team did more than reporting on the need for sandbags and the cresting water; they helped to assemble an army of volunteers to fill sandbags, reinforce levies and build emergency dikes. They got word to the community about impassible roads and traffic conditions. Hennen recalls, "We had traffic jams in a city that has no traffic jams."

"We were able to get actionable information out quickly and reliably at low cost, in a flexible and unique way," Pfeifle remembers. "There were thousands of hits to the Flood Channel website and the ratings skyrocketed."

After the worst is over, you may still have work to do, and people may still expect information from you. Provide it, or tell them where to find it. Alan Eisenson points out that for ongoing emergencies, "If you voice-track, make sure the talent (whether they're in the market or not) re-cut their tracks to reflect the breaking events." You might also want to tell listeners where else they can go in your market, ideally within your cluster, for information that will help them follow the aftermath of an emergency.

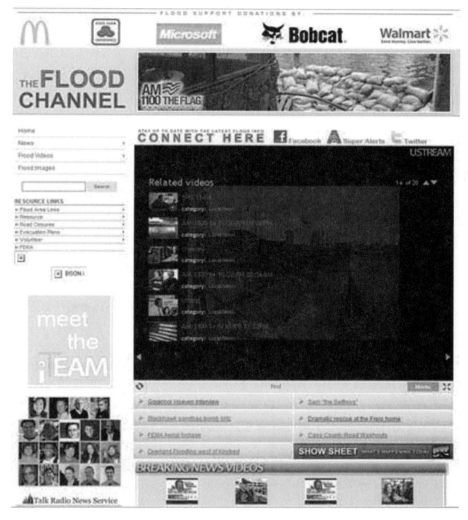

In Fargo, North Dakota, the broadcast staff at AM 1100 and Eagle 106.9 created
The Flood Channel Website to serve their audience with updated information
during the crisis.

Scott Hennen shares lessons he learned from the experience of covering the flood—that may be useful to stations caught in crisis that needs coverage – yet may be without benefit of a large (or any) newstaff:

Scott Hennen's Tips—
Covering An Emergency Without a News Staff

- Cultivate relationships with professors of communications or journalism at local colleges or universities. Recruit the best students to potentially become reporters for your station.

- Have a budget for emergency supplies and equipment, or a trade account at a place where you can get them.

- Contact your best clients during the time of crisis and see what they can do to help. Don't forget to ask what you can do to help them.

- Use all media: video, web, radio, phones. You can set up a Flood Channel, an Earthquake Channel or any other emergency channel within hours.

- Get out your PDA or your contact files and remind yourself of whom you know. Friends and business associates will all want to help, and some of them may be experts.

- During the heat of the crisis, drop regular programming—go to full coverage of what is happening.

During Disaster Coverage: Surviving at the Station

Is your station ready? Do you know what supplies you need to have at the station if a disaster strikes? From bottled water to self-fueled heaters to backup batteries and breakfast bars—you need to pack a "Station Emergency Kit." Howard B. Price, Director of Business Continuity and Crisis Management for ABC News, has practical and carefully prepared lists of what you need in order to survive at your station in case of emergency. You can find all of this information on his website: *http://www.mediadisasterprep. com.* The site contains information on personal and professional preparedness. Price warns:

In a "worst-case scenario" emergency, assume you will get no outside help for seventy-two hours. Staffers may be away from their families for some time, depending on the nature of the emergency. So help them develop their own personal emergency plans, including an emergency communications plan, to keep relatives safe and in touch while their loved ones are away.

It's important for anyone planning for any kind of crisis to understand there is a difference between managing that crisis—responding to the needs of the moment (disaster response)—and maintaining continuity of operations (the process of bringing your operations back roughly to where they were when the crisis hit).

You may think you have no time for emergency training...until there's an emergency. If your staff meetings can spare even ten minutes of time, that's time you can devote to reinforcing some of these strategies. It's time that will pay off well, on the day disaster strikes.

CHAPTER 21

Beyond Powerful Radio
Citizen Journalism

"The most fundamental change we're witnessing
today is the power returning to the audience.
Choice is suddenly in their control
and they intend to use it."
—*Mark Ramsey, author* Making Waves

Everything Old is News Again...

As many news staffs at radio stations have been cut to the bone, for economic reasons, newsrooms have increasingly been relying on "Citizen Journalism." Although that's a fancy new name for it, citizen journalism has been around since the early days of news-talk radio. Broadcasting has historically been interactive, with extensive use of the "eyewitness report." Whenever there's a major local or national event—an earthquake, hurricane, or car accident—news and talk radio have always utilized phone lines to allow audience members experiencing or witnessing the events to participate.

One of the first instances of Citizen Journalism in video format was the "Zapruder film," footage captured by a bystander of the assassination of American President John F. Kennedy in 1963. A man with a movie camera, in the crowd, filmed the tragedy for the nation to witness. What has changed over the decades is the technology. Now, with recording devices cheaply and readily available, more citizen journalists are walking around with cameras and phones in their pockets. Citizen journalists are literally everywhere. Whether it's footage of a natural disaster, a soldier's view from a war zone, celebrity news, or a major traffic jam, radio and TV stations all want to have access to this growing universe of raw audio and video for their airwaves and websites. From school shootings to global terrorist attacks, news and talk radio have come to expect and rely on instantaneous reports and contributions from members of their audience to help cover events. In many cases, citizen journalists are being used to replace or augment paid staff broadcasters formerly sent to cover these events. The work formerly done by professionals, who once gave these events context and perspective, is now often delegated to citizen journalists who "work" for free.

Anyone Can Become a Citizen Reporter

Information is coming from everywhere. Witnesses using Twitter, the micro-blogging instant messaging service, got word to the public of a gunman who had invaded a cable TV network headquarters near Washington, DC. The news, including a photo of the armed man, was out within minutes of the intruder entering the building. It came to some viewers as radio or TV news, and, much later, as a newspaper story. But it arrived first and fastest in the form of a text or tweet, to screens in people's pockets and on their desktops. As with other big and fast-moving news events, like the landing of a jet airliner in New York City's Hudson River in 2009 and the 2008 Mumbai massacre, millions of Twitter clients and IM users functioned as amateur news reporters.

Tech users are also, with more deliberation and purpose, becoming international gossips, opinion mongers, and tastemakers. Who needs the paparazzi when the guy parking cars at an expensive restaurant is willing to snap a photo of today's hot video star and her new BFF (best friend forever) fighting over a lipstick, then send it to a snarky website that also has a branded TV show? For those who prefer more "serious" applications for new media, there's plenty of opportunity to use Twitter (and by the time you read this, there may be several other sites filling the same function, or an entirely new one!) and texting or IM services to spread word of traffic jams, accidents, and fires.

In addition to the breaking news, research shows that listeners and viewers are flocking to websites to get "the rest of the story…" or to "see" photos or video of what they're hearing on the radio. They're using new media tools to share information with each other, and they're willing, in

"Would you please elaborate on 'then something bad happened'?"

fact they are happy, to share it with you. But citizen journalists present another issue: there is a lot of information coming forward that needs to be checked out. "We don't have the personnel to look into everything," Millennium Radio New Jersey VP of news and network programming Eric Scott, told *Inside Radio*. Scott compares tweets to eyewitness reports that don't always mesh with the facts but are still useful. "It may give you something you can go on when you're investigating the story further." (It's worth noting that Millennium Radio New Jersey newsroom has a staff of twenty.)

Some broadcasting managers have cleverly taken the natural affinity of a generation to communicate instantly and fluidly with their peers, transported these consumers of new media to their news rooms, trained them, and made them part of their teams. A not-so-secret "secret" about footage being posted to stations' websites is that some of the best of it is coming not from citizen journalists, but from the stations' own staffs, who may not have carried cameras or video recorders in the past. The audience doesn't care who took the footage; they care that it helps tell the story. But, is the story accurate?

Accuracy—Making Sure You Get It Right

The benefits of using citizen journalists are great. Ask any news director, and you're likely to hear that he or she depends to a certain extent on being able to send and receive "tweets" or instant messages to and from the audience. But these same news directors will readily admit that having un-vetted information flowing into your station is risky. At some point, before a report from a "citizen" goes into your news, you need to check it out. In other words, if the public is to be able to rely on your product, at some point a real journalist is going to have to work on the story. That's your quality control.

Credibility Check

By using citizen journalists, you expose your station to the possibility of putting out incorrect information, and damaging your reputation as a credible news resource. There's the scenario where someone with an axe to grind or a political point to make will feed you images that have been cropped or altered to slant the story. It's happened, and when it does, it is hard to take back. One example: An international news reporting service telling the story of a political incident between soldiers and a crowd of protesters that turned violent aired citizen journalist video of the soldiers attacking an unarmed man. The citizen journalist had cropped out the portion of the man's hand that showed both sides were armed. Be aware: There are hoaxes, and publicity seekers. There are well intentioned people who simply don't know what to make of what they're seeing or hearing.

These things have happened, and they are bound to happen again. When events of the day affect the lives, well-being or safety of the audience, that's when you not only need the news, but you need news that is trustworthy. You have a chance to serve your public by broadcasting reliable information. It's an opportunity for your news or talk radio station to grow its base by attracting new audiences to your format—people who may come to check on the big event and then perhaps stick around.

Many listeners regard the news as their insurance policy. They listen to make sure the world is safe. But what about an insurance policy *for* your news? What is to stop the station from broadcasting audio or video that's been concocted on someone's home computer editing station? How do you know whether what you are seeing is real? As always, it will come down to your people. Your people, though you may have fewer of them, now must become more expert editors, fact checkers, skeptics and, as always, powerful storytellers.

Give Context—Not Just Content!

A responsible, trained and credible producing, programming, and on-air team will be more important than ever in giving the stories covered more context and meaning. Raw video or audio is just that—it usually tells only part of the story. The background and the story's possible implications need to be provided by your station.

Your station's *reputation* is what you have to offer "citizen journalists." Your good name, call letters, branding, and credibility are the reason they want their photos and sound posted on your website and on your airwaves, as opposed to simply putting them on their own blogs or posting on You Tube.

There is a benefit to both sides. Without your news and talk personalities, it's just pictures and sound. As anyone who has ever conducted an interview or taken a call on the air can tell you, not everyone with a story to tell is a good storyteller. And when you *do* get a story from your audience that sounds almost too good or too spicy to be true, check it out. Maybe it is.

The advice on "hiring right" in Chapter 19, *Creating Powerful News,* from *ABCnews.com* executive Bernard Gershon is even more important when you consider choosing "citizen journalists," or using their content. To use "citizen journalism" responsibly, you need someone in the editor's chair who can take that raw footage or audio and use it to tell a truthful story that will touch your audience. But by using Gershon's criteria, you might find that one of your citizen journalists could become your next great hire.

Citizen journalists can work hand in hand with your staff to generate talkable topics or human interest stories on a slow news day. If someone has filed great audio or video for you from the street, keep their contact information and invite them back if you think they can add something to your product. With all the talk about citizen journalists as the future of the industry, creating powerful communication in the age of citizen journalism will depend at the end of the day on something as old as communication itself: Tell the truth, make it matter and never be boring.

*Note: There's find more about using Citizen Journalists in Chapter 20, *In Case Of Emergency.*

CHAPTER 22

Beyond Powerful Radio
Traffic & Weather Together

"The ability to communicate color, content, and drama
in thirty seconds is rare and glorious."
—*Doug Harris*

Traffic and weather "together" are important. Traffic and weather are often the reasons people tune in regularly to news and news-talk radio. Traffic and weather reports should be accurate and delivered consistently during key drive times. Some stations provide this service twenty-four hours a day, and the information is often available online.

Since most traffic and weather information can be instantly obtained from a variety of sources, the advantage radio has is in the personalities who deliver the data. It is useful to know that there has been a four-car collision on the road ahead of you caused by a sudden hailstorm, but it feels better to know that the person giving you the information understands what it is like to have your new car hit by a piece of ice the size of a golf ball.

Another Hot One

Listeners respond to and seek accurate information. While many radio stations or networks may choose to have a relationship with a TV meteorologist or an accredited weather service to provide forecasts, trained meteorologists may not be the most scintillating personalities.

It is best if your station can have weather reports given by someone who sounds likeable and conversational. If possible, help train your weather presenters. Make sure they talk as if they are speaking to only one person, and not "all you folks out there."

A lot of explicit data about high-pressure systems or other technical information may be very interesting to the meteorologist and his or her colleagues, but unless the forecast concerns something extreme, such as a tornado, flooding, or a snowstorm, stick to the basics.

What would most people say if someone asked them, "Is it going to rain?" "How hot is it going to be today?" or "What's it like outside?" The answer is what should be in your report. Listeners need to know what to wear, how to dress their kids, or whether to bring an umbrella. Toward the end of the week, people begin to plan their weekends. Tell them what they can expect, in plain language.

Non-meteorologists often do a great job with the weather because they are not experts. One Los Angeles announcer consistently engages his listeners with creative brief weather updates, such as: "Aren't you glad you got that haircut? Another hot one today. Sunshine, high of 83."

Traffic: Bad for Commuters, Great for Radio

If you have ever been stuck in a traffic jam, you know how vital the information can be. Even satellite radio networks offer local traffic updates. Stations have found ratings and financial benefits by promoting and delivering frequent reports at specific times. Audiences will tune in at the exact minute they have been trained to expect the latest traffic report.

Since so much of the information that radio provides can be found elsewhere, once again, it is the presenters who can make a big difference here. Personalities make your information not simply accurate, but genuinely powerful radio. Broadcast personality Caroline Feraday was the "Flying Eye" over London, first for Capital Radio, then for BBC Radio's Five Live.

> Your listeners are counting on you to make them feel better. If they are stuck in a jam, they need you to validate their frustration, anger, or annoyance with that delay.
> I know this sounds obvious, but it is easy to be blasé about a traffic jam that will really mess up someone's day. Every single person that is in their

car is there for a reason. Maybe it's because they have to be somewhere on time? Perhaps they have to pick the kids up? Or they want to make a good impression at a job interview or a first date? Maybe their favorite TV show starts soon.

Whatever the reason, listeners want to know if they are going to be late and they want to know why. It makes them feel better. Maybe they can call ahead? Perhaps leave extra time for the journey or travel a different route? Maybe they can do nothing but wait, but, either way, that mention of their problem works psychologically.

Credibility Matters

Be on time, get it right. Never say, "There are no stalls or accidents." You are tempting fate. Instead try "No reports of any stalls or accidents." If you declare, "It's all clear," the situation may immediately change and you'll lose credibility. What you said moments ago may no longer be correct.

On the other hand, some facts do not need to be repeated day in, day out. Caroline Feraday says this:

> A gripe of mine is telling a bunch of commuters the stuff that they can work out for themselves. Don't waste their time. If there is always a half a mile backup at the Blackwall Tunnel, then do you need to tell them every bulletin? At the very max remind them sometimes, "Usual jam at the Blackwall Tunnel. How do you put up with that every day?"

One frequent listener complaint is: "I tune in to find out what is happening on the roads, but they almost never report on the mess I'm stuck in, or they'll report an accident that doesn't exist. While I'm hearing that, I'm sailing through that area. They just don't get it right."

To counter that complaint, if you report traffic make sure to check periodically to find out if accidents you have reported have been cleared or not.

Keep your listeners from becoming bored during traffic reports. Each person should be able to "see" what it is you are talking about. Caroline Feraday stresses the importance of making a movie in the listener's mind:

> Try to talk in pictures, and say what you see. If you can't see the crash but you can see smoke, then tell the listener that. If you can see the ambulance coming along the hard shoulder, then tell them. Make it visual.
>
> Very rarely will a story change as rapidly whilst you are on the air, nor will it matter to people as much as the travel news does. How we are all addicted to watching those car chase tapes on the television! Have

you watched how the traffic slows down to see a crash? We're naturally voyeuristic.

Very few of your listeners will actually be stuck in a traffic jam at the moment you mention it, so for the rest of them—make it interesting.

I once did a travel bulletin for BBC Radio Five Live in which I mentioned that a church roof had blown off in high winds. A famous film director visiting the studio remarked, "What an amazing vignette of life." It was true—you can say so much about life in those 60 seconds. That church roof was now blocking the main road through a sleepy Devon village.

"Where" Before "What"

Give the location of the traffic holdup before you detail what happened. People first want to know, "Is this near me?" Caroline Feraday puts it this way:

> Travel the listeners' journey with them. If there's a queue, or backup, on the motorway, it's no good saying, "there's an accident on the M25, causing it to back up." As a driver, you'll hit the back of the mess first. "You're going to come to a halt at around Leatherhead. I know it's miles up, but I can see that the traffic doesn't really start moving again until you've passed the accident the other side of the Staines turning!" Oh, and people don't know the numbers of the junctions, so tell them exactly where they are. On what road is it? Where on that road? In which direction? Also, listeners hate a mispronunciation. Plus if there's a colloquial name for a junction, or landmark, learn it.
>
> By the way, if you know the roads where the problems are, then I've found it helps to be able to picture it in my head. If you can do that, then you'll barely use your script. "Heading around the M25—you know the stretch where it goes down to two lanes just before the A10? Well, I know you get stuck there most days, but actually, it's going to take you about twenty minutes more today because some poor guy has broken down in the inside lane."

What Is Your Source?

Traffic presenters—make sure you know where your information comes from and how old each item is. Cultivate a healthy relationship with the police department or highway patrol. Can you easily contact them to obtain the fresh, updated information? Does your newsroom monitor police and highway patrol scanners or websites and check press releases from the state about highway construction projects?

Maintain an accurate phone and contact list with twenty-four-hour emergency numbers and keep it where anyone who might need it can find it in the event of a big problem during off hours. Your list should include not only highway patrol contacts but fire department, power and gas, and airport and railroad contacts, since these are all areas where an unusual incident can affect traffic and you may need to gather relevant information quickly.

Calling On the Cars

Does your station use "traffic spotters"—listeners who call from their mobile phones to report on various traffic jams? If so, credit your valuable resource, the caller: "NEWS 105 traffic spotter Ben in Hampton says he's looking at the big rig truck that lost its load of chickens on Highway 5; Ben tells us he's watching the police try to round up the birds. It sounds like it may take a little while to get everything back to normal since the chickens are outrunning the cops." To keep current, ask the spotters to call you back or find out if it is all right to phone them back, to see if there is new information.

There is a place for personality and humor in traffic and travel reports. Obviously you never fool around with a serious situation when lives are at stake, but there is a lot of room in the mix for having fun and playing off the show personalities and presenters.

I once heard a traffic report about an accident involving an overturned truck carrying condoms. Not only did the spill cause a twenty-minute backup; it generated lots of comedy in the studio and for listeners stuck behind the "road full of rubbers" as well. The traffic story also became a news report.

Career On-Ramp

Traffic announcing and reporting can also be a great "entry" into broadcasting. Many have found that if you start out reporting traffic and do a professional job, it may open doors to other parts of the business for you.

Caroline Feraday moved from reporting travel conditions in the United Kingdom to more prominent on-air roles. She offers some lessons she has learned:

> If you want to be part of a team, you simply have to play. Any anchor wants to be sure that you will make their show sound good. If you sound good when they ask you a question, then they will do it again and again until that is part of your role. If they feel nervous that you won't spark when asked to deviate from your script, then they will definitely try it less. It is worth trying, and you will soon get a feel for how much or how little you

should say in a segment. Don't feel you have to show off or be wacky for the sake of it. The listeners simply want you to be good company.

What about that script then? I reckon the fewer words you have on it, the better you'll be. It's not a memory test, though, so keep any facts you need at hand. If you can keep the information in front of you down to the basics and chat around it, then you're more likely to speak like a normal human being.

Lots of on-air personalities have worked as traffic reporters. It is a good way either to start your broadcasting career or take it in a new direction. Many traffic services also offer newscasts to their client stations. If you work for a traffic service, you may have a chance to add news writing and anchoring to your list of skills. This area of the business tends to provide a little more job security than other parts of broadcasting. As long as there are people in cars, there will be a need for traffic reporting.

CHAPTER *23*

Beyond Powerful Radio
Newswriting

"Write to express, not to impress."
—*Mervin Block,* Writing Broadcast News

The Long and Short of It

Anyone who writes knows it's harder to write shorter, but less is often more effective. Newspapers and the Internet specialize in detail. Radio cannot compete for sheer tonnage of information. Radio's job, and yours, is to get information out quickly and succinctly. When you hear it on the radio, it's news. When you read it in the paper, it's history. Put in the big stuff, the important things that you would tell friends. Give enough information so listeners can think about a story and discuss it at their dinner tables.

Author George Orwell was deeply concerned with the effect of words, especially those that cause confusion. In his essay "Politics and the English Language," Orwell set down the following writing rules that will probably serve you well, regardless of which language you are using.

Never use a metaphor, simile, or other figure of speech you are used to seeing in print. Never use a long word where a short one will do. If it is possible to cut a word out, always cut it out. Never use a passive phrase where you can use the active. Never use a foreign phrase, a scientific word, or a jargon word if you can think of an everyday English equivalent. Break any of these rules sooner than say anything outright barbarous.

Mervin Block is America's newswriting guru. He wrote the news for CBS television for years. Many generations of American news journalists have read his books or attended his television newswriting workshops at Columbia University in New York. He has written several books. What follows is from Block's book, *Writing Broadcast News*:

Bad News

- ***Don't label news as good or bad.*** What may be bad for some listeners is good for others. Heavy rain may be bad for pedestrians, motorists, and sunbathers, but it can be good for farmers, taxi drivers, and umbrella vendors. "Good news" abounds on broadcasts when the prime rate drops, but for listeners, a drop in the prime can be either positive or negative. Anyone who takes out a home improvement loan will benefit from lower prime rates and could save on adjustable rate home mortgages and similar borrowings. However, for other listeners, lower rates are "bad news." Many consumers like high interest rates because they are able to earn strong returns on investments like money market funds or U.S. government securities.

- ***Don't tell your audience that a story is distressing, interesting, or amusing.*** The best policy is to stick to the facts, tell the news, and let the listeners decide. If the "good news" or "bad news" is tied to a specific person or group, characterizing the news may be valid. For example: "Mayor Murphy received good news today from his doctor," or, "The IRS has bad news for taxpayers."

Lead-Ins, Lead-Outs

There are some definite do's and many don'ts for writing into and out of correspondents' reports and actualities. In *Writing Broadcast News*, Mervin Block advises:

- ***Don't use the same key words the reporter uses, and don't introduce him or any speaker with the very words he starts with.*** Violation of this rule produces "the echo-chamber effect." It sounds—and resounds like this: "Good evening. Governor Goober warned today he's fed up with state employees who loaf on the job." Instantly, we hear Goober say: "I'm fed up with state employees who loaf on the job." Listener: "Haven't I heard that somewhere before?"

- *Don't steal the reporter's thunder.* Although the lead-in for a hard news story should hit a few highlights, the anchor shouldn't skim off all the reporter's best material. Otherwise, the reporter's account will seem anticlimactic and will seem as though the reporter got his news from the anchor.

- *Don't write a soft lead-in for a hard news story.* A soft lead-in may work for a feature story, but a hard news story calls for a hard lead-in. A lead-in is something like a store's display window. A dime store doesn't dress a window with diamonds, and a diamond merchant doesn't display dimes. Hard news, like diamonds, deserves an appropriate showcase.

- *Don't write a lead-in that conflicts with the reporter's script.* This may seem basic, but every once in a while we hear a reporter say something that contradicts what the anchor's lead-in has said. That's a mislead-in.

- *Don't overstate or oversell.* The lead-in should not promise or suggest more than the reporter is going to deliver. It should adhere to standards of journalism, not hucksterism or showmanship.

- *Don't be vague.* Sometimes, because of the way newscasts are put together, we don't know precisely what the reporter in the field is going to be saying, or which segment of a speech is going to be used. We have to write "blind" (i.e., without saying anything specific). We put down only enough words to allow the report to start: "The chairman of the city transit agency, Lionel Train, spoke out today on the agency's problems..." Writing "blind," like flying "blind," can be risky. Wherever you can, say something substantive: "The chairman of the city transit agency, Lionel Train, said today he'll clean up the agency's problems within six months..."

- *Don't use a faulty "throw line" at the end of the lead-in to introduce a reporter.* If the next voice we're going to hear is not that of the reporter but of a woman taking an oath of office, you'd confuse a listener by saying, "Jerry Jarvis has the story." One way to handle that "throw line" is to say, "Jerry Jarvis looked on as Mary Barton took the oath..."

- *Most lead-ins run less than twenty seconds, and a few run barely five seconds.* No matter what it takes to do the job, no matter what the length, every word matters. The shorter the lead-in, the greater the need for every word to carry its weight.

Words Count

Everybody complains about bad writing. Broadcast journalism trainer and author Deborah Potter worked for years as a news reporter on CNN and CBS-TV and radio. Potter maintains:

> Your staff won't learn if no one teaches them. Much of what we hear on the air is badly written. Good writing is not magic. It is a craft. It can be learned and it can be improved, but first everyone has to know that it matters.

Potter adds it is important to offer regular feedback about writing. "Words count. If you want listeners to tune in and believe what they hear, you need to care about what is being said. Praise good writing and you will get more of it."

Deborah Potter's "Write Stuff"

1. Take time at the front end to understand the story. Candy Crowley of CNN puts it this way: "The less time you have to write, the more time you should take to think about it." Try telling someone in six words or less what your story is about. If you can't, you will have trouble writing it.

2. Choose information that will tell the story best. Avoid the cramming impulse. Select specific details—the brand of beer, the make of the car—that will bring the story to life. Leave the rest out.

3. Organize your information in a logical way. If it helps, make an outline. Keep related facts together. Answer questions as they come up. Know where you are going before you start.

4. Tell it, don't report it. Imagine that every story you write begins, "Hey Mom, guess what I just found out!" Or, "Honey, you won't believe what happened today!"

5. Rewrite. Revise what you have written by looking at it backwards. Look closely at the end of every sentence, paragraph, and story. That is where you want the strongest words, because that is where they have the strongest impact. Crisp endings are one simple way to sharpen your writing.

6. Put your writing on a diet, and think of adjectives as empty calories. Particularly the adjectives so overused in broadcast news: senseless, horrible, tragic, ironic, and the like.

7. Do use active verbs that add energy to your writing. The right verbs do more than convey information. You build understanding and make the audience care. It's the difference between a story saying that a bus was involved in an accident and a story that tells how the bus skidded down an embankment, rammed into a guardrail, and flipped into a ravine. Active verbs in the active voice are the hallmark of writing that communicates clearly. The active voice tells you who. Then leave out all the words you do not need.

See it on Your Radio

People do not think of radio as a visual medium. But a talented storyteller who writes with dazzling detail can tap into all of the imagery and emotion stored in the listener's brain and make him or her feel that they really are "seeing" the story. While telling a story in just a few words is key in writing powerful news copy, the visual element is important to keep listeners engaged. Many songwriters have mastered this in their lyrics. Take for example, Bob Dylan's "Mr. Tambourine Man." When you hear the line "To dance beneath a diamond sky with one hand waving free," you can see it. And that makes it more powerful.

In 2004, I was in Australia during the Athens Summer Olympics. Part of my job was to listen to some of the Australian Broadcasting Corporation's coverage of the events. I didn't have much enthusiasm for an item that began, "Up next, it's the women's archery competition..." until I heard the reporter tell the story.

REPORTER: This young woman picked up a bow and arrow when she was just a child. Her parents are right here beside me. Now here's what she's got to do: Hit a black target the size of a grapefruit, across three football fields.

Two minutes ago, I could not have cared less about the women's archery competition. Now I was paying attention and fully engaged in the story being told. If you can get a listener to "see it" or "feel it," then they will care and pay attention.

Visual descriptions are especially important to men. Brain research shows that men are more stimulated by visual details, and language that describes events with accurate visual elements tends to make them pay closer attention to a story.

Sports announcers are the best in the business at visual description. They are mostly men, talking to men, in a way that men understand. If you have ever attended a baseball or football game, you will notice men listening to radios while they watch the game with their own eyes. The play-by-play announcers enhance the visual experience for these men.

Women, on the other hand, are emotive. If a woman can "feel" an emotional connection to a story, she is more likely to listen closely and take in the information. For a story to appeal to both men and women, it should deliver information using both visual and emotional language.

Here's an example from England. A reporter, working from a camera phone video taken by a bystander, paints the visual and emotional scene of a pit bull attack on a small child. He uses both kinds of language to make men and women see and feel what happened in this story:

> The boy and the pit bull were about the same size. The dog had its jaws embedded in the little boy's neck. The child screamed in terror and pain. Within moments you couldn't tell the difference between the red-and-white pattern in the child's shirt from the blood. And can you imagine how his mother felt, standing by helplessly as the vicious beast attacked her child?

Speak In Pictures

You can improve your visual writing and learn to speak more visually by imagining you are talking to a blind person. Start by seasoning your everyday off-air conversations with descriptive details. Use all the colors in your verbal paint box. Make observations of little things in life a part of your normal speech.

Get out to places where you will have a lot of interesting things to see. Find new places where you will experience things to talk and write about. Build and stockpile files of mental imagery. Describe events so loaded with sensory information that the audience actually feels transported.

Where Have All the Writers Gone?

Writing expert Mackie Morris is an advocate and teacher of effective broadcast newswriting. In an article for Radio-Television News Directors Association's *Communicator*, Morris warned managers that it is up to them to encourage good broadcast newswriting: "The best writers are those who have something meaningful to say. Unless our newscasts begin to communicate…with clear and effective writing, we may not have any audience left. Our audience will have gone elsewhere for information and inspiration."

Mackie Morris offers three suggestions to managers who are training their staffs to write better news copy:

1. Require your people to read.

2. Challenge them to think, and reward them when they write well.

3. Establish a standard of good writing that applies to everyone in the newsroom.

Mackie Morris first put out the "Good Writer's Dazzlin' Dozen" during his teaching years at the University of Missouri–Columbia School of Journalism. The "Dozen" is a list of what to look for and how to do both radio newscasts and news reports right (see the list below that follows on page 272). Even if you broadcast in a language other than English, there is much usable wisdom here.

Mackie Morris' Dazzlin' Dozen

1. **Write factually and accurately.** The best technique and the finest form mean nothing if the copy is wrong.

2. **Write in the active voice.** Your copy will be tighter, complete, easier to listen to, and more interesting. Do whatever you must to avoid the passive voice or past tense (examples: "He says" instead of "He said"; "tells" instead of "was told").

3. **Write in the present or present-perfect tenses.** They make your copy more immediate—and immediacy is more interesting.

4. **Keep your writing simple.** Write one thought to a sentence. Do not search for synonyms, since repetition is not a sin. Do not search for complicated intellectual language. Give the audience a better chance to understand the story.

5. **Be complete.** Make sure your quest for brevity and conciseness does not cause you to omit necessary information.

6. **Be creative.** Stick to the rules, but develop your own style. Try to say the same old thing in a new way. Make use of the "rule of threes" ("Lions and tigers and bears, oh my!" or "Life, liberty, and the pursuit of happiness") and other effective writing devices that cause copy to be more interesting.

7. **Write to be heard.** Maintain a sense of rhythm in your writing. All life has rhythm, and rhythmic writing is easier to hear. Be careful of confusing homonyms. Always, always test your broadcast copy by reading it aloud.

8. **Avoid interruptives.** Do not force the listener to make difficult mental connections. Put modifiers next to what they modify. Do not split verb phrases.

9. **Avoid commas.** A comma demands a hitch in your reading and the result is a jerkiness that frustrates the listener. Avoiding commas also will eliminate awkward subordinate clauses. Such clauses kill the impact of copy, especially if they come at the top of a story or sentence. Put a comma only where you intend to pause.

10. **Avoid numbers.** The listener has trouble remembering them. Instead of "48 percent of a population consisting of nearly nine-hundred and eighty-seven thousand people," try, "About half the population of nearly a million..." It is easier to "see" and remember.

11. **Avoid pronouns.** If you must use a pronoun, make sure it agrees with its antecedent.

12. **Create word pictures** so the audience can "see it." Use the medium of imagination.

What Listeners Want

The essence of news is the well-told story. If informative, entertaining, and up-to-the-moment, the story will always work. Most listeners turn on the news and want to know: Is my world safe? Did a nuclear bomb land somewhere or can I go about my business and lead my life today?

After that, audiences want to hear about the world they live in, their community, and what is happening. They want "talkable topics," weather, sports scores, and updated traffic reports. Breaking news aside, research shows that listeners shut off news, talk, or information broadcasts for the following two reasons:

1. "It's too depressing."

2. "It's boring."

Using the Powerful Radio methods takes care of the problem of being boring. The other challenge is to work to keep audiences who find the news depressing, who say, "I just can't take any more. There is nothing I can do to fix this problem."

A steady stream of stories detailing human suffering, environmental destruction, homelessness, war, and natural disasters can overwhelm people. Audiences become uneasy, then shut down or tune out.

Find a Solution

You can do something to prevent the listener fatigue that results in listener tune out. Each time you report a "problem story," try to find and present some sort of solution. That will lift the audience and be more effective in keeping your listeners.

One example of this was the American coverage of hurricane Katrina in New Orleans in 2005. The first images of flooding and human suffering were followed by details of the disastrous official response. After days and weeks of watching and listening to the suffering of the newly homeless, many turned away. They simply couldn't stand hearing any more.

But one reporter found a few uplifting stories in the midst of misery. First came hopeful stories of animal rescues. Then the story of a nine-year-old boy who had been living in New Orleans with his unemployed, drug-addicted mother. Malnourished and barely able to read due to sporadic school attendance, he had few friends. He told the reporter that in his old neighborhood, the other kids had regularly beaten him up.

But now everything had changed. The boy had reached an emergency relocation center in Houston where his mother was given medical care. He was attending school and had made some friends. His new teacher asked him to stand up and tell the class what it was like to survive a major hurricane. With a donated backpack filled with books, this child was now in an individualized reading program, getting proper care and eating a hot nutritious lunch in the cafeteria every day.

Hurricane Katrina gave this boy a new chance. That little bit of good news uplifted the audience, giving them a small but much needed break from the horror they had been witnessing for weeks. Presented with a "solution" story, people could listen longer.

CHAPTER 24

Beyond Powerful Radio
News Anchoring

"Stories are as essential as the air we breathe and the
water we drink. They captivate our imaginations,
enchant our minds and empower our spirit."
—Matthew Kelly

"May you live in interesting times."
—Chinese saying

If you anchor or present the news, whether you or someone else on your
staff did the actual writing, it's you that the audience connects to. Yours is
the name the public knows and yours is the voice they hear. If the job is
well done, listeners stick around, ratings result, and management applauds.
If you do not communicate powerfully, listeners leave.

Zen Rules of News Anchoring

KOA Denver managing news editor Jerry Bell could paper the walls of a
mansion with the awards he has won for news excellence. The following are
Jerry Bell's "Zen Rules of News Anchoring."

Background, Not Foreground

It is shocking for some talent to realize that the listeners do not sit with their hands cupped to their ears to make sure they are hearing everything you say on the radio. A good newscast demands attention and must cut through the clutter of everyday life. Imagine your newscast as it is being heard on the car radio. Mom and Dad are driving their three screaming kids to school. At least three different conversations are going while the radio is on. What is going to come out of that speaker that will silence the crowd for even a few seconds? That is your challenge. Guess what? Your audience is not hanging on your every word!

To Err Is Human

Get your facts right, but cast off the nasty baggage that it is unacceptable to flub now and then in your on-air delivery. What is more important is taking risks and being able to put yourself out there without fear. The beauty of radio is that mistakes travel quickly to the void of outer space and are soon forgotten. So you make a goof—no big deal. It is not the end of the world.

Radio Is a One-on-One Medium

Use the word "You" in a newscast. You are storytelling to one person at a time. If your news copy is written in a detached way and you speak at and not to your listener, you miss the essence of the medium. Radio is portable and personal. It travels with people. Aim your newscast at the individual, not the collective group.

What, Why, and How before Who, When, and Where (Most of the Time)

As mentioned, good radio leads are not good newspaper leads. The newspaper gives you the old who, what, where, when, why, and how. In newspapers, the most important part of the story is where and when it happened, and who was interviewed. But in radio news, the more compelling radio leads usually deal with the effect the story has on the listener. Quite simply: (1) How will the story affect you? (2) What is the reason for it? (3) Why is a change taking place?

Here is a good radio lead: "Your taxes are about to go up."

That works better than: "Legislators at the State House voted last night to raise the property tax levy…"

Be a Person, Not a Newsperson

Read this lead:

> Police are beginning a probe into a probable homicide at 361 Elm Street. A thirty-five-year-old woman was found slain. The suspected murder weapon, a Colt 45 revolver, was found next to the woman's corpse. Homicide detectives say the slaying reported has similarities to five other homicides in the neighborhood this year.

What is wrong with this lead? Everything. You have words no one ever uses in normal speech and it sounds so pompous as to be almost silly. Instead, try this lead:

> A murder on Elm Street—and the cops say the killer left his gun at the scene. Police are investigating the death of a thirty-five-year-old woman and think it may be the work of a serial killer. Five other murders in the neighborhood have the same M.O.

Sound Paints a Picture and Creates Energy

A good radio story should have sound that imprints pictures in the mind of a listener. You could read a story about a flood and get all the facts. But if you add the sound of the flowing water, a cry for help, or the motor on a boat going down what used to be a highway, then you use our medium best.

Sound is not just sound effects. Most stories you hear on the radio have an audio segment somewhere in the middle. That is predictable and very dull. Clever news anchors will lead with sound or even use multiple sound bites to tell a story.

A Pause Refreshes

The small nuances of announcing separate the men from the boys and the women from the girls. Use a fraction-of-a-second pause for emphasis. The ever-so-slight elongation of a word will stress its importance. These are techniques used for centuries by the best orators in the world.

Take the "I Have a Dream" speech of Dr. Martin Luther King, and imagine how it would have sounded being read by a dull monotone news reader. The beauty of this speech is in the power of its words, the ups and downs. The elongation of key words and the changes in volume and pace give the speech motion and emotion.

These speech techniques, toned down a bit, can make your newscast come alive.

Fight Your Fears

Jerry Bell adds:

> Everyone wants to do the perfect, flawless newscast. That is a good goal, but a fear of making mistakes may end up being just the thing that keeps you from being a good news anchor. How? If you fear making a mistake, you will never take a risk with your voice. You will be so uptight that you will constrict your voice and cut off all the power and fullness that can come when you use your full vocal instrument. If you read every word individually, while being oh-so-careful, you will sound like a robot instead of a human being. You will be boring and lifeless on the air.

If It Were So Easy, There Would Be Tons of Great News Anchors

The sad fact is that most news anchors sound exactly the same: dull and predictable. Here is why:

- Fear to go beyond the acceptable to reach the exceptional
- Lack of hard work
- Lack of coaching or airchecking.

Final Zen Notes

If you are learning this trade:

- Make airchecks of your work, constantly.
- Send your work to people you know and trust. Ask for and accept their harshest critiques.
- Acquire mentors who can coach you to greatness.
- Make daily airchecks, and listen back to your own work. Be your own worst critic.
- Becoming a good news anchor does not just happen. You have to work at it to make it happen.

Mystery List

I picked up the following list years ago. When I found it, tucked inside an old journalism reference book at a public library, it had already been well used. It was covered in coffee stains and torn at the corners. I never knew who wrote it, but I carried it in my wallet, copied it for fellow broadcast journalists and friends, and used it all the years I worked in broadcast news.

Create Radio News with "Ear Appeal"

- **Open your news with a sounder or great story** to grab attention and set it apart from the other entertainment on the station.

- **Use the station name or call letters:**

  - at the opening of the newscast

  - at the close of the newscast

  - going into the commercial

  - coming out of the commercial

  - in the sports segment

  - in the weather segment

  - within at least one story ("Mayor Grover tells K101 News").

- **Ditch all wire service copy.** Rewrite every story in your own words. Tell the story—do not read the story. Rewrite multiple versions for ongoing stories.

- **Put "what" before "who."** Never start a story with a source. Phrases like "Police say...," "Senator Joe Jones says...," or "The Red Cross reports..." make weak openers because these guys say things all the time. Most of the time it is what they say, what is in it for listeners, and what happened that is important, not who is saying it.

- **Open with action words**. Use powerful verbs that clearly tell immediately what the whole story is about.

- **Keep actualities and sound bites short and colorful.** Avoid using sound just for the sake of using audio. Remember, a good movie director leaves a lot of film on the cutting-room floor. Try to put only the great stuff on the radio. A rule of thumb is "one thought per actuality."

- **NEVER put on a dull spokesperson.** If you can say it better and quicker than a boring expert, do it yourself.

- **Commercial radio is a headline service.** No matter what a newswriter thinks, a story becomes bulky and hard to digest after about three lines unless it is an ultra-hot breaking event. Research indicates listeners feel most satisfied when hearing a lot of items, rather than a lot of details on a few items. In your newscast, try fitting in more short stories instead of a few longer ones.

- **Promote your newscast about ten minutes before it airs.** Bring on the newscaster to deliver a couple of quick teases. In talk radio these can provide many magic moments. The best two stories to tease are usually the top story and the kicker.

- **Don't sweat it.** How long should it take to write a story? Not long. If you understand your story, it should take about as long to write as it does to tell. Read it out loud as you write to make sure it sounds conversational.

Basics

Use a checklist when training new broadcast news anchors, reporters, and producers. Just as a pilot does his or her checklist before taking off in an airplane, double-check the "list" before you go on air. Avoid the "disaster" of incomplete stories, or items without purpose or focus that are boring.

Make sure all your news stories contain all of the following: who, what, where, why, when, and how (how it happened, how it affects people, how much it costs, how it can be solved). And ask a final "how": How would you tell this story to a friend?

Checklist: Powerful News

- What is the subject?

- Is this new information?

- Who cares? How will this matter to your audience?

- Would you have a conversation with someone about this story off air?

- Does this story affect health or safety, human emotions, money, or other concerns of our listeners? How?

- Who are the "characters" or people involved in this story? Do you care about them? Will the audience care?

- Is it visual? Can a listener "see" this story in his or her "mind's eye"?

- Is the writing clearly understandable? Do you understand this story? Could you tell the story on air without reading it?

- Go global: How big can the story be? Can a huge national or international story be told with a local angle? If so, how? Think local:

  Example: "Best Oil company has been ordered to pay one hundred million dollars to cleanup the largest toxic spill ever to hit the American Southwest. But right here in Franklyn, the Environmental Protection Agency reports some dangerous pesticides leaking into our own groundwater. The cost of cleaning that up will be high."

- If there are several angles to the story, can multiple versions be made? Does this story have a second-day angle or potential for Monday morning? Can it be used on a slow news day?

- Double-check your work before it goes on air. When you are pressured or in a hurry, it is easy to leave out one or more important elements. Make sure the story contains everything important.

CHAPTER *25*

Beyond Powerful Radio
Multi-version News

> "One theme with endless variations, like life itself."
> —*Photographer Alfred Stieglitz*

Multi-*what*?

It is a given that good newsrooms update stories as new information becomes available. The multi-version method is different.

Multiple-version or multi-version reporting is the evolution of a news or feature story over time; or the retelling of a single news story in a variety of different ways by using a different mix of writing and sound in each version. The story takes on new forms, angles, and voices each time it is presented to the audience. This replaces the former technique of simply recycling and repeating the identical story in full detail for hours at a time.

Any one version of a story written in this manner will leave out some details and include others. In this way, each multi-version piece should be able to exist alone, containing who, what, why, when, where, and how. However, if listeners hear all the parts of a multi-version story, they should have a deeper and more complete comprehension than one could get from any single part.

What Can Multi-version Do for Me?

Because multi-version lets you tell the same story many ways over the course of time, even if the facts don't change, it's never boring. A listener hearing several versions gets something different each time. The result: your audience stays engaged.

Multi-version is a natural way to create content for multiple platforms. You can recycle the same story, for each different delivery system—texting, your website and on air—to maximize the potential of a story and get the most "mileage" out of it.

With the competition to earn listeners with news, the multi-version method gives reporting a story variety. It breaks the story up into pieces to keep people listening longer. A good multi-version report is powerful radio; it prevents the audience from being bored and tuning out.

Multi-version can serve as an audience teaser enticing the listeners to stay tuned or come back later. For example: "Coming up in the news at five, more of our report on man-eating alligators loose in city parks. How did they get out?" Who would want to miss that?

In America, multi-version reporting is fairly standard. It is not uncommon for a news reporter on his or her way out to a story to ask the assignment manager these two questions:

- "When do you need it?"
- "How many do you want?"

Why Multi-version?

Multiple-version reporting became popular in America in the 1980s. For years, news had been the venue through which most stations fulfilled the majority of their federally mandated public service requirements. When the Federal Communications Commission deregulated, many of these long-standing rules disappeared.

Because news was expensive, many stations immediately cut their news staffs down to the bone. Thousands of FM stations were left with just one morning news reader. It became clear that if news was going to be part of commercial radio at all, it would have to earn its keep by generating both audience and revenue, just like any other element of a station's programming. Public radio has also adopted multi-version. They want to attract listeners too.

Why did they put the news back if they didn't have to have it? Some stations discovered, after shaving their news departments down to nearly nothing, that people in the audience wanted their radio news back. They preferred radio as their source of news and information. When news happened and no one was around to cover it for radio, stations lost listeners and credibility. It is no accident that the top-rated stations in the top fifty American markets are news-talk. Talk programmers and hosts are grateful for the interested and informed audience that a successful multi-version newscast can bring.

The Theory of Evolution: Adapt or Die

The result is that American news is now packaged better than it was before deregulation. People want news, and they know how to get it. They can pick up a newspaper, go online, turn on CNN, or they can use their radios. Your station is competing with these and many other news sources. Your presentation must be shorter, sharper, faster paced, and very interesting.

Let Them Know

In any market, it's not uncommon to find a station proudly proclaiming—on buses, billboards, and, if the station can afford it, TV—"If it's happening, you'll hear it here on Z-97." Since for many stations the five-minute segment has been cut to three, two, or even one minute of news every half-hour or hour, that news better be darn good radio. If your station has a news commitment, work hard to promote it.

Local Builds on National

Here is another way multi-version can work. Your local newsroom can now build on what national network news is sending. For example, if there is a big trial involving a violent gang, your local newsroom might add the hometown angle of that story in a multi-version format. You can promote that hometown angle and save some feature pieces for the next day's morning news: "Our neighborhood schools, overrun by gangs. Join us tomorrow morning for part four of 'Your Kids and Crime' after the news at seven."

Multi-version can also be your secret weapon against Monday morning "no-news" doldrums. Leaving a multi-version feature in progress guarantees a few minutes of interesting material on a day when there may not be much happening.

Multi-version can be applied another way. When a story is going to be part of your news all day long, you don't want the audience to get tired of it, even if the basic information isn't changing. By rewriting lead-ins and changing the actualities, you can make it sound different enough to hold the audience's interest.

The Method

Everyone figures out his or her own way to do multi-version. I actually make four sets of notes, on paper, one for each version, before putting them into the computer. I like to have four versions when I begin, instead of going back four times to write the different versions. I plug in all the facts about the story on each page, and then assign each page a different angle and its own sound bite covering a different part of the interview. No two pieces should be the same. If a listener hears only one version of your report, he or she should feel "satisfied," but if listeners hear all of the parts, they should feel "full." Taken all together, the collective minutes of your multi-version reports should resemble an in-depth documentary piece.

In the case of a feature story, you can think of multi-version reporting as a miniature soap opera. Build your audience through the morning and leave them with a "cliffhanger" to bring them back tomorrow. Multi-version is ideal for features that can be held.

For example, "Now that we've told you about the shocking death of the baby monkey, be listening tomorrow at eight as the drama of animal abuse at the city zoo continues to unfold."

A caution: If you bring your audience back for a second helping, there must be something new and substantial in your next feature segment. Don't just rearrange a few words.

Lee Harris is the morning anchor on all-news 1010 WINS in New York City. His job requires a constant updating of news stories. Harris offers his tips on the multi-version method as applied to breaking news:

> While covering a news conference or other event, start writing the story in your head while the information is conveyed. Listen for usable cuts. Mark them. When you have five or six of them, presumably the most exciting of

the bunch, you have the ingredients you need to produce multiple versions of your story.

Here's how you can crank out three or four versions of the same simple news story in a hurry: Use a lead-in, then an actuality (pre-recorded interview statements). In the next story, paraphrase that actuality, then use a new actuality. Work your way through your best audio in this fashion, creating as many versions as you need, or until the story changes.

Advanced Techniques

Sometimes on a "charge and reaction" story, you can create several versions by focusing alternately on the charge, then the denial. As an example, an attractive, successful fashion model has mysteriously disappeared. Police are investigating the photographer of her last known assignment.

Story one could be an interview with the police investigator talking about why evidence points to the photographer. At the end of the story, you would mention that the photographer has hired an attorney and denies all charges.

Your second piece could feature an interview with the suspect's attorney talking about what an insult it is that his client is under suspicion. At the close of version two, mention that the police continue to investigate the photographer as their prime suspect.

In both stories, the information conveyed is essentially the same, but the stories will sound different because the narrators are so diverse in their voices and views.

Another multi-version technique that can give your reporting depth and set it apart is to briefly give the meat of your story, then focus on an interesting element. For example, a building with many housing code violations bursts into flame. One of the firefighters working on the blaze is killed. Sad as the story is, it doesn't take long to give the hard facts. You have a sound bite of a resident who is sobbing that the building was a deathtrap.

Using that audio adds depth to your story without detracting from the necessary information that must be conveyed. With this technique, the entire story can be colorfully told in several different ways, each less than a minute long. Multiple versions might include sound of the reactions of the firefighters, eyewitnesses, the arson investigator, and housing officials, along with a spokesperson for the Red Cross describing emergency services available to those displaced.

If time permits, you can let the news anchor handle the hard news story and select one of the angles with or without an accompanying actuality. The anchor will then hand the story off to a reporter, who can add yet another angle with or without audio.

By mixing the angles and assigned introductions, still other multi-versions of a story can be created. If there's not much time, the anchor-presenter can handle the hard facts, and the sidebar multi-versions can be done by the reporter in the field. Again, this works best if the anchor can handle the basics of the story in his or her lead. Remember, the key to multi-version is alternation.

Example: "A seven-year fire department veteran is dead. Twenty-six-year-old John Jones was killed while fighting a fire in a downtown apartment building this morning. The building had multiple housing code violations and the fire is considered suspicious." Now that the anchor has given the basics, the reporter is free to do multiple versions of follow-up.

The following pages contain a few multi-versions of a single story about a blizzard in New York City that aired on 1010 WINS. The station had already broadcast reports on the traffic tie-ups, interviewed storm experts and city officials, and reported on electrical outages. In short, all the "hard news" on the blizzard had been reported, yet the snow still came down. Harris's assignment was to continue to cover this story and to get the "human angle."

Harris went underground to one of the more central subway stations in Manhattan, where people were sheltering from the storm. He filed these four reports, which work well with all the parts together, and equally well with the individual pieces alone, the hallmark of a good multi-version.

NEW YORK BLIZZARD: MULTI-VERSION ONE

This first version does not use an actuality. It just describes the scene.

The Columbus Circle Station is a pretty strong argument for placing the rest of the city underground and having New Yorkers evolve into a race of mole people. I mean it's dirty and you can't understand the announcements, but at least there's no slipping and sliding down here, because there's no snow down here. About the only hint of the weather above is that a lot of folks are dressed in clothing usually associated with Arctic exploration. But nobody looks any more testy or miserable than they usually do.

Lee Harris, 1010 WINS, at the Columbus Circle Station.

NEW YORK BLIZZARD: MULTI-VERSION TWO

Lee Harris uses a quote here, but the woman is difficult to understand, so he repeats her statement and leaves it in the report.

Well, there's no snow down here in the Columbus Circle Station. In fact, there's very little indication of the situation topside at all, other than the arctic-explorer look favored by many of the commuters this morning, and the above-average number of homeless people who came down to get out of the storm. This 35-year-old woman says she actually likes this kind of weather because it tends to make people more generous, and she needs the help:

WOMAN: I'm off the streets and I'm eight months pregnant. Welfare's finding me a place pretty soon.

HARRIS: You are eight months pregnant and you slept on the street last night?

WOMAN: I sleep on the street, that's right.

HARRIS: And she says she slept on the street the last time she was pregnant.

Lee Harris, 1010 WINS, at the Columbus Circle Station.

NEW YORK BLIZZARD: MULTI-VERSION THREE

Well, on top of everything else, the weather is apparently making a bad impression on some of our foreign visitors. This businessman from Hong Kong just doesn't see the charm in having his flight delayed thirty-six hours, and waiting almost that long to get a cab.

MAN: Well, it's interesting. But it's not…very impressive.

HARRIS: Oh, uh, I suppose the weather is better in Hong Kong?

MAN: Well we are having a tropical climate over in Hong Kong. So hot, wet, wintertime you are up to like 50 to 60 degrees!

HARRIS: That's OK if you like being comfortable. And that sort of thing.

Lee Harris, 1010 WINS, at the cab line at the Sheraton, New York.

NEW YORK BLIZZARD: MULTI-VERSION FOUR

We're back at the subway station with the woman who's pregnant and homeless.

One of the reasons the subway was put below ground was to make it impervious to days like today. And below ground it looks like just another day. Including the usual contingent of people who call the subway home night after night. This woman says she's been homeless for eight years, but weather like this has its advantages.

WOMAN: Even though it's colder, street people have a tendency to be more friendlier—if it's snowing, if you're homeless. And they do help you out more than when the weather's nicer.

HARRIS: By the way, that woman claims to be, and appears to be, eight months pregnant.

WOMAN: With my last kid, I slept on the street also.

Lee Harris, 1010 WINS, in the Columbus Circle Station.

Fitting It All In

Most news professionals have found individual ways to make their news fascinating and brief, yet thorough. If you have written news for broadcast, you know how much harder it is to write short.

An expert at the craft is CBS News Anchor Jim Chenevey. Chenevey's talent is understanding that you cannot explain *every* detail of a story. If you've tried to write effective text messages or Twitter feeds, you already know that it's tough to fit complex stories into 140 words, but it can be done. The art is not only what you put into each story, but also what you *leave out.* The art of this craft is deciding what gets left on the cutting-room floor, to be used in another version, while still giving enough information so your audience understands what happened.

When Chenevey anchored and wrote eight newscasts per morning, each averaged five or six stories, a kicker of some type, plus a piece of sound, all in *one minute.* His advice to newswriters and anchors: "Cut out extra words, write the piece, then go back and CUT."

Jim uses the culture for material. His style is conversational. He varies the audio and rotates the good stories, just as is done with the music in music formats.

Chenevey includes "A," "B," and "C" stories in each cast, varying the rest. He adds the new, breaking stories into the mix but uses multi-versions of the ones that would run all morning.

The best way to illustrate this is to actually show you his scripts that he read over the course of one morning. The newscasts on the following pages aired years ago. While the copy is dated, you can still pick up the basics of multi-version methodology from the Chenevey news scripts.

CBS Spectrum
Chenevey Newscast

6:00 AM

Good morning. This is a CBS Newsbrief.

The Toronto Blue Jays have won the American League pennant...

"Q... It was a tough year and they came through for us..."

One of the ecstatic Toronto fans. The Jays will play either Philly or Atlanta in the World Series beginning Saturday night.

Bell Atlantic has scheduled a news conference this morning, reportedly to announce it's agreed to buy Tele-Communications Incorporated, the nation's largest cable TV outlet. This would create a mega-media company, number six on the Fortune 500.

President Clinton has cleared 65 million dollars in emergency funds to help fight public health problems resulting from the flooding in the Midwest.

In Sydney, Australia, a twin-engine cargo plane crashed after hitting two kangaroos on the runway. No one was hurt.

In Concord, California, voters will cast ballots for or against a school voucher program. But one group plans to cast spells. A coven of witches wants to open a pagan school under the voucher program and hopes to whip up some votes with a little black magic.

From CBS News, I'm Jim Chenevey.

CBS Spectrum
Chenevey Newscast

6:30 AM

Good morning. Here's a CBS Newsbrief.

Two more Americans are Nobel Prize winners. Russell Hulse and Joseph Taylor of Princeton have won the prize for their studies of gravity. Doctor Taylor I presume?

"Q...It certainly is a great honor and it's a very humbling one."

Bell Atlantic reportedly wants to buy Tele-Communications Incorporated, the nation's biggest cable company. The deal would create a sixty-billion-dollar media giant.

Toronto has won the American League pennant, beating Chicago last night six to three to take that series four games to two.

Several students at Oakland University in suburban Detroit are being tested for HIV. They were not informed that a lab they were using was also being used for AIDS research, utilizing a live virus. So far, none has tested positive.

Police in Schenectady, New York, are looking for a few good "Johns"—men who would be willing to hit the streets looking for sex, as part of an undercover prostitution investigation.

From CBS News, I'm Jim Chenevey.

CBS Spectrum
Chenevey Newscast

7:00 AM

Good morning. Here's a CBS Newsbrief.

A "monster merger" is in the works. It could be the biggest ever:

"Q...Bell Atlantic Corporation, Tele-Communications Incorporated, and Liberty Media Corporation today announced that they have signed a letter of intent to merge."

She's with Bell Atlantic. If approved, the deal would create a sixty-billion-dollar multimedia giant. Number six in the Fortune 500.

American scientists Russell Hulse and Joseph Taylor of Princeton University have won the Nobel Prize in physics. This for their work on the study of pulsars and Einstein's theories. Relatively speaking...

Toronto has won the American League pennant, beating Chicago last night to win the series in six games.

Fire officials in Austin, Texas, say three recent fires were set by kids who say they got the idea from MTV's "Beavis and Butt-head" cartoon.

The mayor of New Haven, Connecticut, says it felt like a bee sting, but it was a bullet that hit him in the leg. Police say it went through two steel doors and a wall before it bounced off Mayor Losure's leg. He's OK.

From CBS News, I'm Jim Chenevey.

CBS Spectrum
Chenevey Newscast

7:30 AM

Good morning. Here's a CBS Newsbrief.

Bell Atlantic has announced a major merger. It plans to buy cable giant Tele-Communications Incorporated and its Liberty Media subsidiary.

Russell Hulse and Joseph Taylor, both of Princeton University, have won the 1993 Nobel Physics prize for their studies on Einstein's theories.

Some students at Oakland University in suburban Detroit are upset about not being informed that a lab they were using was also home to AIDS research using a live virus...

"Q...We have absolutely no indication that any of these students were exposed, however we are discussing this matter with the students to alleviate their concerns."

The school's David Dissen.

Rats are nothing new to ships, but this ship is the space shuttle Columbia. Forty-eight rats are now on board the orbiter, preparing for tomorrow's scheduled launch.

Deputies in Citrus County, Florida, were chasing Daniel Benock, wanted on a probation violation, when Benock jumped into a lake and tried to swim to freedom—that was until he saw a seven-foot alligator floating nearby. He's now in jail. Glad to be there.

From CBS News, I'm Jim Chenevey.

CBS Spectrum
Chenevey Newscast

8:00 AM

Good morning. Here's a CBS Newsbrief.

Somali warlord Mohammed Farah Adid has today vowed to release captured U.S. pilot Michael Durant and a Nigerian peacekeeper. Adid says the two hostages will be released today or tomorrow.

The Philadelphia Phillies will take on Toronto's Blue Jays in the World Series beginning Saturday night. The Phillies beating the Braves six to three last night to win the National League pennant. Phillies manager Jim Fregosi:

"Q...I guess we're going to be the underdogs again. It's not a bad way to go."

The space shuttle's fueled, and so far all systems are go for the launch later this morning.

The Rite-Aid and Revco drugstore chains are expected to announce today they're suing several drug makers for alleged price-fixing.

Quite a scene during a radio debate featuring Nylo Yuri, a candidate for mayor of Hialeah, Florida, and suspended incumbent mayor Raul Martinet. Yuri claims that during the debate, Martinet stood up and spat at him. Martinet says he was just blowing. A third candidate, Salvatore De Angelos, says it was all very embarrassing.

From CBS News, I'm Jim Chenevey.

CHAPTER 26

Beyond Powerful Radio
Integrating News & Talk for Radio, TV & the Web

"Art—a means of communication by which mind reaches mind
across great gaps of space and time."
—*Francis Hoyland*

"Share, and share alike."
—*R. Edwards's "Damon and Pithias," 1556*

Research tells us that most audiences for news-talk radio perceive both the news and the talk elements as equally important. But due to tight budgets and restrictive formats, many full-time news-talk radio newsrooms have been cut down, and now may consist of only two to four people, sometimes fewer, and not all of them are full time.

Some newsrooms work with a lot of syndicated content and the staff is often comprised of people who must be responsible for producing both news and talk, or a hybrid of both.

It is not the ideal situation. Image is not reality. There is a growing trend with "digital newsrooms" working across all platforms to blur the lines between news and talk, or commentary. Of course, it's better to have a large professional news staff. But if you just have a couple of talented news reporters and anchors, you can make it work.

It is possible to maintain a news image with very little actual news reporting, because when talk hosts discuss news stories and current issues on their programs, the station conveys the impression of being "on top of the news."

News-talk stations short on people use a lot of smoke and mirrors. They may have any or all of the following: several network news services, special reports from the field, or people with mobile phones calling in or texting to report traffic tie-ups or as eyewitnesses to breaking news stories. (For more on this, see Chapter 20, *In Case of Emergency* and Chapter 21, *Citizen Journalism*.) Some stations use their talk hosts in live remote or outside broadcasts from places where news is happening. Savvy radio news people and talk hosts call on their friends and connections at newspapers, TV stations, and magazines to debrief them on the air about stories they may be covering.

Good reporters and news presenters work very, very hard. The fact that most stations now have smaller news staffs does not mean less work—it means more. Being number one is never an accident. Radio news is not for the lazy.

Break Down the Brick Wall

Have you ever noticed a psychological "brick wall" between the news and programming departments? It bears mentioning because news and talk should always work together, but often don't. News and talk presenters are often surprised to learn that audiences don't differentiate if they have heard a certain item on the news or in the talk shows. Somehow, the news department got separated from the rest of the programming. This is the old "Let's take a break for the news" routine. In the news-talk format, this is not a good thing. You must break down that brick wall, or at least put some holes in it.

Remember, your audience does not know there are two "camps" at work here; they only know that their radio is on, and, if you are lucky, they know which station they are listening to. They want interesting, relevant talk. Listeners do not care whether they get their information from a guy wearing a news hat or a talk hat. Fight the war against the competition, not each other.

Failure to Communicate

Why don't we talk to each other? Because:

- Talk and programming says: "The news writers, reporters, and producers are always so busy, we don't want to bug them."

- The news department says: "The talk hosts are in their own world and don't bother to talk or listen to us."

- Management says: "Keep them separate because news is fact, talk is opinion and entertainment. Mixing them would damage our news credibility."

On winning talk stations, however, news reporters, anchors, and hosts talk to each other both on and off the air.

They share resources, knowing their product is a marriage. In fact, the best news-talk radio happens during times of crisis. That is when the lines of demarcation blur, and everyone pitches in to do what they can to help each other get the full story on the air quickly.

News is the chronicling of events. Talk is the discussion, the "why" behind the events and how people feel about them. But, your audience will be well served if they hear the truth, no matter who tells it to them.

A perfect example of integrating news and talk is New York syndicated morning host Don Imus and his newsman Charles McCord, a credible "news personality." There are no brick walls here. Imus is at his best discussing the news of the day, and McCord is an integral part of the show. McCord retains total news credibility. One of the most important parts of the Howard Stern Show is when Robin Quivers does the "news," albeit in a nontraditional style. The late long-time syndicated radio commentator Paul Harvey regularly blurred the lines between personality and newsman as well.

A word about the credibility factor: Audiences today are much more sophisticated. They know the difference between a newsperson being serious and one who is fooling around. Some newscasters even read commercials and manage to keep their credibility. Audiences know when they are seeing product placement, and they can spot a commercial, even if it is delivered by a newsperson, a mile away.

When a huge event affects the lives of listeners—a war, an earthquake, a flood, radioactive leaks—there is no fooling around. News anchors today have come to understand that much of the news is in place as an insurance policy. It is there in case you need it. Of course, when you need the news, it had better be there.

Look for Talkable Topics

Another way to build the relationship between the news and talk staffs is for the news people to keep a lookout for "discussable" news items. There is not much to say about a fire, flood, or breaking story other than giving the facts and information as they become available. After the facts are in about the massive car crash on the bridge, the talk show topic may actually be: "Why are citizens willing to endure life-threatening conditions to save ten minutes on their commute?"

A hard news story can generate a softer talk topic. Train your people to save the stories about Supreme Court decisions or any polls or items about which people are likely to have strong views. Peel the "onion" that is your story to find material for an in-depth, open-phone talk show.

The Crossover Talents

Opinion traditionally had no place in the news. On the other hand, talk has not been a forum for chronicling the facts. So, hybrid news-talkers such as Dave Ross are rare. Wearing both hats, they manage to bridge the gap. When Ross does a newscast, the listener can tell what he thinks; on the other hand, listeners know what an objective and conscientious newsman he is when hearing Ross's talk show. Ross hosts a daily talk show on KIRO/Seattle and presents news feature commentaries on the CBS Radio Network. Over the years, KIRO has sent Ross around the world to cover big news events such as the fall of the Berlin Wall. Dave Ross has found the equation to marry news to talk: Keep a unique voice and retain credibility in both.

It is impossible to describe Dave Ross's creativity. Sometimes he sings his commentaries, often uses humor, and has a cynical "bright eye" on the world around him. If you have not heard his work, a sample script—archived from a CBS Radio commentary—is an interesting twist on the health care cost issue in the United States.

DAVE ROSS CBS RADIO NETWORK SCRIPT
Health Care That's Always There

The simple solution to health care costs.

I'm Dave Ross on the CBS Radio Network.

It's an appealing motto, "Health care that's always there." The big unknown is, at what cost? The President says that the savings are obvious. You can cut paperwork to one claim form, encourage preventive care, and end the billions of dollars of unnecessary medical tests.

Well, I understand the paperwork, the insurance industry is ready to do that anyway. I understand preventive care… but how will you stop the testing? If a patient wants a test, does a doctor say "no" and risk a lawsuit? The key is to get the patient not to want the test. But how?

I was talking with Dr. Nancy Dickey with the American Medical Association, also a family physician in Texas, and she told me an interesting thing. Whenever she offers her patients a medical test, the first thing they ask is not "How much will this cost?" since the cost is usually covered by insurance. What they ask is: "*WILL THIS HURT?*" That's what they want to know: "Will this hurt?" And I suddenly realized that's it!

We've been going about it all wrong. For years, doctors have been saying, "This won't hurt a bit." WRONG! The doctors should say, "Well, yeah, this is gonna hurt a little," and he kinda glances toward a big old four-inch-long needle sitting over by the sink.

That's why people didn't have as many tests thirty years ago, because those tests hurt! "Health care that's always there" is a great quote, but here's another one: "You bet that test is paid for, I'll just go and get the needle!"

I'm Dave Ross on the CBS Radio Network.

Develop a Daily System

If you want to integrate your news-talk product, it takes extra effort. The list that follows is a system to develop news-talk integration:

- *Work together.* Meet with the producers, talk show hosts and the news assignment manager or news director every day. Compare what you know about the news and events of the day. If it cannot be done in person, do it for five minutes on the phone, by instant messaging or e-mail.

- *Take today.* Go through the list of today's topics, discuss:

  - What will news do with the stories?

  - What will talk do with the stories?

  - Any ideas that anyone else has.

- *Prospect for gold.* Share the loot. Everyone should look through the wires, newspapers, and any other usual source materials. Talk about multi-version reports or anything that can be done in short-form news, then moved into a long-form talk.

- *Pick the right talent for the subject.* If a newsperson or host has an affinity for a specific topic, he or she will do a better job. Why not send your baseball fanatic out to do the baseball story? Utilize your talent's natural interests, background, and experiences. This means you will really need to get to know your talent. If you don't know, ask. "Is anyone interested in alternative medicine?" Again, interested is interesting and powerful.

- *Be flexible. Things change quickly.* You've got to be ready to change plans.

- *Listen to everyone's ideas.* If people are assigned stories or topics they do not like, ask them to give you better ideas. People always work better when the idea is theirs.

- *Communicate.* If things change news-wise or events happen throughout the day, talk to each other. This is a team effort, and the listeners are not necessarily aware that there is a brick wall between the newsroom and the talent area.

- *Listen to each other.* News departments, when they can, ought to be aware of the content of the various talk shows and whatever else is on air. Keep the radio on at the station. Talk hosts: Listen to the news!

- *Create a future file.* When notices arrive regarding future events, designate a person to file them in the computer in daily calendar form. Both news and talk should utilize these lists for topic and story ideas. Newspapers work these types of files as much as five years ahead.

- *Create a follow-up file.* On dull days when not much is going on, look back. Did the station cover any stories that need to be updated? An updated news story might ask:

  - "Where are they now?"

  - "Did the child in the custody fight live happily ever after?" "What happened to the neighborhood after the rapist was released?"

Looking ahead is good, but you can also do mighty powerful radio when you look backward.

- *Do not fight over guests.* If there is a guest or an interview that a newsperson has set up and the talk host wants to interview him- or herself, work it out. Protect the on-air product, not your territory. Perhaps borrowing a clip, or piece, of that interview audio from the news department will be enough to get discussion going for a powerful talk show.

Conversely, if something noteworthy is said during one of the station's talk shows, use it in the news. You'll have an exclusive. Producers: Endear your host to the news staff by getting that audio to the newsroom fast!

Be a Team. Be a Station. Be Number 1!

Work together. Cooperate. Powerful radio is a collective effort. William Shakespeare said, "The play is the thing." Put egos aside. Forget the players. Focus on the play.

Let the news people know what types of material you are seeking for your show. Ask them to save anything they come across. Talk hosts: Do the same for your news team.

People are usually glad to help, and may have a lot of ideas and material that may not be appropriate for their own department or show but could work for you.

Break Format When News Breaks

This is when news-talk is at its best. During times of national or local catastrophe, go ahead and break format. Have a procedure (whom to call, commercials to move, etc.) in place in the event of an urgent news story. Get the information on air right now. Nobody cares about your "cover story" or "topic A" when all hell is breaking loose and lives and property are at stake.

Drop what you had planned and go with the breaking story. Debrief news reporters on the air. Ask them questions about the story. If it makes sense to do so, have them stay on the air and take calls. Talk hosts: Give the news department all the time it needs to get information on the air, even if it cuts heavily into your show.

Always Archive

Remember to keep audio and, if you have them, video files. If you have the archived audio and video accessible, you can easily re-purpose magic moments on air for promos, or later for awards submissions.

Some of the most effective news-talk managers are those who have worked on the air themselves. Bob Christopher is one of those people. Christopher ran the Florida State Network, anchored at KTAR in Phoenix, Arizona, and was a manager at WWL radio in New Orleans, where one integrated newsroom served four stations.

Bob Christopher's Creating Powerful Radio Points

- Understand your listeners: where they live, where they shop, and what they want and need from you.

- Create an emotional bond with your audience.

- As often as possible, deliver more than you promise to listeners and advertisers.

- Surround yourself with people who want to win.

- Take time to talk to them and smile at them in the hall.

- Develop personalities your listeners will love.

- Focus on the positives in your corner of the world.
- Dream up fascinating promotions or special events.
- Remember, it's marketing!
- Know your competitors.

CHAPTER 27

Beyond Powerful Radio
Integrating Radio & TV News

> "The business of every art is to bring something into existence."
> —*Aristotle*

Every TV news director I work with says the same thing: "Our best people come from radio." That's because radio people know how to communicate and tell stories; they can work without a script, and can spontaneously improvise. Many TV-only broadcasters look back wistfully, remembering their days in radio as their happiest, when they did their best work.

Smart broadcasters use TV for what it does best, presenting pictures to show events as they happen. With the Internet, most radio personalities and programmers are becoming more experienced working with video to post on station websites. But radio is great training if you want to make the move to television. Many broadcasters have found they enjoy doing both, and again, with the digital newsroom, you may be *required* to do both! It's like being bi-lingual. Each medium has its own strengths—but if you can be versatile and learn to work effectively in both audio and video, you will be more valuable as a broadcast communicator.

Great storytelling and powerful communication are the keys to both. Radio broadcasters are often curious about working with pictures and would like to give television or creating video for the web, a try.

I'm seeing more and more TV and radio newsrooms around the world moving toward combining their efforts into a digital newsroom integrated product. Bi-media, or combined newsrooms, started as a cost-cutting measure, but it can be beneficial overall. When a TV and radio station are under the same roof, or even on the same floor, it makes little sense to send two sets of reporters to the same press conferences, the same fire stories, and to interview the same local figures or celebrities.

"A Face for Radio?"

Talented radio people can and do make it on television. Radio broadcasters should take it upon themselves to do as much as possible not to discourage television stations from utilizing them. If your radio station is often a source for TV footage, always be ready to make an appearance. The audience no longer expects their TV news to be delivered by people who look like movie stars. A small amount of coaching, grooming, and effort may be all it takes to convert a successful radio talent into a shining television personality.

Producing the Pink Elephant

A lot of TV interview, discussion, or "talking head" programs are really just talk radio shows with cameras pointed at them. Managers can enhance the level of creativity for personalities doing these types of shows by allowing them to work in both media. Talented TV people can be taught to speak "visually" for radio reports.

Radio people can be taught to leave space in their writing for pictures. A good assignment manager for either TV or radio can decide which stories fit best with either medium. There's another great benefit in using reporters who work in both media: TV and radio can promote each other, increasing visibility and audience.

A bit of history: CNN (Cable News Network) was first to try the all-news radio format on TV. CNN hired a lot of radio reporters. They worked cheaper, and they had the necessary skills. CNN realized that the basics for both radio and television are the same: You must tell an interesting story in a fascinating way. Each medium has assets and drawbacks. On radio, if you want to talk about a pink elephant, all you need to do is describe one and people "see" it. On television, if you want to talk about a pink elephant, you must actually produce one.

In the early days of television, reporters and hosts alike had backgrounds in either print or radio. Where is it written that broadcasters cannot be great at both TV and radio? Here are some techniques that we use at Geller Media International to help make the transition from TV news to radio news easier.

From TV to Radio

1. Speak to ONE person listening! When on radio, speak visually. Paint word pictures. Imagine you're talking to a blind person—how would you describe things? Don't refer to pictures—the audience can't see them. Use details, small things that you notice.

2. If you are stuck for a way to begin a report, pretend the anchor has just asked you a question or write the question into your report: "Why are six hundred nursing mothers converging on a small theater in suburban San Francisco? To get into the *Guinness Book of World Records*—it's the Third Annual Nurse-in."

3. Use TV to promote radio and radio to promote TV. On morning or "breakfast" TV shows, try saying, "When you get in your car on your way to work this morning, don't miss the interview coming up on Z-97. The mayor, his mistress, his wife, and his mother will all be on live with host Jim Smiley."

4. It's OK to promote your TV news coming up on the radio. Most people now in their cars will be checking out the pictures tonight on the TV news anyway. Why not send them to your channel?

5. Whether on radio, TV or the web, promote within your programming. Let your audience know what is coming up next. Tease them with exciting tidbits about upcoming stories so they stay with you.

6. Use TV anchors and special reporters as regulars on radio shows. They get a chance to express themselves as people instead of sticking to a tight script. Conversely, television viewers are often curious to see what their favorite radio personalities look like. At many stations, the meteorologist, the sports guys, and the traffic reporter all do both radio and TV. If you have talent, that is all that matters. If someone has talent, he or she can make it on radio or on TV. (If you are interested in more on cross promoting, and using TV and radio together – there's more on this in Chapter 29 *Promotion* and Chapter 20 *In Case of Emergency*).

7. Keep a radio ON in the newsroom. Even though you can hear most radio stations over the Internet, people are often busy at their computers doing other work. Make sure there is a radio monitor that comes in clearly in your television newsroom so the reporters can actually hear themselves on the air.

8. Use multi-version. We've covered this for radio (see Chapter 25, *Multi-version News*), but it's an important tool in television as well. Remember, you may need extra footage and additional comments. Use details and small things you notice.

9. Remind the audience how the story affects them, whenever possible. Try to present a solution to every problem when you can.

10. Remember to make it matter. Ask yourself: "Why is it important?" Make sure your story explains.

From Radio to TV

Consultant John Catchings' background includes both radio and television. He managed newsrooms at KGO-TV and KPIX-TV in San Francisco. Catchings is a brilliant problem solver, never taking "it can't be done" for an answer. Here are some of his ideas to help radio people create powerful television news:

- **Play to the visual.** You witnessed it, but the photographer missed it! Never assume that because you saw it with your own eyes, the picture was taken. Look at what the camera is capturing. Do this while you are on a story. Do not wait until you are back at the studio editing to realize you do not have the right shots. It is better to make your photographer mad at you than your news director—or worse, not do your best for the story.

- **Start with the best video.** Be the director of your piece and use your best pictures. Avoid the temptation to start the story with a stand-up shot.

- **Put movement into each shot.** Do not be a human mic stand! (I've heard reporters who stand like statues in front of a building referred to as "living lawn ornaments." Don't become one.) Get involved in your shot. Choreograph the shot, be engaged, demonstrate your stories and ideas. Keep it moving forward. Walk around, move, point.

- **Let the pictures tell the story, but let the story breathe.** Do not allow it to become boring. Watch for length.

- **Make good use of natural sound.**

- **Do not overwrite.**

- **Use graphics, charts, and your own imagination** to jazz up less-interesting stories.

- **When you edit, do not hang on too long to the good shots.** It's tempting, but keep it moving. Be creative.

- **The essence is storytelling.** Never forget that. Do what it takes to tell the story.

Grab the Spotlight

Money can't buy happiness, but it can buy TV exposure. If you can afford it, purchase commercials to advertise your radio station on TV. A TV ad campaign is expensive, but if it draws in new listeners and brings higher ratings, it is worth it. If you're interested, there's more about this in *Promotion*, Chapter 29.

Still the most time honored use by American radio of American television is and has always been the free "plug" or mention on the air. Get all the free TV publicity you can! Do things on your radio station that are newsworthy and attention-getting, and the TV stations will come knocking on your studio door. When they come in, make sure they see your call letters. American radio stations learned the "mic flag" trick long ago. Mic flags are designed with television coverage in mind.

When your station is taking calls from listeners on issues of the day, it makes a good TV "public opinion" story. Many TV assignment managers have learned to send a reporter and camera in to tape live radio talk shows for multi-versions of hot news stories. Radio managers: Don't be shy. Call up the TV stations in town when a particularly controversial or important subject is being discussed on your airwaves, especially if TV coverage on the story has been intense.

Benefit from All Information Media

People do not make distinctions about where they get their news. Whether they read it, hear it, or hear about it, or watch it. Television, radio, the Internet, video, audio, photos, and text are all part of their information network. Broadcasters: Take a lesson from our audience. Eliminate all of the barriers that keep us from using ALL of our resources to bring listeners and viewers the most compelling information and news product we can produce.

PART IV

Beyond Powerful Radio
Working Across Multi-Platforms

CHAPTER 28

Beyond Powerful Radio

Audio Communication Across Multiple Delivery Platforms: Broadcasting, Streaming, Video, Social Media, Podcasting, & Beyond...

"At Google, we worry first about creating an application that will work to benefit a user, rather than worrying first about how it's going to make money."
—*Chris Sacca, Head, Special Initiatives Department for Google*

There has never been a more exciting time to work as a communicator. Commercial radio in America has been around for more than 90 years, and radio's audience is still expanding. Now it's easier to access because a radio can be in your pocket, your phone, your computer, your iPad, *and* your stereo system. What's great about the digital world is that it's mobile and convenient. You can receive messages anytime, from your computer or phone, wherever you are, whenever you feel like it.

Because this plethora of accessible new media allows your show, message or content to instantly get out into the world in many ways, there's a lot of opportunity to expand on creating content. Working across multiple platforms is your "highway" not only to create the programming and content, but also the opportunity to market and promote it. The playing field has leveled. If you've got a computer and a microphone, plus a mixer and a digital recorder, you can produce state of the art audio. You can create a show or even your own station, online.

The delivery method or *how* the audience receives the content isn't what's important. It's time to reinterpret philosopher Marshall McLuhan's famous phrase: "It's no longer the medium, it's the message."

Avoid Useless Chatter

Just because you *can* say or show something, doesn't mean you should. As a communicator, if what you have to say isn't relevant, it doesn't matter if it's broadcast, podcast, texted, or tweeted; it won't have the desired effect. Avoid useless chatter. Because media outlets *can* post whatever comes down the pike, the temptation is there, but people might not appreciate a constant never-ending data feed—unless it is relevant to them or it's interesting. If you make a regular practice of "tweeting" for the sake of saying you "twittered," or blogging so you can say you have a blog, you'll be wasting the power of these different platforms.

What works across all platforms, in any medium, is powerfully communicating a message or story that informs, entertains, inspires, persuades, or connects with people. Powerful storytelling. Because the web offers the chance to "narrow" cast, by targeting those with special interests, you can offer a variety of, or multiple, feeds for different audiences. You never want to be seen as adding to the pile of commercial clutter.

In this chapter, some of the top experts at the forefront of broadcasting share their experience, advice, and wisdom about using all forms of media. As we navigate the new world of multi-platform distribution, the key to success, just as with any other creative process, is to try things and see if they work.

Sifting and Refining

It's easy to be overwhelmed. There's a lot out there. To quote air personality and author, Turi Ryder, "Think of all the available content as crude oil. There may be a lot of it, but it's no good to you unless it's refined." If your organization can act as a "refinery" for content, that's one way of making yourselves useful, and a content destination for your listeners, readers, viewers, or advertisers.

Your Audience is Multi-tasking

People are busy. Their time is valuable. In radio, we already know our listeners are multi-tasking. Since a significant number of at-work listeners are in front of their computers during the day with the radio playing in the background, part of the challenge of working in multiple platforms is finding ways to encourage listeners to move from on air to online and back.

Daniel Anstandig, President of McVay New Media, says, "Multi-tasking is nothing new to radio listeners. For generations, listeners have incorporated radio into working, driving, cleaning, cooking, and socializing. It's the ultimate passive medium—as a listener, you can engage as much or as little as you want. Successful radio programmers have even used "usage imaging" to teach listeners how to multi-task using their stations.

Examples of "usage imaging" include well-known liners like "listen while you work" or "turn it on in the car"—phrases that instruct the audience to multi-task with the radio. (Current research indicates consumers want a sort of "all-purpose magic device" containing radio, phone, video, and other functions to manipulate or access content. Some companies have already responded by creating or adding applications for devices originally designed to do just one thing, such as downloading and reading books, so that they do more, like play radio stations in the background.)

In fact, radio's nature as a multi-task-friendly medium is one of its most underutilized strengths when it comes to digital opportunities. Radio is a medium that listeners are trained to use while doing other things. Producing online content that is relevant to the station's broadcast might just be the key to easily getting more page views and "time spent connected" from your audience.

A study from Nielsen sheds light on the multi-tasking phenomenon among television viewers. Nielsen reports that three out of four Americans surf the web and watch TV at the same time—and half of them say that they do it daily. How much time do people spend with the TV and web *simultaneously* (usually using e-mail, Facebook, or other websites and mostly unrelated to the content of the TV show they're watching)? Turns out it's an average of about two hours per day.

This points to an obvious opportunity for television—to create online content that ties in to on-air programming. If it's done effectively, it might just get more mileage out of each viewer by attracting them to use the station's website simultaneously.

Numerous studies show that the people who visit radio station websites are often P-1s or P-2s who can be converted to P-1s. (The P-1, or "parallel 1," listener is someone totally committed to your radio station, a fan, who has it on much of the time. P-2 is second tier; they listen to you but not as loyally.) Knowing that Portable People Meter measurement (PPM) numbers are driven by high P-1 listening, your ability to move listeners from sphere to sphere could ultimately even impact your ratings.

Make your show more compatible for multi-taskers, and for people who want to access your brand in many places at once. Block your competition by getting more time from your listeners—don't give them the chance to multi-task with someone else.

Using the Audience

If you want to engage and keep the attention of your audience, involve them.

An interactive component to your product allows your audience to get involved. This aspect of multi-platform media is important, whether you are broadcasting music, news, or talk. In the old days, listeners had to call a radio station or write a letter to be heard. Now listeners can interact with the station immediately—online, using Twitter, texting, and instant messaging. All are powerful and indispensable tools in today's interactive media ecosystem.

Interactive media also offers this benefit: Your audience can become a source of content, helping you acquire or build your local news product. If you ask for pictures, you'll get pictures. Ask for stories, voila! (There's more about this in Chapter 21, *Citizen Journalism*.)

"This Way to the Show..."

How will your audience find you, or know what's on offer? How will people hungry for content locate your "restaurant" in the first place? Digital platforms require some way of letting the audience know there is more of your branded content elsewhere: on the web, podcast, reporter blog, digital station, etc. When adding digital or online stations to your mix, your radio can be like the aroma of good cuisine that leads the audience to something different or more of what they like online, or that lets them know you have content they cannot get over the air. Having unique content on your website is important. Don't "cannibalize" your radio station. To give the audience a reason to come to the web, show them a benefit: If they come, they can get *more* or hear something different.

Offer More

Rick Jensen, program director and talk host at news-talk WDEL in Wilmington, Delaware, stresses the importance of offering something on your site that cannot be gotten elsewhere.

> Start by focusing on your station's core competencies. Think back to the days when the big Top 40 station would leave a list of their "pick hits" at local record stores. They were often sponsored—the goal was to get Top 40 record buyers to listen to your station. Then "fast forward." Ask: "What is it your station does better than anyone else? How can you market that to non-listeners?"
>
> Get your website on e-mail lists of influential groups who can benefit from your station and website. Maybe your station is the most reliable for severe weather reports and school closings with unparalleled resources on the air and on the Internet. When schools, association and others with large member databases include this information with the message "Listen to..." or "Go to..." they are not just promoting your station or your website, they are providing service to their members.

Backpack Journalists for Digital Media

Many broadcast networks and radio news-talk stations routinely send their reporters out with cameras in addition to audio equipment, allowing them to post video or footage for their station's websites as well. At WDEL, reporters produce a daily video newscast, much like any major market TV newscast, that can be viewed online.

Driving the Hit Counter Up: "Come See the Half-Naked Lady"

Driving up the number of "hits" on your website is crucial for getting into search engines. That's how Google and the other search engines offer up your station's website in higher placement for someone seeking general information on a story. Cross-promoting the website on the station is important to drive up hits. But there are other ways to get your station to "pop up" at the top of the search engine listing on a topic.

Fox News reporter Eben Brown, while working for WFLA in Tampa, learned that what brings people to your news site may *not necessarily be the news itself.*

> At *www.970WFLA.com* we used a lot of photo and video galleries. I was often the local radio pool reporter for Presidential visits, which allowed me to get quite close and take stellar photos. I'd post a gallery, especially if he's visiting local sites or posing with local celebrities. Once, the President took a few minutes to give a pep talk to our unlucky football team, and those pictures were quite popular among our website viewers. We watched the counter rise continually. We left it up for a while and it continued to get a fair amount of attention.
>
> [Animal rights group,] PETA often uses women in bikinis (or less) to bring attention to their demonstrations. I interviewed and shot video of one lady protesting outside a KFC. The radio story was admittedly a bit boring, but we mentioned that video of the bikini-clad twenty-something was available on our website. The hit counter went through the roof.

If all your station is doing is streaming the same content online that you broadcast over the air, you're wasting big opportunities. You have video and print and instant interactive capabilities. With these come many more chances to create and deliver content, and ways of establishing deeper relationships with your audience. Your website is a great marketing tool, but it's so much more. A powerful website does what all powerful content does: It informs, entertains, inspires, persuades, and connects people to one another.

Create & Use Video

Daniel Anstandig, who navigates the multi-platform world for his clients, suggests, "Create your own videos and post them online. These videos should have three characteristics: they should be short, entertaining (usually funny), and brand-oriented (though not a call to action)."

Anstandig notes that the most head-turning midday personalities in your market today may not be on the radio at all. Instead, you might find them on YouTube, iTunes, or another popular audio/video on-demand site.

In fact equal-opportunity stages like the above-mentioned sites have made stars out of so many living room dwellers that it's a wonder more program directors aren't scouting for talent online.

By the time you're done reading this, over five million people will view videos on YouTube. That's 11,574 views per second. And, they may be taking TSL (time spent listening) away from YOU! Neilsen recently reported that over sixty-five percent of online videos are viewed between 9 a.m. and 5 p.m.—the majority happening between 12 p.m. and 2 p.m.

"We try to do videos about things that people are talking about," says Ben Relles, the founder of popular YouTube channel "Barely Political." His strategy has worked, attracting over 255 million views in the last three years. Relles and a team of five people work together to produce one or two videos per week with each video taking about two days to produce. One of their most popular videos was the "Obama Girl" music video (you may remember…"I got a crush on Obama" from 2008?). Barely Political is just one of many YouTube channels attracting millions of viewers annually—some rivaling the reach of major media outlets.

The on-demand audio world has also drawn millions. Creative people don't need tall towers anymore to get an audience. They need a fifty dollar camera or microphone and an internet connection!

You can create your own stage. What better place for a media outlet (like a radio station) to find new talent than to hire online entrepreneurs—people who have so much to say that they created their own stage! Those creative people are deserving of an interview when companies are looking for new talent. Get yourself a Flip Video Cam and start a YouTube Channel. Or, buy yourself an inexpensive USB microphone, and start a podcast.

If you are an on-air personality, ask yourself: "What am I doing for my career when I'm not on the air?"

Use Digital Media to Grow Your Audience

Most on-air personalities are rewarded if they can grow web traffic in addition to reaching ratings goals. If you're a manager, consider structuring some sort of incentive for your staff to increase traffic and awareness of your brand *everywhere*. Whether you are paid a bonus on your digital performance or not, interactive media can help you to grow your audience, using your on-air and online presence synergistically.

Daniel Anstandig offers these ideas to help encourage listeners to visit your website:

1. **Develop online content about something you LOVE.** Strong web traffic starts with strong content. The only way that you will realistically stay passionately engaged in creating content is to create something personally meaningful to you. Don't waste your time developing online content about things you don't like. [Working with subjects and topics you care about] makes the work easier and more fun. If you are passionate about fashion or health and fitness, write content for your site (or station's site) that is specific to your passion. Become the "Health and Wellness editor" for the station's website. If you are into the local club and bar scene, you should maintain the local events calendar and "local blog."

   Do not limit writing privileges to the on-air team. If someone in traffic, billing, or sales is passionate about a topic like kids and families, consider giving them the role of "Family Content editor" for the site. Everyone has a voice. (Although not everyone should get to use it on your website. Be sure to vet people's contributions carefully.)

2. **Promote specific content from your site on the air.** What is on your site *today* that is fresh, interesting, and will make a difference in the lives of your audience? You should be able to answer that question with something substantial every day. Then, it's easy to promote that content on the air. Keep in mind that if you are posting content about topics that you are passionate about (see point #1), cross-selling that content on the air to your audience should be easy! Let your passion do the selling.

Consider creating an opportunity for the editor of your website to record or go live on air each day with a promo letting your audience know what's on your site *today*. If your web master would like to be a "video star," but it's not logistically possible to have him or her live in your studio every day, perhaps a camera or microphone in the "nerve center" of your station's website would solve the problem. It also gives your audience another connection to your web content, and puts a human face on your site. "Melissa, what's on the WXXX website today?" "Jane, I just posted listener photos of the pet costume contest from the station party last night, and there's a link to sign your kids up to be dancers in the Hollywood movie that's filming downtown."

3. **Optimize your site's keywords and metadata to increase referred traffic from search engines.** Making your website more search engine friendly can dramatically increase your traffic. Make sure your website's "meta tags" are completed properly—those are keywords and descriptions of the content found in your site that is hidden in every web page's code. Also, be sure that your site has a Google site map. Consider using free services like SEO Ranking Monitor to track the position of your website in major search engines.

4. **Use "Sharing" links to let your audience easily refer their friends to specific content on your site.** Over one million sites use *AddThis.com* to allow web surfers to easily share content with their friends. [You can] get a button for your site that will allow your audience to share your page on Facebook, Twitter, and other popular social networking sites. Other sharing services include "Share This" and "Add to Any."

5. **Get more page views out of each visitor who comes to your site.** When someone lands on your site, be sure that they are easily enticed to view other content and information. Make sure your site is user-friendly and easy to navigate. Every page should have a clear path to "go deeper" into the site. The average amount of page views for any visit on any website is three. If you can get more than three page views per visitor, your site is above average in average page views per visit. More page views means more opportunities for sponsorship inventory (more impressions). (Be careful how much commercial advertising your visitor has to wade through to get to content. If it's too much, they'll leave.)

If You Are Streaming...

Here's how to grow your online audience:

1. **Make your "Listen Live" button obvious and clearly placed.** Make it easy for your audience to find your stream. Place a "listen live" button somewhere clearly in the header of your site. Don't force listeners to go searching for it, or you'll lose their tune-in. The best sites have the "listen live" button consistently and predictably placed, and it is big and obvious. (Put one on every page.)

2. **Put links to your show's stream in your e-mail signature.** Each day you are interacting with your community via hundreds of e-mails. Those e-mails are almost always going to listeners, buyers, and business partners in your audience. Posting a link to the station's audio stream in every e-mail signature can immediately increase your tune-ins. You can even include an actual "listen live" button in your e-mail signature. This is a great way to build a streaming audience with people who know you and are likely to tune in.

3. **Add your show and station to internet radio "yellow pages" type directories.** The most popular radio station streams to attract listeners from a variety of sources. Your own website is just one way to tune in. There are a number of large internet radio station/streaming directories online that can help to direct more traffic to your stream—and it doesn't cost anything to get listed.

   Here are four major directories for online streaming:

   - *Radiotower.com*: This is a directory of stations, podcasts, MP3s, and videos.

   - *Web-Radio.fm*: This directory allows listeners to search for stations by call letters, format, state, country, and internet-only vs. broadcast stations.

   - *Streamfinder.com*: Listeners can find new stations, bookmark their favorite stations, and add new streams that are not already listed.

   - *Penguinradio.com*: Stations of many different countries and languages are listed here.

4. **Promote your stream on air.** Tell your audience "Turn your computer into a radio."

The reality about radio is that it may be more convenient for some listeners in the workplace to "tune in" using your stream on their computer or phone than it is for them to use a radio. If you are not promoting your stream as a way for listeners at work to use your radio station, you are missing a major opportunity. Most online listening comes from people in their offices. Use the words "turn your computer into a radio," encouraging listeners to use their computer at work to listen. Sell the convenience of listening online from their computer.

5. **Keep your current listeners.** Just as it is easier to keep a current customer than develop a new customer, it is always easier to keep a current listener than to find a new listener. Program directors should monitor and police the online audio stream with as much vigilance and responsibility as they lend to the on-air audio. In some cases, if your station is filling spot breaks with "filler audio" or other commercial inventory, the audio online can be very different than what is heard on the air. Many radio stations use lousy audio to fill time in their spot breaks online. They'll run the same "elevator music" to fill commercial time in every break and miss an opportunity to really entertain the audience during breaks on their internet stream. Get creative. Fill your stream with interesting content. Run great archived audio from your show. Share lifestyle news and information. Make use of every minute you have with your audience to excite and interest them. (Good PDs program their entire audio presence. Be as picky about what goes in your stream as what goes out over the air. It's also a good way to audition material for air, if listeners to the stream respond positively. For content, don't forget to check your network; they may be already providing content that you can use.)

Creating Your Website

Most major market stations and big brands understand the importance of hiring a professional to create an online environment that's consonant with their brand and their image. But it's surprising how many smaller organizations decide to make their new media presence an "afterthought," whether from thrift or lack of awareness, and hand over their brand to an intern or somebody's cousin who is "good with computers." If you would allow your sister-in-law's nephew's best friend to drive your new sports car, by all means, hand him the keys to your station's website.

Your reputation is on the line anytime you put your name on something. That is especially true of your online presence, which can be copied and linked and sent around the world in seconds. Make sure you hire a professional, whether in-house or as an independent contractor, who is smart and understands your brand. Don't expect that because you are known in your marketplace that whoever you pick will instinctively be aware of how you'd like to be perceived in new media. Take the time to train, and make an effort to collaborate with, the person who will be managing your brand in a new media setting. Once somebody has put your logo on a web page featuring photos of a syndicated host's wet tee shirt contest, it's too late.

Take steps to ensure the security of your website's visitors, to the greatest extent that you can. It's a balancing act. As a website provider, you naturally want to collect as much information as possible about each person who visits your site. Tom Demos, president of PortlandMediaMonitor.com, points out that "every website logs some information on its visitors." But the minute you start asking for minute details of somebody's personal life ("Do you own a pet? Are you single or married? What's your household income?"), there is a risk of alienating that person.

McVay New Media/Digital Strategy VP Jon Erdahl looks at the other side of that equation: "Broadcasters tend to shy away from drilling down and mining deeper data from their audience. Think about how much info YOU give up to sign up for a free website. Don't be afraid. Ask away and start gathering real intelligence on your audience." Demos says, "Lots of news sites set up 'portals,' or registration points, through which a visitor must pass to get deeper or more detailed stories. Often, the content is 'free,' but the 'price of admission' is your data."

Safety Measures to Protect Privacy

Nobody likes to have his or her privacy invaded. So, while you should collect e-mail addresses and contact information on visitors to your site, you owe them, at minimum, a commitment to make sure any financial transactions, such as buying station merchandise or donating to a charity you're supporting, are made through a secure merchant site.

Post, very clearly, your site's privacy policy before you ask anyone to register for any services you are offering. Do not use anyone's e-mail address, even for station events, unless you have specifically asked them if it's "OK." This gives site users a sense of comfort and control, and will build loyalty to your site, and your brand.

Scott Woelfel, managing partner of the interactive strategy and design agency, Armchair Media, LLC, advises asking these questions when planning your site:

- "Why would anyone spend time here?"

- "Why would anyone tell a friend about it?"

- "What is your strength and what are you doing to promote it?"

With vast experience in designing successful media websites, Woelfel knows what to do (and what not to do) when creating your site.

Armchair Media's Website Do's and Don'ts

DO:

- **Put yourself in the position of the user.** Think like the person you want using the site, not like someone who is creating it.

- **Keep your index pages simple,** but present the user with many options at the story level. Users respond better to fewer choices when hunting for something, but then look for options when they complete a task.

- **Anticipate what a user would want to do next** — then offer him or her that choice. Checking a baseball box score might indicate an interest in tonight's pitchers. Make it easy to get that info, without clicking if possible.

- **Use images sparingly.** Users tend to ignore large images and are much more likely to click on text links.

- **Become the authority.** Links to sources outside your site don't lead users away; they bring them back more frequently because you become the authority on that topic.

- **Use other media and platforms.** Figure out what works best on the web, on mobile, on Twitter, etc., and create a suite of products to reach your audience wherever they might be.

- **Optimize your site for search.** You are many more times likely to get traffic as the result of a search than by browsing, and if you aren't getting that search result then your competitor is.

DON'T

- **Try to be everything to everyone.** Know your target audience and find ways to engage them.

- **Apply linear thinking to a non-linear medium.** Save the tickers, scrolls and uncontrollable audio/video for television. The user should always feel in control of his or her experience.

- **Try to be an electronic "newspaper."** Almost all news sites present content in the same way—subjects divided into hierarchical sections. No one consumes information that way in the age of Google and smart phones. Find new and better ways to present the content that makes you better than your competitors.

- **Think what works today is going to work a year from now,** or even next month. Technology changes fast and users are very fickle. Keep up on trends and be ready to move with them when they happen.

Daniel Anstandig agrees. He says "Whether you are developing a multi-platform strategy for a radio station, show, TV show, or even a product like paper towels, there are some fundamental questions that should be considered as you create your plan.

Below are a few of the questions Anstandig suggests reviewing as media companies enter the digital space. Each of these questions can be placed into one of these eight categories: content, community, communication, commerce, monetization, movement, management, and measurement.

1. Content

- Who is this site targeting? Who is the average user?

- What type of content will be featured on your website?

- Who will be responsible for producing this content?

- How often does content need to be refreshed—and who will be responsible for its implementation?

- Will the content be delivered in the form of text, audio, or video?

- What type of technical platform will this content require?

- Is the content going to be syndicated to iTunes, Shoutcast, or any other "Internet Yellow Pages" site?

- Will the content require any "RSS" (Really Simple Syndication) feed functionality? Are you going to share your content with other sites?

  (*Example*: Tim McAteer, managing editor for online content at all-news 1010 WINS in New York, says 1010 WINS has gained listeners by providing news for specific communities using RSS feeds. "We've increased our hyper-local news coverage, to reach new, non-radio audiences. In return we have advertisers who can target their ads to specific boroughs. 1010 WINS news content is placed on local websites. Users may then turn on the station for more.")

- Is any of your content going to be repackaged for e-mail distribution?

- What is the mobile experience of the people who are using your site? Can this site be optimized for all mobile browsers? Kevin Gossett, Clear Channel Phoenix's Digital Program Director says, "Leading edge websites are already doing subtle redesigns to look really good on the iPad, and with dozens of new tablets coming out in the next year, there's going to be a rush to make sure your site looks good on that form factor."

- How is the site going to be optimized for search engines?

2. Community

- Does your site give the audience freedom to establish a community around your content? This may be in the form of "social networking" forums or comment-posting functionality.

- Does your content lend itself to augmentation from "user generated content?"

- How are you harnessing the traffic on your site? Are you managing a database of users on the site?

- Is there any incentive for your users to communicate with each other on the site?

- Are you maintaining active e-mails as part your user database? E-mail is still one of the most effective digital marketing tools. Don't act like it's dead, because it's not. Do not forget the value of simple e-mail marketing. We have heard from a number of political fundraisers and strategists that e-mail is the strongest (and most "profitable") marketing tool for keeping in touch with donors.

- Can you use Facebook Connect or another community API that will make it easier for people to join your site or social network? (For those less well versed in technology, API stands for "Application Programming Interface." It's a way that you can make one application talk to another. Speaking in loose layman's terms, API is like a "socket" on a program that allows other programs to "plug into it.")

3. Communication

- How will visitors interact with your brand?

- Do you have a dedicated "Listener Relationship Manager" at the station who is designated to reply to all general communication that comes into the station?

- Who will be responsible for monitoring Twitter, Facebook, and other social networks for mentions of your brand—and responding to them?

- Do you have a policy for air talent on how quickly listeners should expect a reply to any e-mail or other communication?

- What type of technology will you use to facilitate communication between visitors and your station staff? Are you going to limit communication to e-mail? Or, are chat rooms, instant messengers, and/or "live operator" modules going to be available?

4. Commerce

There are two sections of this checklist that account for revenue. "Commerce" is the part of your revenue strategy that accounts for business-to-consumer transactions. This may be in the format of merchandise: t-shirts, hats, concert tickets, etc. It may also be in the form of digital downloads or digital access, such as online classified ads, loyalty clubs, or password protected content.

Some of the questions that must be answered in this portion of the strategy are:

- What type of store front/shopping cart functionality will you need for your site?

- Do you have a secured merchant account?

- What is your strategy for controlling inventory in your store?

- Who will serve as the customer service representative at your station when a visitor has a problem?

- Are there products that should be promoted on sites outside of your own? (eBay, Amazon, and other online commerce portals?)

5. Monetization

The second section of this checklist that accounts for revenue is "Monetization," which pertains to business-to-business related transactions.

- What exact product will you be selling online?

- Who will sell the product, and what type of training do they require?

- Do we need to recruit someone to lead the interactive/digital media sales efforts?

- What is the revenue potential in this marketplace? (This analysis can be provided based on regional revenue audits.)

- What is the best way for this station's sales staff to integrate selling interactive—without distracting important attention from the core product (on-air advertising)?

- At what point will your company bring on additional sales resources?

6. Movement

This portion of the strategy accounts for how you will "traffic" listeners onto and through your website. This includes recruitment of audience onto the site as well as navigation through the site.

- What is your strategy to move visitors onto your website?

- How will you utilize search engines to direct interested customers to your site?

- Has your site been optimized for search engines, and what is your plan to maintain healthy search-engine-friendly sites?

- What type of on-air cross-promotion will be utilized to support the website?

- If you are streaming, are you diligently cross-promoting to your on-air properties?

- How will you retain visitors on the site for more than three pages (the average number of pages viewed on any site)? Clear clutter from your website. Too many banners and tiles and no content drives down visits and page views.

- What information will be stored about your user during each site visit to ensure that they are served the best and most relevant content and/or products?

7. Management

- Who will lead this initiative inside the radio station?

- Do you have a Content Management System that is accessible to the entire staff, so that content may be manipulated online by anyone?

- What systems do you have in place to traffic your ads?

- Who will manage your streaming technology, and who is responsible for technical problems?

- Who will lead the sales initiative for interactive? (In many cases, it serves radio stations best to have someone other than the general sales manager responsible for championing interactive sales behind the scenes.)

- Have your compensation packages been reconfigured to reward people for action on the digital plan? (Without incentive, people are unlikely to give it the attention it needs.)

- What type of education, coaching, or internal guidance do you have available for your sales and content teams? How will you help them to transfer their "analog" skills into the digital world?

8. Measurement

Responsible tracking of your site's metrics is essential. You will need to have an analytics program such as Google Analytics or WebTrends. These analytics/measurement systems will help you define popular areas of your website, how long visitors are staying, and where they are coming from. Remember that streaming measurement is just as important as website measurement; make sure every tune-in or view is counted.

- What metrics program will you use?

- Is it necessary to commission third party audits for this site? (This is dependent on your sales strategy.)

- What types of reports will be opened to the sales staff on a regular basis?

- How often will our consultant review the metrics with us to refine our content strategy? (How can our content creators learn from the metrics?)

- Have you set up a system for regular audits of your statistics, so that you can learn from how your audience is using the website?

Without thoroughly considering and planning for any one of these areas, the digital media strategy of that company may be vulnerable."

Revenge of the Pod People

Many "online only" shows are building large audiences. Because of this, even though monetizing the Internet is still a challenge, one area that is generating financial rewards is the podcast. That's because it's easy to verify who's using your product. Then, of course, you can sell to them.

In 2009, when CBS changed the direction of FM talk station KLSX, in Los Angeles, the station pulled its popular morning personality, Adam Carolla, off the air. Carolla had material prepared for his program that he never got to deliver—rants and comedy that nobody had heard yet. He wanted an outlet. A podcast, without federal regulations on what you can and cannot say, and a chance to talk about how unsatisfied he was with the state of radio, seemed like a good idea. When LA's traditional print media, and various trade publications, contacted Carolla for his comments about the format change, he used the opportunity to let his listeners know they could hear "his last show" in podcast form. Downloads reached a million by the end of the day. Clearly, there was a market for what Carolla had to say in any medium.

According to iTunes downloads, Carolla's podcast audience is around 2.8 million listeners per month. There are ads, and it makes money. Adam talks a lot about cars, so Ford motors signed on. He talks about sex: another sponsor: Adam & Eve Adult Products. They pay top dollar for the online commercials and web ads.

Carolla is also a stand-up comedian. His podcast is a way to let his fans know about his upcoming live comedy club events. Another source of revenue: Musicians make money from concessions; Carolla makes money selling signed t-shirts and DVDs at his live appearances. Carolla's relationship with his former employer, CBS, continues. CBS radio handles ad sales for his podcast.

The Blog

Powerful radio creates a bond between a listener, the radio station, and its personalities. Digital media offers many opportunities to enhance that relationship.

Blogging, or keeping an online journal, is another way to deepen the connection between a personality and the audience. Writing a blog is hard work. It takes a lot of time to consistently create new content. What's hard for you should be simple for your listeners. They should be easily able to "sign up" for your blog from the station's website, with the option of receiving it directly, or reading it from your site.

If you aren't much of a writer, or are not willing to commit the time it would take to compose regular blog entries, you still have a really good option for giving your audience a chance to interact with you in an informal and very personal way. The growth of Facebook, and other social networking sites, has made it possible to offer brief daily updates on your whereabouts, both literally and figuratively, personally and professionally. For example, your Facebook page can contain your thoughts on topics that didn't make it to the air, or a more considered response to a listener's comment. You can direct your audience to information you think may be helpful to them, and, of course, post video and photos for any purpose.

When you use social online or digital media for professional purposes, make sure you use it carefully and well. Audiences, no matter how devoted, probably do not care what you ate for breakfast. They will care if you saw the members of a famous music group singing "Happy Birthday to You" in harmony with somebody's daughter at a local breakfast spot, especially if you recorded it.

Personal, Not Private

If you have a Facebook page or website for your family to use, consider creating a separate one for professional use. Don't mix the two. If you "friend" your mom on your Facebook "work" page, make sure she understands that when she posts there, it's like visiting you at your office.

Daniel Anstandig is a big proponent of using Facebook for your station as a whole.

> Your listeners are there. You should be too, but be smart about it. Don't just put a link on your [station's] site to Facebook. That just creates an exit door. You need to give your audience a way to use Facebook that drives traffic and interest back to your brands. Use sharing and collaboration tools, like the Facebook Connect API, which enables your audience to seamlessly integrate your site into their Facebook experience.

CHFI Toronto's air personality Erin Davis (for more on Davis, see "How the Internet Saved the Radio Star" in Chapter 30, *Branding— Building the Brand Beyond Radio*) is an example of how blogging can maintain your career, and grow your brand. Davis set up her website and began her blog a few months before she lost her job. As she puts it, "Blogging kept my career alive."

She says, "It used to be that when a personality was taken off the air, he or she simply disappeared. No one at the station was allowed to tell you where he or she had gone; all you could do was hope that your favorite host, DJ, or newscaster would resurface and you'd find them again." Blogging offered Davis a way to keep in touch and to communicate with her fans and listeners through regular, personal, online posts. Here Erin Davis offers her best advice on keeping a blog.

Erin Davis's Top Ten Tips on Blogging

1. *Set aside a regular time to write.* If you want your blog to become part of a listener's day, you have to commit to making it a part of yours.

2. *Once you start it—keep writing!* How many times have you gone to someone's website only to find the same blog that was there last time you visited? If there's no promise of something new on a set basis, what incentive is there for someone to check in on your thoughts?

3. *Be prepared to answer e-mails in response to your comments.* Often a reader's feedback can provide food for thought for a future blog, or can be excerpted (either anonymously or with their permission) in a follow-up "feedback" journal.

4. *Let listeners feel like they're missing something if they don't visit your site regularly.* It can be your "take" on current events, your random thoughts or even some behind-the-scenes stories about the latest goings-on during your show; give them an "inside" look that they might not be privy to anywhere else. Never be boring!

5. *Be open*, but at the same time be careful about revealing too much about your personal life. Too many details can engender resentment or erode the image that a listener has of you. If you spend your Friday and Saturday nights drinking or partying hard, that can be "too much information" when it comes to the respect that listeners have for you.

6. *Remember that anything you write is open to the world.* Your blog may have just fifty readers, but it only takes one to cut, paste, and send it to someone that you "dissed," or to a potential employer. The written word can last forever. You don't want your 40-year-old self paying a price for what 25-year-old you, said in anger or jest.

7. *Unless you're saying clearly that you're doing it, don't use your blog as a means of promoting products or services.* If you were invited to a restaurant by its owners, tell your readers that. Then tell them what you thought of it, but be honest. Your integrity is not a renewable resource. If a reader feels used or manipulated by your blog, then your opinion is no longer worth anything. Be as honest and transparent as you can. Listeners often perceive radio hosts as being easily bought off. If you want them to trust you and read your blog, don't abuse their loyalty.

8. *Do feel free to let listeners know where you're going to be appearing publicly, and invite them to join you.* Your blog can be a wonderful tool not only for letting readers know what your radio station is doing but also for self-promotion. The caveat here is the same as it should be with your on-air content: Make sure you ask yourself "what's in it for the reader/listener?"

9. *Write about you, but write about them, too.* You will find that the blogs that touch the most people are the ones where you're sharing an experience that is not only personal, but universal. It can be

funny (like the guy next to you at the concert who sang louder than the performer you paid to hear) or somber (the loss of a pet), but if it strikes a chord of familiarity in a reader, you've made just another connection with that person.

10. *Keep it real.* There's a reason that listeners become readers. Reward them for visiting your blog with fresh insight, humor, or information, and they'll keep coming back. Loyal listeners who become loyal website visitors can prove the difference between a prolonged and successful career, and just another faceless voice. Your blog adds another dimension to who your listeners think you are. Honor them by sharing yourself.

Short, But Sweet

Social Mediaologist Jessica Northey has accumulated over 40,000 Twitter feed followers by texting insightful, fun, or useful messages. Northey now works professionally with everyone from "A" list celebrities to corporations, such as banks and hospitals, and individuals—coaching them all to connect with their fans and customers to "go viral," using social media. She also writes a regular column for *www.allaccess.com*.

Northey says, "Don't fall into the 'analysis paralysis' mode. All of the information and platforms, support applications, mobile phone interfaces can make anyone's head spin. It's not that hard. Use all social media. Text frequent, but relevant, messages. If someone follows you on Twitter, follow them back. This gives people a sense of being personally connected to you."

Jessica Northey's Action Plan for Social Media

Northey says, "Keep it simple. Be clear about why you are using social media. Set your goals and manage your own expectations from the beginning."

Typical goals:

- Building relationships
- SEO (improve website ranking)
- Growing targeted following
- Owning the story online.

Reaching Your Goals

Jessica Northey suggests:

1. *Create a business plan that defines your target audience.* Understand how and when your target audience uses social media, (i.e., their gender, age, and geography) and be *there* when *they* are there.

2. *Understand your purpose.* Is it for awareness, entertainment, or to sell the audience something? Do you want branding, loyalty or a call to action? Does your audience know about you today? A solid strategy will translate across all platforms.

3. *If you are driving traffic to a website make sure it's in aesthetic shape.* Change your background on platforms that allow you to do this (Twitter, YouTube, MySpace). Hire someone who can create custom work, if you can. Most stations have social media platforms with empty tabs, no photos, no videos, no notes. That's no good.

4. *Your 'Social-ality' should reflect YOU.* This is what shows your character. Include your brand's unique attributes: behavioral, temperamental, emotional and mental. Are you sassy? Entertaining? Educational? Motivational?

5. *Content is king!* Without giving value to the audience, you will inevitably get, "so what?" [Your content might] vary by market/geographic location, but remember to target your audience, and think about what you should talk about that will be interesting to *them.*

6. *Speak WITH your audience not AT them.* Social media is all about *communicating* and user generated content. Forget 'What am *I* doing?' and ask your followers 'What are *they* doing?' This is why I have thousands of followers. I am constantly engaging them and asking about them. They feel I care. If you are not having success on social media, it might be in direct proportion to the kind of person you are in real life. No one can help you with that except maybe a good therapist."

Jessica Northey recommends the following to improve your social media profile:

Cross-promote your social media involvement on air and online. Connect your website to platforms using widgets, 'Like' buttons, etc. Please remember that whoever you designate to tweet, post or blog for your brand represents your brand. Add social media platforms participation links to business cards, letterhead and other broadcast and print media.

She also advises:

- When you are out in public, consistently talk about social media and all the ways listeners can connect with you. Add social media applications to your phone.

- Put your Twitter or other social media addresses on everything including T-shirts, coffee cups, bumper stickers, billboards, ads, the station's van or vehicles.

- Offer social media-only promotions—with a deadline. Don't forget to invite followers to your events. Include links where they can register.

Finally, consider using new media to partner with advertisers—offering them specials through venues like "Groupon," "Gowalla," "Foursquare," or other online discount coupon companies or services that invite customer participation; this will help to build your brand and help your audience to save money. There are uncountable ways you can now place your brand in front of your audience by offering them something useful or special. Perhaps your station, "The Mix," would like to offer a custom blend of coffee, "The Morning Mix," at a local chain of coffee shops? You can e-mail them a coupon for "a free cup, today only." There are dozens of new media platforms you can use to get your name, and your advertisers' names, out there. By the time you read this, there are likely to be dozens more.

The great advantage of new media is that it costs very little to try something new. Unlike spending money for t-shirts, billboards or newspaper ads, the cost to promote yourself or your brand in the virtual world is little, changing your strategy takes almost no time, and the benefits can be huge.

In the box on the following page are a few tips (and warnings) from the RTDNA.

While some of these points are covered elsewhere in this book, they bear repeating. Though these were written with journalists in mind, they apply to ALL broadcasters working on-line and using social media.

Now you have the playbook. The creativity is yours to supply.

Social Media Tips

From the RTDNA - (Radio & TV Digital News Association)

To protect your brand and credibility, social media comments and posts should meet the same standards of fairness, accuracy and attribution that you apply to your on-air or digital platforms.

- You should not write anonymously or use an avatar or username that cloaks your real identity on newsroom or personal websites. You are responsible for everything you say. Commenting or blogging anonymously compromises this core principle.

- Remember that what's posted online is open to the public (even if you consider it to be private). Personal and professional lives merge online. Newsroom and all broadcast employees should recognize that even though their comments may seem to be in their "private space," their words become direct extensions of their news organizations. Search engines and social mapping sites can locate their posts and link the writers' names to their employers.

- Avoid posting photos or any other content on any website, blog, social network or video/photo sharing website that might embarrass you or undermine your journalistic credibility. Keep this in mind, even if you are posting on what you believe to be a "private" or password-protected site. Consider this when allowing others to take pictures of you at social gatherings. When you work for a journalism organization, you represent that organization on and off the clock. The same standards apply for journalists and broadcasters who work on or off the air.

PART V

Beyond Powerful Radio
Marketing Content

CHAPTER 29

Beyond Powerful Radio
Promotion

"Promotion is the exploitation of opportunity."
—Doug Harris

What Is Radio Promotion?

Simply, promotion is anything that puts the word out about your station. Promotion gets people talking about and listening to your product.

Promotions are events such as contests, publicity stunts, and outside advertising on billboards or TV. "Promos," on the other hand, are the spots or segments you run on your station that support your own programming.

Radio promotion has two goals: To draw in new listeners and to get current listeners to tune in more often. Promotion is also a sales tool for additional revenue while expanding the station's audience.

Doug Harris, marketing and promotions consultant, believes that marketing and promotion professionals are often the most misunderstood and underappreciated people in a radio station.

When operating budgets get tight, all expenses related to marketing become suspect, and because the effects of good advertising and promotion are not always immediately apparent, these funds are often the first to be cut. As the radio industry has become more cost conscious, traditional advertising campaigns for radio stations have become scarce, reserved for station launches, the debut of new morning shows, and the occasional cash contest. The current trend in the marketing and promotion of a broadcast property is to "get results with less."

That's not an impossible thing to do, but it requires a certain amount of creativity and planning. Doug has a couple of great stories of stations that launched successfully by "out-thinking rather than outspending" their competition:

> Alternative rock station KPNT-FM, "The Point," launched in St. Louis, Missouri, with a special press conference. All the invited journalists were from local high school and university papers. At the "First Student Press Conference," these amateur journalists got the professional treatment, including interviews with the new station's personalities and a hot new alternative music artist. The station awarded a $500 educational grant for the best article, resulting in a great deal of press about KPNT in student publications around the city and an implied endorsement by the writers and their papers. Within two ratings periods, KPNT became a Top 10 radio station in a crowded marketplace, and a leader among school-aged listeners.

> KTBZ-FM, "The Buzz," in Houston, Texas, was looking for a memorable way to inform its listeners about its scheduled move up the dial from 107.5 to 94.5. Reading from a supposedly "official" letter from station management, the station broadcast announcements that on a certain date, "The Buzz would cease to exist at 107.5." Panic swept through the loyal audience, and thousands of people called the radio station to protest. The station invited people to "Save The Buzz" rallies across the city, encouraging them to write, call, and e-mail The Buzz's management. Weeks later the station announced that because of the audience's support, it would be getting a new, stronger signal. Then the station invited the audience to a free "I Saved The Buzz" concert. Although the signal switch and even the free concert had been planned months in advance, the station was able to maximize the impact of these events by giving listeners credit for "saving The Buzz." What could have been a disaster (and indeed was for the station that took The Buzz's place on the dial) helped loyalty among Buzz listeners that has lasted for years.

Getting into Listeners' Minds

What does it take to earn a place in the mind of a radio listener? Harris says:

> People remember what is important to them, that which makes a profound impression. These are usually the things or experiences that they perceive to be either first, biggest, or best. As an example, many people can tell you that the name of the highest mountain in the world is Mt. Everest. Far fewer could give you the names of the second or third highest peaks. So, the trick becomes to convince your listener, or target listener, that your station is or has the first, biggest, or best of something.

What types of promotions make a lasting impression? Harris describes them with the amusing and memorable acronym "SAFO SHRIMPS":

The SAFO SHRIMPS Theory of Consumer Interest

Sex—also romance, love, and relationships

Achievement—songs in a row, award-winning programming

Fantasy—contest prizes or an experience with element of fantasy that cannot be bought

Outrage—edgy content, dramatic publicity stunts, and "shock talk"

Spectacle—uses "theater of the mind," station "roadshows," and live broadcasts; gives audiences something they've never seen before

Humor—major personalities, morning shows, comedy bits

Rescue—blood drives, fund-raising efforts, human interest stories

Injustice—news of the day; bad judgment calls by sports officials, politicians, etc.

Money—contest prizes, lottery results, stories on government spending

Patriotism—love or affection for sports teams, community, country, or home

Scandal—gossip, celebrity news

To decide which of the Safo Shrimps tactics your station will use to lure listeners, Harris advises, "Learn as much as you can about your target audience and their needs." There are, of course, lots of research companies you can pay to provide this kind of information, but if you don't have the budget, your station can benefit from simply reviewing the news headlines that other media, like broadcast, print, and the Internet, are using to grab the attention of the same people you are looking to interest.

Keeping Your Promise

Doug Harris is also an expert on "branding" radio stations. "Branding" is often spoken of in hushed tones, as if it were a mystical phenomenon. But a one-word definition can simplify and clarify the meaning and importance of branding. In the world of broadcasting, a brand is a "promise." Every time a listener encounters a radio brand, that station's "promise" must be fulfilled. A station that promotes a safe haven for listeners and their families cannot allow its personalities to use racy or "blue" humor. Ever. If a listener lured by this "safe and fun for the whole family" promise tunes in to hear a dirty joke or even something slightly inappropriate, the "promise" has been broken. If a station does something out of character from its image, it risks changing that image in the minds of the audience and devaluing its brand. A brand is the collection of emotions and beliefs that comes to mind when a consumer hears the name of that radio station, sees its logo, or meets one of its personalities. A successful marketer protects his brand by ensuring that all of these contacts promote a single, pure image (more on this in Chapter 30 *Branding—Building the Brand Beyond Radio*).

The same phenomenon works for radio stations. A radio station or station personality must do something significant in order to be remembered by a listener. It must be something that the listener cares enough about to form an opinion. Most markets have dozens of radio stations, and most listeners are "button-pushers". If the station, its personalities, or its programming are going to be remembered, they must send a compelling message, from a credible source, in a dramatic fashion. And this message must be sent with frequency and consistency.

Doug Harris breaks the process down into the steps described in the following subsections.

Define the Target

"The programming and marketing teams should identify a primary target, describing your intended listener's age, gender, and programming preferences." Harris continues:

> Your programming team may have purchased research to find the "hole" in your market, that segment of the listening audience which is not being served by another radio station or another piece of programming.
>
> The research may point out the radio stations from which your new station hopes to steal its audience. Your marketing team may visit some of these stations' events to see the audience in person. Other general information from research companies may reveal your intended listeners' tastes in reading materials, entertainment, automobiles, vacation destinations, and even food. Before you set your marketing strategy, look at all the research available. Know as much about your audience as possible.
>
> By knowing your audience, you ensure that you are promoting something that will be of genuine interest. Address a real need, giving listeners a real solution to a real problem. Offering a three-week vacation for two to another country may not be as useful to your target listener, a 33-year-old mother of two young children, as a weekend at Disneyworld. Promote the right thing at the right time to the right person.
>
> It may help you to follow the practice of many radio stations of creating a profile of a fictitious person with a name and a life story in order to imagine your target listener. Some programmers have even been known to place a photo of a stylized, fictitious family of this type in their broadcast studios to keep the on-air hosts focused on the target.

An additional tool for visualizing the target listener is "LifeStage Demographics." (You can read more in Chapter 33, *LifeStage Demographics.*) Whatever strategy you use to create and promote powerful radio, it is important to know who you're talking to.

Identify the Emotional Needs of Your Target

People remember the things they connect with emotionally. A message like "Ten songs in a row" or "More music in the morning" would seem to be a great selling tool because it is fact based. It's true that claims like "The Rock Station" or "Hot Talk" tell the listener what to expect and can help differentiate a station from its competitors, if the audience cares about the claim. But emotional slogans like "We're with you" and "The sound of the city" often connect with a listener's lifestyle or feelings. Some programmers have found that this emotional imagery is more important than making an empirical claim about music or talk.

The very name of your station can add an emotional component to its positioning message. "The Edge" suggests a cutting-edge approach to music. "The Beat" connotes a rhythmic music presentation and hints that the station is in touch with the "beat" of the market. Monikers like "The Hawk," "The Colt," and "The Eagle" suggest that the station has the characteristics of those animals, like a feisty, proud, or playful spirit. And station names like "Jack" and "Alice" are meant to help promote a "we do what we want" kind of programming that appeals to a particular audience and positions the station as having a "personality" of its own.

The personality aspects of stations are an additional tool in positioning your station, as it works to compete with the flexible and individual choices listeners can make using their portable media players and custom computer music channels.

With micro-positioned formats on the rise, marketers and programmers may be best served by promoting an attitude, in addition to their music position and dial position, to earn a lasting place in the listener's memory.

Along with Doug's thoughts about building an emotional connection with creative and meaningful slogans and names, it's important to promote the on-air personalities at every opportunity. The emotional connection and relationship that a listener has to an on-air personality or presenter is a powerful incentive to select your station. For example, promoting your evening host taking requests for love songs at a set time builds an additional personal bridge to your listeners.

Give Me a Sign

To get the most use out of your station's logo as a marketing and promotional tool, Doug Harris makes these suggestions: "Your logo is part of building an emotional connection with your listener. Make sure that the artwork and the image it represents engages rather than offends or confuses your audience."

Take a trip to the grocery store. Companies spend millions of dollars researching which colors and packaging styles appeal to different sexes and age groups. Learn from their work. Compare a beer bottle or a can of charcoal lighter fluid with household cleaning supplies and shampoo. You'll notice a big difference that you may incorporate into your station's "packaging."

Be careful. Doug recommends that a logo be unique and distinctive but, more importantly, easy to read and identify. "Many stations make the mistake of using elaborate artwork that overpowers the call letters and dial position. It may look gorgeous, but if it is hard to read and/or remember, you have not effectively promoted your station."

Doug mentions some other forms of "logo abuse" that include "use of colors that do not read well at night (a concern for billboards), or a font size that is too small or too fancy (how's your audience's eyesight?). Since logos are often reduced to black-and-white versions for use in some forms of media, good marketers must make sure it translates well. When it comes to creating a logo, stick to professional artists and a simple approach."

Even though Doug Harris is strong on research, when crafting a marketing and promotional identity, he still points out that "legions of successful stations have been launched on 'gut feelings' of brave programmers and marketers." There's no substitute for life experience. Research alone won't get you there. Your best asset for promoting a radio station is having a great product to promote.

Product, Permanence, and Promotion

Your product is what you do. Ideally, you have built a fine station with creative elements, good shows, interesting news and information, plus top personalities.

Permanence involves keeping those shows consistent by running them at regular times so the audience can develop the habit of listening.

Now comes promotion—letting the audience know where you are and what you are doing. You can promote any element of your radio station, as long as it's good, interesting radio. Don't knock yourself out barking people into the tent if the circus isn't great.

Promotions have to be as good and creative as the rest of your station. If your station is intense, dynamic, creative, funny, and passionate, your promos should be too. If they are not, you're missing an opportunity to generate revenue, get new listeners, and create powerful radio. A powerful promotion should:

- Promote the station's image as well as its product

- Build passion, emotion, and listener loyalty

- Involve your listeners

- Ensure that people who are not participating will still enjoy hearing the contest.

Technology makes it possible to monitor listeners' habits in real time. This is changing the way stations schedule promotions. In the United States, it has made sense to run promotions in connection with the big Arbitron ratings books. Many stations have had success starting their promotions on Thursdays because that's when listeners begin keeping track of what they're listening to in the Arbitron diaries.

Promoting the News

Your own airwaves can be one of the best vehicles available for marketing the news and information you offer. Take a small excerpt from a reporter's "magic moment" on the air, or a piece of a great interview on a breaking story, and create a powerful image-enhancing promo. It might sound like this:

If you weren't listening to Z-97 news yesterday at noon, here's what you missed: [insert audio of magic moment]. *For news as it happens, it's Z-97!*

This "performance promo" lets the audience know that if they're not listening to you, they're really missing out. This method applies to more than news programming: Record audio of everything. Save "magic moments" from callers, talk shows, contests, and monologues. They make great promos! Magic moment promos have an extra benefit. Often, listeners who hear the promo genuinely believe they heard the show from which it came. Your entertaining promo can get you credit for listening that didn't actually take place.

If your production director doesn't recognize a powerful radio moment when he or she hears one, or can't spend time listening during the day, it's something a good producer should save or note. Make sure your station has a system in place to get these creative moments into the production studio and back onto the airwaves with a minimum of delay.

You can also create promos around specific station personalities. At one Arizona station, a news promotion was built around individual reporters, including the then-morning police reporter. Here's the basic script:

> *While you're asleep, KTAR's Rod Petersen is out cruising the streets, looking for trouble..."And I'll find it too,"* [says Rod]. *The best police and crime coverage on KTAR, Newsradio 620.*

A Scoop for a "Scoop"

Another way to engage your listeners while promoting your news product is to ask the audience to help you. Texting and e-mail make it easy. Most news and talk TV and radio stations employ some version of the "tip line." And viewers or listeners may do more than just alert you to breaking news stories or events; they may be able to provide eyewitness reports or actual video or audio that you can use. Don't underestimate the attraction for many listeners in hearing their name on the radio or getting credit for a "scoop." This works for traffic tips as well. You will hear many radio stations thanking "mobile [or cell] caller Bill" for the information on the load of chickens that fell off a truck blocking the three left lanes of a major highway.

Many stations take this to the next level and thank listeners who participate with modest cash awards or gifts. A promotions director in San Francisco, with a limited budget, came up with the idea of "a scoop for a scoop," asking listeners to call with news tips. Whenever the station used one, the caller would receive a coupon good for free ice cream. Listeners from three counties called in to get those free scoops of ice cream. The tip line is not a contest, the "reward" or prize is a "thank you."

You can look at listener tip lines in one of two ways: as a lot of extra work screening the phone messages for veracity and tracking down leads, or as an opportunity to eclipse your competition by getting first crack at new stories that no one else has. For much more on this see Chapter 21 *Citizen Journalism.*

Let callers know on your outgoing message that this is not the place for anonymous sourcing. If a listener wants credit for letting the public know that a neighborhood grocer is storing toxic waste in the back room, he will probably receive it. If he wants to keep his job as a grocery store cashier at that market, the tip line is not the place to leave a message.

People who call in or text with news stories are likely altogether different than those who would enter a contest or competition. Instead of "winning," they want to be part of the station and believe they have something of value to share. And the station gets another promotional opportunity. When someone's story is on the air, he is going to get all his friends and family to listen. You could not ask for a better promotion for your radio station than a personal recommendation from one of your listeners.

"I Won! I Won!": Doug Harris on Creative Contesting

Contesting is about fantasy, big or small. We live in a cynical world, but many dream of winning big. In the best contests, everyone is a winner. Listeners get to play a part in an adventure or game, where nothing negative can happen, and even if you lose, people walk away feeling that it was fun to play.

The audience likes to imagine what life would be like if they met their favorite star, won a million dollars, drove a red Ferrari, traveled around the world, got their dream kitchen, or owned their own home.

The goal for an effective contest: to get people to believe that if they listen to this radio station, their lives could change.

Doug Harris breaks contesting into several different categories. He points out two factors controlling the likelihood that a listener will participate in a contest. "Generally speaking, the harder or more complicated your contest is to play, the fewer people will play it, and the bigger the prize or payoff, the more people are likely to enter.

The Pros and Cons of Contests

Designated Caller Contests

The on-air personality offers a prize or a chance to play a game to caller X. This is easy to do and easy to understand, but it limits participation to the most active audience members. Most people never call radio stations and believe their chances of winning are very small. Generally it is not exciting radio, unless the winner is extremely animated. However, many programmers believe that "teasing" the audience with an upcoming contest makes people listen longer.

Trivia Contests

The on-air personality solicits an answer to a question. Because the audience gets to "play along," even if they are not actually calling in, there is some added entertainment value. This is also a very simple contest to explain and conduct.

Recall Contests

This requires a bit more from your listeners. They are asked to tune in at a particular time of day to hear a code word, phrase, or song. They must then listen again later that day for a chance to call in and repeat the information to win a prize. The purpose of this form of contesting is to promote listening to a number of dayparts.

E-mail, Fax, or "Snail" Mail Contests

In all of these, a listener gets to choose his or her own time to participate. With a longer time frame, more people can participate. Mail-in responses require more time than fax or e-mail contesting, but all three remove the "run to the phone" or "stay by the radio" obstacle. These contests can be trivia or recall based, or can simply ask for a listener's contact information for a random drawing. Here you can also get more complex responses, such as for an essay or photo contest. (E-mail and instant- or text-message contesting can occur in real time and has produced some great talk radio. Personality shows can generate content in the form of audio for on-air use, photos and videos for the station's website, and stories or information that can be used in a variety of ways.)

Performance-Based Contests

Listeners may be asked to perform a stunt or a task over the phone or in person at a specific location. Of course, the more difficult, labor intensive, or potentially embarrassing the stunt, the smaller the potential universe of players becomes. In most cases, a substantial prize is required to get people to participate in these contests, but when they work, they can be a lot of fun. If they're theatrical enough, they can get your station covered on TV and in print.

Here are some examples of contests that got a lot of TV and print attention:

To position its morning show as outrageous, contemporary hit radio station WZZU-FM in Spokane, Washington, conducted a search for the hairiest back in the city, inviting male listeners to come to a nightclub and show off their "pelts" while dancing. The winner got a cash prize and a laser hair removal treatment.

That's the same feeling rock station KLOL-FM in Houston, Texas, was going for when it invited men who weighed over 300 pounds to enter the Fat Man's Dance Off at a local nightclub by offering a $500 cash prize. Over a dozen men participated and the winner got a standing ovation and left with a pretty blonde.

For years, WEBN-FM in Cincinnati, Ohio, punned on the American national holiday of Labor Day by staging a "pregnant bikini contest." It drew huge crowds, and a lot of TV cameras.

All of these contests took advantage of the public's interest in the bizarre and unusual. In addition to all the free press, stations that can post photos of these types of spectacles on their websites can get more "promotional mileage" out of them.

Performance-based contesting can work over the radio, as well. KRBE-FM, in Houston, Texas, challenged listeners to have an on-air telephone conversation with their mothers during which the listeners would say something so outrageous that the moms would use foul language. "Make Your Momma Curse" has been used by dozens of radio stations around the world.

In both on-air and off-air performance contesting, this rule of thumb applies: The more difficult or more potentially embarrassing a contest is, the bigger the prize must be.

Can You Buy an Audience?

A Chicago radio station once ran a promotion called "The Million Dollar Minute." It threw a million one-dollar bills on the floor of a bank vault and a single listener was given sixty seconds to scoop up as much as she could. The station calculated she would walk away with about $10,000. But, owing to a series of errors, the winner managed to grab $106,083. And the station dropped in the ratings. Many stations have tried giving away huge cash prizes, cars, and cruises, only to find listeners deserting when the contest is over.

While a powerful promotion can initially bring large numbers of new listeners "into the tent," unless you build a connection with them, no matter how big the prize, no matter how creative the contest, you cannot truly "buy an audience." Over the long haul, unless your station entertains and informs, providing a real sense of connection, you won't keep the listeners who have come for the contest. Listeners may love their prizes or sell them for a profit later, but providing content is ultimately the way to keep your prize—the new audience you have won.

The launch of a new station or show is one instance where a massive promotion or marketing effort can really pay off. Your objective is to bring people into the tent long enough for them to get a sample of your programming. Doug Harris calls this the "jet-assisted takeoff," resulting in a short-term spike in ratings.

Even though the majority of new listeners are coming to play the contest, if your programming is deserving, enough of them will stay to justify the expenditure. Another time to spend promotional or marketing dollars is when you've lured a high-profile show away from your competition and you want listeners to know where to find their favorite host. That expenditure nearly always gets a positive result.

Lots of small prizes often work better than one major prize. More people can win, and, more importantly, more people believe they can win. These promotions can be less costly and they achieve the same goal of getting people to talk about what's happening on your station. Added up, the more winners, the more people are thinking good thoughts and spreading the word about your station.

The Bake Sale

Some of the best promotions in radio are spontaneous, developing from programming on the air. Here's a wonderful example: Dan's Bake Sale.

The idea for Dan's Bake Sale came from a conversation between talk show host Rush Limbaugh and one of his listeners. Rush publishes his own newsletter, available by paid subscription. "Dan the Listener" from Fort Collins, Colorado, said he'd like a subscription but was short on money and couldn't afford one. In keeping with Rush's political philosophy of entrepreneurship and independence and his sense of humor, Rush decided to have a "bake sale," selling chocolate chip cookies to raise money for Dan's subscription.

It became a huge event. Newspapers reported all flights into Fort Collins booked for the weekend of the bake sale. People planned camping trips just to be there. Rush flew into town and thousands of fans turned out to meet him. It was huge, it was fun, it promoted Rush's show, and it created a news event covered by TV, radio, and the national press. It also sold a lot of subscriptions to Rush's newsletter!

Other Favorite Promotions

Some of the best promotions tie into public service, benefiting your community while getting the word out about your radio station. They don't have to be expensive. A good promotion generates press that your station couldn't possibly buy. Listed below are a few success stories.

Orange Barrel Holiday

When Albuquerque, New Mexico, was plagued by road construction projects, traffic was a mess. Drivers were going crazy trying to maneuver around orange construction barrels, which were closing off lanes and streets everywhere.

The market's full-service station, KOB, decided to have some fun with a bad situation. The station contacted the company that made the orange barrels and devised the "Orange Barrel Holiday." Listeners signed up to win an all-expense-paid trip to the small town in Indiana where the barrels were manufactured. Highlights included a tour of the barrel factory and lunch in the plant cafeteria. The promotion worked by combining a sense of community involvement with a sense of humor.

The Ugliest Weed

One drought-stricken summer in California's San Joaquin Valley, radio station KFBK/Sacramento urged its listeners to send in the ugliest weed growing in their fields or gardens. This idea struck a chord in the largely agricultural area. Listeners responded in a big way. KFBK got so many tumorous growths, many of them enormous, that they filled up several storerooms and part of a warehouse.

The grower of the ugliest weed won a cash prize and some free gardening supplies from the sponsor and became a local celebrity. People in town talked about the contest, and it generated free publicity for the station on local television and in the newspapers. This is a great example of a promotion fitting a station and its community.

Mystery History

At the same time each day, WABC/New York played bits of audio from an actual historic moment. Listeners had to guess who was speaking to win prizes. Since politics, news, and discussion of current events fill much of the broadcast day, "Mystery History" works well on news and talk radio stations. It helps if a talented production director puts this contest together.

Singles Night at the Supermarket

This promotion combined knowledge of audience lifestyle with practical considerations such as sex, food, and revenue. The sponsor was the largest supermarket chain in California. The station, KIOI-FM/San Francisco, broadcast live from a store location and invited its target listeners, singles in their 20s and 30s, to meet the disc jockeys and each other. The station handed out free t-shirts with the station logo, and listeners wore them as they pushed their shopping carts through the aisles.

More than a thousand listeners turned out and several romantic relationships and one marriage resulted. The sponsor loved the promotion because it brought lots of people to the market. The event created great word-of-mouth publicity for the station and its client.

Go to Hell

This falls under the category of "geography joke" promotions. Stations often give away trips to the usual places. With a little creativity and an atlas, however, you can go the extra mile. WMIR in Lake Geneva, Wisconsin, created a Halloween promotion.

A check of the map turned up the town of Hell, in nearby Michigan. On-air promos promised listeners an all-expense-paid trip to Hell on Halloween, complete with dinner at the Devil's Den restaurant. The fact that this particular "Hell" was in Michigan was mentioned only once in each promo, and not very prominently.

The promotion set the town "on fire." Thousands of people signed up for the opportunity to go to Hell...and come back. A little research may turn up many such opportunities within driving distance of your station: "Win a free trip to Tokyo (Nebraska)," and so on.

A Promotion Checklist

"The promotions or marketing manager is the 'PD' of the off-air side of your radio station," says consultant Michael Hedges.

Michael Hedges's Tips for Creating Powerful Radio Promotions

- *Ask, "Does this promotion make sense?"* Every promotion must make sense within the marketing objectives of the radio station.

- *Less is truly more.* Choose your promotions carefully. When presented with five (major) promotional ideas for a month, choose the ONE that has the greatest likelihood of succeeding. Do that one.

- *They remember!* Every time the radio station is presented to the public, an impression is made. These impressions are cumulative in the mind of the listener. Listeners are equally likely to remember your faults or your merits. Your very polite listeners will never call to tell you how disgusting and dirty the remote van looked, but you can bet one will tell ten friends that your station looked tacky.

- *When designing a promotion, always ask yourself how it can be made bigger.* Radio is show biz. Show it to them!

- *Don't outsmart yourself.* Complicated promotions rarely succeed because listeners just don't have time to participate. You can build interest in a promotion only to the extent that the listeners see a payoff. The promotion will fail if the length of the rules promo goes over thirty seconds.

- *It's the details.* Think thirty times about each step through which the gentle listener must pass to play the game, attend the event, and win the prize. Use their eyes and ears, not yours. The wrong telephone number, url or e-mail address on an entry form is totally inexcusable.

- *Remember the payoff.* Sales promotions can work if, and only if, each and every listener-participant comes away from the event feeling that the time and energy he or she spent participating was in some way compensated.

- *Remember to get paid.* Plan for local media coverage. Think of ways to make your promotion interesting to them. Make sure that every local editor knows about your promotion well in advance. Have photos of every contest winner published in the local or community newspaper.

- *The promo is better than the bit.* Former Dallas radio personality Ron Chapman's "first and only law of promotion": The production must be the best element on your radio station. The writing must be tight, smart, and crisp. If a promotion, event, or contest doesn't sound exciting on your radio station, listeners will never hear it.

- *All promotions are equal.* Listeners don't necessarily know the difference between programming promotions and sales promotions and they don't mind being sold products or services compatible with their expectations of the radio station. Anything sold in an entertaining way is, well, entertaining.

Consultant Jaye Albright advises:

Create priority and focus with your station promos. Narrow the focus to only the most important promo topics—devote your entire inventory to these. The more you ask of your listeners, the less impact each request will have. Each week, there will be dozens of priorities that all seem worthy of promo mentions. Unfortunately, the more you promote, the more clutter you create and the fewer things your audience will actually remember and respond to.

Think of every promo as a favor you are asking of your audience: attending an event, listening to your morning show, participating in a contest, or friending you on Facebook. Network TV is a good example of using promos effectively; each of the major networks airs thirty to fifty different programs each week, yet they heavily promote fewer than a dozen.

Steer Clear of Contest Junkies

Warning: There is a group of people who live to play radio contests. Make sure your contest is legal and restrictions are clear. You can tailor your rules in order to weed out the contest addicts. Your rules should be structured in such a way as to give the average person the best chance of winning.

Avoid Disasters

Whatever your promotion, plan it carefully. Do a little informal research. Run your promotion idea by a few people around the office. See if they can spot any obvious flaws.

A storyline about a contest was dramatized on the 1980s TV show *WKRP in Cincinnati*. Although this contest played out on a network sitcom, it could easily be an example of a real station promotion gone horribly wrong: It was the standard American "Thanksgiving Turkey Giveaway," with a twist.

Instead of handing out coupons for frozen turkeys, the station would drop live turkeys from a helicopter to glide down to listeners waiting in a parking lot below. Unfortunately, the promotion department overlooked one important consideration—turkeys can't fly. As fictitious newsman Les Nessman reported live on the air, "Turkeys are hitting the ground like bags of wet cement!" Be certain your promotion will "fly" before you drop it on the public.

No Budget? No Problem

For some reason, many station managers do not believe in spending money on marketing. When faced with this challenge, Doug Harris says, "Use OPM." What is "OPM"? It's "other people's money" or "other people's media." How does one get hold of other people's money? Actually it is not very hard. As Doug Harris points out: "Clients of a radio station have cars, electronic products, restaurant gift certificates, trips, tickets, spa days, and access to places and people all of which can be incorporated into station giveaways." All those clients ask in return is airtime and maybe an appearance by you or one of your presenters from your station van. Here is where the sales department can be your best ally. Of course, they will expect advertising revenue in return, but that is fair.

If the sales department is unable to help, or if you are promoting a non-commercial radio station, you still have options. As a member of the media, you have access to cultural and entertainment events and items that your listeners do not.

One example of creative problem solving to promote a show in America came from public radio. A quiz show, just starting out, had no money for prizes, so the promoters talked one of their network's news presenters into recording an outgoing message on the voicemail system of each week's winner. And they made fun of themselves for not having money for better prizes. The audience got the joke, and now, several years later, though the program is a success, listeners still demand a chance to win that news presenter's voice on their phone answering machine. Now that bit is an integral part of the show.

Let's say you work at a non-commercial jazz station with no funds to spare. Ask a band that gets a lot of airplay from your station to put on a concert just for your listeners, and borrow a local jazz club for the venue. Everybody wins—the club gets exposure, the band gets airplay, and your audience feels special and appreciated. Cost to you: zero.

Although you may not be spending any money on your event, it is advisable to detail in writing the value of the things your station is providing, and the value of the products or services you will receive in return. Make sure all the necessary people sign off on the event, and you can avoid some nasty surprises later.

Do not be afraid to use your contacts to arrange experiences for listeners that they would not otherwise have. Celebrities are often loyal to the stations that first recognized their talent and promoted them early in their careers.

"OPM" Programming

Make sure to use what Doug Harris calls "other people's media" (OPM) every chance you get.

> Listener polls, publicity stunts, and the traditionally wacky things that radio stations do are often attractive to television stations and print outlets, provided that they are sufficiently out of the ordinary to be of interest to the public. Of course, a good place to look is at your own company if it owns newspapers, magazines, TV, outdoor, or other media. But don't stop there. Create relationships and educate yourself on the needs of other media outlets in your area. And be prepared to give them content in a form that they can most easily use.

Most cities have a media contact list published by the visitors' bureau, or you can do a little homework and create one. Then find someone on your staff who can write good press releases on a regular basis. Use this list to promote station activities, events, and personalities. Remember, these outlets and electronic media like the Internet are always in need of fresh entertaining content. If you can provide something interesting or exciting for them to cover, they will.

Approaching Television

You can use video to promote your radio station online by posting videos both on your own station site and using YouTube along with other internet video service sites, but how do you get a TV station to promote your radio station? Former New York City television assignment editor, Howard Price, is an experienced gatekeeper for those trying to getting their stories covered by WABC TV. Price suggested you keep in mind the following points when trying to pitch a radio story to television:

- Think about how you can break through the thousands of e-mails spewed daily onto the assignment editor's desk, the nine phone lines that ring constantly, and the 330 channels of scanner chatter that must be monitored.

- Don't get frustrated if you call a TV news desk and they are brusque with you or if you hear "no." It just means they are busy. Try again another time.

- Get a feel for what plays on the station you are pitching to. Like radio's many formats, each TV station's programming targets specific audiences and demographics.

- Call once. Fax once. E-mail once. And never call when the newscast is on the air. Make sure your faxes and e-mails contain the facts—that's what the stations really need.

- Pitch things that dovetail with the day's news—especially if you are a news or talk station—and don't pitch a goofball story on a serious news day. It may work better to promote your "light" story to a TV station on a slow news day.

- Keep TV posted regularly, and with as much advance notice as possible, on your scheduled guests.

- Know the TV station's deadlines. Most coverage for morning news shows is locked in by 4 a.m.; for noon shows, by 10:30 a.m.; for the 5:00 and 6:00 p.m. news, it's about 3:30 p.m.; and for 10 or 11 p.m. newscasts, by about 9:30 p.m. The exception, of course, is for legitimate breaking news.

- Start your events on time, but run them long enough for latecomers to have a chance at getting some pictures and sound. Deliver what you promise on your press release or pitch to the newsroom.

- Plaster your call letters everywhere. To make sure your name, dial position, and images get the play you want, post them all over your studios and at your events. That way, even if they aren't mentioned, the audience will see them.

- No pictures—no story. TV is a visual medium. Compelling pictures are what drive it. A bunch of folks sitting around a radio studio don't make for exciting TV, unless of course they are high-profile folks making news exclusively on your air.

- Be "TV friendly." Create broadcast spaces inside and outside your studios that TV crews can easily negotiate to get the shots you want them to get. TV crews need extra time to put their trucks in place, string their cables, etc. Make sure there are electrical outlets in your studios that they can access. Giving them time to edit your story helps, but remember, "live" is TV's magic word.

- If your radio station is co-owned with a TV station, labor every day to strengthen that partnership. Share resources when it counts and each station will reap the rewards. If you are not co-owned but your station has a network affiliation, partner with your network's local TV outlet. Your network will love you, your TV partner will love you, and, most important, so will your audience.

Piggyback on Your Advertisers' Advertising

Doug Harris suggests "doing a little homework to find out which advertisers in your market spend the most money on television, print, and outdoor." He continues:

Find a way to include one of the station personalities or a station logo in that client's advertising. The client might like to use one of your station personalities as a spokesperson for his or her product or service instead of an anonymous actor.

This is a way to get exposure for your radio station's call letters, logo, or personalities at little or no cost to you. Of course, co-promoting a major event is a great way for your station to look larger than it would if it were doing this project alone. And if two media entities are willing to share the limelight, you can put your station's logo and personalities in front of a much bigger audience.

Other resources—a branded website, an online newsletter, or an interactive phone system (such as a movie theater's recorded schedule on the phone message recorded by your afternoon host)—can all offer additional exposure for a particular personality, program, or promotion.

These cost-effective examples of "other people's media" will enhance and amplify your marketing attack, especially if traditional, more expensive avenues of external marketing are closed.

While on-air messages are usually short-form (10 to 60 seconds), more details and features of a promotion may be easily explained on the station's website. The website is also a great place to post photos of contest prizes, previous winners, contest rules, and other key information, too cumbersome for air.

Doug Harris' Action Plan for Success

Here is a seven-step process for planning in advance and putting things in writing to build an annual marketing plan for your station, personality, or program.

Step One: Each department at the radio station should prepare a list of goals, needs, and wants. The needs of the programming department are quite different from those of the sales department. Both are important. This list should include equipment upgrades, additional staff, and other expense-related requests. It should also include ratings and revenue goals and marketing targets and achievements. If your programming department wants to "own" the concert-going public, then the marketing and promotion department needs to target concert venues and ticket outlets. Meanwhile, the sales department can target concert promoters and related activities and products such as soft drinks and guitar stores.

Step Two: Create an eighteen-month calendar beginning with the start of the next month. If that seems too big a job, try one year or even six months, but start planning now for the future. Keeping in mind the goals that have just been identified, here's what a planner might put on a calendar:

- National, regional, or local events and holidays
- Religious observations
- First day of school, university classes begin
- Days when banks, schools, and public offices might be closed
- Major sporting events
- Celebrity birthdays of interest to the target listener
- Station events or anniversaries
- Special station programming
- Ratings periods.

A marketing manager should be looking for anything that might interest or distract the target audience. He or she should be looking for a "good parade" in order to "get in front of it." Promotion is the exploitation of opportunity.

Step Three: Marketing, programming, and on-air staff should meet to decide which of these calendar dates are most important and how the station will tie into them. If the team is not comfortable planning Christmas promotions in March, then at least acknowledge the need for a Christmas promotion and stockpile some airtime or station resources. For promotions during ratings periods, reserve funding and promotional airtime in an imaginary "war chest" for later use. You can decide later what your specific strategy and tactics will be. In commercial stations, talk to your sales department about their potential needs for these calendar periods. Ideally, the needs of sales should be integrated with those of programming to share costs and maximize revenue.

Step Four: Calculate your budget for each promotion or promotional period. If you know you'll be doing four concert remotes per weekend and giving away one hundred station t-shirts at $5 each, add that to the cost of having your staff at the event for two hours, special banners, etc., and budget the cost of running that promo each weekend. If you know that each weekend you send your staff out with prize packages costing $800, it's simple to put your budget together. Identify other costs like morning show giveaways and special opportunities as specifically as possible.

Be sure to leave some contingency dollars for "unscheduled" opportunities that may come up at the last minute. You don't want to miss a spontaneous moment to promote your station because you didn't leave any budget for it. For ratings periods, planning for a billboard campaign at one price and a TV campaign at another price will prepare you for either scenario.

Step Five: Defend and explain your budget by writing a story, or narrative, to go with your proposal. It should show the department's goals and how they work with the key periods you've identified. Your manager will review this budget, so requests need to appear reasonable, logical, and beneficial to the station. Financial managers are paid to keep costs down, but if you've done a good job with step four, your figures will not look like guesswork. Budgets are NEVER approved on the first pass, and you will be asked to reduce your request. A good marketer knows this. Ask for everything you need, but prepare to settle for less.

Step Six: When asked to reduce the budget, a marketing manager may wish to show the narratives to other department heads. There may be ways to cut expenses by sharing costs with other departments. The narratives explain marketing goals to everyone. Perhaps individual requests can be scaled back in order to meet group goals.

Step Seven: Review your progress and your spending every month. "Mid-course corrections" may be necessary if your plan is not having its desired effect. If you have launched something that is not working, the marketing and programming teams should take steps to correct it. At the end of the year, your station should be able to look back on a series of successes and a minimum of disappointments.

Remember, the most common mistakes in marketing and promoting broadcast properties and personalities can be avoided by following two simple rules:

1. *Plan in advance.* Why wait until the last minute to plan promotions? The dates for all national holidays, many sporting events, and the ratings periods that affect any market for the next year are all available today.

2. *Put everything in writing.* If a marketing manager must tell his or her tale over and over, it will slow things down and sap its strength. Have written rules about promotions and how they get on the air. Everyone involved in the process needs to know and follow these rules.

Use Your Own Airwaves and Website to Promote

Of course, your station already has the two most powerful tools you need for keeping your listeners and attracting new ones. Since your website has the ability to be "searched" by anyone anywhere, it makes sense to add exciting content at every opportunity. Don't miss a chance to put up something great. Have a digital camera with you everywhere you go, not just at station events. Is your station's bumper sticker stuck on the back of the governor's limo? Get it onto your site fast. The most powerful tool to keep people listening longer or to give them an idea of what they can expect from your station is the powerful promo.

Up Next—Powerful Anticipation

One of the most highly paid positions at a major market radio station is that of production director. Radio stations are not known for throwing money around needlessly, so there must be something rare and special about a non-managerial position that can command almost as much salary as is spent on a morning show.

Creativity is the "X factor" that makes the production director such a valuable member of your team. Radio imaging pro Mark Driscoll says, "Your product is the station's package. Your promos are the wrapping paper and the bow on that package. Having great promos makes the listener want to open up the box and see what's inside."

Create Expectations

Innovatively produced promos for your station and your shows make the audience feel they will miss something if they tune away.

Maybe a listener is not interested in whatever is on the air at the moment. However, if you can create excitement and anticipation about an upcoming event, the listener may give you five or ten extra minutes of his or her time, or come back later.

Pick the Highlights

Promos can establish your station's "personality," or image. Some call it "stationality." You know you have a great station when you have trouble deciding which moments to promote.

Station promos are a lot like film promos. They incorporate peak experiences and show highlights to create excitement, energy, and, most of all, the desire to "be there." Like many movie trailers, the promos may often be better than the shows themselves.

Seize Opportunities

Anything from an upcoming appearance to the top-of-the-hour ID can become an opportunity to creatively promote your station. There's just one rule: If it is pre-recorded, it has to be perfect. Make sure you have a good-quality, reliable audio recording system in place in order not to miss the chance to utilize a "magic moment" for a show promo. You may come across some of these moments during aircheck sessions, and it is very frustrating when the quality of the sound is too poor to use for a produced promo.

You do not need to have a huge budget to run great promos on your radio station. If you have creative air talents, you can harness their abilities to promote not only their own shows but the station itself.

Listen to some of the hundreds of audio feeds from various stations' websites. There you will find a mix of hot promos, parody songs, and creative spots. In addition, many production directors maintain their own websites featuring examples of their best work.

Remember, when you make your promos, formatics count. Don't miss an opportunity to give call letters, dial position, and the station's name.

Promo Points: News-Talk Radio

Teases and Promos Are Best When Short

If you err, err on the side of brevity. It is better to leave the audience hungry than to overfeed them.

Cross-Promote Like You Mean It

Having each air personality enthusiastically mention other shows and events on the station promotes and personalizes both the hosts and the station. There is nothing like a word of endorsement from a listener's favorite host to make that listener give another show a chance.

If you are not a particular fan of the show you are being asked to promote, find one or two genuinely good things you can say, and say them. For example, "Sam's show got rated number one in the Reader's Choice Poll of *City Magazine*!" You don't have to lie; you just have to realize that when someone on your team succeeds, you win too.

If you are the number one show on the number seven station, it is not nearly as rewarding as being the number one host on the number one station.

Many of the biggest syndicated personalities in America take the time to cross-promote others on their local stations and their affiliates as well. Cross-promotion gives your schedule a feeling of continuity.

Do It Yourself—Get Your Own Outside Press

You can use your own website to promote events. Cultivate people of influence in the online world. Social networking and appearing in online chatter and other people's blogs is a great way to "virally" get the word out about your show and what you are doing. Promotions consultant Pam

Baker is a big proponent of doing it yourself. She says that talent shouldn't expect the station to do all the work:

> If you are a morning show personality and your show's events or antics are not receiving any press coverage, do it yourself. The sales team works hard to develop relationships with clients. You should do the same with the media. Be active on your own account. Positive public relations can not only boost your ratings, it helps establish you in the marketplace, making you more valuable. Consider the benefits of hiring your own public relations representative.

Throw Out Stale Bread

It is tempting to use great promos over and over again. I've heard stations use the same old promos for days, weeks, even years. Do not give in to that temptation! Even if you have produced the most hilarious promo—distinctive, memorable, and featuring seven of the biggest stars in Hollywood—after a while, it gets boring. In fact, if a listener hears the same promo over and over again for weeks, it can make your whole show sound boring. If a promo is really that fantastic, run it for a little while, store it for several months, and then recycle it.

Keep a library of stand-out promos that are not date-specific, in the event you are unable to produce a fresh one for some reason.

Change your promos like you change your underwear. If someone complains and says, "But I did a great one last week," remind him or her that creativity leads to more creativity.

Stay "Up" for It

If you cut your promos last thing before you leave the station, there is a danger of sounding tired and unenthusiastic. After all, you have just spent three hours on the air, you want to go home, and you are holding your car keys. Try running into the production room prior to today's show and see what you can come up with to promote tomorrow's show. The promos will have that sound you have when you first go on the air—spirited and full of energy.

Get It Right

When you work with pre-recorded elements, make them perfect. Live on the air; you cannot possibly control everything that happens. But when you record, you can. Make it flawless. Here you can create radio art.

Creating Powerful Promos

You can creatively "promo" or promote anything. There's no excuse for a boring promo. TV "magazine" shows and tabloids make a business of promoting the most mundane details of stars' lives as if they were shocking new information. It's not until you've waited through 59 minutes of other news that you find that the "newly discovered nude photographs of today's biggest big screen star" are actually baby pictures. The purpose of the promo is to entice the listener to come back later or stay longer to hear what you've got.

Here is an example of a radio station bragging about increasing its transmitter power—something not usually considered exciting. Broadcaster Tom Bodett, a spokesperson for the Motel 6 chain, did the spot. Bodett made famous the Motel 6 tag line: "We'll leave the light on for you."

PROMO: KGO TRANSMITTER UPGRADE

[Soft country-style music plays behind the spot]

When a radio station has been around as long as KGO, some of that electronic stuff's bound to wear out. Well, since it did and not everyone can talk real loud like that Ronn Owens or Bernie Ward, KGO went and got one of those new jillion-watt transmitters to squirt those sound waves out there.

[Electrical-sizzling sound effects]

Well, sure, it's a big deal to the baby harp seals up in Nova Scotia that are now getting a fuzzy earful of KGO at night, but what's it mean to you?

Well, not much except you might not need to use that microwave to heat your Lean Cuisine anymore and you probably won't have to actually switch on the lights either. Just turn on KGO and stand back...

I'm Tom Bodett, and we've cranked up the power for you on KGO News/Talk 810.

To write, produce, and create powerful promos, begin by thinking of how you could be enticed to tune in. A great promo will intrigue the audience with a promise of something interesting coming up. Although research shows they will be disappointed should the actual item not stand up to the promo, listeners tend to keep trying if the promo is really that good. There is a risk.

If you consistently fail to deliver what you promise, you can lose credibility and audience. Often, those tabloids really DO have amazing photos. Remember that promos are "the fancy bow you wrap around your station's package." Your station needs to have something real to promote, or you'll have only a wrapped box, with nothing inside.

There are various styles of promos. If you want to experiment with your station's image and build continuity between shows, try to create the image that the radio station is like a family and all the hosts listen to and support one another. When done well, it really works. The "inside" promo is the method of one host promoting his or her show within another host's show. Your talkable topic or engaging question can make a good promo, as well.

Listen to your station's other programs. Then you'll really know the product you are promoting. For example: "Hi, I'm Sam on WKXW, The Talk Station. You are listening to the Dr. Paula Show, but I'd like to invite you to join me later on this afternoon. We'll be taking calls, the mayor will check in, and you'll get a chance to meet the number one singer in America right now. That's today at 2 p.m. here on the Talk Station."

Direct Promos

Example: "Up next with Bill Jones on WWXX, you'll meet the man who saved California's gray whales, and later in the show, Joe Jones's lawyer. He's defending a notorious author and death row inmate. Coming up, on WWXX."

That's an effective promo, but it took only fifteen seconds. It includes the name of the host, the station's name, the time coming up, and a teaser.

Parody Songs

Creating the Powerful Parody

Promos with parody songs can be a powerful way of getting a message across in a unique manner. If you're musically creative and you like to sing, this may be a method that works for you. Parody songs[*] can also be used to get your point across in a fun way.

---

[*] *The Green Book of Songs* by Jeff Green has song titles listed by topics; it is great for parody songs. You can also try working with karaoke music.

To create a powerful parody song, find a current event, news story, or a celebrity you find humorous—then do one of the following:

- Pick a song that has a "hook" close to your topic.

- Pick a very popular current tune that is easy to sing.

- Use a nursery rhyme.

CHAPTER 30

Beyond Powerful Radio
Branding—Building the Brand Beyond Radio

"Things do not change, we change."
—*Henry David Thoreau*

"If you can identify, capture and keep customers, then marketing is easy, but if you lose sight of the customer and their needs, marketing a brand gets more difficult."
—*John Parikhal*

Branding in an Overcommunicated "Always On" World

How do you build and maintain a brand? Author, consultant, researcher and Joint Communications President John Parikhal shares wisdom from his years of experience establishing and marketing brands. He's worked with some of the top companies and corporations in the world, including helping radio and TV stations research, create, and grow their brands.

Parikhal says, "Audiences live in an always-on, over-communicated world, addicted to the immediate, to the instant, to the latest and the newest. We are drowning in options and we want more. People are conditioned to believe that there is always something better coming—and, that it's coming really soon."

Because people are overloaded, it requires a lot of mental juggling. Parikhal says, "Our brains are on overtime trying to keep up with all the options. Anything that helps reduce the juggling makes our lives easier. And, brands help reduce the juggling. That's why we want as many *clear* brands as possible—so that we don't have to think about them. We want to reduce choices to the strongest and most reliable."

Parikhal continues, "Things are moving so fast these days, we even want *people* to be brands—to stand for something, to offer clear benefits, promises and guarantees. Unconsciously, you brand yourself, with your clothes, accessories, social networks, and photo-journalism. People are millions of micro-brands in motion."

Brands Are a Promise

Parikhal explains, "A strong brand is a promise, a guarantee specifically that the buyer will get what he or she expects, that it will satisfy their particular need, and that it will do it consistently. A customer doesn't have to think much to use a strong brand. They already know what it will do for them—satisfy a particular need. Strong brands usually have history—they have been around for a long time, consistently delivering on a promise. And, many of the strongest brands don't really have slogans."

Parikhal mentions a few recognizable brands as examples, along with audience/customer expectation:

Honda is a brand—the promise is simple: A very reliable vehicle with high resale value. And, if something goes wrong, the company will fix it. You are *safe* buying and driving it. No slogan. Millions of people love Honda. Apple is a brand. It's technology that is simple and easy to use. And, pretty to look at. It makes your life easier and better. It *thinks for you* and wants to *make you happy*. No slogan. Millions of people love Apple. Tide is a brand. This laundry detergent is branded as a product that gets your clothes whiter than other detergents, a fact that is particularly important to new brides and new mothers. It gets clothes *clean* and says you are a *good mother*. Millions of women love Tide.

Now, think about a radio or TV station. Do you really love it? Despite thousands of slogans through the years, do you know many people who do love their favorite radio or TV station? If there aren't a lot of people who love you, you aren't a brand. You are a "wanna-be" brand.

If a brand is strong, the people who use it turn themselves into passionate unpaid salespeople. How many of your friends try to persuade you to buy a Honda? How many of them hound you to buy a Mac?

Now, think about how many of the people you know who try to get you to watch a particular TV channel or listen to a specific radio station. Probably not many. Too many wanna-be brands. It requires too much energy to think about them.

If your radio, TV, or online business isn't getting noticed, you can do something about it, but first, here are a few basics of marketing.

Marketing 101

Before getting into developing your brand, it's worth a quick review of the basics, because your brand is only one part of marketing. If you know Marketing 101, it's easier to maintain and evolve a strong brand.

The magic words are "maintain and evolve." That's because some products become brands before anyone has thought about how to market them. They are simply so great, and there is such a huge pent-up demand, that people often "brand" them before they even start marketing.

Some examples in past years include *Rolling Stone Magazine*, MTV, Google, Amazon, and Ben & Jerry's ice cream.

The Five Elements of Marketing

Marketing is a process. The process is designed to connect your product with an identified customer. In its simplest form, marketing is based on five elements...

1. **Create a customer.** There has to be *a customer* for your product—a product that exists or one you believe there is a market for. You must engage and satisfy this customer, both before and after they use your product.

2. **Differentiate.** Your product must have at least one really *strong* differentiating "benefit"—something special that makes your product *different* from (and superior to) other products that might meet this need. Often, the benefit is psychological (more on that later in this chapter) rather than "practical."

3. **Get their attention.** The customer needs to *know you exist*—that you are there to fill the need(s).

4. **Location knowledge.** They have to be able to *find you* (online, on the dial, in the store, or wherever you are). And, they want finding you to be easy.

5. **Value.** In the customer's mind, the *value proposition* has to be right. Value is what it "costs" the customer relative to what they get—and it's not always about money. *Warning:* the customer's mind is often irrational and value is not logical.

Based on the five elements, using tools such as market research, advertising, promotion, and public relations, you can identify and connect customers with the product and help evolve the product. If you do it right and do it consistently, your "product" will become a brand.

Now, on to Branding 101.

John Parikhal's Branding 101

1. A brand is a *promise*. It's a *guarantee*. It's a form of *trust*.

2. A brand promises that the product will *meet one or more practical or emotional needs.*

3. It promises to *be reliable*—to give you what you expect each time you use it. And, if it fails you, it promises to "make good" as quickly as possible.

4. Brands usually *take time to grow*. But, they die quickly if they consider themselves more important than the customer.

Brand history is littered with examples of how fast a brand can die.

At one time Perrier was a top brand in "pure" sparkling waters, but after a problem was discovered with benzene in its bottles it damaged the brand.

At one time, BP (British Petroleum) was on its way to becoming the top brand in "green" oil companies. However, after a cap failed on one of its undersea drilling rigs, causing a disastrous oil leak, its "green" brand was dead. At one time, someone put poison in Tylenol and yet, today, that brand of pain reliever is stronger than ever.

Why? What's the difference between Tylenol and Perrier or BP?

Tylenol kept its promise that it was *safe*. It spent over $100 million dollars to replace every bottle of Tylenol, developed safety packaging to make sure their packages were tamper-proof, and *constantly* told the public what they were doing and why. No cover up. No spin. Just keeping their promise and rebuilding trust.

Perrier and BP tried to avoid the problem, hoping it would go away. But in the always-on, always connected world, it never goes away.

5. *Branding isn't hard.* It just takes honesty, time, a good product, and a willingness to bite the bullet when things go wrong. So, if you find it hard to be honest, to create a good product or to fix things when they go wrong, stop now. Work on those things you find hard.

There are some who would say that both commercial radio and TV lost sight of creating a great product, as many stations and networks began opting for "less expensive" productions, hoping that the audience, its customers, would "put up with it." That may have worked better in the past when there were more limited options for the customer who "settled" for what was on TV or radio or in the magazine. But the Internet changed the rules. The *good news*: You can make your product better, you can understand your customer, and you can keep your promises. You can create a brand.

6. *Think of yourself as a brand.* It's more important than ever to be a "brand", whether you are an on-air host, a recording artist, an actor or actress, or a website. It helps you stand out from the crowd and makes it easier for your "customers" to put you at the top of their list.

It's important to protect the image of "YOU" as a brand. Be aware that your public image is based on all impressions you make—with instant media (be careful, information you make available about your life or experiences may appear on open websites such as Facebook), or what you say in public. Certain actors, public figures, and politicians have all had their reputations and brands "ruined" or diminished due to stories, photos, or videos that have appeared online with or without their knowledge or approval.

John Parikhal—How to Create, Establish and Build a Brand

1. *Review* the points in Marketing 101.

2. *Understand the competition and you.* Make a list of all the great things about your "product." Make a list of the great things about your top two competitors. If you don't know who they are, find them.

3. *Focus.* Strike out anything on your product's list that is also on the competition's list. What's left is what's really different about you. Once you know what's really different about your product, you have one or more of your brand "attributes." Now, look at the attributes you've identified in point 2 above. If there are any you need to add back in to support your brand, do so. Just remember that they aren't unique.

4. *Use your "difference" for leverage.* Focus on your "meaningful difference" and use it as part of your thinking about how to position the practical and emotional benefit of your product. Understand and *articulate your "promise."*

Work on your "brand attributes." What is special about your brand? Attributes can be "tangible," such as the most helicopters covering traffic in the area, or psychological, such as "when I wear a $2000 watch, people will think I'm more successful and I will feel more confident."

5. *Improve.* Review your quality control procedures and work constantly to innovate and make your product better. Keep your promise—and show it with "brand deeds."

6. *Act like your brand.* Your brand's "deeds" say everything about you. Brand deeds can range from the "fair value" that Starbucks pays for its coffee to Martha Stewart supporting and using organic supplies for her own vegetable garden to a radio station that raises money for kids who need medical treatment. Your brand deed should always be rooted in your brand "attributes."

7. *Stay close to your customers.* Check in with your customers often. Use formal and informal research. If you get complaints, fix the problem. If you get compliments, work on using that feedback to make the product even better.

8. *Never stop.* Review the list above at least every few months or days to see what might need attention or adjustment.

Reaching the Customer

Marketing guru, Ted Chin, suggested that the best way to reach a customer is to understand who they are. He called them your "Prime Prospect"—the person most likely to use/buy you or your product.

1. *Identify prime prospect.* Who is your customer? How do you know? Use research of every kind to understand them: informal feedback; online polls; segmentation research; focus groups. Everything you can. Make sure your research can be validated. Share the knowledge of the customer with everyone who works for your company—it helps them to help.

2. *Identify prime prospect's problem.* What "problem" will your product solve for your prime prospect? Is it *practical* (I want a TV news show at 6 p.m. or I want to buy cheap anti-virus software) or is it *emotional*? Most "problems" have a powerful emotional component.

3. *Solve the problem.* Using design, advertising, technology, promotion, and every other tool you need, "solve" the problem.

For example, when New York radio station WCBS-AM (all-news) tried to compete against WINS (all-news), they focused on a "practical" but "emotional" need of their prime prospect, who was feeling overwhelmed with information and couldn't keep up. WCBS's solution was a campaign that was tagged with "When I can't read about it, I hear about it on WCBS."

Prime Prospect Problems—Emotional

Online, on the radio, on TV, and in print, the same "needs" or problems are dominant. John Parikhal explains:

1. *Accompany me.* The most basic human need is for companionship. Radio hosts, TV anchors, crowds—they all "accompany."

2. *Reassure me.* Make me feel safer, more comfortable—with my ideas or my circumstances. Conservative talk hosts, financial experts, TV doctors, and even Oprah meet this need.

3. *Thrill me.* A very popular emotional need—from battlefield news footage to football or CSI, everyone loves a thrill.

4. *Reward me.* Give me something for what I've done or given you. It can range from money to recognition.

5. *Teach me.* People love to learn. (In the USA, NPR meets this need. As does the TV show, *Jeopardy*.) The Internet excels at this.

6. *Help me escape, imagine or dream.* A huge category. The biggest. You can fill in a dozen examples from TV, radio, print, or online. Most perfumes, credit cards, beers, and "contests" work best on this emotional category.

Prime Prospect Solutions

The best way to "solve" the above problems in media or online are...

1. S*hows, songs, or stories I like.* Create "shows" or "songs" that meet one or more of the "emotional" needs and you will win with it. "Shows" can be as short as a YouTube clip. Make almost everything into a "story."

2. *Polarities.* Frame things in terms of Winners and Losers or Good Guys and Bad Guys. It always works.

3. *Things I need to know.* Traffic and Weather. News headlines. Analysis. Context—the biggest category of all—make sense of it for your prime prospect.

Advertising is easy. Creativity is harder.

The Three Rules of Advertising

1. **Advertise a benefit, not a component.** Steve Stockman is a filmmaker who makes great commercials. He once said that if radio or TV people advertised Charmin toilet paper, their slogan would be

"Made from wood pulp that doesn't scratch...". In other words, they would focus on what the product was made from instead of the "benefit" of "softness."

Every time a radio station says "Your at work, soft favorites," it is selling wood pulp. Sell the benefit of "softness."

2. **Develop a strong tagline.** Think rhythm and rhyme. They help. If you can sing or hum it, even better. "From Worst to First" was a nervy challenge for a budding Z100 as they told New York they weren't just going to get better, they would be number one. To New Yorkers, joining someone on a run for #1 is an emotional benefit.

Have you come up with a line that *truly* differentiates you? If you have to explain your tagline, it isn't working. If people can't remember your tagline, start again.

3. **Media plan.** Decide which media are best for you. What's the benefit of radio, billboards, TV, online, promotion, contesting, transit ads, toilet stalls (and other "untraditional" spots)? Once you know the right media for you, create ads or promotions for the medium.

Cross-Platform Branding

Parikhal says, "In the multi-media age, you want to be on as many platforms as possible. Keep these in mind..."

1. **Review Before You Start.** What differentiates your brand? What are your "meaningful benefits?" What brand "deeds" will support your brand. Who are your biggest fans? How can you reach them to help you share the benefits of your product? What is your budget—how much can you spend? Who are your competitors? What are they doing to get better? What are you doing?

Review your tagline. Is it really strong? Which one of your competitors could use it—and have it fit them, too? If it can fit one of them, go back to the drawing board.

2. **Brainstorm.** Use the formal rules of brainstorming to come up with effective places and ways to advertise.

3. **TV.** If you advertise on TV, focus on emotional benefit—using visuals and melody whenever possible. Don't pay too much. A lot of TV is overpriced but old habits die hard.

4. **Radio.** Listeners think of on-air promos as "ads for the station." Make sure these "ads" are strong. Get rid of noisy production and outdated "sounders." Treat your audience as if they are your best friends.

5. **Print.** It has a place. Billboards can be very powerful—if you change the copy and update them, turn them into a "story." Newspaper has some uses—depending on your customers. And, taglines can go anywhere.

6. **Online.** Use social media. Connect with every *"qualified" blogger* who might like your product. Ask for their honest opinion. Whenever possible, get reviewed. Connect with your *fans*—using the most up-to-date methods, Facebook, at the moment, is king. Optimize *search.* Know why people come to your website. Make it easy for them to get what they want. Do *usability testing,* often. Read Steve Krug's *Don't Make Me Think* and keep up to date with Jackob Neilsen. *Cross-promote* by contacting *webmasters* of sites who might be a good fit for you. Most important, *check your site often* to make sure that links are still good, that everything works and that you are getting a lot of traffic. Notice where you get the traffic and evolve based on this information. And, keep an *eye on your competition*—what are they promoting, what works on their site, how are they getting better?

More About Using the Net

Individual personalized targeted marketing builds brands as well. The Internet is blossoming with one-to-one marketing. Online companies have worked hard trying to make their customers happy. Amazon, eBay, internet radio, Google—they all want to know more about their customer. Online word-of-mouth to build a brand has become the most powerful new tool in history. Broadcasters began to move their money and, far more important, their brightest people, to learn more about digital and online.

Too Much Choice

Parikhal points out the Internet didn't just offer a *new* way to connect with the customer. At the same time, it *increased the number of choices* in every known category from radio to shoes. It increased choice for the media, and it put time-shifting on steroids.

> Instead of two radio stations that played your favorite music, there were a hundred. Instead of waiting for summer reruns on TV or for a movie to come out on DVD, you could download it (illegally in most cases) or watch it on new platforms such as YouTube. That was a game changer.
>
> Prior to the Internet, there were some advantages to being an established broadcasting brand. You couldn't just start a TV or radio station without putting up some serious money for towers, buildings, staff and marketing. The old rules have been re-written and marketers are still learning, and trying to figure them out.

The New Rules

The new rules start the same way the old rules started. You need to know what the customer wants. But the difference is that today's customer is much more sophisticated about what they want and how to get it. They still like to buy. They just don't want to be sold. They don't want you to find them and interrupt what they are doing to give them your message.

They want to find you, when they want, and to learn about you before they buy. You can't spin them. You have to win them.

And, that's why brands are more important than ever. They make it easier to "win them."

When the Brand is YOU

A hallmark of success is to *become* a brand (e.g., Martha Stewart, Oprah Winfrey, Tiger Woods, etc.). How can you become a "brand?" Based on the power of a personal blog, and using social media, here's the story of how Erin Davis, a top rated on-air personality in Toronto, did just that.

How the Internet Saved the Radio Star

In June of 2003, 98.1 CHFI-FM in Toronto, the radio station for which I'd co-hosted mornings for 15 years, decided to go in another direction and pursue a different audience. (I like to joke that it was a smaller one.) That new direction did not include me, despite years at the number one or number two position in the ratings in Canada's largest radio market, and like many of my fellow broadcasters, I had the unenviable experience of learning that my last show had indeed been MY LAST SHOW.

Except, it wasn't. Just three months before my firing, I'd set up my own website *www.ErinDavis.com* and begun a daily blog, a "journal," writing thoughts, sharing experiences and giving listeners another way to connect with me and for me to connect with them. Despite having only about thirty readers to start (and my husband asking why on earth I was spending so much time each day writing for so few), I kept on. After that fateful day in June, the numbers grew exponentially as listeners learned that I had a website, that I was alive and well, and that I could tell them daily how I was doing, what had happened, and so on. In the first week after my firing, I received 1500 e-mails.

Also, for reasons I don't fully understand, CHFI maintained a message board on its website, and hundreds of listeners were permitted to voice their anger and frustration surrounding my dismissal.

Two weeks later, a Toronto newspaper picked up the story of listeners' support online, and published my website and e-mail address. My inbox swelled to 5000.

I answered every one of those e-mails and saved the addresses so that when I had big news, I could send it to them personally. I was able to tell them when I'd been hired at another radio station, and the numbers there almost immediately reflected a sudden and sizeable arrival of new listeners.

To give this story an even sweeter ending, in September 2005 I returned to my (former station) home and my chair at 98.1 CHFI. To our unending gratitude, displaced CHFI listeners returned, too.

Of course, CHFI launched an extensive and expensive ad campaign announcing my return—and the arrival of my terrific new partner, Mike Cooper—but I know in my heart that had it not been for that daily journal, had listeners not had a way to stay abreast and correspond with me—my story might have had a much different ending. As it is, contrary to what the Buggles might have sung (and please forgive the word "star"; it's theirs, not mine): Video may have killed the radio star...but the Internet saved this one."

Note; More on Erin Davis' blogging tips in Chapter 28 – Working Across Multiple Platforms

Air Personality Erin Davis' daily blog helped maintain her profile and grow her audience, even while between jobs.

PART VI

Beyond Powerful Radio
Making Money

CHAPTER 31

Beyond Powerful Radio
Sales & Commercials

> "We are all in sales"
> —*Pat Bryson, Bryson Broadcasting International*

> "Do anything you want on the air ...but you still have to be able
> to sell it. If a sponsor is afraid to be associated with it, you lose."
> —*The Greaseman (Doug Tracht, syndicated personality)*

There once was a time when an on-air personality would ask, "Why should I care about commercials?" The answer was, and is, because they pay the bills.

"Whether or not you ever intend to derive your income from commission sales, *we are all in sales!* Trying to increase the audience for your brand, convincing your boss to adopt your ideas, getting hired by a prospective employer, getting a date or a spouse—we sell! These are all *sales* situations. Recognizing these situations and understanding the basic process of sales will take you miles ahead of your competition." These are the knowing words of Pat Bryson, sales trainer, consultant and president of Bryson Broadcasting International.

An understanding of the revenue side of the industry will make anyone a more valuable asset to the station. With an economy that has ups and downs, more on-air personalities and programmers have found a knowledge of sales to be important.

It was remarkable in the past, how little some air personalities knew or bothered about the importance of commercials. They saw the spots as a "break" in the programming instead of an integral part of the on-air package. But a poorly done or boring commercial can be as much of a tune-out as any other bad programming. If a commercial is done right, and creates powerful radio, it will keep listeners engaged.

"It takes both sides of the hall to run a successful radio station: sales and programming," Bryson continues. "When these two departments work hand-in-hand, the station flourishes. Both are concerned with meeting the needs of the customer. To the programmer, the customer is the listener. To the sales person, the customer is the advertiser. Pleasing these two groups, the listener and the advertiser, should not be a mutually exclusive undertaking. In the new world order, we add the power to reach both of these groups through the Internet. Once again, programming and sales must work together to utilize this powerful new 'touch' to its fullest potential."

Turn It Up!

Salespeople listen to and view the station differently than the rest of the staff. That became very clear to me one night on the way to dinner with friends in sales. The car radio was on. Suddenly the conversation was loudly interrupted: "Quiet, turn it up!" A client's spot was on. Sales people are just some of the people who turn the radio "up" during commercial breaks. That's their work. It's important to them. It's the way they and their stations make money.

Creative, effective, powerful commercials are important. And there's big money in making good ones. Televised sporting events like the Super Bowl or the Olympics are now watched nearly as much for the creativity of the commercials they carry as for the efforts of the athletes involved. But, in sales and advertising, as in sports, before you get to the big leagues, you have to practice, train, and learn the ropes.

Sales is from Mars, Programming is from Venus

Salespeople are a different breed from the programming or on-air talent. We need both types to make a commercial radio station a success. For

*"The dip in sales seems to coincide with the
decision to eliminate the sales staff."*

years I've been doing a seminar as part of the Creating Powerful Radio/TV workshop (with apologies to John Gray): "Sales is from Mars, Programming is from Venus."

For an on-air personality, the need to earn a living is there, but most chose their careers because of a need for creative expression, a love of performing, and a desire to be in the spotlight. It is essential to the happiness of an on-air talent to have an audience. But the motivation for a sales person is financial reward. Experienced account executives may have a background in selling products or services other than radio. It may not matter much to them what product they are selling. Nevertheless, a good sales person, no matter what he or she is selling, cares about the quality of the product and wants to see it succeed. They can be every bit as passionate about selling as talent are about their shows.

Break Down the Brick Walls

The way sales and programming view one another can affect the success of a station. It's important that each side respects the work of the other. If key members of your sales department resent your morning host as the guy who leaves the building at 10:30 a.m., they probably don't understand his day began with show prep and a pot of black coffee at 2:00 a.m. Conversely, you have a problem if the morning personality sees the account executive as an unapproachable guy in $500 shoes.

A lot of time is wasted because of distrust between sales and programming. Sales people often view talent, particularly on personality radio stations, as a liability. A sales person lives in fear of the one careless remark that will blow up an account he or she has been working for months to acquire. The talent, meanwhile, believes the sales staff would be perfectly happy running commercials fifty-nine minutes out of every hour. Hosts feel that sales have no respect for the product they are selling and little idea of what it takes to build credibility with an audience. With some effort, both sides can reach an understanding.

An opportunity presented itself one April Fool's Day. Station management agreed to an experiment: We made a switch. First thing in the morning the sales team was surprised to learn that instead of their regular duties, each was being given a shift on the news-talk radio station. On-air personalities were handed a list of potential clients they would have to meet with and convince to buy advertising on the radio station. The sales manager smiled. He thought it would be fun, "Going on the radio, how hard can it be? I talk all day long." After about an hour, midday host "Bob the Sales Manager" had sweat stains the size of soccer balls under each arm. His hands were shaking. Here is what listeners heard.

> FIRST CALLER: *I want to talk about that ancient tree they are about to cut down on Main St.*
>
> *(Silence from the host.)*
>
> NEXT CALLER: *I want to talk about the verdict in the Lawson murder trial.*
>
> *(Silence from the host.)*

Finally someone took pity on Bob and asked for some advice about getting a selling job.

At last, a subject Bob understood. He'd made it through the hour, but just barely. Here's what he said afterward: "You never appreciate how hard it is until the pressure is on, and you have to hit the ball yourself." Here are some excerpts from the talk show host's appraisal of his day:

> I can't believe how hard it is. I hate wearing a suit. There's a lot of math, percentages, and numbers. I couldn't take it. I heard the word "no" more today than I have in my entire life. This is hard. If I had to do this every day for a living, I'd be miserable! I couldn't take the rejection.

After the experiment, talent showed a new respect for the efforts of the sales team. Now they bring in sales leads. Today, when this station's talk hosts meet someone with a business, product, or service, or an executive who could be a potential advertiser, they collect business cards and hand them to the sales manager. This has led to new revenue for the station, based on relationships and connections with people who previously did not consider radio commercials as an effective advertising tool. The air staff now happily goes on sales calls to meet clients and the sales team has a new regard for what it takes to do the work. They like each other better now. That new respect has also paid off when talent are asked to do live copy or produce creative commercials.

The Live Copy Advantage: Credibility Sells

Some of the most effective spots are ad-libbed or "live copy" because there's room for fun, spontaneity, and personalization. Here's how it works: The host may be given either a fact sheet or a script. He or she highlights what is best about the product or service being advertised. Storytelling skills and personal experience are worked into the sell. If the host is credible, the spots are entertaining, and if the product is decent, listeners are likely to buy. That, above all else, makes advertisers happy.

Credibility is paramount. American personality Howard Stern's sponsors pay enormous rates for his live spots, even though he sometimes seems not to be selling the product at all. Once in a live spot for a life insurance company, Stern created a brilliant show "bit." He advised male heads of households not to buy too much life insurance from his sponsor. As he explained it, after you die, your wife's new boyfriend will convince her to give him the insurance money to start a mail order business, which will subsequently fail, and then, bankrupt, your children will starve or wind up on the streets as teenage hookers.

The moral of Stern's commercial: You need this life insurance, but don't buy too much of it. That was an original and powerful commercial, and it was funny, too.

Many products in America are on the map today because of the personal selling and live copy spots done for them by personalities.

Another Live Copy Advantage: Job Security

Air personality Mike Siegel is quick to point out that tying air talent to advertisers through live copy spots makes it easier to ride out a couple of bad ratings periods. The advertiser believes it's the talent's personality that is selling the product. This creates financial security both for the station and the air talent. Even if numbers are down-trending, if you're bringing in big dollars for live spots, management will be reluctant to get rid of you. If management does show you the door, your satisfied advertisers, who believe your commercials help their business, may follow you to your next destination.

One broadcaster who recently left her long-term air shift after a company downsizing, took her program to the Internet. One of her biggest live copy clients went with her. To the financial benefit of both, the advertiser continues to benefit from her large and loyal following and is prominently featured on her website, and at live events.

Siegel encourages the relationship between the talent, account executive, and the client. He advises: Before it goes to air, look over the ad copy. If the account executive or the client writes a script for the campaign, the talent should have an opportunity to read the copy, give feedback, and give suggestions for modifications. Account executives: Make sure you record live copy spots and always follow up with the client to confirm not only that the script is satisfactory, but also that the spots are working.

Siegel believes that if you're selling a product, you'd better know it and use it. Eat at the restaurant. Drink the Washington State-grown cherry juice. Drive the car. Get the skylight installers to put one in your house. Siegel warns, "Don't endorse a product you don't know, and don't endorse a product you don't like. The spots won't ring true. The audience won't believe you, and they won't buy."

I remember a TV segment about the late legendary veteran commentator Paul Harvey, who was known for his innovative live commercials. Most of Paul Harvey's sponsors had been with him for decades, and listeners had come to associate these products with him. As a test of the listeners' devotion, the reporter traveled to a rural factory and asked a group of women working on the production line to hold up their thermal beverage containers. Each woman proudly displayed the container manufactured by the company recommended and endorsed by their hero, Paul Harvey. That's the power of creative live copy selling.

The Sales Call

Before you walk out the door to meet a client, or potential client, keep in mind the following principles from Pat Bryson.

Bryson Broadcasting International's Sales Principles

- People don't buy radio advertising; they buy what it will do for them.

- If they won't give you their time, they won't give you their money.

- People buy emotionally and justify it with logic.

- We need to access the client's world, understand the client's world, and live in the client's world.

- It's not what you *say*, it's what you *ask*.

Mike Siegel recommends going with the account executive to meet sponsors. "Get to know them personally. Raise any questions you may have about any possible flaws or problems with the product or service at that time. Learn enough to be able to convey your personal enthusiasm. Consider including a brief interview with your client in the spot. Be sure you endorse only one product in each advertising category. (This is one of the reasons live spots demand premium pricing.) Follow up on any listener complaints." Again, Siegel warns, investigate thoroughly before endorsing.

If a spot doesn't work one way, be flexible and willing to change the approach. Don't treat commercials like a separate part of your show. The audience is sophisticated enough to know why the commercials are there. If the products and services are good, and properly targeted at your audience, you can make the commercials as informative and entertaining as the rest of your show.

All of this seems like a lot of work, but when handled properly, live spots can be a gold mine for everyone involved.

The Pareto Principle—Become One of the Top 20

One of Pat Bryson's keys to training successful sales people is "The Pareto Principle." This principle was named after Italian economist Vilfredo Pareto, who noticed in 1906 that eighty percent of the land in Italy was owned by twenty percent of the population. He also observed that twenty percent of the pea pods in his garden contained eighty percent of the peas.

Translated for sales, the Pareto principle states: "eighty percent of the business is brought in by twenty percent of the sales force."

Bryson finds the Pareto Principle bears true in both broadcasting and in life.

> Program directors may recognize the Pareto Principle as "P-1 listeners." Most sales managers will admit that eighty percent of their station's billing is produced by twenty percent of their sales staff.
> The Pareto principle applies not only to sales people, but also to the station's clients—twenty percent of the people who buy advertising time will bring in eighty percent of your station's business.

Assuming the Pareto Principle holds true, what is it *exactly* that the twenty percent are *doing* to get eighty percent of the business and to be so successful?

New Prospects

"Sales is a process," explains Bryson. "Understand the process, work the process, and revenue will be the result." Some parts of the process are harder than others. Even the difficult work can be made easier. For example, Bryson ranks the ways you can contact prospective clients as follows:

- **Cold Calling:** "Cold Calling" is hard. Cold calling means contacting strangers, people you do not have a connection with. Statistically, only five percent of the cold calls you make will actually result in a sale. That means you'll hear a lot of "No's" to get each "Yes."

- **A Lead:** But if you have a "lead" of some kind or information about a business that shows you they might need to advertise, the likelihood of closing goes up to fifteen percent.

- **A Referral:** When someone you know allows you to use their name, it pushes the likelihood of closing a sale to fifty percent.

- **An Introduction:** Introduction calling will make you rich. If you can get an *introduction*, you will close ninety to ninety-five percent of the time. The twenty percent of sales people who write eighty percent of the business live in the world of referrals and introductions.

How it Works: Three Phases to Win in Sales

Phase 1. The top twenty percent organize their day so that it includes time for talking with new prospects.

Phase 2. Then they make "discovery calls"—to gather information from these prospects.

Phase 3. And they "present solutions," and ask for money.

Presenting Solutions

Part of your solution may come in the form of your own prepared commercial for your prospect. Bryson says, "Have your thirty-second commercial ready. When approaching a prospect for the first time, top sales people don't say, "I sell radio advertising." That description comes from *our world*. They instead position what they do in relation to the *client's world*. Top twenty percent sales people explain the benefit of why someone should give them their time with their opening lines:

> *Hello, my name is _____ and I work for KXXX. I don't know if we have anything to talk about or not, but I work with business people who are experiencing frustration. Some are feeling the effects of the slow economy or having trouble finding and keeping good people. Others have seen profit margins shrink with the advent of strong competition, like large discount retailers like Wal-Mart. Which of these might be of concern to you? [at least one of these will be a problem for your prospect]. Would it make sense for you to invite me over to discuss this? How about Thursday or Friday?*

The first five minutes are the most important.

Bryson reminds her trainees of something your mother may have said:

"You never get a second chance to make a first impression." The Bernieri Study uncovered some interesting (and scary) data. The University of Toledo analyzed the performance of job applicants during a twenty-minute interview. The interviewers were asked to rate each applicant on attributes such as ambition, intelligence, and competence.

A group of observers was asked to watch just the first fifteen seconds of the interview. The results showed the impressions of the group who watched fifteen seconds of the interview almost paralleled those who participated in the twenty-minute interview.

Establishing trust with prospects starts the minute they first see you. Dress professionally, smile, shake hands firmly (but not vice-like) and give the person a reason to spend more time with you.

When you meet your client make a point of using the time wisely. And, before you can present a solution, you need to understand your client's challenges. That involves research. As Bryson puts it, "The top twenty percent understand the use of questions. It's not what you tell; it's what you ask! Sales today is the art of asking good questions to uncover the client's needs and pains. The top twenty percent learn to master the art of moving prospects through Level 1 questions, to Level 2 questions, to Level 3 questions. It is at Level 3 that the top twenty percent find the big, long-term dollars.

Level 1: What is the biggest challenge facing your business today?

Level 2: What effect has this problem had on your business?

Level 3: What effect has this business problem had on you personally?

Again Bryson says, "It's all about accessing the world of the client and living there. Top sellers create 'solutions' to appeal to the emotions of their clients. *People buy emotionally and justify it with logic.*" The most successful sales people craft written solutions that speak directly to the needs and pains of their prospects. They spend the majority of their time with the client talking about "solution," which is the client's world, and only a small amount of the time talking about the station. *People don't buy radio advertising: They buy what it will do for them.* Your proposals should reflect this."

Bryson concludes, "It's important to check back with the client after the commercials have run. Honest feedback is important. Instead of asking your client: '*How am I doing?*' which will probably prompt an '*OK*,' try asking: '*If I could change one thing about what we did for you, what would it be?*' This encourages your clients to help you improve your service. Surveys are fine, but nothing gets better feedback than spending one-on-one time with your clients."

Selling the Talk

Broadcast executive David Baronfeld's decades of experience in sales and management have made him a believer in the benefits of selling news-talk. "Although we have seen huge growth in listening options over the last few years, some of the most consistent performers have been the news and talk formats. And while syndicated talk has become hugely popular, it is the local sponsorships like traffic, news, business reports, weather, sports, etc., that create premium revenue opportunities."

Baronfeld offers the following pointers, including successful techniques he has developed and learned through the years, to sell radio, in particular talk radio, and live copy commercials.

1. **Create promotional alliances.** Identify twenty-five quality, high-profile local businesses. Multiple locations are preferable; however, a strong single location store can act as a magnet. Target one company per category and create an annual or semi-annual promotional event that you can do together for years. Examples would include: banks; casinos; home improvement stores; car dealerships; electronic, furniture, and jewelry stores; cosmetic surgeons; and sporting goods stores.

2. **Create media partnerships.** It is advantageous for radio to join forces not only with other TV and radio properties within your group or cluster, but also with competing media. Having a relationship with either the daily newspaper or leading TV station tells your advertisers that you are the "go to" dial position for breaking news, weather, sports, etc. Shared resources provide the opportunity to put your station's name in print or on the screen at no charge. You add name recognition and raise the level of your station's credibility with your listeners.

3. **Think brand names.** Brand selling is different than a co-op or non-traditional revenue deal. By prospecting for business generically, millions in potential revenue are never realized. Prospecting should be focused. When asked "What's your favorite soft drink?" people don't say, "I'm a cola drinker." They say, "I like Coke."

   For potential advertisers, paint a picture of your listeners with real-life examples of the products they buy and own: "They are Lexus owners who use Dell computers and stay at the Westin." Using brands as part of your presentation allows you to charge a premium for your brand.

4. **Take a good look at your listener.** Years ago, I worked with an AOR station to help improve their local sales effort. The sales people couldn't get beyond their image of the audience's "band T-shirts and bad teeth," but they had to make their budgets. So I brought

a camera to the next station promotion and took pictures of their listeners. One visual emerged. No matter what they wore, their hair was fabulous.

Two days later, I walked into a sales meeting, showed the pictures, and suggested they call on the Conair blow dryers guy, the Aveda shampoo rep, and the distributor for Head and Shoulders. Less than 72 hours later, the station closed an annual contract, worth nearly six figures, with the area's largest beauty supply house.

That's just hair. Now think about how much money you could generate if you saw your listeners in a different light, as brand buyers and brand users of everything from mortgages to cars, phones, home improvements, travel, and so on.

5. **Understand your advertiser's needs.** The people I like to sell to are those accountable for hitting or overachieving their budgets. It makes most sense to talk about using radio directly with the people who are responsible for maximizing those sales. Shoot for the top. Call or write the company's president or CEO. Tell him or her you have an idea that can maximize sales and save them money. Nine times out of ten, you'll get the appointment.

6. **Let your air talent sell for you—Part I.** This is the sales perspective that Mike Siegel talks about. Everybody loves to meet the station's prime talent. Bring along a camera, and chances are good that a picture of them (ideally, wearing your station logo) and the client will occupy a prominent wall position. Do this in fifty companies with more than fifty employees. Soon you'll have thousands of "impressions" per week in the workplace. Make the goal to be in 540 offices in the next three years. That is a lot of exposure, and all you'll need is a digital camera.

7. **Let your air talent sell for you—Part II.** If you allow and encourage talent to earn income from revenue streams separate from salary (i.e. promotion fees, endorsements, live copy), you'll be viewed as talent-friendly, which is a good thing, especially at contract renewal time. Most on-air personalities understand that the better their relationship is with sales, the more the account executives will pitch them to clients, and the more money they'll make. Studies show that air talent who spend at least five hours a week with station sales-people can almost always equal and sometimes double their regular salaries.

8. **Let your air talent sell for you—Part III.** Perhaps you remember or have heard about the late talk personality Alan Berg. The movie *Talkradio* was loosely based on his life. We spent at least two to three hours per week making sales calls together. One day we had two calls to make. The first was with the owner of a Chinese restaurant. We walked in and made some small talk. In just minutes, Alan jumped in and said, "I can only endorse one Chinese restaurant. And if you'd like me to endorse yours, you'll need to buy a twenty-six week schedule." In less than thirty seconds we had the order.

Twenty minutes later, we're meeting with the owners of a Rattan furniture store. As I begin my presentation, Alan says, "I can only endorse one furniture store. And if you'd like me to endorse yours, you'll need to buy a twenty-six week schedule." Again, within two minutes of the start of the meeting, we closed the deal. All I had said was, "Hello."

Selling Alan, or rather letting Alan sell, was truly extraordinary. Look around you. Your best salesperson may be a member of your air staff.

9. **Hire a sales staff that lives the lifestyle of the format.** If you are selling news-talk, hire salespeople who use news and talk radio. At some clusters salespeople can sell most, if not all, of the station formats. At others, there are separate sales staffs. In my opinion, that is the better way to go. As an example, Toyota has separate sales staffs and facilities for Toyota and their premium brand, Lexus. Don't hire a group of music radio listeners to convey what it's like to be a sports talk fan to your client.

Instead, assemble a staff of sellers who love the format, can describe its attributes, understand the variety of people to whom they will be selling, and share similar interests with the client. For example, hire a former business owner or someone who has sold the types of products your station will advertise. I'm not saying that non-news-talk listeners can't sell this format, just don't have an entire sales staff of them.

10. **Create as many premium avails as possible.** Each week you have several hundred premium available spots for sale. Make sure your sales staff understands just how valuable these commercials are. Live reads, business and sports sponsorships, traffic and weather reports, news updates—don't let these golden nuggets go to waste. And don't give them away either. These are your "beachfront premium units." They are worth more, and you are entitled to charge more for them.

11. **Have fun.** If you sell news-talk, you are involved in a format that appeals to more potential advertisers than any other in town. Your air-talent is the best known. Your listeners are the most active. Welcome to radio utopia.

Making the Sale: Networking vs. Cold Calling

To excel at sales, just as on the programming side, it helps to be a good communicator. Your people skills and knowledge of how to make connections can lead to potential business and will serve you in all areas of life, not just broadcasting. Most people who gravitate toward sales are genuinely social individuals. Developing relationships is an important part of prospecting and growing sales contacts.

Business leads are all around you. The person exercising next to you, your uncle Dave, your kids' nanny; everyone in your circle can potentially lead to business. With the help of the Internet, you can make your own "coincidental meeting" occur by seeking out individuals who may already work for or work with companies you're looking to contact. Try using on-line Social Networking Services to find business connections you may not have realized you had. Most of them are free or cost next to nothing to use. It may not be too long before the "cold call" becomes a rare event. It seems you may already be just a couple of acquaintances away from the person you thought you could never reach.

Sales trainer, consultant and author, now PR/PR Public Relations President Pam Lontos, has more than twenty-five years of sales experience, from selling health club memberships to being vice president of Disney Broadcasting. Her books, *I See Your Name Everywhere: Leverage the Power of the Media to Grow Your Fame, Wealth and Success* and *Don't Tell Me It's Impossible Until After I've Already Done It*, are bestsellers.

Lontos suggests:

It is much easier to approach prospects on the recommendation of their friends. But if everyone knows this, why aren't more people doing it? It's very hard to "cold call" a prospect, but if there is a prior relationship or connection in place, things become easier. Proper networking techniques are the secrets of the superstars in sales.

Tracking news sources and gathering clients are based on similar principles. The more people you know, the more ways you can follow a story or a business lead. Although there are effective shy sales people, the job is a more natural fit for outgoing personalities. (You will find more about this in Chapter 7, under Right Casting.) I once watched "Michael," a top sales manager, work a room. Michael seemed genuinely interested in what was happening in the lives of each person he talked to, and he remembered everyone's name. All those people felt significant, special, and important.

If Michael had asked them for the entire contents of their wallets and purses at that moment, they would have cheerfully handed them over. He "works" his clients the same way. Michael understands that businesses are run by people. When you get the person on your side, you'll get their business.

Meeting the Right People

Pam Lontos advises: "Go meet the people who can make the sale. Attend charity events, or business social functions where the decision makers are. One salesman went to a local pub every Friday after work. He didn't go there to drink. He went there because all the advertising agency decision makers met there every Friday."

Once you've connected with the decision maker, Lontos suggests, it does no good to go up and say: "I'm Joe Blake with WXYO. Do you want to buy some advertising?" Instead Lontos advises:

> You must focus on and ask them about themselves to establish rapport. Find out how they got started in the business and what they enjoy most about their industry. Ask what they do in their spare time when not working. Put yourself in the prospects' place. Ask: "How would I know if someone I'm talking to would be a good prospect?"

How Can I Help?

Be of genuine help. For example, if you realize that two people you have met at an event don't know each other, introduce them. This is an easy way to be seen as a helpful person. Ask existing clients if they know anyone who would benefit from advertising on your station. Help them focus on a particular group. If they are golfers, ask about anyone in their foursome. If they belong to a civic group or organization, ask about the other members. It's not that people don't want to give you referrals; it's just that they truly can't think of anyone if you give them their whole world to choose from. You've got to help them narrow it down. After someone gives you a referral, ask what he or she thinks the referral will be looking to accomplish. This will give you a little preliminary information.

Also ask if you can use your contact's name. When you do call, say, "Susan asked me to call you and I promised I would."

Finally, Lontos says, "The secret weapon in sales is to be genuinely interested in other people":

> When you ask people about what they do, they will eventually ask you about what you do. Have a great benefit statement ready: "I help business-people with their advertising and marketing plans so they can increase their bottom line." Most people will respond by asking how you do that. Now you can start talking about what you do and how you can help them. That's a lot better than a cold call.

Pam Lontos's Sales Tips

- Understand your clients. Question and listen to the prospects and uncover and meet their true needs.

- Qualify the buyer. Always get to the top decision maker. Don't waste time with people who are not in a position to make a decision.

- Listen with the intent to understand. Only when you understand can you respond. Listening is more important than talking. The client will give you the information to sell him or her. The next thing you say should be based on what the client just said.

- Understand the power of questioning. You can qualify the buyer, establish rapport, eliminate competition, build credibility, identify needs, find hot buttons, get personal information, and close a sale, all by asking questions. Have powerful questions at your fingertips.

- Sell benefits, not features. Clients care only about what's in it for them. Sell the end result of what they want. You can find this out only by asking questions and listening.

- Use the power of testimonials. The best sales tool you have is a reference from a satisfied client. Use testimonials to overcome objections and build trust. Testimonials take the fear out of buying and make it easier to close.

- Learn to recognize buying signals. Prospects will tell you when they're ready to buy. You must pay attention.

- Remember, the best buying signal is: "How much does it cost?" Don't give prices until you're first shown value. Don't offer the price until you are asked.

- Know the difference between a stall and an objection. "I want to think it over" isn't an objection—don't waste time treating it like one. This prospect has an unanswered question. Find out what the prospect wants to think about, answer it, and continue selling more benefits.

- Uncover the real objection. Prospects usually won't tell you their true objections at first. Due to the fear of making a decision, they often give false objections at first, to stop you from selling to them. Ask questions to find the real problem.

- Anticipate objections. If you've been selling for your station for two months, you already know the ten or so standard objections. Have answers to them written out and rehearsed. Create questions that eliminate objections before they are even mentioned.

- If you don't make a sale, make a firm appointment to return. Make some form of "sale" each time you call.

- Never argue with a prospect. If you win the argument, you still lose the sale.

- Redefine rejection. You're not being rejected, your offer is.

- Treat each client as though he or she is the most important.

- Satisfy client complaints in less than twenty-four hours. This will lead to added sales and a great reputation.

- Understand that hard work makes luck. Years of hard work went into making successful people "lucky." You can get just as lucky by learning how to sell and seeing more prospects.

- Use the power of persistence. Take "no" as a challenge. Learn from children how profitable persistence is. [Pat Bryson says "objections are your friends."]

- Have a sales call scheduled immediately after your sales meeting. Try out what you have just learned. Do it over-and-over, day-after-day, until that technique becomes automatic.

- Learn the ABCs of sales. Read, go to seminars, and participate in webinars. Listen to CDs. Adapt the techniques you learn to your own personality. Use your car as a school. Download and play sales training talks or motivational CDs as you travel.

You've Made the Sale. Now What?

Pat Bryson says, "The top twenty percent of successful sales representatives realize that what they do *after* the sale is just as important as what they do *before* and during the sale."

After the sale, Bryson lives by these two maxims:

- It is five times more expensive to generate new customers than to keep existing ones.

- More sales are lost each year due to neglect than any other reason.

The best sales people know this. They cherish their clients. After the client has said "Yes", the sales person pulls out his or her day timer or PDA and logs the following: expiration dates of the contract, service calls, copy changes, bi-annual reviews. They send a hand written thank you note *and* they provide client information so that their sales manager and general manager can write thank you notes also.

The best sales people give "notice of the new advertiser" to on-air personalities and front office people. If a potential customer calls about an ad they have heard, all station employees should be able to direct them to the correct client. The top twenty percent know their clients' important dates, i.e., birthdays and anniversaries. They never forget to "sell the sold." They keep clients updated on changes at the station. They take advantage of station "freebies" to pass these along to clients. They send information about the client's industry (with the Internet, how easy is this?).

The Sale Is Not Complete Until the Money is in the Bank

The top twenty percent of winning sales people recognize that a sale is not completed until the invoice has been paid.

And if the Client is Slow to Pay...

Rather than view collections as someone else's problem, successful sales executives have a system for making collection calls to avoid charge backs. They start with a friendly call at thirty days past-due to ferret out any potential problems. If the money has not been received by forty-five days, they call again and ask to "save them a stamp and come by and pick up the check." By sixty days, any past-due account should be called to the attention of the business manager or sales manager. After ninety days, the ability to collect diminishes significantly.

Produced Spots

Make the Commercials Powerful Radio

The Creating Powerful Radio principles apply to commercials: Will the commercial engage a listener? Does this product or service affect "health, heart, or saving money or transformative topics?" (How can this product or service transform someone's life in some way, to make it better?) How? How does it benefit the listener? Remember to paint word pictures. Think and speak visually. Personalize; be a powerful storyteller. Keep the message on point. Be creative. You'll always win over your listener if you make him or her laugh. Make it matter, be truthful, make sure to always emphasize what is "in it" for the listener.

The Radio Advertising Bureau suggests these guidelines:

1. The most important rule in radio advertising: Mention the client often. Make sure the listeners know where to find the client.

2. Play up the advantage to the listener. What's the unique selling proposition of the product or service? What does it offer that is not available elsewhere?

3. Grab attention. Use noise, music, unusual voices, whatever is appropriate.

4. Zero in. Pitch directly to your target listener. "If you own an aging, overweight cat, listen to this!"

5. Be easily understood. Copywriters who use big words gratuitously (there's one now!) often lose the audience.

6. Get to the point! Don't delay the unique selling proposition.

7. Use action words—"Now" and "Today"—when you're announcing a sale. Radio's and interactive media's greatest strength is its immediacy...use it!

8. Make the listener part of a word picture. Don't just talk about that new car. Using sound effects and music creates a mood and puts your listener behind the wheel.

9. Avoid clichés such as: "We're known for our excellent quality and great customer service." Try, "Our quality sucks and we'll ignore you from the moment you come in until you leave in a huff." The audience will pay attention.

10. Be accurate. Make sure the spot is checked by the client or other responsible party before it hits the air. Nothing says "We're sloppy and don't deserve your money" more than a spot with factual errors that's rushed onto the air.

Turn It UP

Your station may have the greatest production team in the world waiting to do your clients' bidding, but there's no rule that says a great car dealer is also a good copywriter, and you have certainly heard clients voice their own spots so poorly that their commercials sound like parodies.

Producing good commercials for your customers is where you'll really have a chance to win their trust and help them build their businesses. But what, exactly, makes a "good" radio spot?

Have you ever turned the radio up to hear a commercial? Audience research shows when a spot is well produced and fits the station's target audience, the listeners perceive that spot as new or useful information about products or services they may want to try, or special pricing on an item they may already use or need. They may actually pay special attention to that spot. Conversely, a bad or boring spot about a product or service that's not relevant or does not conform to the Powerful Radio principles involving health, heart, money, or transformation—that does not persuade, entertain, inform, or inspire—will drive listeners away from your station.

For some creative people, ads that work seem to fall like rain from the sky. For the rest of us, there's Maureen Bulley. Bulley is president of "The Radio Store." Her books include the popular *Write Good Copy Fast*, and she holds seminars and workshops for industry professionals. She's managed to take what is often perceived as a highly creative and quirky process and put it in a form that anyone can use. Here she shares the techniques she teaches to create powerful ad copy:

> The correlation between audience tune-out and "commercial breaks" is no coincidence. But if we view breaks as an interruption of programming, so will our audience. Advertising jargon such as "stop set" or "commercial break" implies that we are stopping or breaking away from entertainment to broadcast commercials before we return to regular programming. Not coincidentally, it is also the time we lose listeners to the competition when they scan the dial to see who is not playing commercials at that moment.

You can persuade your audience to stay with you for every minute of every hour. Commercials are a valuable part of your programming. You must treat them with the same respect as the rest of your show.

Give careful thought to the placement of commercials in the context of the programming hour. Know when your competition schedule commercials and for how long. If they are about to lose their audience because of a commercial "break," be ready to receive and capture that audience with compelling programming.

Be aware of how many spots in a row your station is airing. Not only will your audience wander, but long commercial clusters do a disservice to your advertisers. If no one stays to hear their commercials, no one can respond to them.

Check computer-generated logs, paying attention to the sequence of commercials. Has the computer scheduled a hard-sell ad in the first position at 6:30 a.m. when the majority of your audience is waking up? Try a less jarring commercial in that important first position. Spots will often be an exit point for listeners, but don't hold the door open for them as they leave. Treat them like an old friend who came over for coffee and encourage them to stay for "just one more cup."

If you are the talent for the spot, read commercials with a new attitude. Enter the studio in a positive state of mind. Prepare to focus, and contribute in a creative and meaningful way. Improvise in scripts whenever possible to add a personal touch or to make an awkward script easier on the ear.

Preparation is Gold

A well-organized session makes the finished commercials sound better. If a talent needs to run down the hall for a pair of working headphones, a bottle of water, or a functioning timer, you may lose the mood of the session or stop a creative process cold. If you're in charge of the studio where the commercials are produced, it's your job to make sure everything is in order ahead of time.

Scripts should be double-spaced and appear clean and uncluttered. NEVER include anything in the body of the script that is not meant for air. Copywriters should provide a pronunciation guide for words the talent may not know how to say, such as proper names and brand names. Show numbers as digits, not words. The eye recognizes "250" but stumbles over "two hundred and fifty." Scripts should be proofread and timed by reading aloud. This allows the writer to identify and correct word combinations that are difficult to say, or sentences that are too long to read in one breath. Focus on the end user when preparing a script for production.

The order in which scripts are read in a production session is also important. If the talent has just completed an airshift, his or her voice is warmed up and ready to perform. If production is scheduled before an airshift, allow time for the voice to warm up. Read easier scripts first, and build up to ones that are more demanding on the voice. A talent's voice is his livelihood. Treat it with respect.

Create Powerful Copy

The first step in creating powerful copy is gathering information and establishing clarity. What is this copy intended to do? What is its goal?

The advertising goal must be specific and measurable. Indicate precisely what you want to happen when people hear the commercial, and how often you want it to happen. Clarity will help you create a script that gets the desired result.

If your clients want to increase traffic to a website through their radio advertising schedules, advertising goals would specify how much more traffic they desire in measurable, quantifiable statements. By design, the script must include a call to action that sends the listener to the website. The script does not include a telephone number or street address, because that information would only distract listeners and would not help advertisers achieve their goals.

Jeffrey Hedquist, with Hedquist Productions, and author of *The Ultimate Radio Commercial,* creates stories he can use as advertising. Hedquist gives the following advice specifically for people who need to tell a story in the form of a powerful commercial. He calls them his "Six Story Starters":

1. Google for insights.

Go to Google and type in: "What are [the people in your target audience] feeling?"

Remember, it's feelings that will establish the emotional connection for your client.

The best most effective stories are emotional. For example: "What are single moms with two kids feeling?"

A recent search yielded about 285,000 results. You'll get more. You don't need them all. Look at the first five results and you'll have pertinent stories to relate to your client. It's the beginning of a fresh campaign that picks up on the most current concerns, interests, and feelings of the people you want to reach for your client.

Be very specific with your search. For example: "What are men with bad haircuts in Hartford, feeling?" About 3,270,000 results. Go figure. The first five can be story commercials for that salon you've been trying to get on the air.

2. Do field research.

[*All of the experts in Beyond Powerful Radio recommend this.*] Buy something at your client's store, or over the phone, or online. Eat at the restaurant, visit the club, browse through the merchandise, talk to the service staff. Do the same with your client's competitors.

What's the shopping/purchasing experience like? Look for unique qualities, services, approaches, or people. Take notes or record your impressions as you do it. There's your campaign.

3. Talk to your client.

Probe for stories. Whether you're writing the commercials yourself or you're handing the information to a creative production team, gathering the juiciest input is the first step to make writing a commercial easy. The stuff for stories may not be found in the client's newspaper ads, their yellow page ads, or on their websites.

Do an Audience Needs Analysis, or "ANA." What does your client's audience need? What's their pain? What are their dreams? What are their concerns?

Get them talking. Record the conversation. You can't take notes effectively enough to catch all the good stuff that will come out. An offhanded comment may lead to a great campaign. I've had this happen again and again.

Here are some suggested ANA-type questions to ask:

- How do your customers feel about you now?
- How would you like them to feel?
- How did you get into the business?
- What's the worst thing that's happened?
- What's the best thing?
- What do people not know about your business that they should?
- What do you do that's special and different that no one knows about?
- Why do customers buy from you?

- What's the most surprising, unusual thing that's happened to you or to a customer?

- What keeps *you* awake at night?

- Do you have any secret recipes, techniques, skills, or history?

- What do your competitors have or do that you don't?

- What do you have or do that your competitors don't?

These questions are starting points. Your client's answers may lead elsewhere. Just follow the threads and see where they lead.

When you hear something that's unique, or has a potentially strong emotional connection with your customer and the audience, make note, and *tell your client*. At the conclusion, remind your client [about specific parts] of the great input they gave you. It gets you both on the same team—creating the campaign together. Then when you come back to them with a story commercial, they'll understand that you've taken their thoughts and created magic with them."

Pat Bryson, Jeffrey Hedquist, and Maureen Bulley all stress that sales is, at core, an emotional decision. So you need to find out: "What *emotional* problem should this advertising solve for your customer?"

Hedquist "peels the onion" to get to the inner layer of his client's customers' needs. For example, your client sells golf equipment. What's the emotional need? Your client will say: "To play better golf." So you might ask: "Why would he want to play better golf?" Client: "I don't know. I guess to get a sense of accomplishment, to feel better about himself, to be cool." Now we're getting closer. "Why would he want to feel better about himself?" Finally, you and your client discover together that the reason for purchasing new clubs is so that your customer can compensate for feelings of inadequacy, to combat peer pressure, and to feel like more of an equal with his friends. Well, that's a long way from where you started.

"The answer to emotional buying questions," Hedquist says, "will be a basic need: love, acceptance, validation, etc. This will be the core around which to build your campaign."

4. Talk to your client's staff.

Get their unique perspective. You may discover someone with unique skills or experience to build a story on the chef who was trained in Europe, the dog groomer who cared for a celebrity's pet, the hardware store employee who's a former remodeling contractor. You will unearth treasures.

5. **Talk to customers.**

Stand outside the client's business and ask twenty customers why they bought there. Their reasons may be quite different from what the client thinks.

The pattern of responses will give you ideas on what to base your commercials on. The client who thinks his three generation reputation for exceptional service is what brings people in may find that it's his location across from the post office that accounts for most of his traffic. That's what you should build on.

Let the customers tell you how to advertise to them.

6. **Talk to yourself.** Use your own life, people you know and their stories that may relate to the product or service the client is selling to help create a powerful commercial... *(For more on techniques to learn storytelling from your own life, check the chapters on Storytelling, Fundraising, Show Prep, and Producing.)*

The Copy Navigator

Maureen Bulley, president of The Radio Store in Toronto, designed and created *The Copy Navigator.* When writing scripts using the Copy Navigator, brainstorm based on what you know about the product or service and the problem it will solve for consumers if they purchase it. Gather any other data that the advertiser thinks may be useful. If your station has access to research that may help position your client in the market or better target the client's ad, be sure to have it ready.

Perhaps you know that your listeners, twenty- to forty-year-old mothers, frequently use a certain city playground as a place to bring their kids and socialize. Perhaps you know that your client's car dealership is just a few blocks from this popular spot. Your automobile-repair client might not have thought "We're just a two-minute walk to Playland" and that this could help sell auto tune-ups, but if *you* do, it can help that client get a result.

Broadcasters pay a lot of money for research about their listeners. Make sure your clients get to take advantage of that investment.

Once you have the information you need, you may still need a little help creating just the right copy. To fill that need, try working with Bulley's

Copy Navigator. The Copy Navigator can be completed by the copywriter, account executive for advertising copy, or the program director or promotions director if the goal is to write effective promotional copy. (For a sample of Bulley's Copy Navigator, see page 419.) You may find it useful to ask additional questions to get the answers you require. Ask questions like, "Why should I buy from you? The store down the street has similar products." Or, "If I bought one of your products and I wasn't satisfied, what would you do?"

Write Good Copy Fast—Maureen Bulley's Copywriting Techniques

All commercials require a beginning, a middle, and an end. In fact, some writers start by deciding how the commercial will end and work backwards. This is a style decision that you will make on your own.

One of the most common problems with scripts is that they introduce a theme or an idea at the beginning and fail to revisit that idea again at the end. If you state a problem at the beginning of a script, and then use the middle to state your client's approach to that problem, be sure to refer your listeners back to the original problem and how your client will solve it for them at the end of the spot. For example:

> *If your car is acting a little sluggish lately, it may be time for a tune-up. It is time to save on a tune-up at Ed's Garage. Ed's will have your car running smoothly in no time with a fifty-six-point check and tune-up special for just $49.99. Ed will tune up your engine, and check all the fluid levels too. If they need topping off, he'll do it, all for under fifty bucks! Car a little sluggish? Perk it up with a tune-up special at Ed's Garage. Call 566-CARS to book your appointment.*

Notice how we refer back to the opening "problem" of a sluggish car at the end of the commercial. This theme could be made even stronger by adding sound effects of a sluggish car at the beginning, and replacing them with sounds of a smooth-running car at the end.

Regardless of whether you are writing a narrative, dialogue, or any other style of commercial, review all of your scripts with the "beginning, middle, and end" concept in mind.

1. Writing Narratives

Maureen Bulley teaches thousands of people around the world how to write copy in a variety of styles. Here's an excerpt from her Certified Radio

Copywriter© program that will give you an idea of how to write five basic types of advertising copy.

Great narratives include all the necessary product information, but you hear it in a natural way, within the context of a story. That's the secret.

A narrative is also known as a single-voice commercial. This is one of the most frequently used techniques in broadcast writing.

One of the most common mistakes made with narratives is writing them too long. They end up being read so fast they lose all meaning. They become an irritant, compromising your station's programming and any results the advertiser had hoped to achieve.

Write a narrative as though you were writing a letter to a friend, or speaking to someone on the telephone. Write the way people speak. People don't talk in complete sentences, and they do use slang. This will help you fit the entire thought in to the allotted time. Pick one theme or storyline to concentrate on, and then weave in the details as required.

Another key to a good narrative is to know the skills and personality of your voice talent. If you write with a particular voice talent in mind, it becomes easier to develop the script to make it sound like something he or she would actually say. When you write your next narrative commercial, read it aloud the way you want your voice talent to read it. Then ask yourself if you can read it comfortably within the allotted time period, if it sounds natural, and if it convinces you that trying this product would be a good thing.

Commercials that blend in to your programming and complement it, instead of intruding on it, are much more effective. If your station's programming is high-energy, a narrative can mirror that programming without becoming a high-pitched scream-fest. Think about how one of your listeners might tell that story.

2. Writing Dialogue

They say that when two people really "click," they can finish each other's sentences or read each other's thoughts. That is how a great dialogue commercial sounds. In fact, allowing the talent to complete each other's thoughts is a great technique for writing and producing effective dialogue. Above all, dialogue, like narrative, should sound natural.

Prove it to yourself by writing your next dialogue commercial "short," giving the talent time to make it sound natural. Allow them time to pause and respond to what the other person is saying. If you don't have particularly strong acting talent, cast two people in the commercial who have complementary personalities, or appear to get along well in the halls or at the coffee machine. Your chances of achieving your goal of better dialogue will be greatly improved.

Let them work with the script by giving them only basic copy points, then ask them to converse with one another about the advertiser and the products. Your client may hand you a veritable grocery list of products to promote. Remember, though, that your obligation to your client is to achieve his or her goal. A dialogue ad that sounds like a list won't sound very natural, and is not likely to be effective.

Good dialogue makes the listeners feel like they're eavesdropping on a private conversation. So, try recording two people having a conversation about your client's product or service. You will probably get some great natural responses that make for a very realistic commercial. You can either excerpt portions of that session for your spot or use the actual dialogue as the "script" for your recording session with professional talent.

Finally, when you're choosing the voice actors for your commercial, be sure their voices are not similar. Otherwise it can be difficult for the listener to identify who is talking, and who is saying what.

3. Testimonials

A testimonial commercial could be from a satisfied customer, a celebrity endorsing a product, or a commercial voiced by the client. Whoever is doing it, the most important feature of a testimonial ad is that it must be believable. The other challenge with testimonials is making sure that they sound good in the execution. This can be achieved with good recording techniques, whether in-studio or on the street, and with people who simply sound good and give coherent, succinct comments.

If you and your client have chosen a local celebrity to be your spokesperson or to endorse your product, be sure you have explored all the positives and negatives of this type of approach. There's always a risk that the person you've chosen may do something later to embarrass the client or risk the reputation of the product. If you do involve celebrities, be sure to involve them in the creation of the script. Ask them what they would actually say about the product, and try to incorporate their honest feelings and words into the copy. This will give credibility and integrity to your celebrity testimonial spot, and the listeners do know the difference.

The final type of testimonial commercial is the client-voiced commercial. Before you cast a client in a commercial, be sure there's a perfectly legitimate reason for him or her to be there. If it's simply ego, that's not good business for either of you. If ego is at the root of your client's desire to appear in his ad, an ad that talks about your client can sometimes do the job. For example, John Jones might feel just as good about hearing a professional voice promote his business this way: "John Jones has been greeting customers at the door of his restaurant with a cup of his wife Mary's homemade chili for twenty-five years."

With endorsement commercials, it is always good to include the client in script development. If the client is in the spot, work to get the best possible voice delivery from him or her. Remember, your goal is to make the client sound genuine, not like a professional announcer.

4. The Art of Storytelling

While all commercials require a beginning, middle, and end, it is sometimes difficult to express all of the important points within the prescribed time period. The key to successful storytelling is being able to complete it within the number of seconds provided. This is a challenging writing style, but with practice you can master it! (For more on storytelling see Chapter 17, *Becoming a Powerful Storyteller.*)

The best advice is to use fewer words. If you can say it in two words, don't use four. If you can make a statement with music or sound effects, it will help you to move the storyline forward without spending valuable time.

Never overlook your most important job of selling product for the advertiser. Ask yourself why you are using the storytelling technique, and decide if it's really appropriate. Do not tell a story for the sake of telling a story; make sure it introduces the product in a beneficial way, and "asks for the order."

One of the unique benefits of advertising with sound is that it gives us the opportunity to convey the story and have the listeners develop their own images about its details. Because they play an active role in completing the storyline, listeners tend to remember the message longer. They may also be able to relate personally to the story, or know someone who can.

When you work on your storytelling skills, begin by writing the story out, using as many words as it takes to tell it. Then go back and remove all unnecessary components that don't contribute to the storyline or sell the product. Once you have that first edit, look for places to economize on words. Look for opportunities to convey your message with sound. Even the voice reading your commercial will add to the story's overall texture. Keep paring down your script until it works within the prescribed time. Be sure to allow the announcer(s) time to tell the story at an appropriate pace. You'll defeat your purpose if you ask them to rush through the commercial to include all your copy.

5. Humor

Perhaps one of the most difficult techniques to master is humor. Humor is powerful when done properly, painful when it is not. Humor is also a high-maintenance style. Humorous commercials tend to become tiresome fairly quickly and can go from being entertaining to annoying if the listener is overexposed to them. Humor is also culturally specific and differs from one target group to another. Use humor with caution, and be sure to have fun with the audience. Never make fun of your audience in an effort to sell a product or service.

The fundamental rule for writing a humorous commercial is to ensure that it stays true to the product. Many times people remember the joke in a commercial but are unable to identify the product or service advertised. So when you're deciding whether or not to use a humorous spot, ask yourself, "Does the humor serve to promote the product and encourage trial?" Remember, the job of advertising is to promote the product.

Common themes of humor spots include the following:

- **The human condition**—If the listener can say, "I have been there, I know about that," the humor is based on the human condition. These situations are funny because we can relate to them.

- **Incongruity**—This form of comedy consists simply of putting things together that don't belong together. Incongruity can be achieved either in the script writing itself or in the production style. Perhaps the music is completely the opposite of what people are expecting, or the voice talent is exactly the opposite of what the listener expects to hear.

- **Exaggeration**—Exaggerating or minimizing a situation can make for memorable comedy. Exaggeration can be achieved through words, but it can also be conveyed through the characters in your commercial, the selection of sound effects, or the choice of music. Think about what naturally belongs in the commercial for the product or service you're writing for, and then try using the polar opposite.

- **Puns or double meanings**—A pun or double meaning usually goes along with some type of misunderstanding. This launches the comedy and helps establish the humor in the situation.

Using Maureen Bulley's tools for exciting and effective copywriting, powerful radio can happen *in*, as well as *around*, the commercials on your station. Below is Maureen Bulley's Sample Copy Navigator.

Sample Copy Navigator

Date: _____ Account: _____

Marketing Goal: *What does the Advertiser expect to achieve over a specified period of time? That is, increase awareness/ increase sales 10 percent over last fiscal year.*

_____

_____

_____

Advertising Goal: *What does the Advertiser expect to achieve with this advertising campaign? That is, increase inbound calls by 150 per week.*

_____

_____

_____

Best Potential Customer: *Describe the best prospect for this commercial. Include as much detail as possible.*

_____

_____

_____

_____

What's in It for Me? (Benefit): *What is the problem I am trying to solve with this advertising? That is, I'd love to take the whole family out for dinner, but it's too expensive. At Our Town Restaurant the whole family can enjoy a meal out, while saving money.*

_____

_____

_____

Why Should I Believe You? (Support): *This will back up the "What's in It for Me?" statement with reasons why the customer should believe what we say; that is, at Our Town Restaurant, children under 6 always eat free.*

_____

_____

_____

How Should It Sound?: *Describe the tone or manner of the copy, the same way you would describe the product's personality; that is, a sense of humor, a serious money-saving message.*

_____

_____

_____

Things to Include in Each Spot: *Elements that must be in every spot such as jingle, use of a specific announcer, or a slogan.*

_____

_____

_____

More On Powerful Storytelling

Jeffrey Hedquist teaches the following technique to help create ads. As his base he uses "The Story Spine" method, created by Kenn Adams, Artistic Director of "Kenn Adams Adventure Theater!" and author of *How to Improvise a Full Length Play: The Art of Spontaneous Theater*.

Hedquist shows how he uses the Story Spine to create an ad based on the following:

Client: Carroll's Home Design Studio.

Condensed client background: remodeling—garages, basements, kitchens, bathrooms, gutters, windows.

Prices—better than custom lumberyards, more than big box stores. Do really good work.

Market: empty nesters, disposable income.

Typical customer profile: DIY wannabe and spouse (Ed and Doris).

The Six Step Story Spine Method

1. Once upon a time...

Doris and Ed lived in a house that, like all houses, needed some things repaired. Ed was a halfhearted do-it-yourself wannabe, and Doris was a pragmatic "let's just get it done right" person.

2. Every day...

Doris would remind Ed that something in their house needed repairing but Ed would keep putting it off.

3. But, one day...

Ed finally agreed to make the repair, but Doris had already called in the professionals from Carroll's.

4. Because of that...[you can have a couple more 'because of that...' s]

Ed was secretly relieved. He never really wanted to do it himself anyway.

5. Until finally....

The team from Carroll's home Design Studio arrived and started work, and Ed knew he was off the hook.

6. And ever since then...

Doris hasn't had to nag Ed about the door. And now that they've found a good solution to getting repairs and remodeling done, she's got all kinds of projects to complete.

On the following page is how Hedquist used the Story Spine to transform an outline into a script.

CLIENT: CARROLL'S HOME DESIGN STUDIO
Radio Spot: 60—"Professionals"

Do: Ed...

Ed: Mm hmmn...

Do: You know you're very special to me.

Ed; Mm hmmn...

Do: You're a good provider, a loving husband...

Ed: Where is this going Doris?

Do: But, as a home repair guy...

Ed: Yeah?

Do: You're a good provider, a loving...

Ed: It's the front door isn't it?

Do: Well, it needs replacing, and I've been asking you to do it for...

Ed: What...a year?

Do: One year, 3 months, 14 days.

Ed: All right, I'll get to it...

Do: I've taken care of it.

Ed: You? What do you know about...

Do: I know enough to call Carroll's Home Design Studio.

Ed: Well, they do have good prices on doors...

Do: They sure do. That's where the professionals get their stuff. And Carroll's can do the whole installation.

Ed: Really?

Do: They have a team of installers who're experienced in...

Sound Effect: Doorbell rings

Do: That's probably them now [calling out]. OK guys, you can start on the front door.

Ed: Do I know these guys?

Do: No, but Carroll's guarantees their work.

Ed: Think they need my help?

Do: No. But I won't have to nag you anymore about the front door.

Ed: Great.

Do: Now, about these kitchen counters...

Ed: Just go to Carroll's.

Do: You know what their commercials say...

Ed: They're on Route 1 South in Fairfield...

Do: Next to Ace Hardware.

Ed: In Ottumwa, on the corner of Iowa Avenue and Main.

This commercial had huge results. Hedquist explains, "I think it was because we captured what their target market was feeling and we told stories that resonated with them. To paraphrase an e-mail from one of their customers: 'You could have saved money and just recorded these commercials in our kitchen. These are exactly the kinds of discussion I have with my husband!'" It will also help you write better copy if you answer the nine story questions from Chapter 17, *Becoming a Powerful Storyteller.*

Both Maureen Bulley and Pat Bryson, who are world renowned sales trainers and consultants, emphasize that becoming successful in sales is an ongoing process. Bryson puts it this way:

> The best sales people never stop learning. They recognize that yesterday's sales and marketing skills are not enough to be successful in the new world order. They devote a part of each week to studying marketing. They embrace new technologies. They recognize that we do not sell radio: We sell solutions! Today, those solutions may include radio selling messages, website presence, interactive phone campaigns, and social networking sites. You must offer more than a low rate to earn clients' business.

Maintain Balance

Keep it in perspective. You can't sell them all. Successful sales people plan well, work hard, and maintain a balanced life and, in addition to work, the most successful salespeople make time for family, health, exercise, recreation and spiritual pursuits. They have tremendous powers of focus. To be at the top of their game requires more than spending all their waking hours at the office.

Learn to balance the personal with the professional. The sales people in the top twenty percent have the same twenty four hours in each day as everyone else: they simply understand how to use those hours wisely…"

There is more on selling, sales techniques and how to connect with clients in Chapter 32, *Fundraising & Giving.*

CHAPTER 32

Beyond Powerful Radio
Fundraising & Giving

*"If you have much, give of your wealth;
If you have little, give of your heart"*
—Arab proverb

Money hasn't always been a problem for broadcasters. In Europe as well as in the United States many non-commercial stations historically received a substantial amount of their funding from government grants or taxes. They never had to think about bringing in money to survive. Now much of that is changed. Many stations now need to ask for money from listeners and solicit corporate sponsorships in order to continue operating.

While there are different needs for commercial and non-commercial stations, savvy broadcasters know that fundraising and cause-oriented programming go hand-in-hand. Radio and TV continue to be effective revenue-creating tools. Joined by the power of the Internet, you have at your disposal a powerful proven vehicle for producing money, whether you want to raise the funds necessary to keep your station on the air, or to use the power of your access and relationship with a large audience to help a cause you think is worthy. Programming that reflects the true concerns of a community not only enhances your station's image and public profile, but can also keep your station alive.

When was the last time you helped a stranger? When was the last time your radio station did? People everywhere care about making their community a better place. Most want to help others. I work in thirty countries, and everyplace I go, this has been true.

A Gallup survey commissioned by the "World Giving Index" ranked giving in three categories: who gave time, who gave money, and who helped a stranger.

The top five money-giving countries were, not surprisingly, countries where wealth is more abundant. Countries with fewer resources volunteered more time. Countries where poverty is common were most likely to help a stranger in need. So, it's the *type* of giving that varies from country to country, but giving, to help others in need, is universal and for many of the world's religions, giving is a big part of their spiritual practice.

Here are the reasons you might turn your radio station's programming over to fundraising:

1. To keep your station on the air.

2. To live your station's core values, or help others.

3. To garner prestige.

Any fundraising effort that takes your product away (or changes it—your programming is different during pledge or fundraising drives,) even for a little while, should fall into at least one of these three categories. If you want to raise money on air, whether you work in commercial or public radio, whether you're fundraising for charity or to generate funds to keep your station on-air, in this chapter you'll find the techniques that work.

Partnering With a Charity

Today, technology makes it easy for your audience to pledge. Vast numbers of geographically scattered people can pledge or donate instantly—online, or through their phones or mobile devices—amounting to a powerful force for good in the world. During the earthquake disaster in Haiti, listeners were able to tweet or text or call a number that would allow them to immediately donate to the Red Cross, quickly raising millions in small increments.

Choose Carefully

Aligning with a cause or charity gives you a chance to enhance both your own and your station's brand and image, in a way that is meaningful to you and your audience.

Selecting a cause that is on target with your audience is also a part of your programming or marketing plan. Causes you support make a strong statement about your station, your brand, and you.

While this "marketing" helps people in need of assistance, it can also help enhance your brand and image.

Because you will be identified with this cause, before you get involved, or decide to act, ask: "Is this cause or charity consistent with your station's audience and image? Does it meet the goals of your organization? Will it resonate with the audience? Is it something I want to support?"

The reverse is also true. As with any endorsement, should you choose a cause that "doesn't fit" or is outside of what your station stands for, or one that alienates your audience or advertisers, you can not only give yourself a metaphorical black eye, but your decision could have a negative financial impact on your organization.

A case in point is the story of a giant American retail store we'll call "Stains."

Stains chose to back a candidate its directors considered business-friendly. The corporation made a large gift to the candidate's campaign office, without looking at the total package of his views. Imagine their embarrassment when it turned out that the man they had thought would be their strong supporter in Washington DC held some personal views that were offensive not only to a large population of Stains' shoppers, but also to Stains' own employees.

The company's CEO had to make a public apology. The company nearly lost a deal to build several Stains stores in a major metropolitan redevelopment area. To avoid continuing negative press and a possible boycott of Stains stores, the company also promised to set up a review process for future political gifts.

The public relations disaster could just as easily take place at your radio or TV station. Check out the charity, their programs, and anything you ask your audience to support, carefully. Make sure the charity you choose is fully consonant with your station's core values, and that the kudos you may hope to get from your efforts do not turn into rotten tomatoes hurled at your good name.

Where Does it Go?

Before you commit to partnering with a charity, it's important to make sure the organization is legitimate, and that the proceeds you help raise will actually go to the people they purport to help rather go to funding the organization itself.

Al Tomkins, with The Poynter Institute and author of *Aim for the Heart*, cautions: "Do your research to avoid supporting charities that abuse their privilege. A perfect example of this is the organization that claimed to have helped paralyzed veterans—they took in more than $100 million in a year, but more than $70 million of that went to administrative costs and staff salaries."

Take the time to carefully investigate the recipient of your charity. Tomkins adds, "If we are asking people to spend hard-earned money, we should do our homework to be sure the money will be frugally spent and that it will go where the giver thinks it is going."

Al Tomkins takes the responsibility of vetting a charity seriously. He offers the benefit of his experience, and these tools, to help you avoid making an unfortunate choice:

[In America] every non-profit organization must make its tax files public. There's a form, the IRS Form 990, that they have to make available to show where their money goes. I'd make it a rule that before my radio, TV or website promoted a charity, I'd examine the IRS Form 990 first. Every charity, including those that are well known and highly thought of, such as "Make-A-Wish Foundation," should undergo the same examination. After you have looked the form over, give the charity a call and check your data. Clerical errors do seep through. The IRS Form 990 will include a phone number on the front page. Usually all of these charities have these forms from the previous year available on their websites.

The I-990 form will provide the following:

- **Income**—What is the organization's cash flow from donors, grants, services, and investments?

- **Expenses**—Take a line-by-line look at how the group spends its money. How much is spent on executive salaries, office supplies, travel, gifts, contracts, vendors, and consultants? Ask yourself "Does this expenditure help them accomplish their charitable goal?"

- **Assets**—What does the charity own? The possibility exists that a charity may own expensive property, yet have no cash available to spend on its cause. This should be a red flag. Beware of a charity that may actually be a shield for a property owner who does not want to pay taxes on his property.

Tomkins explains, "IRS Form 990 includes a section showing how this charity has performed over the last five years. Look for trends and make sure this year's data is not a one-time fluke. Keep it in context. All charities can have an especially bad or good year."

You can check out *www.charitynavigator.org* to get additional information and see how your prospective charity is evaluated and rated by this independent organization. To check charitable organizations in the USA, Tomkins recommends Guide Star at *http://www2.guidestar.org/* among others.

Before Partnering, Ask:

1. What are you trying to accomplish?

2. Is this issue or cause important to YOU or your staff?

3. Will this issue or cause resonate with your audience?

4. Are there other ways your audience can get further involved with this effort?

5. Investigate the organization, check it out carefully to insure the money will go where is it supposed to and that it is a legitimate non-profit enterprise.

6. Does this charity or cause reflect the image you have or want for your brand?

7. Decide what will be the time limits of your commitment.

Set A Time Limit In Advance

If you've ever volunteered your time, you are already aware that a charity will naturally want as much time and support as you are willing to give it, sometimes even more. You can't blame them, but it's best to communicate clearly to set limits at the beginning in order to avoid possible disappointment later. Be clear. Decide in advance how much time and for how long you want to commit to this fundraising activity, in order to avoid misunderstandings later on.

The relationship between media outlet and charitable organization can be a little like dating, where one person thinks there is a commitment to marry and the other wants to see who else is out there.

Be sure your annual fund drive recipient understands that this year you will be helping with their flood relief effort and, while their needs may continue, your company may decide next year to rebuild earthquake damaged homes on the other side of the globe.

I once worked with a station that supported a charity that helped sick children by giving them opportunities to participate in special events with celebrity support. We had a fruitful five-year relationship. Our announcers were frequently photographed riding circus elephants with the kids and escorting them onto concert stages to meet music superstars before crowds of thousands. The charity received lots of money and celebrity attention.

In the sixth year, our manager's nine-year-old son became gravely ill with a degenerative disease. Of course, our staff wanted to help. So, we decided to change direction and partner with an organization that raised money for research to cure his disease. Since we had never specified a time limit for our support of the first charity, they naturally assumed our relationship would go on indefinitely and they were understandably angry at the change. They not only felt betrayed; they punished our station by keeping us away from their future events, which we would happily have supported in smaller ways, with public service announcements, giveaways, etc. And we missed opportunities to showcase our station in smaller ways at some of their concerts and parties.

If at some point you choose to discontinue your support of a charity, abruptly ending philanthropic gifts can look as though you are abandoning a cause or organization, and that could inadvertently hurt you and the non-profit.

Opening Hearts and Wallets

It's never easy to ask people to open their wallets and give. We've all been asked for money, but is there a secret—a key to breaking through the many requests we get for help so that we respond? Yes. It's the same thing that makes listeners, viewers, and readers respond to your other content—the appeal has to matter to them. The same principles that apply to all great programming, i.e., powerful, emotional, engaging, or entertaining story-telling, will always stir hearts and minds to action.

Powerful Storytelling

When I was hired to work with a radio stations staff along with a hospital medical team, the goal was to work with them to teach techniques they could use to communicate more powerfully for their on-air fundraising drive. Before our workshop, here is a story that went on air:

INTERVIEWER: Tell us about Freddy.

DR. JONES: This eight-year-old male patient presented with a variety of symptoms, suffering from weakness, poor circulation, and shortness of breath. The diagnosis showed that this patient was suffering from a rare genetic birth defect, one that would require a transplant. One sibling, now deceased, suffered the same defect.

That's not much of a story—it's more of a clinical case history. In order to make the audience see Freddy as something more than a file and a basket of symptoms, with a bad diagnosis, we had to paint a bigger, more detailed picture of Freddy and his family. If people could imagine Freddy as a child they might know, with parents who might be friends of theirs, of course they would help him.

After the Powerful Radio Workshop, the staff was able to use techniques they'd learned to tell this story:

Eileen Combs worked in a flower shop. While she arranged roses and fragrant lilies, she imagined her wedding to Donald MacAllen. John Shorter had no plans to marry anybody. He was still in school. One rainy cold night, on her way to meet her fiancée, Eileen's car began making a noise like smashing soda cans, and she pulled over. When Eileen looked into the eyes of John Shorter, the kind man who had stopped to help, she knew her plans had changed. John and Eileen married within the year, and started their family. They never finished painting the baby's nursery, though, because Camilla died three weeks after she was born, of a misshapen heart. The Shorters were devastated, but a few years later, they were ready to try again. At first, all was well. Their new baby, Freddy, was pink and healthy...for a little while.

But something was going wrong. Freddy wasn't growing. He couldn't seem to catch his breath. Fearing the worst, the Shorters took their child to the doctor. Terrible news: Freddy had the same heart problem that had killed his newborn sister Camilla. There was hope, but the family needed a donor, and the hospital didn't have enough beds and equipment to keep Freddy alive while he waited. Each bed and machine cost thousands. Where would the money come from? It came from you. Because you sent money to support our hospital, Freddy could live. With a machine for a heart, he survived the five years it took for a suitable donor to be found. The hospital was able to provide for Freddy the facilities he needed, and today the Shorters are a healthy family of three.

That's what went on air during the station's two-day radio-thon to raise money for a children's hospital for kids who needed specialized medical care. You can see how important it is to tell stories instead of just relating case histories. The Creating Powerful Radio techniques were, literally, lifesavers, enabling the staff to tell stories so compelling that they were able to increase their donations by forty percent.

"Stories that make you feel guilty are never as effective as stories that make you think, laugh, invoke empathy, or inspire," says Hedquist Productions creative director and storytelling trainer Jeffrey Hedquist, author of *The Ultimate Radio Commercial*. These can be pre-produced in advance or done live. Hedquist's ideas work for both pledge drives and charities.

Storytelling works for all categories of fundraising: Non-commercial stations pledge drives, and emergency aid in crisis, and it helps with long-term relationship building when you partner for fundraising with established charities.

Begging For Money—Nobody's Good Time

If you've listened to public or community supported broadcasting, or visited the websites of online communicators, you've likely heard or seen some version of the plea for money. It's no secret that it takes a lot of money to run a media outfit, whether you have a newsroom full of reporters who must be paid, or you're putting together a music website from your dining room table.

The cash has to come from somewhere. What's the secret to getting your audience to pay for something they can enjoy, in many cases, for free? That's a riddle that has not been completely solved yet, but there are some stations and fundraisers who are more successful than others.

Hedquist suggests, "Begin by interviewing previous donors. Encourage them, in their own words, to tell *why* they gave and what they enjoy about your station. Ask for suggestions on what programming they'd like to hear in the future. Ask previous donors to encourage other people to give.

Edit the interviews but keep them real. A natural comment is far better than a canned pitch. Listeners want to know how donating made the donor feel, so they can feel that way too.

Find points of your product (and its financing) that connect to your audience's personal interest. Ask listeners to call in to share their stories about a particular feature on the station, whether or not they're donating. (*For example*: "I don't have a car. I ride the bus but listening to the Car Talk guys makes me laugh. I learn things. It also makes me feel better about taking the bus.") That way you can build support for your programming without having to be the one doing all the selling. Give listeners reasons to act. As you near an hourly, daily, or weekly goal, build anticipation by announcing how close you are getting to your goal. Give donors a sense of accomplishment."

Matching Donations

Tell stories about the generous companies who are multiplying listeners' donations. Don't just announce a corporate matching donation. Connect your listeners to the company that's giving them. For example:

If you have a printing job, you'll never have to worry about someone messing up your job if you go to Apple Tree printers. Because Apple Tree printers cares about getting the details right, they appreciate our news department. That's why they've generously offered to match your donation to WXXX.

Or,

Pruneville Hospital noticed its doctors were listening to WXXX in their offices. Because Pruneville has so much respect for their staff and patients, they want to come onboard by matching any amount you give in the next hour.

Matching Grants

Don't forget to remind your listeners that their own employer may matching-grant fund and, if you can, keep a list of local companies that do this on your website.

Goods and Services

You should be able to accept donations of services from businesses who wish to pledge them either as a simple gift or as an incentive for others to give. (*For example*: "Gwen Laufer will provide vending machine services at the station for a year through her company, 'Snacks to Go,' if we can match her gift valued at $3000, with cash donations.")

Individual Matching Donations

You may get an offer from an individual to match donations for a period of time or up to a certain amount. Even if the individual wishes to be anonymous, tell a story about them. (*For example*: "We have an anonymous donor who listens at her office when she is solving important legal questions; she's offering up to 500 dollars in matching pledge money for the next hour.") Add a little mystery and make it your event.

Special Need

If the station suddenly incurs an unexpected cost, such as a new piece of equipment to replace something that's just failed, tell the story of what happened, and emphasize the immediate need. (*For example*: "Last night, you may have noticed some gaps in our interview with the Vice President. That wasn't your cable company...that was our best camera overheating. We're making do with our old equipment, but if you've gotten used to seeing every detail clearly, we are going to need your help to replace that camera; it won't be cheap...")

Make Sure the Need is Real

Consider the wisdom of your timing. Make sure your need is real. (If you've just completed construction on your high-profile multi-million dollar state-of-the-art broadcast facility, your management team is very well paid, and your audience is aware of it, this may not be the moment to launch an on-air appeal for more money.)

Hedquist suggests, tell "mini-stories" about ongoing items or services the station needs and ask donors to "take charge" of them.

For example, you could challenge your listeners to buy your station a year's worth of electricity, or pay the artists licensing fees you owe for playing their music on your website. Maybe some very neat person would like to treat your community station to a year's worth of cleaning services or supplies.

(Imagine how much your co-worker would enjoy knowing he or she is supplying the toilet paper your most famous host will use during "breaks.") Need a birthday gift for the gardener who has everything? Offer someone the chance to provide floral and plant services at your best girlfriend's public radio station.

Say "Please" and "Thank You"

Donations can take many forms, including cash, products or services that can be turned into cash, or corporate sponsorships. In whatever form the support comes, it's important to acknowledge the generosity of your donors. Jeffrey Hedquist says creative ways to do this are limited only by your imagination.

Honor companies and people who have donated "wish list" items or products or services by putting up a plaque near the copy machine, kitchen, or meeting room, or even your public entry space, acknowledging their support. Use your airwaves: "I'm speaking to you on the Hortense Lackland memorial microphone from the John Sleighter studios at WXXX." Thank people over the air and in celebratory e-mails, tweets, instant messages, or blog posts: "One year of printer and fax paper for WXXX made possible by a donation from James and Suzy Farmer."

Each of these donations should be the exact amount the station spends on the item: "If you'd like to be the amazing person who replaces every light bulb at WXXX this year, call us to pledge $177.62."

If you're offering "thank you" gifts (pledge premiums) for donors, paint a picture of the benefits of owning the premium for your audience. It may be easier to tell a story about an elegant sponsor donation.

If the premium is a T-shirt or coffee mug, you may have to be more creative. (*For example*: "The handsome Community Radio traveling coffee mug is a great way to let someone know you're a classical music fan. We heard last week that the owner of a sandwich shop down the street noticed one of our subscribers carrying the mug and asked her out to a harpsichord performance. It's going very well.") You might try asking your audience members to call with the most outrageous, innovative, interesting use or benefit they've experienced from owning the premium.

If you're fundraising for a cause, disaster relief or a charity event, keep stories of the progress coming. Let the donors know how their contributions are making a difference. If the event isn't local, find ways to tie it to your community with local stories: Did local area doctors fly to a disaster scene? Were those firefighters who spent the weekend sandbagging against floodwaters in a neighboring state from your town? That is where your audience's money is going.

Report Results

Attach the expected effect to donations of differing amounts: "Your gift of $25 can provide a family of four with canned milk for a month." Always approach the story from the donor's point of view, not the station's. Don't berate them, make them feel guilty or bore them. (An exception to the "no guilt" rule is "This American Life" host Ira Glass, who has become famous for his humorous phone calls to never-pledged long-time public radio listeners. Glass solicits the friends of these "freeloaders," then calls the procrastinators and records their excuses for not giving. It seems to work pretty well.)

If I Give, What Do I Get?

When soliciting donations, ask yourself: "What is the benefit for the listener?" Find it, hone it, define it, then deliver it. And don't forget to offer something to your volunteers, perhaps a free pound of coffee to all who took the night shift answering pledge calls.

Corporate Sponsorship—The Invisible Ad

In the United States, non-commercial/non-profit stations are allowed another effective method of fundraising: The corporate sponsorship. Instead of airing a traditional commercial, the corporation or business is *thanked* on air for its contribution, and its product, service, or company is mentioned in a short sponsorship statement.

One public radio station group that has used this tool with impressive results, even during economic hard times, is New York City's WNYC AM/FM and WQXR FM. Under the leadership of President and CEO Laura Walker and Vincent Gardino, Executive Director of Underwriting for Radio and Digital Media, the stations have creatively adapted some techniques from commercial radio sales to obtain significant corporate sponsorships.

Today, WNYC AM/FM and WQXR FM are among the most successful public radio stations in the country, both financially and in audience size.

Even with its history of success, getting sponsorships for WNYC is not without challenges. Public radio lives within strict copy restrictions and guidelines. Before any copy goes to air, it must be vetted by an in-house attorney, and checked against a clearly established set of policy guidelines. Vincent Gardino emphasizes that:

> All on-air spots must feel unobtrusive, like information tidbits. They are a part of the fabric of the programming. And nothing goes longer than fifteen seconds. You need to mention the sponsor but there are serious copy restrictions, including: no hard sell; you can't use slogans or rates; you can be descriptive, but not promotional; no prices; no comparative mentions or repeating of phone numbers or websites; you can't use jingles; no calls to action (*for example*: "Buy it now, the sale ends Thursday!"); no mention of awards. If there's a spot for a film that's won an Academy Award or a Pulitzer Prize-winning novel, or a Tony award-winning Broadway play, in the advertising you can't mention the award.

Because of these rules, many businesses or corporations who buy time on commercial radio won't buy WNYC.

But it works both ways. Many food product companies, tech companies, law firms, and medical centers are among those who are unique corporate sponsors of WNYC. They wouldn't consider buying or supporting commercial radio.

WNYC only does direct selling to clients; they don't use an ad agency. Several people on the staff have come from commercial radio, but Gardino says:

> Even with an experienced radio sales person, it can take months, even up to a year, with a new account executive to train them in non-commercial radio thinking.
>
> But our corporate sponsorship clients get results. Studies have shown that the listener response rate for the products and services mentioned on public radio is eighty-two percent higher than for commercial radio. That's because WNYC delivers a prime audience of educated, affluent, culturally oriented and involved listeners. For WNYC listeners, the station is important in their lives; they're loyal and connected to the programming.
>
> Our audience considers us like family, and are extremely devoted fans of the station. They believe that sponsors who help keep the station afloat and support the programming they listen to are worth supporting.

And Gardino, with his sales team, works hard to maintain strong connections and relationships with clients. In fact, Gardino uses clients, the corporate sponsors, to help get new leads, and it works. He explains, "When I was [in commercial radio] at the ABC radio network, we had an advisory board. You'd have affiliates of the network telling people [other potential sponsors] how great it was." When he got to WNYC, Gardino put together his own advisory board made up of key sponsorship clients, in turn made up of those who share the same ideals, values and perspectives as WNYC. Members of this board have been helpful in suggesting additional contacts and ideas to generate more funding.

Have a Party

WNYC has taken another page from the commercial radio playbook—the dazzling star-studded event for clients and prospective clients. At WNYC it takes the form of the annual client cruise. Gardino explains, "We do this as a thank you for 500 of our closest friends. We don't focus on business on the boat. It's a thank you party. We bring the air personalities and raffle off prizes. The halo affect lasts all year."

Inviting New Sponsors

WNYC has a very active website with over half a million unique visitors per month. They also run on-the-air spots to solicit and invite new or potential sponsors. You might hear: "If your company or business would like to become a WNYC underwriter or corporate sponsor, contact WNYC's Executive Director of Underwriting Vincent Gardino" (and gives Gardino's direct phone number). Gardino says, "The single most effective way to bring in leads has been those on-air announcements. We run one in each daypart, and on average, I get three to four calls or e-mails a day from them."

Showing Off

Vincent Gardino impresses prospective clients by giving them tours of WNYC's studios. Corporate sponsors enjoy getting a behind-the-scenes look at the station and meeting the on-air personalities. They welcome the chance to see and experience for themselves how radio works.

The Only "Magic Formula" is Hard Work

Gardino says, "Obtaining a steady income stream from corporate sponsorships is not easy. In good times or bad, there is no "magic formula." The only "secret" is hard work. It all comes down to basics: client, client, CLIENT! Continue doing the fundamentals, including cold calling. Client contact will tip the scales in your favor. Always deal directly with the decision makers—the CEOs or VPs of marketing. Deal with the people who can say "yes" or "no," and say it quickly."

Vincent Gardino's Top Ten Tips To Attract Corporate Sponsorships

- Form and use a client advisory board for leads.

- Deal only with decision makers, people who can say "yes" or "no."

- Have a thank you party. Bring your on-air staff.

- Remember fundamentals—cold calling and follow through.

- Use on-air spots to invite or solicit sponsors.

- Use your website.

- Bring clients/donors in to tour the station.

- Hire right, then have patience—take the time to train your team.

- In good or bad times, it's HARD work.

- Relationships matter, think: client, client, client!

Seed Money

Vincent Gardino applies commercial radio experience to benefit major market, non-profit New York City stations. At the other end of the size scale, on the other side of the country, Northern California's Melissa McConnell Wilson did the same thing, applying the knowledge and experience she'd gained from many years of success in commercial San Francisco Bay area radio to managing KVHS FM, a non-commercial Active Rock (New Rock) station owned and operated by Clayton Valley High School in Concord, California.

As General Manager, McConnell Wilson found some of her challenges were the same as Gardino's but many were different. Unlike WNYC, which employs dozens of professionals, KVHS depends on high school and adult students, who work for training, experience, and class credit. Melissa transformed KVHS into a highly regarded, innovative new rock station. Today, KVHS is supported by its community, with a large and loyal listening audience. (This small station now shows up in San Francisco ratings and only covers three counties.)

I attend seminars and broadcast industry events every year where I am often asked, "Where do we find talent? Where are our future communication stars?" Stations like KVHS serve multiple functions. Not only do they act as treasured community assets; they often serve as the training grounds for future professionals. Many of the people you'll see profiled in this book got their starts on radio stations like KVHS, but in tough economic times, the school station has become an endangered species. That's why McConnell Wilson's fundraising ideas are so valuable. They can conserve a resource for the communications industry, maintaining a place where young people can learn craft and get experience.

McConnell Wilson says, "If you want to do this, you have to have the heart to do it. It's hard work, but if you make up your mind to do it, it can be done." She should know. The week McConnell Wilson took over KVHS, its funding was cut. At the same time, it became clear the station's basic equipment was in need of costly repairs. KVHS innovatively and creatively found ways to match non-commercial events with commercial businesses and private individuals. These days, McConnell Wilson often gets calls from other non-profit stations asking: "What do we need to do to be successful at *our* station?" Here is her advice:

Your most valuable resource is your signal. In our case, that applies not just to our fundraising, but also our programming. Our format gives us a great opportunity to cover local events and to play local bands.

The station also reaches out to the community with ties to the station. (Try using the same principle that colleges and universities have used for years. Go to your alumni, and their families, for support. They have the most heartfelt connection to your product. Be glad you only need tires for your station van, and not a new auditorium.)

Of course, you can use your signal for on-air and on-location (remote broadcast) fundraising. But since your station has a non-commercial (educational, religious, etc.) license, some kinds of fundraising are not allowed. Check local, state and federal guidelines, laws, rules and regulations and learn how to work well within them. Make sure your prizes are appropriate for your audience. That's especially true if your station belongs to a school or religious institution. But don't miss opportunities to connect your station events to the calendar (like Mother's Day), and bigger happenings in your community (such as an internationally known marathon).

For example, you should get expert advice on what is considered a "lottery." Some kinds of "games of chance" are not legal in many states. (You wouldn't want to print up raffle tickets for a weekend spa stay and orchard tour, then find out that it's illegal to ask people to buy them.) Another example: You need to know whether or not you can, for instance, hold a benefit to raise money for another non-profit organization or charitable agency.

Bricks and Mortar

You can't take basic workplace skills for granted, as McConnell Wilson learned when she came on board at KVHS. "When you work with novice broadcasters, you'll have to teach them everything, including the importance of branding your event and volunteers with banners and attire featuring the station's logo." She advises:

- Set up a business office with communications equipment: phone, fax, voicemail, Internet access. It should look professional, but it doesn't have to be expensive or large.
- Write a telephone contact script so your people can make fundraising calls. This way you can prepare staff or volunteers who don't normally "sell" to do "cold calling."
- Your number one selling point? A "Win/win/win" (yes, triple!) situation for donors to your station:

  1. Airtime for their business interest.
  2. A charitable donation for their business for tax purposes.
  3. Public recognition for their generosity towards your non-profit organization, school, etc. in the community served by your station's signal.

If you work with younger volunteers, they may be well on their way to living in a "paperless" society. So, you may need to stress the importance of having a business presentation package, especially a donation receipt letter, or contributor form/contract. All these should include your logo, and your non-profit status/IRS taxpayer ID documentation, in addition to an electronic press kit. Many businesses and individuals will donate for a tax write-off before the end of their fiscal/tax year. You'll want to make it easy for them to give to you by having a letter ready to acknowledge receipt of their donation.

Your paper presentation or your website should make clear your "spots per dollar" ratio for contributor announcements. That's the number, type, and approximate length of "acknowledgements" the donor will receive as a result of his or her contribution. This correlates with the rate card of a commercial station, though often with considerably lower dollar amounts.

You may want to set a minimum donation amount, for acknowledgements require a lot of work on your part. It doesn't take much to put an "underwritten by" note on your website, but it takes some effort to create a fifteen-second announcement. You may choose to make cash contributions a priority by offering a better package of "thank you" mentions for them.

The Great Outdoors

McConnell Wilson often brings fundraising outside the station, wherever there's a chance to generate revenue for it:

> If you decide to run a live remote/outside broadcast fundraiser, you will first need to check local, state and federal guidelines. In the United States, there are FCC rules and regulations regarding non-commercial licensed stations raising funds for any other non-profit or charitable entities other than your non-profit station. It is usually not allowed. However, public service airtime given to other non-profits is allowed.
>
> If you're planning to partner with a for-profit business on a fundraiser, be careful. If you intend to split the money from ticket sales for a concert you are holding at a movie theater with the theater, you may be on the wrong side of the laws governing non-profit fundraising. The exception is usually if the business is donating *all* of the proceeds (after costs) of the event. They still get the benefit of having community members get to know their facility, and create good will, and that's worth a lot. If you do choose this type of broadcast, be certain to use a "body count" clicker to verify the number of tickets you sell. Don't forget to give yourself plenty of time to generate excitement about your event. Use all media, old and new, to get the word out and cover the costs with more donations.
>
> Create a database. As people donate, it's important to collect and compile as much contact information as you can get, along with amounts/items given. You'll want to be able to reach out again for future donations.

Whether you work in a large or a tiny market, prepare your staff. Even if your front office people are not directly involved in a fundraiser, they're going to get phone calls or e-mails asking, "How do I pick up my premium?" and "What's the number to pledge?" over and over again. Hold one last general staff meeting before your event, where you and your station managers will outline the expectations of each staff member for his or her role in the fundraiser. Then, watch for future stars. Individuals who volunteer and do great work on your station's fundraisers could be good hires down the line.

You'll find more on working with charitable organizations in Chapter 16, *Public Service Announcements.* If you are interested in learning more on fundraising, or "how to ask people for money," there are many resources available including *Fear-Free Fundraising* by Holly Million, one of many books that cover methods of reaching out to individual donors or raising money for non-profit organizations, off air. The Public Radio Program Directors Association also has resources available for pledge drives; go to *www.prpd.org* for more information.

Even though you may be generating money for the most basic needs of your station, to get someone to open up his or her heart or wallet, it's never just about the cash. Pablo Picasso once said: "Artists who live and work with spiritual values cannot and should not remain indifferent to a conflict in which the highest values of humanity and civilization are at stake."

Part of the privilege and responsibility of having a microphone or, sometimes, a website, is serving your community. When the qualities of humanity and civilization are expressed as programming or content, your audience is able to recognize the importance of donating to maintain those values.

PART VII

Beyond Powerful Radio
Understanding the Audience

CHAPTER 33

Beyond Powerful Radio
LifeStage Demographics

"Life is long, but time is short."
—*Eric Schmidt*

Traditional Demographics vs. How We Live

The pivotal moment happened ten years ago during a focus group. As our group began leaving the room, I noticed a young woman in her twenties, one of the participants, saying "hello" to a fifty-one-year-old lady she met in the hall on her way out. As they began to chat, the years between them melted away. Both had young children, attended the same "Mommy and Me" classes, were buying mini-vans, and had stayed at the same hotel in Disneyworld.

Two women, twenty-eight years apart, with the same interests: Both in the same LifeStage. Both comprise the new make up of LifeStage Demographics™.

At that moment a light bulb went on in my head and the concept for LifeStage Demographics was born. We began examining research and focus group results and developed a system that could effectively tap into listeners' lifestyles and LifeStages. Armed with this information, broadcasters could then make programming and marketing decisions based on what was important to their audiences.

From a programming perspective, the ratings growth was astonishing. Stations working with LifeStage Demographics had huge audience increases, and much more time spent listening. We invited sales people to attend my workshops to learn about LifeStage Demographics research. That helped account executives sell ads. LifeStage Demographics brought ratings and cash. It was a win-win for everyone.

The relevance of LifeStage Demographics increases every time a website, cable channel, or other media venue decides to target its product to a particular LifeStage group. Not only are Lifestage Demographics important when understanding how you can serve your audience; they are also the key to understanding how your audience will be using your product.

Different LifeStage groups have widely varying attitudes towards media usage. There's a lot of new research being done about how different LifeStage groups incorporate entertainment and information delivery platforms into their lives.

When I work with successful communicators and broadcasters around the world, they all have one thing in common. Every single one crosses traditional demographic "lines." Why? The reason is that those demographic "lines" were drawn arbitrarily. They *never really existed.* Instead, these highly successful communicators appeal to audiences of a particular LifeStage or interest group. Their form of entertainment works because it provides new and useful information to people in that LifeStage in a way they recognize as truthful, humorous, or engaging. If radio managers and programmers begin to look at their audiences by LifeStages instead of by demographics, the results will be surprising.

It's been nearly ten years since I began working with LifeStage Demographics. The Hallmark Channel and the Entertainment Technology Center at the University of Southern California's "E-Poll" research recently re-confirmed our study—their findings: Individuals in different life stages can have similar demographic profiles.

Cable television found its market, and makes a great deal of money super-serving targeted special interest LifeStage niches. You'll find special programming geared towards animal lovers, the health conscious, independent film fans, golf enthusiasts, home remodelers, political junkies, and gourmet cooks, to name a few.

The publishing world learned about niche marketing years ago, as it migrated from mass circulation "one-size-fits-all" editorial publications, to multiple smaller special interest titles, founded on their readers' common interests. The trend has been to move these titles to a greater Internet presence, with a de-emphasis on print. In many cases, special interest publications now exist entirely online, where elaborate websites can super-serve their readers with content targeted just for their LifeStage and interests.

Media companies traditionally organized their businesses by defining a specific audience niche. They tried to serve what they believed were the needs of that group. In fact, they only served one very specific aspect of a customer's life. The *Wall Street Journal* was for high-powered executives, *Animal Planet* was for animal lovers, HGTV was for women. There were lots of high-powered women executives who loved animals and home decorating. Advertising targeted to women with all those interests and attributes in common wasn't practical then, but it is now.

Assume Nothing

It's time to throw out old assumptions about the audience. Any product or service that people can use can be targeted by LifeStage.

Take a product like Coke™. They market to every LifeStage. Nike™, with its carefully cultivated image of toughness and tenacity, had success using the multi-LifeStage slogan, "Just Do It." The Nike™ image is used to sell across LifeStages and demographics—golf clubs to overweight middle-aged executives, tennis racquets to teenage girls, and soccer apparel to urban teens.

The belief that people make buying decisions based on a common set of needs defined by age, income, sex, and ethnic group is not valid. People have more choices about the ways they live, and make buying decisions based on whole new sets of additional criteria.

In the past, advertisers, programmers, and marketers tended to assume that clichés were true. A typical ad campaign targeted to "mothers in their thirties" might have standard imagery: mini-vans, stressed harried schedules, tender hugs in the kitchen, and bargain shopping. Yet most moms don't drive mini-vans.

With LifeStage Demographics, if you look at a group of friends who are in their thirties, you will probably find some contradictions in the conventional thinking about demographics. Take a group of thirty-three-year-old women. They may shop at the same stores, eat at the same restaurants, and see the same movies as other women of the same race and income.

But in reality, when a thirty-three-year-old woman looks at her group of friends, she sees that some of them are shopping, dining and going out to movies together because they are single and looking for husbands. Some are meeting at the playground with their kids talking about preschool, and renting movies. Others are planning vacations to islands in the Pacific with their husbands or boyfriends. It isn't so much their paychecks, or their ages, that are dictating their lifestyles as choices they have made.

If you follow that sub-group of thirty-something women to the playground—you might also see some older women, some ethnically diverse women, and some men. The age range is 16–65. The unifying LifeStage Demographic—they are all taking care of children at around 2:00 in the afternoon. They are all making buying decisions and lifestyle choices based on the commonality of "responsibility for children."

You might think that the sixty-five-year-old grandmother at that playground, with her high disposable income and her status as a retired person, would buy a certain kind of car, perhaps a sporty, luxury model convertible. Instead, she has a Volvo wagon with toys in the back and cereal imbedded between the seats.

You might think the forty-year-old man pushing the five-year-old on the swing is completely out of place, but he is one of several men at that playground today who work from home and cares for his children. His wife, a physician, is attending to her medical practice. Today he will also stop by the grocery store for disposable diapers, and take his child to a fast food restaurant for a treat. Choices these men will make include: public school vs. private school, soccer camp vs. camping vacation, bottled water or juice boxes, washing the kids' hands with Purell™ or Handi-Wipes™, computer class or music lessons, McDonalds Happy Meal™ vs. a granola bar, video vs. art project. And of course those same people are making decisions about which TV station is on in the family room, how much time each kid is allowed in front of a computer screen or on a mobile device, and what to listen to in their cars. The chronological age of the listener does not matter as much as the LifeStage.

You and You

If you were to talk with account executives or program directors, they might tell you that the most coveted target demographic for broadcasters is adults aged 25–54. In the radio industry we've programmed and sold in terms of targeted demographics for so long that we have missed out on something important: The way people live today is different from how people have lived in the past. Traditional demographic targets were not very accurate then, and they're even less meaningful now. Within each target and format there are different audiences in different LifeStages. They're living very different lifestyles. To determine and super-serve selected LifeStages, while still keeping an open door to a mass audience, is one of the benefits of using LifeStage Demographics.

As an example, a host might want to talk about a specific thing that happened at his kids' preschool. Your station wants that audience of young parents, and your advertisers want them, too. But you also want people listening whose kids have grown, or people who never had kids in the first place. So, instead of saying something like: "When you take your kid to preschool in the morning, you know how you have to run that gauntlet of other kids with colds and drippy noses, and you think to yourself, please let me get out of here without any more germs than I came in with?", he or she might say: "If you made it through years of being a preschool parent, or you're living the preschool parent life now, you know that while preschool is a cheery garden of songs and puppets, and it's also a germ factory, a great place to catch the plague. And if you don't have kids, thank the next parent who cancels a dinner invitation." To put it in the simplest terms, hosts now talk to "you *and* you." That way, you appeal to more than one lifestage, and nobody gets left out.

A cable TV show incorporating LifeStage Demographics might open with: "If you want to sell your home for thousands more, or you're just ready for a living room that *looks* like you spent thousands, Robyn will show you how to give your space a fresh modern feel in two days... ."

Again, the idea is to target your show to a specific LifeStage (people looking to sell their homes and move up), and a general audience (anyone who wants a nicer looking living space). To use an actual target analogy, you can hit the bull's-eye with your LifeStage, and then spread some shots around to hit other areas nearby.

Because many are living longer, enjoying active lives and are in good health in their later years, the stereotypes defining people's lifestyles have been pitched out the window. The stereotyped roles of men and women have changed. Older women have young children. Healthy, fit women are watching and playing sports. Men start new families at sixty. Since people are living longer because of advanced medical breakthroughs, with emphasis on leading healthier lifestyles, those who are fifty-five and over may have more disposable income. And here's big news: The older audience doesn't *consider* itself to be an "older" audience anymore.

Ironically the very people who ought to be aware of this, are often young people who are making key marketing decisions and agency advertising buys, without an awareness of how audience members/consumers in different LifeStages may actually live.

In reassessing what works for sales, advertising, marketing, and programming, it is time to look at LifeStage Demographics™ as a strategy.

The "Google Effect"

LifeStage Demographics is not by any means the only way to target a market. New behavioral databases, pioneered by companies like Google, Netflix, Amazon, iTunes, and Pandora are expanding the methodology of targeted marketing. If you've ever made a purchase, say, bought a book or music from some of these services, you may have been stunned to receive recommendations for other books, music, or films that may seem almost superhuman in their ability to anticipate your interests. How can Netflix™ possibly know that if you liked this year's hit action film, you might also like a twenty-year-old historical drama?

Personalized Targeted Marketing—is personal, but don't take it personally.

By recording the preferences and tracking purchases of millions of music listeners, book buyers, and movie watchers, these companies can now predict, with a fair degree of accuracy, the next movie, song, or book a customer might like. The suggestions these companies offer are founded on a dispassionate statistical behavioral analysis, not a human stereotype with its innate prejudices. These companies work their advertising magic with computer models and statistics, not catchy artwork and clever prose. Because they haven't stereotyped people, their marketing options are almost limitless.

Improving technology allows marketers to define their customers even more specifically by outlook, not just their areas of interest. So if someone is a mother, a wine lover, *and* a computer aficionado, new powerful research systems can find the exact strategy that connects to her mindset and attitude, and track her previous purchases. Marketers can discover the commonality that motivates her wildly varying interests. Soon radio and television will be able to individually target listeners and viewers in this way, allowing programmers to better understand and market to them.

Using LifeStage Demographics™

Whenever I present this material in seminars or workshops—teaching LifeStage Demographics for programming, marketing or sales people, they want to know: "How can I use this? How does this help *us* get ratings, be more effective, market our content, or sell more advertising?"

A thorough knowledge of LifeStage Demographics helps you draw a far more accurate picture of your target audience by giving you a practical understanding of the audience's various LifeStages. Here's how.

Sales

Understanding LifeStage Demographics helps effectively target sales presentations for clients, with proven results.

Knowing your audience and super-serving a LifeStage is invaluable when presenting your station's listener profile to prospective clients. If, for example, you understand through LifeStage Demographics that most listeners without children do not buy life insurance, but as soon as people start having kids and expanding their families, they buy as much as they can afford, that can be useful information when pitching to a prospective insurance agency client and will likely help you get the sale.

A sales force armed with the knowledge of LifeStage Demographics can better explain your station's value to a potential advertiser: "Our classic rock station has an audience of fathers packing lunches for their twelve-year-old kids before those dads go to work. You'll sell a lot of life insurance to these fathers because everyday they think, 'What would happen if I didn't get home from my job? How would my family cope?'" Again, those who are single don't usually buy life insurance, nor do young couples without kids. By using this LifeStage to approach a client instead of the traditional demographic of "men 25–40", you're able to target more the pitch more effectively.

Commercials

LifeStage also helps production directors at stations create better and more successful commercials that net results for the clients, particularly when you can define special interest groups. Common interests elevate awareness for commercials. Advertising in *special interest media* is as interesting to the audience as editorial content. That support means less of the ad dollar is being spent on simply getting attention and more of it goes into defining the message.

Selling LifeStage

Marketing campaigns specifically designed to target the LifeStage of your desired audience will net better results along with increased word of mouth. You will achieve more effective planning of contests, product tie-ins and events. The result: Your audience will feel more connected to "their" station and believe, "They are talking to *me*."

Here is one example of a perfect LifeStage Demographics promotion: An adult contemporary station that had chosen to super-serve young mothers, between twenty-five and thirty-five, held a circus with clowns and prizes for the children. During the event, they also offered a five-dollar oil change and lube job for the busy moms. Members of the station's target audience could attend the radio station function, get a bargain on necessary automobile maintenance and save the time it would take to bring the car into the mechanics shop, all while having fun at the circus with their kids.

Programming & On-Air Talent

Hire staff in various LifeStages. It helps if most are in the LifeStage of the target audience you wish to attract. Learning LifeStage Demographics helps your on-air talent, not only in selecting content and show prep, but helping managers in hiring decisions for new on-air or behind-the-scenes producing talent. Through the use of LifeStage Demographics you will create more powerful, relevant, and targeted programming which will benefit the station by growing and developing the listener base and extending the audience's time spent listening.

Music & Imaging

Using LifeStage Demographics aids your music and research departments in selecting songs, liners, and jingle packages.

Get the Audience You Serve

In other words, LifeStage Demographics help make sure you are speaking to your audience at every opportunity in a language that they can fully understand, and that you fully understand their needs in order to serve them. There is no part of your station, from its logo to the coffee in your break room, that is not affected by LifeStage Demographics.

LifeStage Demographic research shows race and age do not play as big a role in defining audience interests as do education level and social class. According to this research, upper middle class educated Asians, African-Americans, Native Americans, and Hispanics have more in common with upper middle class Anglo Saxons than do those with lower income levels or less education.

LifeStage categories can and frequently do overlap. For example, a person can be a homeowner without being married, and a single woman who is looking to find a husband may have children.

LifeStage Demographics Categories

Kids

There are as many kinds of kids, teenagers, and young people as there are kinds of people. "Kids" are divided into four sub-categories:

- *Academic Fast Track*: "I want to be a doctor so I study all the time."

- *Trendy*: "I spend all my free time at the mall hanging out with my friends. I'll worry about my future later on."

- *Sports Fanatic*: "I play football, baseball, soccer, basketball—any sport whenever I can—and I go to the games."

- *The Perennial Kid*: The "kids" can be eighteen or thirty-five years old! They still may be attending college. They are making important independent spending decisions. Some of these are young people who are done with school. They may have tried living on their own, gotten jobs, or attended college, but, whether due to practical economic or emotional reasons, these kids have returned to the "nest," and are living a LifeStage of prolonged adolescence, remaining at home with their families. Research is showing that the expected age of reaching adulthood has now moved to people's late twenties.

Young Men

This category does not depend on age. We discovered a thirty-eight-year-old man living an identical lifestyle to a seventeen-year-old. Here were men of significantly different ages, almost different generations, living similar lives. Both worked in music/video stores, both rented apartments, both drove sports cars. Both of these men were "not sure what they wanted to do with the rest of their lives." Both were single, dated a lot, got regular, expensive haircuts, ate out frequently, attended concerts, and both visited their families each week for a home-cooked meal. Both the seventeen-year-old and the thirty-eight-year-old also brought sacks of dirty clothes home each week so their mothers could do their laundry!

Young Women

Again, actual age is relevant. A woman could be seventeen or forty-six and might still want to shop at trendy stores, purchase sexy underwear, sign up for gym memberships, or have an interest in romantic gossip about the latest pop stars.

Working People

There are several types of LifeStage Demographics breakdowns in the working world. Among these, we found two main categories: (1) people who still had major career decisions pending, and (2) those who had made a career commitment. The people in these two categories lived very different lifestyles.

1. **Just a job:** This group admitted their "real" lives were outside of their jobs. Someday they hoped to find their true calling, and on that day, would step into the role they were meant to play. At present, they were not committed to or deeply involved in their work. Whether in retail, the corporate world, the public sector, or in fast food services, these people were still trying to "find themselves," and were merely working at their jobs to make a paycheck.

2. **Career commitment:** Those who had made a career commitment lived a very different lifestyle than people who were in the "Just a Job" LifeStage and still had major career decisions pending. These career people were struggling to get ahead in their chosen fields. They spent long or extra hours at work, and many went into the

office on weekends. Some traveled extensively for their jobs. The career commitments cut into their time with family, friends, and leisure activities. Many said they spent time thinking about their work, even when they were not on the job.

Unemployed or Between Jobs

People who are not currently working cross all LifeStages. Whether they are actively seeking jobs or semi- or fully retired, these are people who may have more free time or who spend their time differently than working people.

Renters

Renters lived a vastly different lifestyle than homeowners did. Because they were not under the financial responsibility of maintaining a home, often there was more disposable income available. They also tended to have more flexibility. A notable characteristic of this LifeStage: If need be, they could relocate more easily for work or personal reasons than those who owned their homes.

Home Owners

It was not uncommon to find new homeowners making several trips to a home repair shop in one weekend (and not always to buy items— sometimes homeowners went back just to ask questions!). Depending on income level, extra money that was once used for vacations, luxury items, and evenings out often went into paying extra costs or expenses for the house.

Solo

If someone lived alone, his or her listening, viewing, travel, entertaining, and spending habits were different from those of couples.

Couples

Couples tended to make decisions together, and with more compromising. This included everything from which radio station was playing in the car to the choice of vacation destinations.

With Kids or Without Kids

Those with children lived a very different lifestyle than those who did not have them. Age was irrelevant.

Good Health vs. Ill Health

Age again, is not always a factor here. We found that the lifestyle of an eighty-year-old man in ill health who was spending most of his days in bed, watching TV, online or listening to radio, wearing a bathrobe and pajamas, wasn't all that different from a thirty-eight-year-old woman recovering from difficult back surgery.

Special Interests

Other categories of LifeStages, connect people who had special interests in common, including pet lovers, sports fanatics (with sports divided on several levels—tennis, golf, skiing, baseball, football, hockey, wrestling, etc.), gourmet chefs, etc. Here, age and sex didn't matter as much as similar or common areas of interest. Although there were generational commonalties that should not be ignored, age was not necessarily a factor here either.

When you are formatting, programming, and marketing your station or selecting your content, it is not enough to say, "We want an audience of 25–54-year-old men." A programmer must also ask, "What LifeStages of 25–54-year-old men do we want to serve?"

LifeStages Are Fluid

LifeStages are more fluid than traditional age/sex/income-based demographics. After all, your next age-defined demographic group, if you are in your twenties, is in your thirties, then your forties, and so on. However, if your LifeStage is "With Kids," you may raise a family of young children, live in a child-free house for a while, divorce, remarry, then start all over again with a new house full of small children.

It takes a little more effort on the part of researchers to get used to the idea that we cannot just park people into an age, sex, or ethnic or even income group and expect that they live a certain way.

New marketing tools along with LifeStage research mean more powerful and emotionally connected relationships with our listeners, viewers, and customers. In a world where all kinds of programs are available all the time, on any device, the brands that survive will be the ones that understand their customers as individuals within LifeStages, with unique attributes.

Hire People in the Lifestage You Wish to Attract

There is no substitute for life experience. Your imagination can only take you so far. Most of us base our understanding of the world on direct experience.

It's no longer enough to say we want our audience to be men aged 25 to 54. Whatever your main LifeStage target—"With Kids" checking out schools, "Couples" planning vacations at a resort, "Solo" singles looking for spouses, or active people training for a marathon—if you have not experienced it, it makes sense to have people around you who have.

If you are running a station, or hosting or producing a program, whose target audience doesn't look or live like you (and it is possible that you are), surround yourself with people who are like the audience you wish to target. Their perspective will help you to understand the audience outside of your own LifeStage. Pay attention to these people. They may have insights that do not show up on conventional research. Your show or station's website can also offer opportunities to help you connect with your audience in all LifeStages, in many new ways.

"They say the early forties is the new late thirties."

CHAPTER 34

Beyond Powerful Radio
Research

> "You know the station is a success when people
> who don't listen lie and say they do."
> —*Overheard at a National Association of Broadcasters Convention*

People love to look at research. We open the newspaper or magazine, or watch TV and gobble up those Gallup polls, pie charts, and percentages of who is doing what. We like statistics, metrics, finished products, results. Most of us know it's not the data, but how one interprets it that counts.

Applying research to radio is a challenge. It's easiest with music radio. You ask a group of people what they think about a song, a performing artist, or a jingle. Interpreting "personality" or "news-talk" research is tougher. The reason? You can research only what has gone before. There is no way to predict in a research study what people are going to respond to tomorrow.

Working in talk radio is not for the faint-hearted. It elicits strong reactions. Your listeners will love you or hate you. They're active, and they'll let you know how they feel with calls, faxes, flowers, e-mails, boycotts, and threats.

One clear difference between news-talk programming research and music programming research: Polarization in news and talk radio can be a good thing. Strong listener reaction to a news-talk personality, whether positive or negative, is good, provided there is a balance. Don't be afraid of this intense reaction, it's one of the strengths of talk radio.

In talk radio, negative reaction is not necessarily something to fear, but there is cause for concern if ninety-seven percent of the audience hates your host or show and only three percent love it. If you have an equal number of positively and negatively polarized opinions, that is a sign that whether they love it or hate it, they're listening.

Take strong personalities like Rush Limbaugh, Glenn Beck, or Dr. Laura, for example. People either love them or hate them, but each has an audience of millions. The natural instinct of programmers is that they want their stations to be *liked*. They do not enjoy calming angry listeners, or spending their work days answering accusatory e-mails. But if you have a show you believe in, stick with it. Even if it is controversial, it is worth it. If a programmer can fight his or her instinct to get rid of a show that gets a strong audience reaction, and override the pressure, you will have a valuable product in the end. It may seem like the complaints will never end. Keep in mind that it takes a while to grow a show.

Listeners are creatures of habit. They do not like change. They like it the old way. While some behavior can be immediately altered, according to Dr. Evian Gordon from Australia's Brain Resource Company, co-author of *Integrative Neuroscience and Personalized Medicine*, it takes a thousand repetitions before a human brain is "rewired" to change, and this includes changing listener's habits.

It's only when the new way has a chance to "kick in" that it becomes a habit for the listener. So, (1) if they don't like the host today, they might tomorrow; and (2) if they hate him but they listen (and are counted in the research) that's OK. Don't be alarmed when your research shows that the audience has strong opinions about the hosts on your station. Controversy is not necessarily a bad thing. A station I once worked with printed up t-shirts that read, *"Listen to talk radio, because all great minds don't think alike."*

In just about every radio market, you can hear the story of a beloved host whose name is known to all in the community but who is listened to by very few. Conversely, the mention of certain hosts causes dramatic negative response among many who would never miss a show.

Music radio is both morning-show and music driven. In America, news and talk are very different formats. Obviously both benefit when there is a lot of news happening: a natural disaster, a political crisis, a war, a huge trial, or an election. But talk radio tends to be personality and opinion driven, while news radio is information based and current-events driven.

The news-talk format has splintered into several specifically targeted formats. Under the news-talk umbrella, you can hear hot talk, self-help talk, sports talk, right- or left-wing political talk, Christian talk, male- or female-oriented talk, and youth-oriented talk, among others. There are also thousands of niche-format radio stations delivered online and by satellite that compete with terrestrial, traditional radio, and they cut the target even smaller: Fishing talk, anyone?

What research can do is help you understand your audience and their lifestyles. It can answer questions like: "How can my station better serve my audience?" or "What have they responded to in the past?"

You might be surprised to learn what does *not* change. Frank Magid and Associates, in Marion, Iowa did a research project several years ago based on the question: "What gets people's attention?" What they discovered then is still true today. No matter the delivery system, people will listen or watch when you talk about:

- Health (safety)
- Heart (emotional stories that touch the "heart")
- Pocketbook (money).

There is also a fourth category that has emerged in addition, that captivates an audience's attention: *Transformation.*

Transformative topics include anything that gives a listener hope for the future—that shows how someone's life can be better tomorrow than it is at the moment because of something they've heard or seen in a program. The current trend of self-help, advice, rehab, or fix-it programming is an example of this.

Understanding Your Audience and How They Listen

Before delving deeply into research, it may be helpful to understand how people in your audience actually take in information. There are many more demands on people's attention now than there were just a few years ago, and many more delivery systems where people can find the information and entertainment they're looking for. So if you don't immediately engage your listeners, they're gone. They've got too many other choices for content. Your listeners are busy, and they've been trained to have short attention spans. They are often doing more than one thing while listening. The trick is to break through to each listener in the way that works best for him or her.

Teachers suggest that students absorb information in three ways. Most of us are a mix of all three of these learning styles:

1. Auditory (hearing)

2. Visual (seeing)

3. Kinesthetic/Tactile (touching).

Most of us have one way that works best for us. While radio is not necessarily "educational"—our primary goal is to entertain—people do come to media for news and new information. If you want your messages to "stick" with the viewer or listener, it's useful to know that we now have all the tools at our disposal to reach each type of person in the audience. Radio personality and educator Melissa McConnell Wilson explains, "With traditional radio, you've got just one method, that's 'auditory.' But with a website, you're adding a 'visual' component, and, if your site is interactive, involving listeners, you can expand further to 'kinesthetic/tactile' people."

Of course, people are individuals, not groups. Each person has his or her own interests, but when you hit the core of what people care about— Health, Heart, Pocketbook (money), and Transformation—there's a commonality of human experience.

Research can help you find out what *kind* of "Pocketbook" issue might be affecting people in your audience (for example, Blacksmoke Industries is planning to build a new factory near your city, which will bring needed jobs, but also pollution). If you know what your audience cares about, and if you can tap into that and pay attention to it, you will get ahead. You'll find more on this in Chapter 33, *LifeStage Demographics.*

The Power to Convince

Research can also be an incredible tool for programmers and managers when working with on-air talent and sales people. One project I took on involved a talk station where a minister, a priest, and an attorney all hosted programs. They were dull. Even people with a lot of faith were tuning out. I was called in to help "fix" the shows.

Here's what was going wrong: The hosts were talking *at* the listeners. They were lecturing, orating, and preaching, but not communicating. These men held themselves above their audience. Although each considered himself to be a good listener, not one of them really cared what his audience was saying. As a result, it was not personal, intimate, interesting, or meaningful. It was just very boring.

I met with these hosts as a group, then one-on-one, but could not seem to get them to understand that they were not communicating powerfully. Well-educated, always treated with great respect, and with fairly high self-images, these men refused to believe that they were not fascinating.

It was a focus group research project that saved these shows. We hid our hosts behind a two-way mirror and together we watched the proceedings. The focus group put on headphones and began listening to a recording of the first radio program. Within minutes, most had removed their headphones and were talking amongst themselves.

The priest was outraged. He was shocked that people had tuned him out: "I'm just getting to the important part. They're not paying attention!" I reminded him that in church no one would dare to get up and leave on a Sunday morning, even if the sermon was dull. Parishioners would all sit politely, quietly bored, though pretending to listen. But alone in their cars, at home, or in a listening focus group, listeners do what they please, which is to tune out if a show is boring or irrelevant to their lives.

It was only after all three of the hosts experienced the tune-outs that they were open and ready to learn the techniques of creating powerful radio: storytelling, showing their hearts, being more personal, and listening. They all had the desire for their programs to connect with audiences. They worked hard and today all three hosts have successful shows because they were led to understand that they must become more powerful communicators, and be given the tools to do so.

Research is a necessary tool of modern business. Can you imagine a car manufacturer putting out a new car without test-marketing it first? Big money is at stake. People in business want data before they introduce a new product. They need a realistic sense of how the audience or consumer will react. Radio, TV, the Internet and other forms of media are no different.

Many products we don't think twice about today are in our lives because of quantitative research: single-serving frozen dinners, zipper-lock plastic bags, automobile cup holders, a tire patch in a can.

In the United States, there are pages and pages of names of researchers in media directories. Anyone can hang out a shingle and call him or herself a researcher. Be careful which company you choose. It's a combination of skill and personality that makes good research.

If done right, research can help you get ratings and learn the habits of your audience.

No Crystal Ball

Before you embark on an expensive research study, see who's been there before you. Perhaps the information you seek may be easily findable elsewhere, without having to commission your own costly study. Check Arbitron. They may have data you can use. There may also be research you can access that's already been done by a non-competing business in your market. One radio group successfully used results from research studies done by a local insurance company, a local bank, and a supermarket corporation. All three of these companies had done extensive market research and were willing to share their results in partnership with the radio station. With a better understanding of local consumers and their buying, banking, and insurance needs, both the station's programming and sales departments benefited. There may also be local market data available for free from various professional associations, the Census Bureau and your local Chamber of Commerce.

Researcher Steve Apel emphasizes that market research can't predict consumer behavior. "If it could, no product backed by research would ever fail. What research can do, if used properly, is identify public trends and tendencies." In media, this means giving your listeners something they've been missing or more of what they say they like. There is no crystal ball.

Remember that while there are many research techniques, the basic process involves:

- Asking the right questions
- Compiling the data
- Analyzing and interpreting the results.

Don't Get Intimidated by the Language of Research

Apel advises that if you've hired research professionals using advanced analytical techniques to interpret a study, ask them to explain the techniques they are using. Be sure you're comfortable with the logic. After all, you need to understand and have confidence in this interpretation if you are using it to make changes to your product. Decide before you contract with a research company why you want to invest in the study and what you want this study to reveal. Be clear.

There are two kinds of research studies. "Tracking studies" tell you how you are doing. "Action studies" can tell you what direction you should go in next.

While the "how are we doing?" tracking studies can show you that you are "on the right track," this research is very expensive. Before you contract with a research company, it's important to know your goals. What do you want to find out? Don't let the research company take the lead. Be proactive and help create the questions. The best questions in a research study are not the ones that provide "interesting information." The most effective questions in a study are the ones that lead to real knowledge and change. If a question is not critical to achieving your goals, take it out. Ask questions. Understanding who your listeners are, how they live, what they care about, and how they use media is crucial.

Do You Really Want to Know?

It does you no good to research programming issues if you really don't want to hear the answers. Again, before you begin the research project, make sure you are prepared to make necessary changes. If not, why go forward with the study? If a programming element or personality is something that you cannot or will not move or change, why bother to research it?

One station spent tens of thousands of dollars researching their high-profile morning personality, and looking at a format change. Results: The morning show was the problem, the format was fine. If you were the station manager, you might have considered making a personnel change. But that wasn't going to happen here, because this morning host was under a no-cut five year contract. Perhaps the research money would have been better spent on someone to coach the struggling talent. Obtaining high-cost quality data on something you cannot or will not change is a waste of time and money.

Then there's the research that staff won't implement. One market study showed that a straight-ahead news station with a fine reputation for accuracy and restraint should move towards a more sensational-style newscast. That did not go over well with the news staff, who flatly refused to change their presentation. If that were your station, what would you have done?

Before you do research, know how your staff will deal with the findings. If you want to keep your present team in place, but research says you need to change direction, what will you do? Are you really ready to fire people? Are you prepared to fight it out with your present team? And if they won't change, then what? If you already know that you're not willing or able to do anything differently, save your money.

No matter how thorough or well executed your research project, consultant and researcher Matt Hudson warns that research alone is no way to make programming decisions: "[Research] does not prove or disprove anything. We still need creative minds to understand, interpret, and implement the findings."

Here, Hudson defines some research terms and talks generally about radio research. In some cases, I've provided examples to illustrate Matt's definitions.

Qualitative vs. Quantitative

"Qualitative studies, such as focus groups, involve ten to twelve people and are used to collect indicators that will be tested in a more statistically reliable research project, for example, a phone study. Quantitative studies, such as format searches or perceptual telephone studies, are large sample procedures which yield quantitative results. These can be generalized to the population from which the sample was selected."

In other words, you've got only twenty-eight people at your station and you already know their opinions about everything anyway. So, you get twelve people, strangers who really like your format, gathered in a room. Then you ask them in great depth and detail about whatever you need to discover. These twelve people are a flashlight in the dark. They will illuminate new areas and point you in the direction you need to go for your larger or quantitative study.

This group is like gold. They can teach you things you never believed possible about your station; and the deeper you go, the better it gets. Just as in the focus group that taught the minister, priest, and lawyer how to communicate, when you really listen to these twelve people, powerful things can happen. However, you shouldn't make big decisions like firing someone because twelve people don't like the person. That calls for a bigger, quantitative study.

The questions based on the insight gained in the qualitative study can lead you in a direction of seeking trends in the quantitative study.

Let's say a station's evening talk host is the subject of a small focus group study. Turns out, some of the listeners find him so irritating that they put up with static to hear another host on a station hundreds of miles away. Up until then, the station's management had no idea the distant station could even be heard in the market. Thanks to the small focus group's qualitative results, quantitative questions about the distant station can be asked in the larger perceptual study.

Some researchers say you should never base programming decisions on qualitative research, and all agree that unless designed to do so, results from qualitative research should not be the sole factor in decision-making.

For example, if you wanted to build a new bakery in New York City: If you ask nine people which bakery has the best bread in New York, you'd get nine different answers. They could give you some great ideas on what they'd like to see in the bakery, or whether they prefer store-bought bread. But you certainly wouldn't want to use the results of your nine-person study to determine where you'd put your new store, what types of bread you would bake, or how much you should charge. To make these kinds of decisions, you'd have to ask many more than nine people.

Validity

A test or study should measure what it is intended to measure. The ideal research situation is to have a valid test or study that is also reliable. It is actually possible to have a valid test that is unreliable or an invalid test that is reliable.

As an example, you can ask all the morning host's friends if they like the show. You can do everything right. You can make sure the responses aren't influenced by one another and your demos are properly sampled, but your sample is still a group of your host's friends. The study is perfectly valid; it's just not reliable. If you really want to know what the community thinks of your morning host, don't recruit a group of his biggest fans.

People who call radio stations or write to you are *not* necessarily indicative of who is listening to your station. Research has shown that only one to three percent of your audience will ever call the station. So, create programs for the ninety-seven percent who are listening, not those who call. If you've worked in radio for any length of time you may have come to the conclusion that "normal" people don't usually call radio stations. That may be true, but "normal" people *are* likely to text you, or e-mail you from your website. Most people are still passive listeners, but that's changing. Your listeners are becoming more accustomed to being able to interact with all their media. So take each caller as an individual, even if he or she is not necessarily representative of the greater listening audience.

Because you know your market, work with your researcher to ensure validity. Ask about the criteria your research company uses to select the group. Do a mission statement for your study, then make sure you ask questions that will give you the answers you need. Even though they may not be the answers you want, ask yourself: "Is it skewed or biased in any way?" "Does it really measure what we want?"

Prestige Bias

Respondents tend to give answers that they think will make them seem more educated, successful, hip, financially stable, or otherwise prestigious. A good researcher can control this problem by asking and directing the questions correctly.

Researcher Bias

In this case, respondents provide specific answers because they believe these are the ones the researcher wants to hear. They want to impress and please the researcher. Again, this is easily managed by a skilled professional.

Random Sample

Every person has an equal chance of being selected to participate in a focus group, music test, or telephone perceptual study. A station database is *not* a random sample. If someone has volunteered for your study, he or she could not really have been chosen at random.

Size is Important

What is a "statistically reliable sample size?" It depends on the error rate you are willing to accept. Generally, between seventy-five and one hundred people should participate in your perceptual study for each demographic group, or "cell," you want to measure. For instance, if you want to do a study measuring adults aged 25 to 44, you'll want approximately the following number of participants:

- Women aged 25 to 34 (at least 75 respondents)

- Men aged 25 to 34 (at least 75 respondents)

- Women aged 35 to 44 (at least 75 respondents)

- Men aged 35 to 44 (at least 75 respondents)

This yields a total of 300 participants, generally considered adequate for this type of study.

How to Use a Focus Group

These results should *not* be used to make major decisions. This small sample research technique gives you an indicator; it helps you to devise the next set of questions you will need in your larger group for a telephone or Internet perceptual study.

The Internet is a valuable tool for focus group research as well. Collecting data from willing users to your station site can be useful to learn who is responding to your station's programming, commercials, and public service efforts. Use the data for a further understanding of your audience. Pay attention to the metrics. Who is visiting your site? These are active listeners and users and can be a valuable online "focus group."

What to Find Out

Steve Apel suggests: "Through questions that probe listener knowledge and impressions, you can get a feel for whether people perceive your station's programming the way you intend." In other words, by asking the same question in a number of different ways—using, for example, different descriptive terms—you can get a clearer picture of what listeners really think. The picture "enable[s] you to assess whether or not your station is on target and provide[s] a basic guide for modifying the station to better suit [your] listeners' needs, tastes, and expectations."

For example, during a perceptual study, you might ask the following questions: "Which station plays the best rock? Which station plays the widest variety of rock? Which station plays the hottest rock? Which station plays your favorite rock?" A skilled researcher will be able to interpret the differences in the responses to give you more than just a simple "call letter" answer to the question.

Ask Your Own People

It never hurts to have your target demographic represented in your workplace, and it can't hurt to ask anyone with an opinion to spend a few minutes giving his or her thoughts to you. Be aware, however, of who's speaking. If your chief engineer, a known classical music buff, can't stand your afternoon sex therapy advice show, don't be surprised or make any programming decisions as a result. If, however, your chief engineer is a twice-divorced woman known for her romantic prowess and she finds that same afternoon show dry or pompous, you might want her to elaborate.

The Portable People Meter

In the United States, radio's prime research data gathering system is in transition, moving from diary-based research results to electronic measurement or Arbitron's PPM (Portable People Meter). PPM offers immediate, up-to-the-minute results, twenty-four hours a day.

Here's how it works: Listeners are given a small device to carry with them every day. This device, or meter, then electronically tracks and measures every radio station they listen to and the length of time they spend listening. PPM has moved into most U.S. major markets, though some cities, particularly in smaller markets, still measure listening using diaries.

The difference between using diaries and electronic measurement is the immediacy of the data. Initial PPM results have shown that listeners are more fickle than broadcasters had believed. While loyal to stations they like, when they are bored, that loyalty can quickly shift. The variety of stations people choose was also a surprise. Typical listeners averaged six stations while driving. They might use one for music, another for traffic, yet another for news or talk. They listened to different types of music formats—and most tuned out when they heard long commercial sets. (Because we now know how quickly the listener tunes out if he or she is bored, the principles of powerful radio—making the content relevant to the listener—are more important than ever.)

What kept listeners present through a commercial set was if they were told there was a specific feature (e.g., traffic, sports scores) coming up at a specific time. This strategy is called "appointment listening." Just as programmers in the days of diary ratings programmed "across the quarter hour" to get credit for more time spent listening, programmers are now learning how they can stretch and manipulate listening habits in order to make the PPM work for them.

The "Book"

Since there are still markets using the diary method, also known as "the ratings book," here is how it works.

Listeners either write down what they hear on the radio in a diary or remember what they've heard and then relate this information by phone to a data collection company. Neither of these methods captures "real-time" listening. So, every radio station has a number of listeners for whom they'll never get credit. This phenomenon is called "phantom cume." It's the percentage of your cume that does not mention your radio station when asked to recall which stations they have listened to in the past week, though they *were listening*, they didn't *remember* listening.

Phantom cume is one of the reasons for the creation of the PPM. With the advent of PPM, phantom cume may soon be a thing of the past.

Remember: Research is just a tool. It is one of the many weapons in your arsenal for creating a powerful radio station and online presence. You can have all the research results in the world, but it always comes down to people. You have to use your judgment every step of the way, not just in hiring your staff, but also in choosing your researchers and the participants in your research project. Apply all your creative skills. The rules for creating powerful radio work for research as well.

PART VIII

Beyond Powerful Radio
Final Notes

CHAPTER 35

Beyond Powerful Radio
Final Notes

"Our greatest glory is not in never falling,
but in rising every time we fall."
—*Confucius*

"If at first you don't succeed, try, try again."
—*Proverb*

Working in radio is a great job, with no heavy lifting. In what other profession do you get paid to tell the stories of life, chronicle the times we live in, find the most interesting people alive, meet them, and talk to them? With multiple platforms to work with to reach audiences, it is an exciting time of change.

It is easy to get disillusioned and jaded when concern for profit seems to make creativity a luxury, if not a vice. But those who run the business side of broadcasting need you. They are basing their station's financial future on one idea: that people will listen to what they have put on their radio stations. Your thoughts, your ideas, your words, and your personality are the product they are selling. You matter. It is up to you to use your creativity to make what is on the radio, or online, powerful.

Don't waste a minute of your time on the air. Say your station's name or call letters with pride! Make it matter. Be glad to be there. Tell the truth as you know it to be. Do every show with the same enthusiasm as you did your first, knowing it could be your last. Do not get caught up in pettiness at work.

In the 1700s Denis Diderot made this plea to artists: "Move me, surprise me, rend my heart, make me tremble, weep, shudder, outrage me, . . . then delight me if you can."

In talk, as in all radio, do not forget the important things. Be yourself. Use your life experience. Even though you are talking about the personal events of your life, do not divulge what is private. The powerful radio you create, no matter the delivery system, should be as unique as your DNA, but *always* engage or involve the listener.

Prepare, do the formatics, state your opinions, be courageous, and use humor. Remember, it is never about you, it is always about the listeners. They are the people who are giving you the most precious thing they have on earth: their time.

Acknowledgements

It is impossible to thank all the people whose friendship, insight, and talent have helped nurture, develop, and inspire this work. I am deeply grateful to those who have generously shared their ideas, wisdom, and experiences.

There are no words to thank my editor, colleague and friend, Turi Ryder, without whom this book would not exist.

Special thanks also to Melissa McConnell Wilson, who not only contributed to *Beyond Powerful Radio*, but also created the accompanying *Instructor Manual*, which allows this book to be accessible as a text for Media, Broadcast, Audio Production, Journalism, Communications, and Marketing instructors. Linwood Hagin—thank you for your help as well.

And to extraordinary humorist Leo Cullum who lost his battle with cancer in 2010. He will be much missed as a contributing cartoonist to the *New Yorker Magazine* and to *Beyond Powerful Radio*.

My deepest gratitude to those who generously offered their expertise by contributing extensive sections for this book including Daniel Anstandig, John Parikhal, Jeffrey Hedquist, Jeremy Millar, Tommy Kramer, Pat Bryson (with thanks to Cesco Van Gool and Joyce McCullough for introducing me to Pat), Erin Davis, Doug Harris, and Maureen Bulley.

Many thanks also to Kelli Grisez, and contributors Lee Harris, Sean Ross, Mike Sugerman, Jim Chenevey, Warren Levinson, Michael Haas, Dave Ross, Sharon Katchen, Phil Hendrie, Mervin Block, Scott Shannon, John Catchings, Lynn Jimenez Catchings, Denise Jimenez-Adams, Christine Lavin, Howard Price, Bob Christopher, Sheri Inglis-Schmickl, Jerry Bell, Dan Vallie, Bernard Gershon, Mackie Morris, Jaye Albright, Tom Zarecki, Guy Zapoleon, Randy Lane, Denise McIntee, Alan Eisenson, Lorna Ozmon, Deborah Potter, Ed Walsh, Michael Hedges, Scott Borden, Andy Beaubien, Mike Siegel, Mark Howell, Dave Sholin, David Baronfeld, Ross Brittain, Matt Siegel, Caroline Feraday, Pam Lontos, Matt Hudson, Steve Apel, Eben Brown, Rita Rich, Scott Woelfel, Vincent Gardino, Ann S. Utterback, Ph.D, Susan Berkley, Kenn Adams, Dennis Clark,

479

Jessica Northey, Al Tompkins, Joel Ben Izzy, Pat McCrummen, Tom Taylor and Robert Unmacht.

For their support of this work, thank you to Ken Swezey, Zehra J. Abdi, Henry Leutwyler. Thanks also to Amanda Guest, Erica Farber, Joel Denver, Don Barrett, Al Petersen, June Barnes, Jim Carnagie, Carl Marcucci, Mike Kinosian, Steve Jones, Linda Bracken, Mike McVay, Fred Jacobs, John Catlett, Michael Harrison, Don Anthony, and all the folks at RAMP; Tom Kay and to those involved with the Conclave, also B. Eric Rhoads, and the MIWs—thank you all for your talent, and help and belief in this work.

Special personal thanks to J. Ruth Gendler, Dana Dworin, Anne Chaabane, Adele Scheele, Jennifer Taub, Barbara Blake, Susanne Whatley Miller, Nalini Chilkov, Wendy McLeod, Liz Janik, Fredi Diamond Seraydarian, Diane Jacobs Berk, Valerie Anne Geller (the "other" Valerie Geller), Lauren Walters, Jesica Baker, Cherise Baker Whitehead, Amy Baker Sandback, Kate McCallum, Laurel Ornitz, Carol Archer, Jeff Neuman, Marie Sandgren, Gillien Goll, Christine Henrich, Rhonda Funes, Ron and Alice Lando, Tom Wilson, Doug Kaplan, Scott Adams, Colman Adams, Simon Adams, and Steve Koslow.

Finally, a sincere thank you to all my client stations and to the talented broadcasters around the world who have taken these ideas to heart, have believed in and worked with this material, have risked much, and have succeeded by using the methods in *Beyond Powerful Radio* currently and in years past.

Permissions

Grateful acknowledgement is given to the following people and organizations for permission to reprint previously published materials.

Bonus Books: Excerpts from *Writing Broadcast News* © 1987 by Mervin Block. Reprinted with permission of Bonus Books.

Bonus Books: Excerpts of the *Broadcast Voice Handbook*. Bonus Books © 2000. Reprinted with permission of Ann S. Utterback Ph.D.

Leo Cullum cartoon: "Would you please elaborate on 'then something bad happened'." © Leo Cullum/The New Yorker Collection/www.cartoonbank. com. All rights reserved. Reprinted with permission.

Leo Cullum cartoon: "The dip in sales seems to coincide with the decision to eliminate the sales staff." © Leo Cullum/The New Yorker collection/2002/ www.cartoonbank.com. All rights reserved. Reprinted with permission.

Leo Cullum cartoon: "It's not enough that we succeed, cats must also fail." © Leo Cullum/1997/The New Yorker Collection/www.cartoonbank.com. All rights reserved. Reprinted with permission.

Leo Cullum cartoon: "Never, ever, think outside the box." © Leo Cullum/ The New Yorker Collection/1997/www.cartoonbank.com. All rights reserved. Reprinted with permission.

Leo Cullum cartoon: "Hey, we're sheep. Everything seems like a good idea." © Leo Cullum/2009/The New Yorker Collection/www.cartoonbank.com. All rights reserved. Reprinted with permission.

Leo Cullum Cartoon: "How about a little music to push the plot along." © Leo Cullum/2002/The New Yorker Collection/www.cartoonbank.com. All rights reserved. Reprinted with permission.

Leo Cullum cartoon: "That's not my political opinion. That's just stuff I hear on the radio." © Leo Cullum/2003/The New Yorker Collection/www. cartoonbank.com. All rights reserved. Reprinted with permission.

Leo Cullum cartoon: "It's always 'Get me a Godzilla type,' never, 'Get me Godzilla!'" © Leo Cullum/The New Yorker Collection/2004/www. cartoonbank.com. All rights reserved. Reprinted with permission.

Leo Cullum cartoon: "That's not what you told my screener you wanted to talk about." © Leo Cullum/The New Yorker Collection/2001/www. cartoonbank.com. All rights reserved. Reprinted with permission.

Leo Cullum cartoon: "It's come to my attention that you have a life outside the office." © Leo Cullum/1992. Reprinted with permission of Leo Cullum, Sandhill Arts.

Leo Cullum cartoon: "They say the early forties is the new late thirties." © Leo Cullum/The New Yorker Collection/2005/www.cartoonbank.com. All rights reserved. Reprinted with permission.

Dennis the Menace cartoon: "I like the way you don't ever break for commercials." © Hank Ketcham/North American Syndicate/1998/www. kingfeatures.com. Reprinted with permission.

Pantheon Press: Excerpt from *Bird by Bird: Some Instructions on Writing and Life*. © 1994 by Anne Lamott. Reprinted with permission of Pantheon Books.

Perseus Press: Excerpt from *On Listening*. © 1976 by Carl A. Faber, Ph.D. Reprinted with permission of Carl A. Faber.

The Radio Store: Excerpts from *Write Good Copy Fast: The Broadcast Professional's Guide to Writing Effective Copy for Direct Advertisers*. © 2003 by Maureen Bulley. Reprinted with permission from Maureen Bulley.

The Radio Store: Excerpts from *The Certified Radio Copywriter Course*. © 1999 by Maureen Bulley. Reprinted with permission from Maureen Bulley.

The Radio Store: Excerpts from *Radio Power Tools*, *The Copy Navigator*, and *Creative Advice* by Maureen Bulley. © The Radio Store, Toronto, Ontario, Canada. Reprinted with permission of Maureen Bulley.

Turtle Bay Books, a Division of Random House: Excerpt from *Talk, NPR's Susan Stamberg Considers All Things*. © 1993 by Susan Stamberg. Reprinted with permission of Turtle Bay Books.

Portions of *Beyond Powerful Radio* by Valerie Geller, edited by Turi Ryder, including: "Citizen Journalism" and "In Case Of Emergency," previously appeared in Radio & TV Business Report (*RBR/TVBR*). Portions of the chapter on "Fundraising & Giving" previously appeared in *Radio Ink* magazine.

Resources

Contributors

Kenn Adams
Kenn Adams Adventure Theater
*How to Improvise a Full-Length Play;
The Art of Spontaneous Theater*
E-mail: Kenn@KennAdamsAdventure
Theater.com
www.KennAdamsAdventureTheater.com

Jaye Albright
Consultant, Albright & O'Malley
E-mail: radioconsultj@aol.com
http://www.albrightandomalley.com

Daniel Anstandig
President, McVay New Media
E-mail: dan@daer.com
www.mcvaymedia.com

Steve Apel
Research Consultant
E-mail: steve@apels.net

David Baronfeld
General Manager
KLAA Radio
E-mail: DBaronfeld@aol.com
http://www.am830klaa.com

Andy Beaubien
General Manager/Consultant
Broadcast Programming & Research
E-mail: Andybpr@earthlink.net
www.bpr.com.au

Jerry Bell
Managing Editor/Reporter
KOA, Clear Channel–Denver
E-mail: jerrygbell@clearchannel.com

Susan Berkley
*Speak to Influence: How to Unlock the
Hidden Power of Your Voice*
The Great Voice Company
info@greatvoice.com
http://www.greatvoice.com/

Mervin Block
Writing Broadcast News
Television Newswriting Workshop
E-mail: merblo@aol.com
www.mervinblock.com

Ross Brittain
The Ross Brittain Report
E-mail: ross_brittain@compuserve.com
www.rbreport.com

Pat Bryson
Bryson Broadcasting International
E-mail: pat@patbryson.com
www.patbryson.com

Maureen Bulley
The Radio Store, Inc.
Write Good Copy Fast
E-mail: doradio@total.net
www.theradiostore.com

483

John Catchings
TV Production and Consultation
E-mail: JC@johncatchings.com
www.catchingsandassociates.com

Jim Chenevey
CBS Radio News
E-mail: jch@cbsnews.com
www.cbsnews.com

Dennis Clark
Executive Producer
The Ryan Seacrest Morning Show
E-mail: dennisclrk@aol.com
http://ryan.kiisfm.com/main.html

Erin Davis
Erin & Mike in the Morning—
98.1 CHFI Toronto
E-mail: erin@erindavis.com
www.erindavis.com

Tom Demos
Web consultant/expert
www.PortlandMediaMonitor.com

Alan Eisenson
Operations Manager
KFBK/KSTE
E-mail: alaneisenson@clearchannel.com
www.kfbk.com

Caroline Feraday
Air Personality
E-mail: caroline.feradaytv@googlemail.com
www.carolineferaday.com

Vincent Gardino
Executive Director of Underwriting
WNYC AM/FM & WQXR
E-mail: vgardino@wnyc.org
www.wnyc.org

Nic & Becky Gaunt
Nic Gaunt Photography
E-mail: nic@nicgaunt.demon.co.uk
www.nicgaunt.com

Bernard Gershon
Vice President/General Manager
ABC News.com
E-mail: bernard.l.gershon@abc.com
www.abc.com

Dr. Evian Gordon
Chairman/CEO
Integrative Neuroscience and
Personalized Medicine
(with Dr. Stephen H. Koslow)
The Brain Resource Company
E-mail:
evian.gordon@brainresource.com
www.brainresource.com

Doug Harris
Creative Animal International
E-mail: dough@creativeanimal.com
www.creativeanimal.com

Lee Harris
News Anchor
1010 WINS New York
E-mail: lee@harrismedia.com
www.1010wins.com
www.harrismedia.com

Michael Hedges
Follow the Media
E-mail: newsletter@followthemedia.com
www.followthemedia.com

Jeffrey Hedquist
Hedquist Produtions, Inc.
The Ultimate Radio Commercial
E-mail: jeffrey@hedquist.com
www.hedquist.com

Phil Hendrie
The Phil Hendrie Show
http://www.philhendrieshow.com/

Mark Howell
E-mail: mark@markhowellnews.com
www.markhowellnews.com

Matt Hudson
Music Test America
E-mail: musictestamerica@comcast.net
www.musictestamerica.com

Joel Ben Izzy
Storyteller
Author: *The Beggar King and The Secret of Happiness*
E-mail: jbi@aol.com
www.storypage.com

Lynn Jimenez-Catchings
News Journalist
KGO Radio
¡Se Habla Dinero!
E-mail: lmcatch@hotmail.com
www.KGOam810.com
www.sehabladinero.info

Tommy Kramer
Tommy Kramer's Coaching Handbook
Talent coach
E-mail: tommy@tommykramer.net
www.audiencedevelopmentgroup.com

Christine Lavin
Artist/Singer-songwriter
www.christinelavin.com

Henry Leutwyler
Photography
Neverland Lost:
A Portrait of Michael Jackson
www.henryleutwyler.com

Warren Levinson
Journalist, NY Bureau Chief
Associated Press
E-mail: wlevinson@ap.org
www.ap.org

Pam Lontos
President, PR/PR Public Relations
I See Your Name Everywhere:
Leverage the Power of the Media to
Grow Your Fame, Wealth and Success
http://www.prpr.net/

Melissa McConnell Wilson
General Manager
KVHS-FM Radio
E-mail: MelissaDJ@aol.com
http://www.melissamcconnell.net/
www.kvhs.com

Denise McIntee
Powerful Radio Productions, Inc.
E-mail: Denisemac1@aol.com
www.powerfulradio.com

Jeremy Millar
Australian Broadcasting Corporation
E-mail Millar.Jeremy@abc.net.au
www.abc.net.au

Mackie Morris
The Magid Institute
E-mail: Mackie.morris@magid.com
www.magid.com

Jessica Northey
Social Mediologist
E-mail: jessicanorthey@gmail.com
www.FingerCandyMedia.com
www.FullThrottleCountry.com
www.GetSocialForm.com

Lorna Ozmon
Consultant
President, Ozmon Media, Inc.
E-mail: lozmon@aol.com
www.ozmonmedia.com

John Parikhal
President, Joint Communications
E-mail: jointcom@aol.com
parikhal@aol.com
www.gomediafix.com

Deborah Potter
Broadcast Journalism Instructor
*Advancing the Story: Broadcast
Journalism in a Multimedia World*
www.rtnda.org

Howard B. Price
Director of Business Continuity and
Crisis Management
ABC News
E-mail: Howard.B.Price@abc.com
http://www.mediadisasterprep.com

Rita Rich
Rita Rich Media Services
E-mail: info@ritarichmedia.net
www.ritarichmedia.net

Sean Ross
VP/Music and Programming
Edison Media Research
E-mail: sross@edisonresearch.com
www.edisonresearch.com
www.theinfinitedial.com

Turi Ryder
Air Personality
E-mail: turi@shebopsproductions.com
www.shebopsproductions.com

Scott Shannon
PD/Morning Personality
WPLJ Radio
www.trueoldieschannel.com
www.scottshannon.com

Dave Sholin
Astralwerks Records
E-mail: yourduke@aol.com
www.astralwerks.com

Mike Siegel
Major Attractions
E-mail: mikesiegel2000@yahoo.com
www.mikesiegel.com

Tom Taylor
Executive News Editor
Radio-Info.com
E-mail: Tom@radio-info.com
www.radio-info.com

Al Tompkins
Author: *Aim for the Heart*
The Poynter Institute
http://www.poynter.org

Ann S. Utterback, Ph.D
Broadcast Voice Specialist
E-mail: AVoiceDoc@comcast.net
http://www.avoicedoc.com
http://utterbackpublishing.com/

Dan Vallie
Vallie/Richards Consulting, Inc.
E-mail: valliedan@aol.com
www.vallierichards.com

Scott Woelfel
Managing Partner
Armchair Media LLC
E-mail: scott@armchairmedia.com
http://armchairmedia.com

Guy Zapoleon
Zapoleon Media Strategies
E-mail: info@zapoleon.com
www.zapoleon.com

Tom Zarecki
Chair, Department of Communication
& Broadcasting
Lincoln College of New England
E-mail: TZarecki@LincolnCollegeNE.edu

About the Author

Internationally acclaimed broadcast consultant Valerie Geller works with top stations and broadcast groups throughout the United States and around the world, coaching individual talent, programmers, and managers and conducting Creating Powerful Radio™ workshops. A radio veteran with more than 30 years of experience, Geller programmed WABC in New York, has served on the Associated Press board of directors, and has held various management, news, and on-air positions at several major market U.S. stations.

A noted seminar and workshop leader, Geller trains broadcasters and communicators throughout the world. In addition to her work in the United States, Geller's international client roster of more than 500 stations in thirty-one different countries includes the BBC in the UK, ABC in Australia, and radio and TV stations throughout Europe, Canada, Mexico, South America, Singapore, and Africa.

As a keynote speaker, Geller is much in demand. She has presented sessions at numerous national and international broadcast gatherings and at various U.S. State broadcast associations. She's guest lectured at Columbia University's Graduate School of Journalism and at New York University.

Named as one of the "Most Influential Women in Radio" by *Radio Ink* magazine, in 2010 Geller received The Conclave's highest honor, the "Rockwell Lifetime Achievement Award for Broadcasting."

Beyond Powerful Radio: A Communicator's Guide to the Internet Age" is Geller's fourth book. Her third, *Creating Powerful Radio: Getting, Keeping & Growing Audiences* was published by Focal Press in 2007. Geller's second book: *The Powerful Radio Workbook: The Prep, Performance & Post Production Planning* has been used to teach the Powerful Radio techniques to broadcasters in sixty countries around the world. Her first book, *Creating Powerful Radio: A Communicator's Handbook for News, Talk, Information & Personality,* has been translated into several languages and is regarded as a "bible" by many broadcast professionals throughout the world.

Visit Valerie Geller at www.gellermedia.com, or follow her on twitter at www.twitter.com/vgeller

Index

Notes

Notes

Rec
July 2011

DATE DUE

LIBRARY
NSCC, WATERFRONT CAMPUS
80 MAWIO'MI PLACE
DARTMOUTH, NS B2Y 0A5 CANADA

DISCARDED